PandoraHearts

Jun Mochizuki

CONTENTS

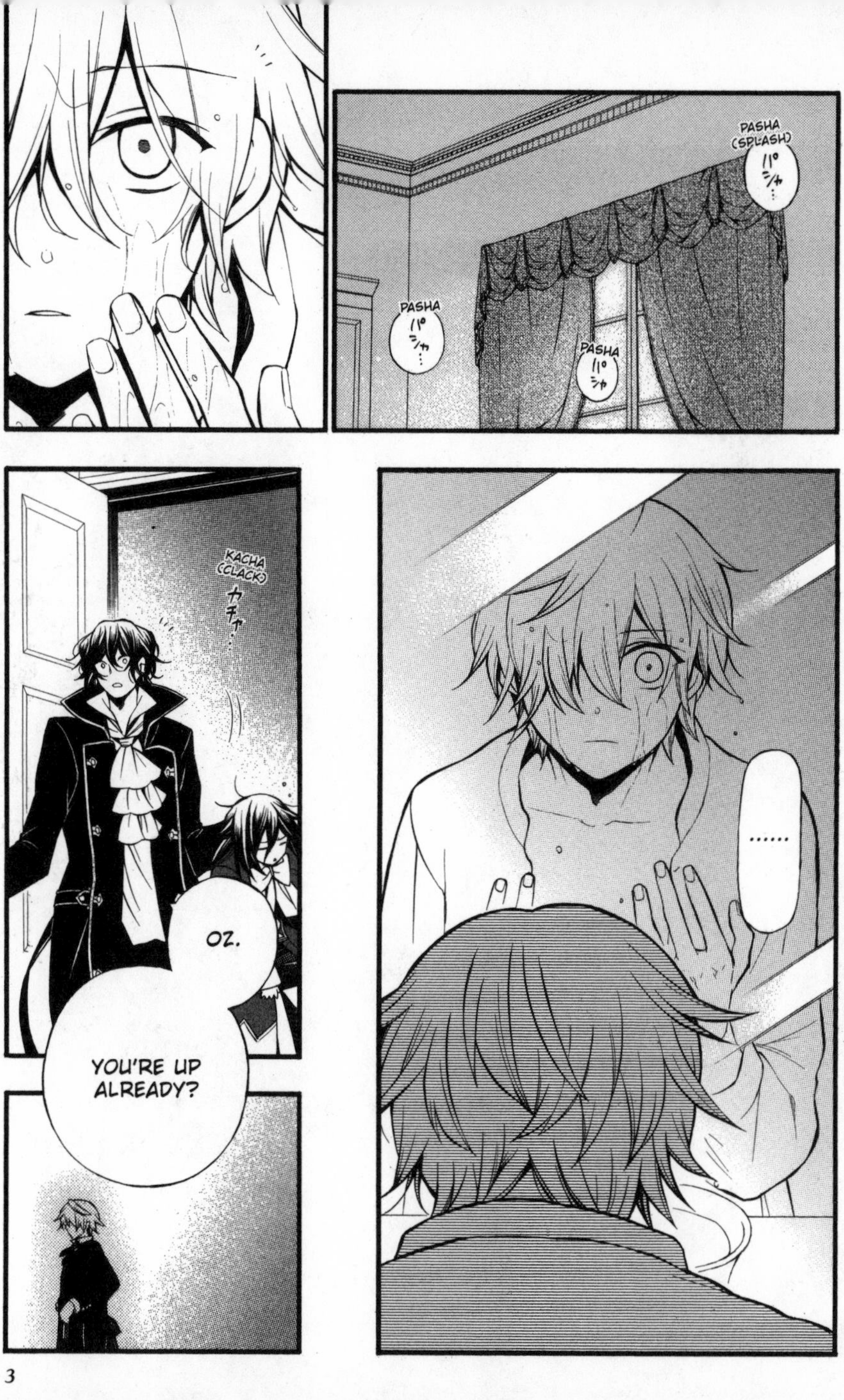
PASHA (SPLASH)
パシャ…
PASHA
パシャ
PASHA
パシャ…
......
KACHA (CLACK)
カチャ…
OZ.
YOU'RE UP ALREADY?

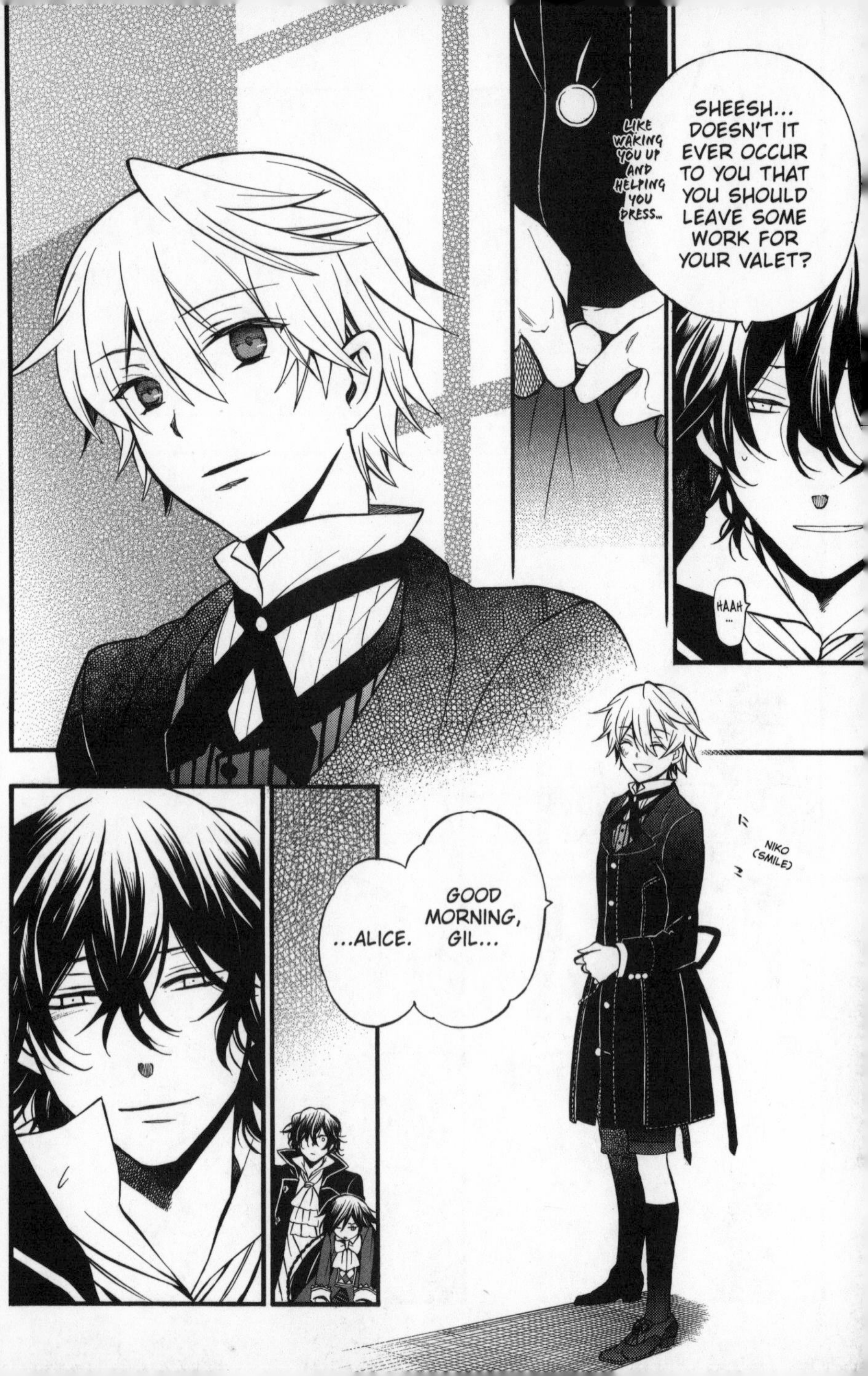
SHEESH... DOESN'T IT EVER OCCUR TO YOU THAT YOU SHOULD LEAVE SOME WORK FOR YOUR VALET?
LIKE WAKING YOU UP AND HELPING YOU DRESS...
HAAH...
NIKO (SMILE)
GOOD MORNING, GIL... ...ALICE.

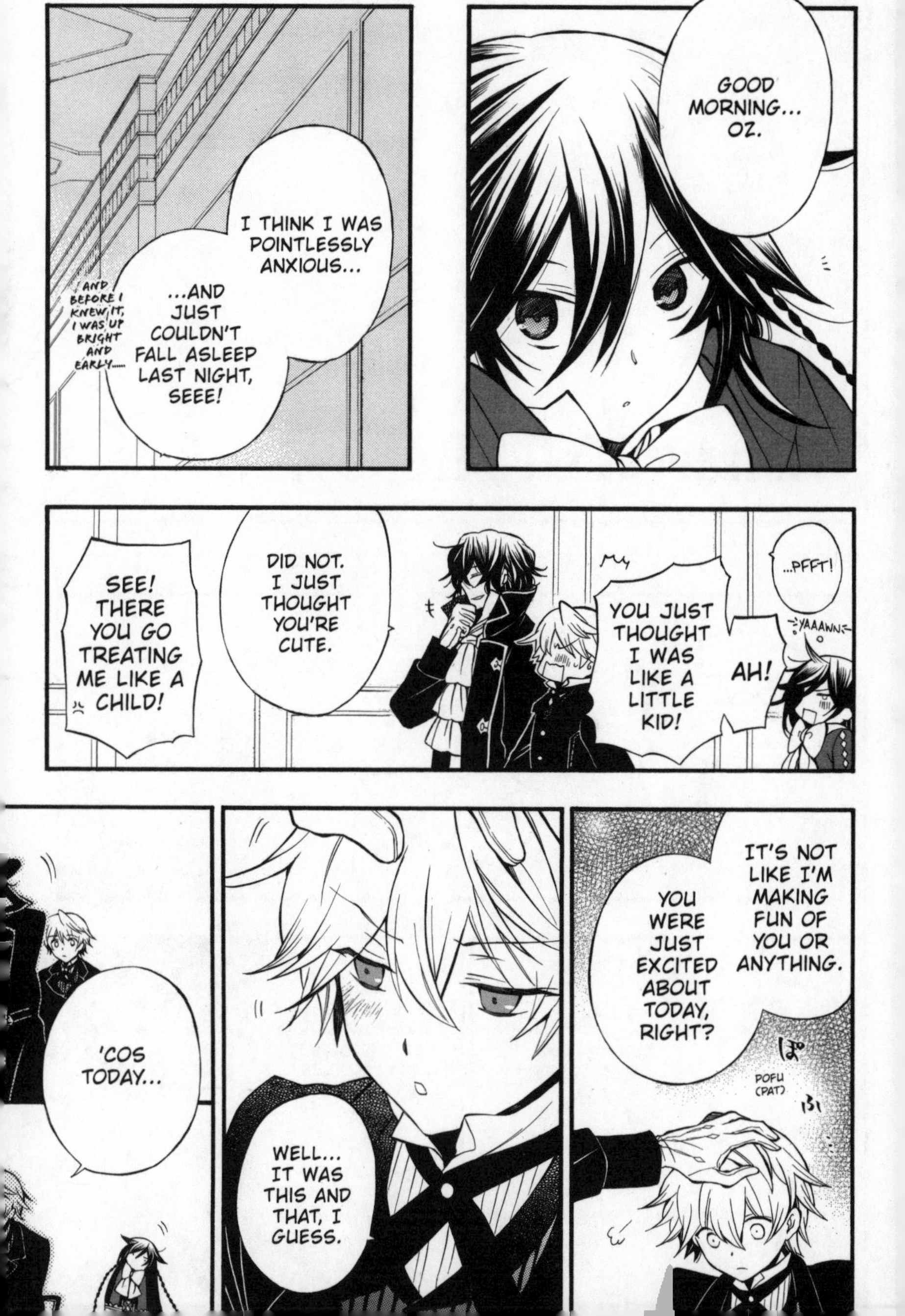
GOOD MORNING... OZ.
I THINK I WAS POINTLESSLY ANXIOUS...
...AND JUST COULDN'T FALL ASLEEP LAST NIGHT, SEEE!
AND BEFORE I KNEW IT, I WAS UP BRIGHT AND EARLY......
...PFFT!
YAAAWN
AH!
YOU JUST THOUGHT I WAS LIKE A LITTLE KID!
DID NOT. I JUST THOUGHT YOU'RE CUTE.
SEE! THERE YOU GO TREATING ME LIKE A CHILD!
IT'S NOT LIKE I'M MAKING FUN OF YOU OR ANYTHING.
YOU WERE JUST EXCITED ABOUT TODAY, RIGHT?
ぽふ
POFU (PAT)
WELL... IT WAS THIS AND THAT, I GUESS.
'COS TODAY...

Retrace:LXII Repose

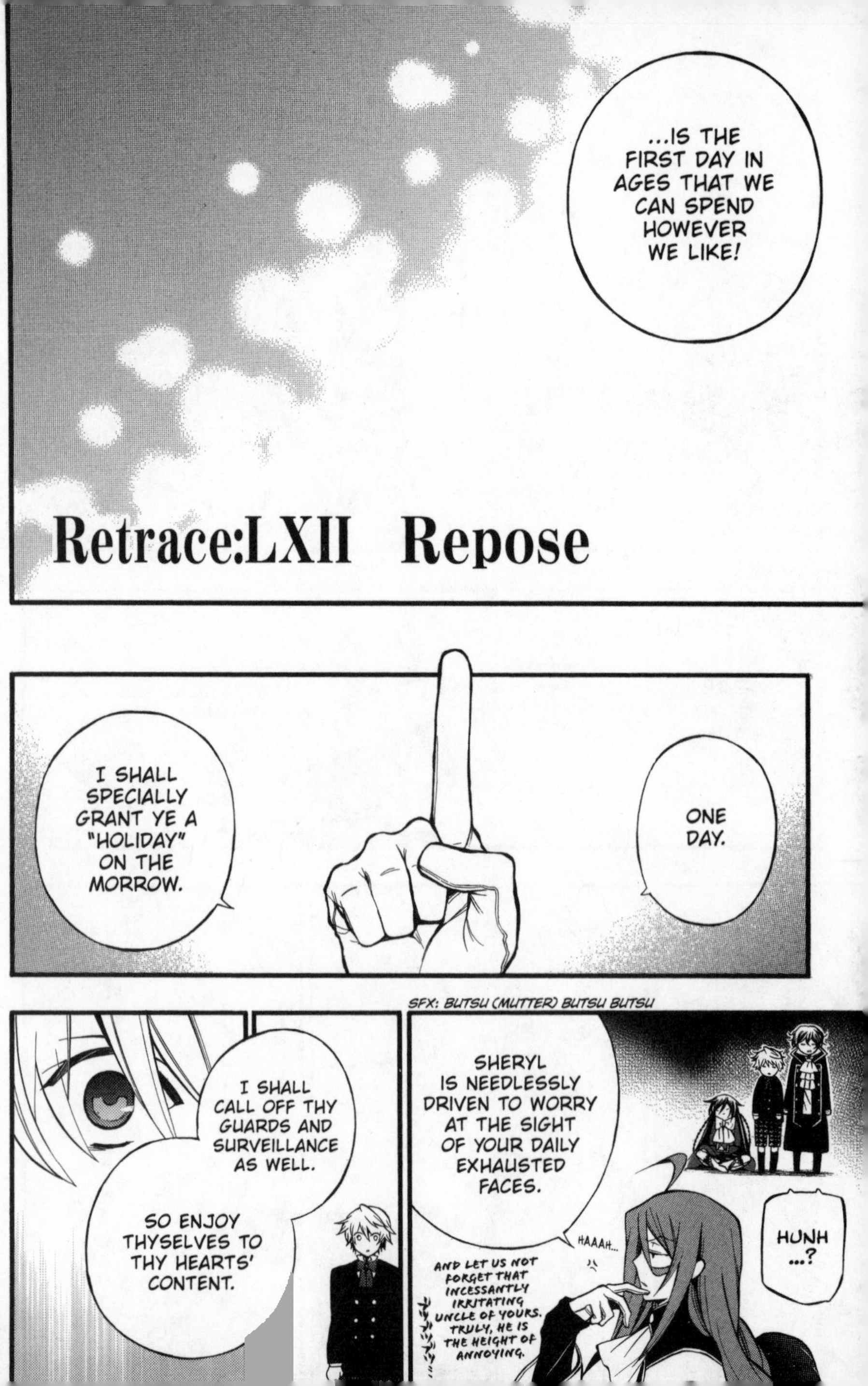

...IS THE FIRST DAY IN AGES THAT WE CAN SPEND HOWEVER WE LIKE!
Retrace:LXII Repose
ONE DAY.
I SHALL SPECIALLY GRANT YE A "HOLIDAY" ON THE MORROW.
SFX: BUTSU (MUTTER) BUTSU BUTSU
HUNH ...?
SHERYL IS NEEDLESSLY DRIVEN TO WORRY AT THE SIGHT OF YOUR DAILY EXHAUSTED FACES.
HAAAH...
AND LET US NOT FORGET THAT INCESSANTLY IRRITATING UNCLE OF YOURS. TRULY, HE IS THE HEIGHT OF ANNOYING.
I SHALL CALL OFF THY GUARDS AND SURVEILLANCE AS WELL.
SO ENJOY THYSELVES TO THY HEARTS' CONTENT.

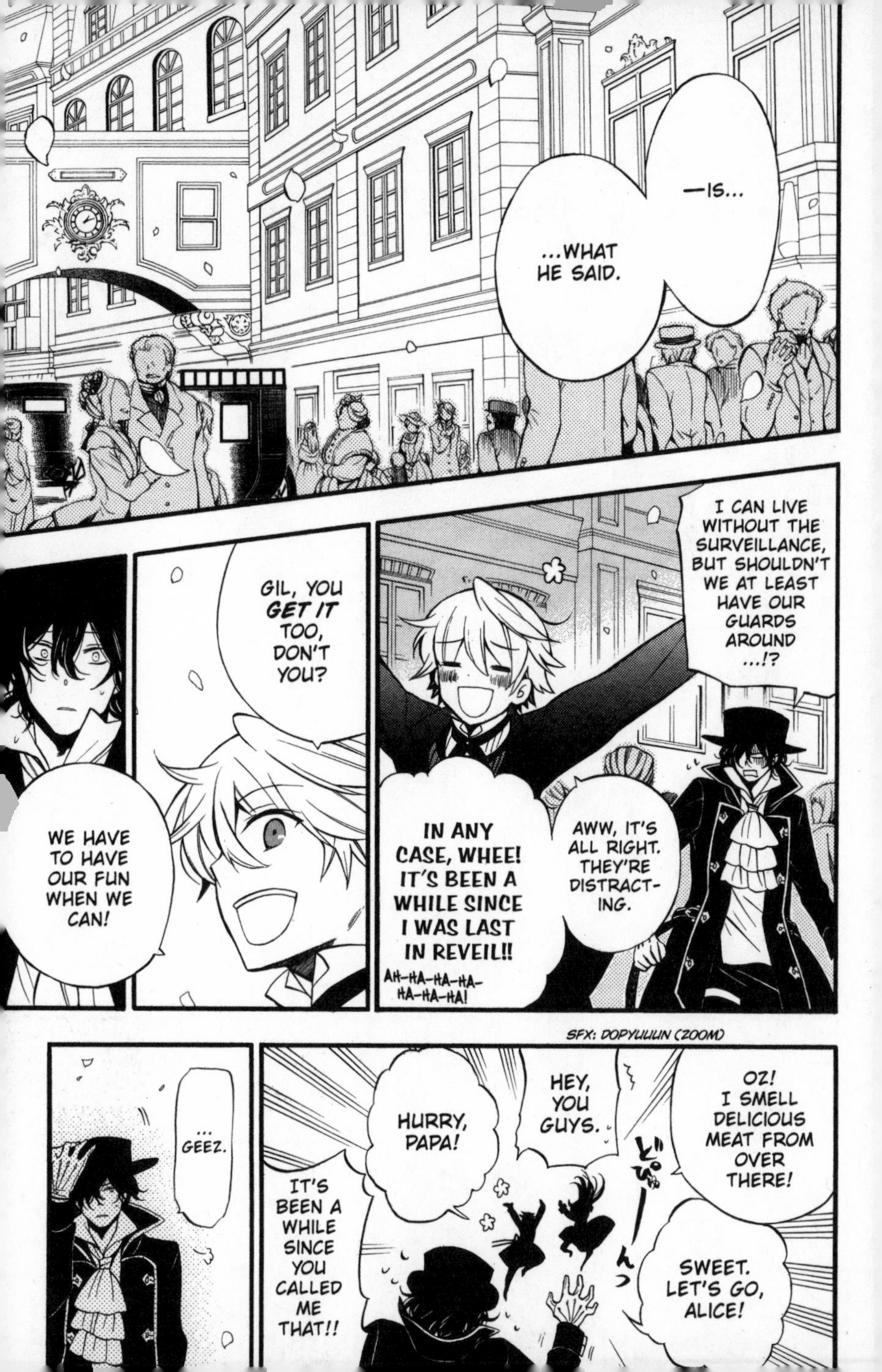
—IS...
...WHAT HE SAID.
I CAN LIVE WITHOUT THE SURVEILLANCE, BUT SHOULDN'T WE AT LEAST HAVE OUR GUARDS AROUND ...!?
AWW, IT'S ALL RIGHT. THEY'RE DISTRACT-ING.
IN ANY CASE, WHEE! IT'S BEEN A WHILE SINCE I WAS LAST IN REVEIL!!
AH-HA-HA-HA-HA-HA-HA!
SFX: DOPYUUUN (ZOOM)
GIL, YOU *GET IT* TOO, DON'T YOU?
WE HAVE TO HAVE OUR FUN WHEN WE CAN!
OZ! I SMELL DELICIOUS MEAT FROM OVER THERE!
HEY, YOU GUYS.
HURRY, PAPA!
どぴゅーーん
SWEET. LET'S GO, ALICE!
IT'S BEEN A WHILE SINCE YOU CALLED ME THAT!!
... GEEZ.

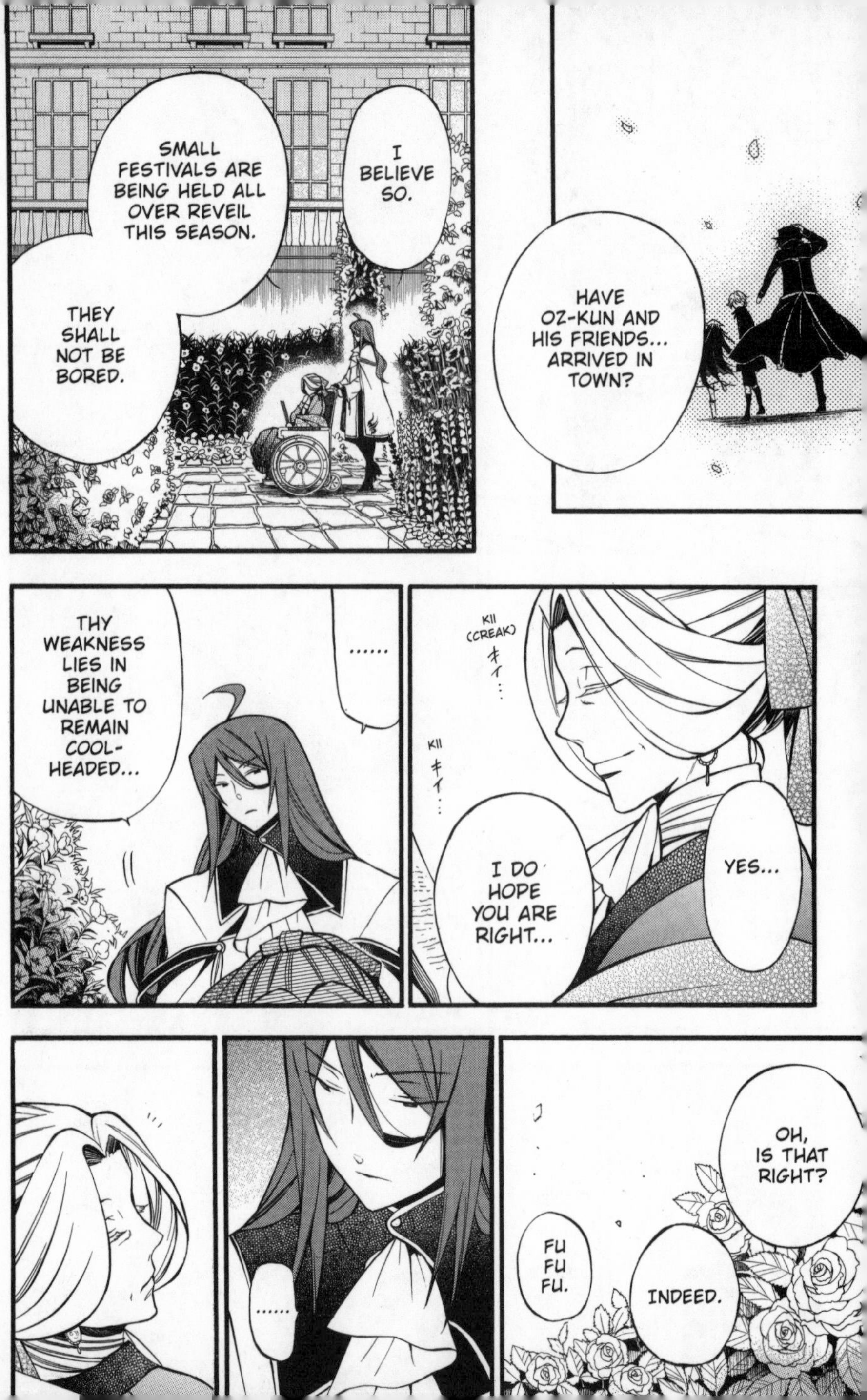
HAVE OZ-KUN AND HIS FRIENDS... ARRIVED IN TOWN?
I BELIEVE SO.
SMALL FESTIVALS ARE BEING HELD ALL OVER REVEIL THIS SEASON.
THEY SHALL NOT BE BORED.
KII (CREAK)
キイ…
KII
キイ…
YES...
I DO HOPE YOU ARE RIGHT...
......
THY WEAKNESS LIES IN BEING UNABLE TO REMAIN COOL-HEADED...
OH, IS THAT RIGHT?
INDEED.
FU FU FU.
......

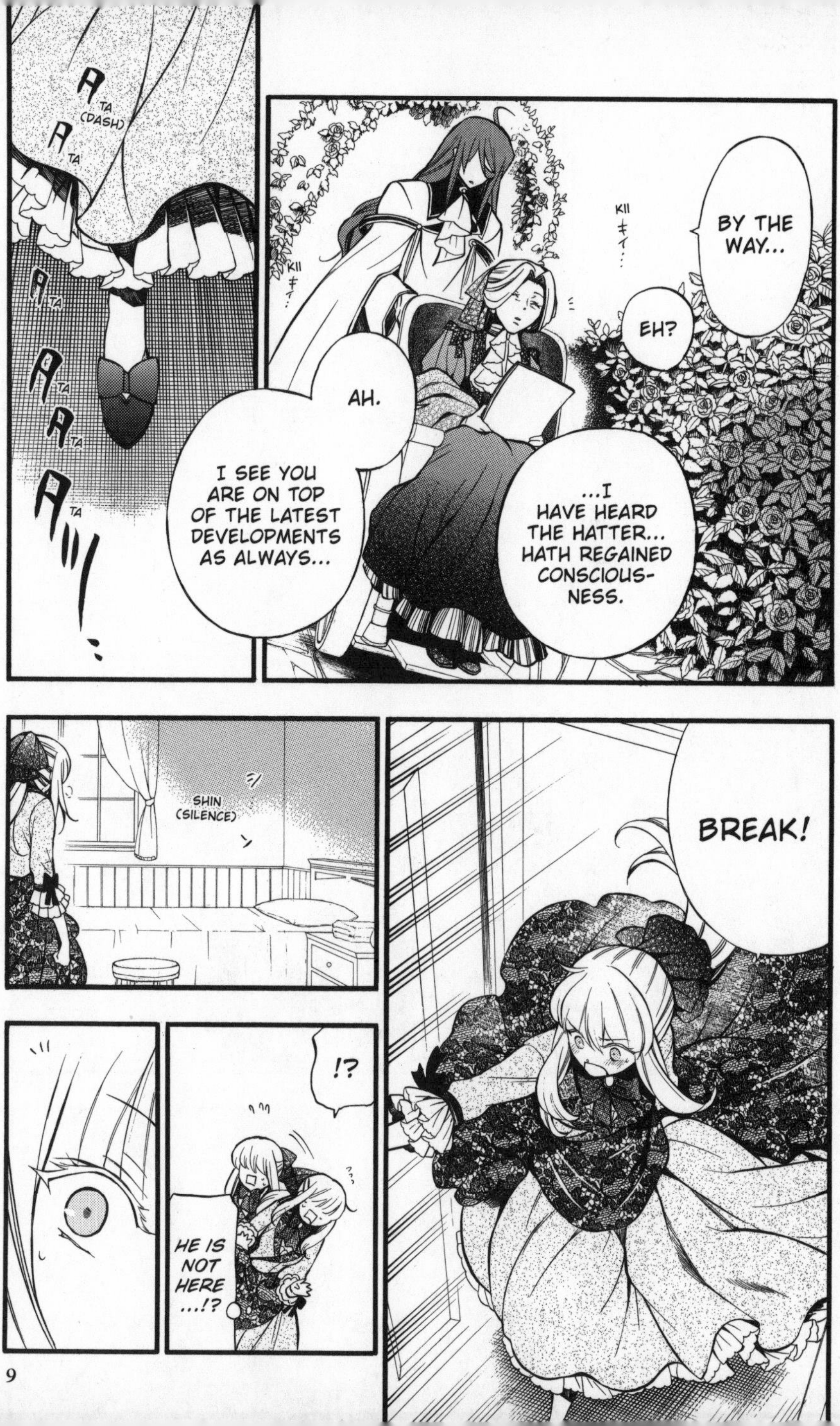
BY THE WAY...
KII
キイ…
EH?
...I HAVE HEARD THE HATTER... HATH REGAINED CONSCIOUSNESS.
AH.
I SEE YOU ARE ON TOP OF THE LATEST DEVELOPMENTS AS ALWAYS...
KII
キイ…
TA (DASH)
TA
TA
TA
TA
TA
BREAK!
SHIN (SILENCE)
!?
HE IS NOT HERE ...!?

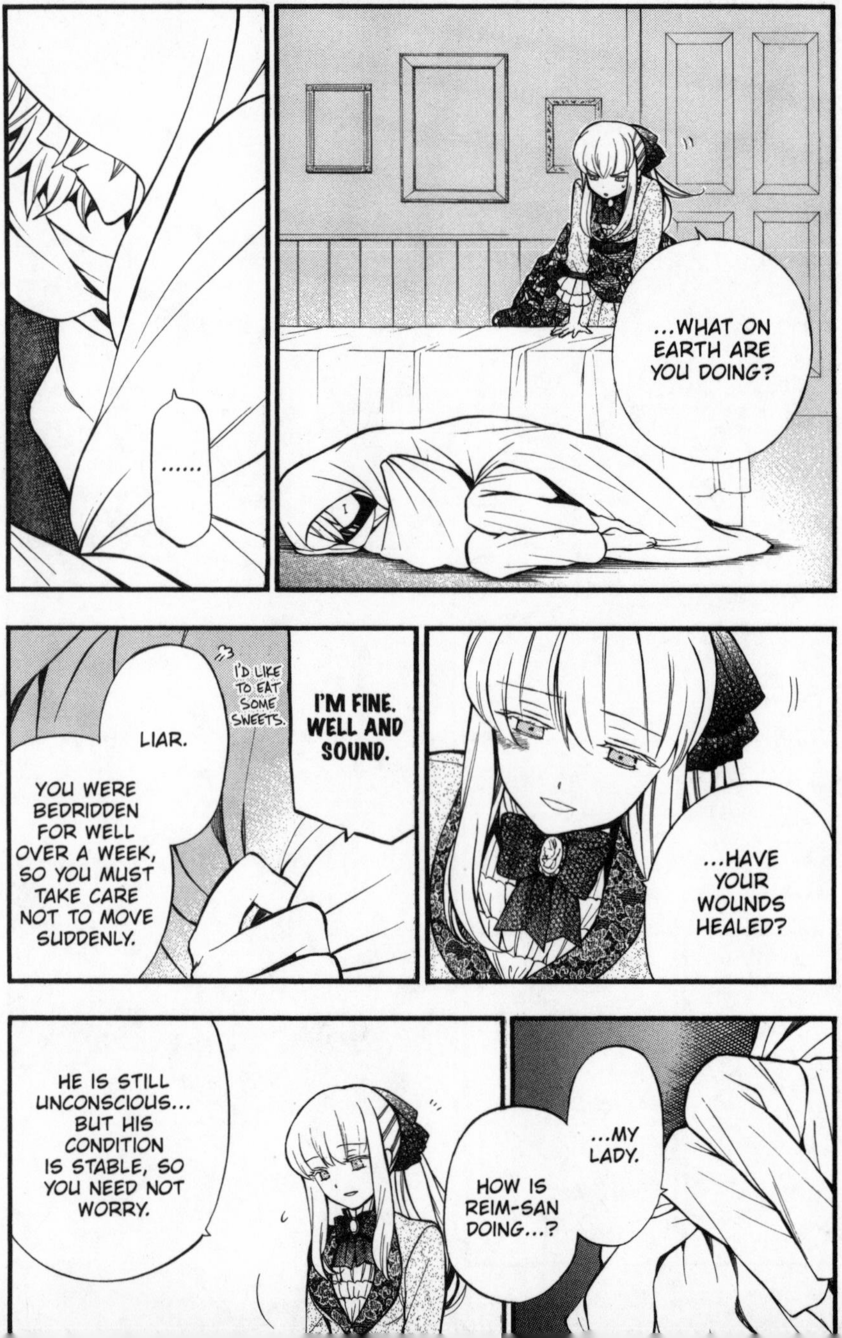
...WHAT ON EARTH ARE YOU DOING?
......
...HAVE YOUR WOUNDS HEALED?
I'M FINE. WELL AND SOUND.
I'D LIKE TO EAT SOME SWEETS.
LIAR.
YOU WERE BEDRIDDEN FOR WELL OVER A WEEK, SO YOU MUST TAKE CARE NOT TO MOVE SUDDENLY.
...MY LADY.
HOW IS REIM-SAN DOING...?
HE IS STILL UNCONSCIOUS... BUT HIS CONDITION IS STABLE, SO YOU NEED NOT WORRY.

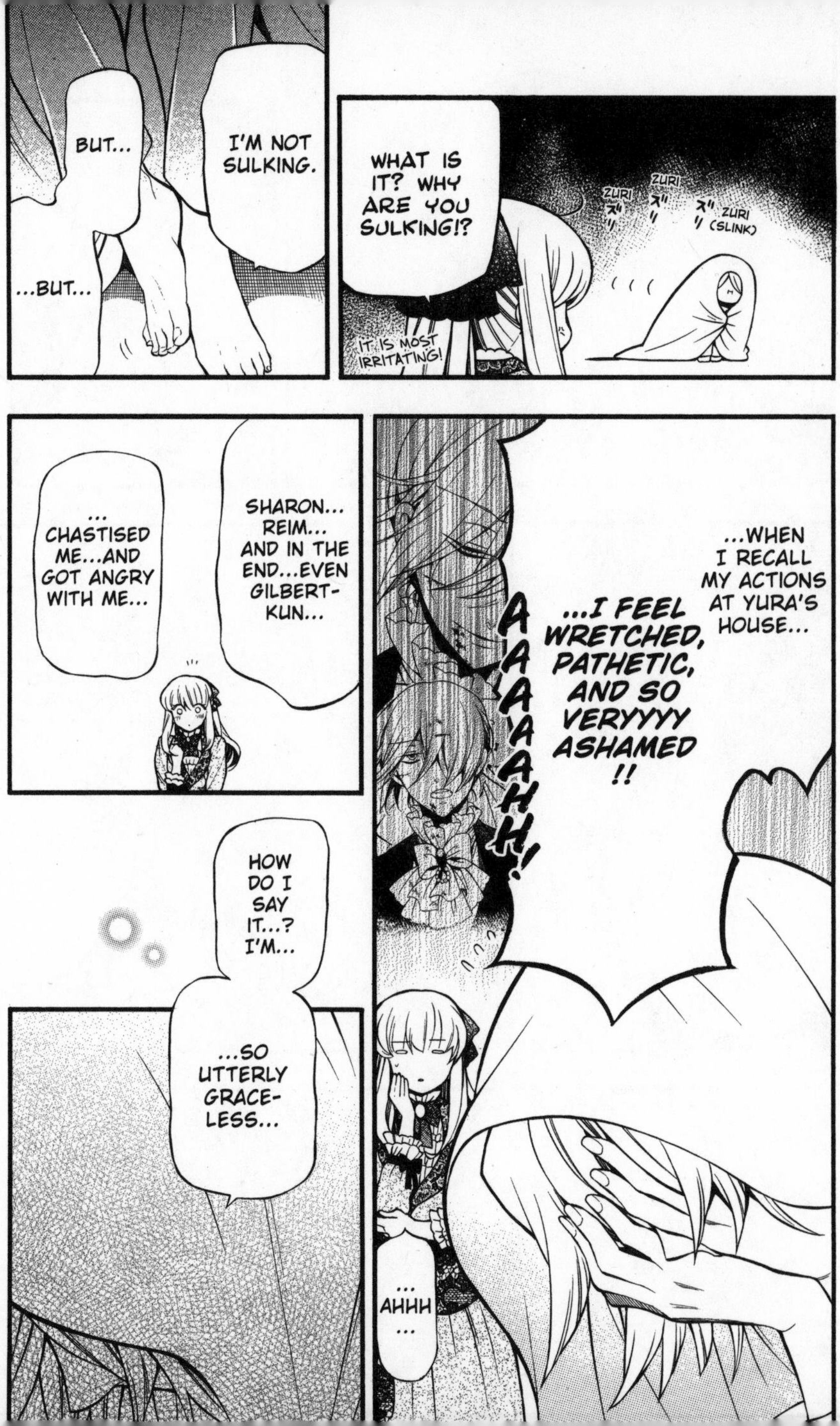
WHAT IS IT? WHY ARE YOU SULKING!?
IT IS MOST IRRITATING!
ZURI ズリ
ZURI ズリ
ズリ ZURI (SLINK)
I'M NOT SULKING.
BUT...
...BUT...
...WHEN I RECALL MY ACTIONS AT YURA'S HOUSE...
...I FEEL WRETCHED, PATHETIC, AND SO VERYYYY ASHAMED!!
AAAAAAHH!
...AHHH...
SHARON... REIM... AND IN THE END...EVEN GILBERT-KUN...
...CHASTISED ME...AND GOT ANGRY WITH ME...
HOW DO I SAY IT...? I'M...
...SO UTTERLY GRACELESS...

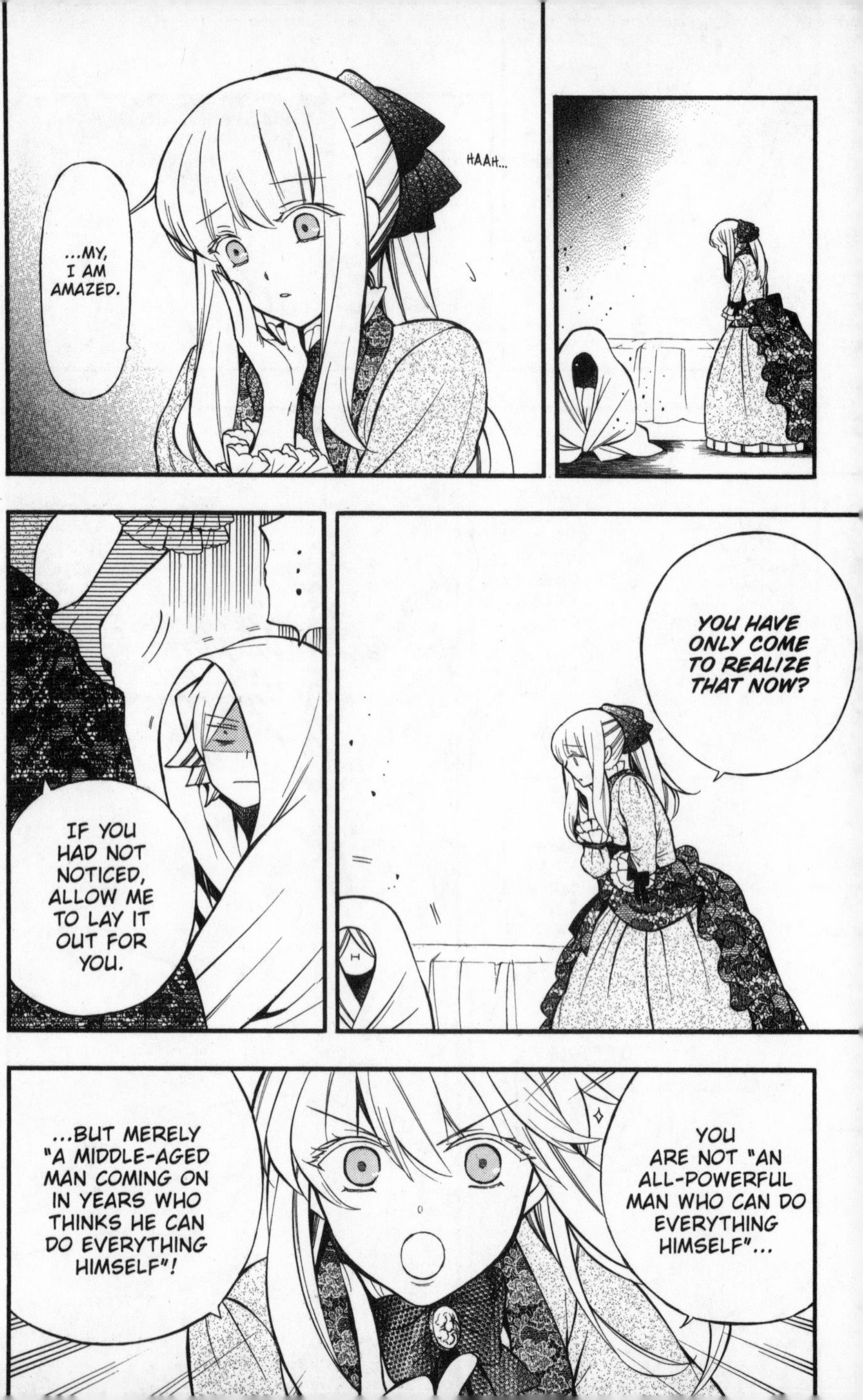
HAAH...
...MY, I AM AMAZED.
YOU HAVE ONLY COME TO REALIZE THAT NOW?
IF YOU HAD NOT NOTICED, ALLOW ME TO LAY IT OUT FOR YOU.
YOU ARE NOT "AN ALL-POWERFUL MAN WHO CAN DO EVERYTHING HIMSELF"...
...BUT MERELY "A MIDDLE-AGED MAN COMING ON IN YEARS WHO THINKS HE CAN DO EVERYTHING HIMSELF"!

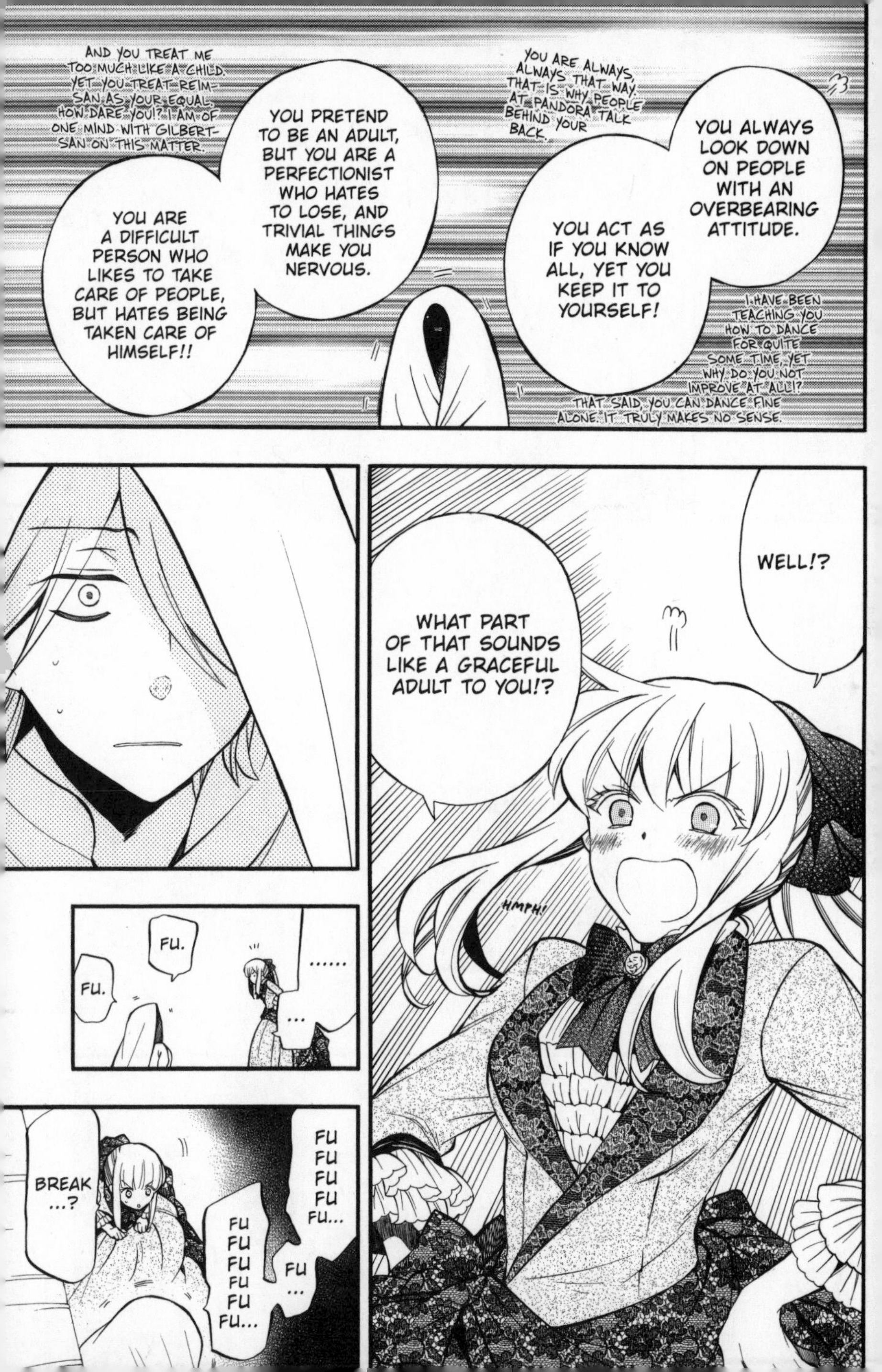
YOU ALWAYS LOOK DOWN ON PEOPLE WITH AN OVERBEARING ATTITUDE.
YOU ARE ALWAYS, ALWAYS THAT WAY. THAT IS WHY PEOPLE AT PANDORA TALK BEHIND YOUR BACK.
YOU ACT AS IF YOU KNOW ALL, YET YOU KEEP IT TO YOURSELF!
I HAVE BEEN TEACHING YOU HOW TO DANCE FOR QUITE SOME TIME, YET WHY DO YOU NOT IMPROVE AT ALL!?
THAT SAID, YOU CAN DANCE FINE ALONE. IT TRULY MAKES NO SENSE.
YOU PRETEND TO BE AN ADULT, BUT YOU ARE A PERFECTIONIST WHO HATES TO LOSE, AND TRIVIAL THINGS MAKE YOU NERVOUS.
AND YOU TREAT ME TOO MUCH LIKE A CHILD. YET YOU TREAT REIM-SAN AS YOUR EQUAL. HOW DARE YOU!? I AM OF ONE MIND WITH GILBERT-SAN ON THIS MATTER.
YOU ARE A DIFFICULT PERSON WHO LIKES TO TAKE CARE OF PEOPLE, BUT HATES BEING TAKEN CARE OF HIMSELF!!
WELL!?
WHAT PART OF THAT SOUNDS LIKE A GRACEFUL ADULT TO YOU!?
HMPH!
FU.
FU.
......
...
FU FU FU FU FU...
FU FU FU FU FU FU...
FU ...
BREAK ...?

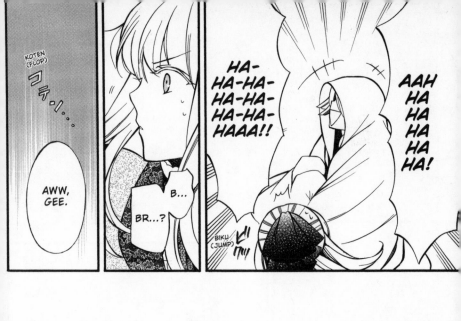

KOTEN
(FLOP)

AWW,
GEE.

B...

BR...?

HA-
HA-HA-
HA-HA-
HA-HA-
HAAA!!

AAH
HA
HA
HA
HA!

BIKU
(JUMP)

I'M
HOPELESS.

...
HOPELESS
...

...I'M
WELL
AND
TRULY...

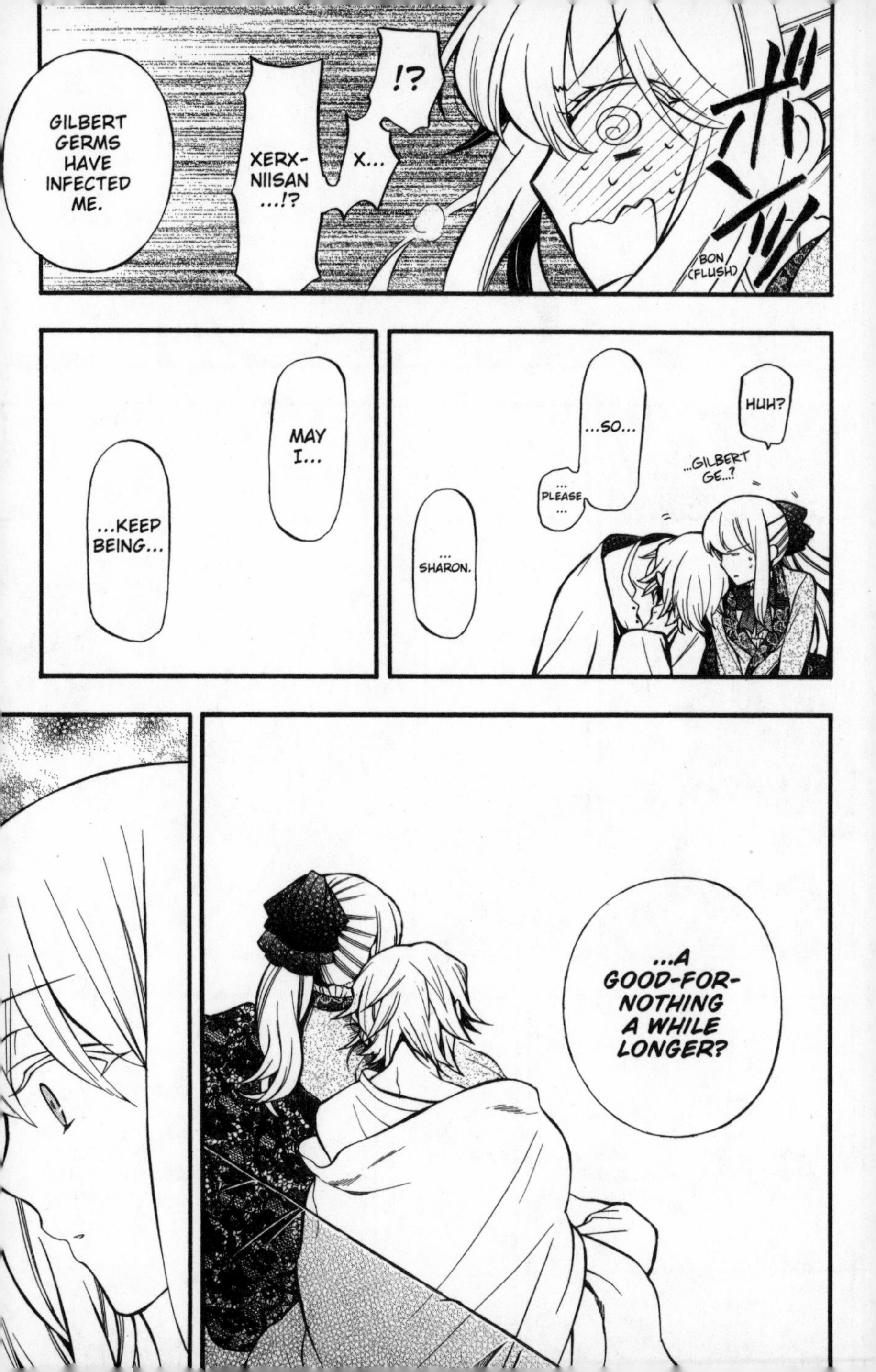
BON (FLUSH)
!?
X...
XERX-NIISAN ...!?
GILBERT GERMS HAVE INFECTED ME.
HUH?
...GILBERT GE...?
...SO...
... PLEASE ...
... SHARON.
MAY I...
...KEEP BEING...
...A GOOD-FOR-NOTHING A WHILE LONGER?

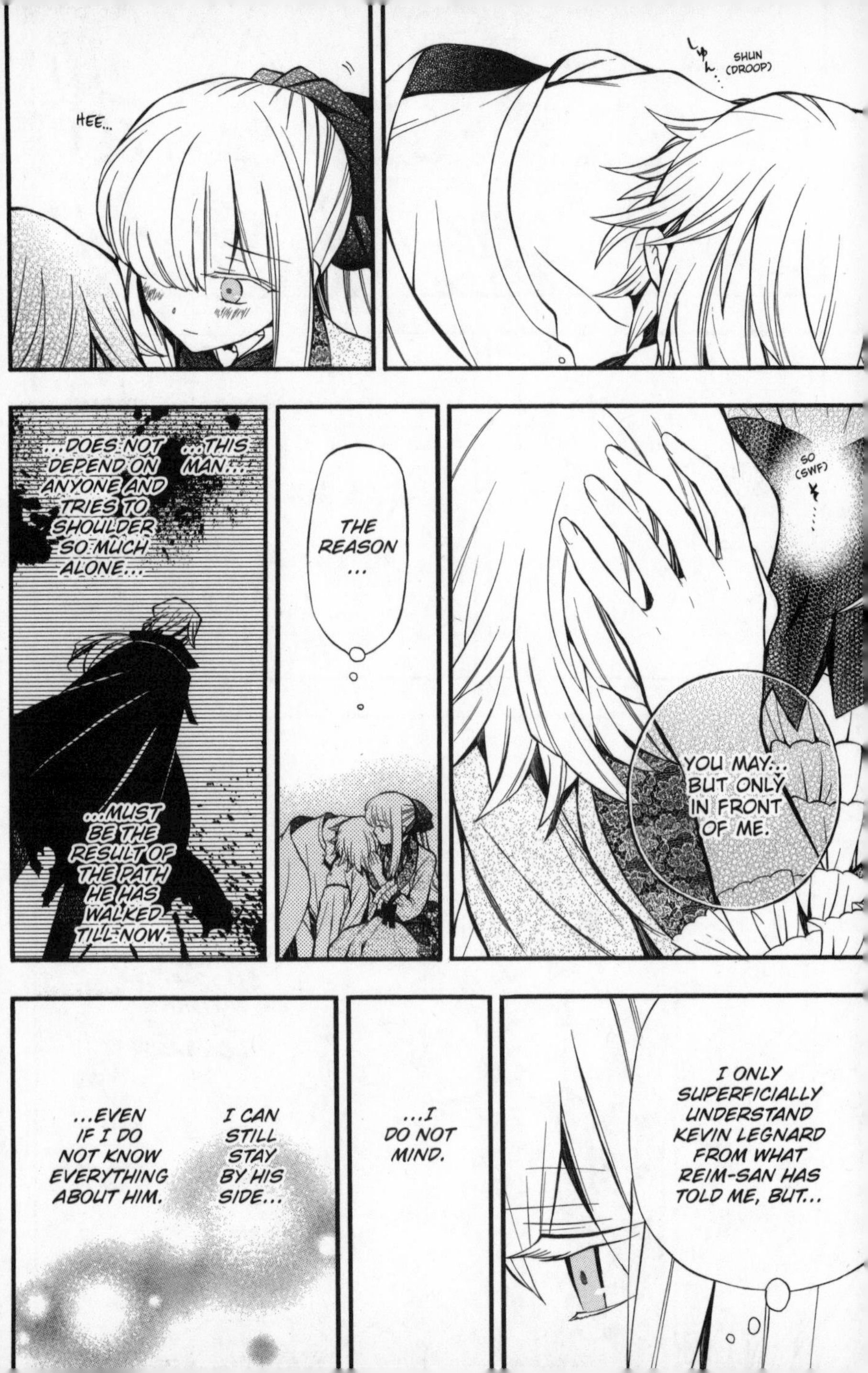
SHUN (DROOP)
HEE...
SO (SWF)
YOU MAY... BUT ONLY IN FRONT OF ME.
THE REASON ...
...THIS MAN...
...DOES NOT DEPEND ON ANYONE AND TRIES TO SHOULDER SO MUCH ALONE...
...MUST BE THE RESULT OF THE PATH HE HAS WALKED TILL NOW.
I ONLY SUPERFICIALLY UNDERSTAND KEVIN LEGNARD FROM WHAT REIM-SAN HAS TOLD ME, BUT...
...I DO NOT MIND.
I CAN STILL STAY BY HIS SIDE...
...EVEN IF I DO NOT KNOW EVERYTHING ABOUT HIM.

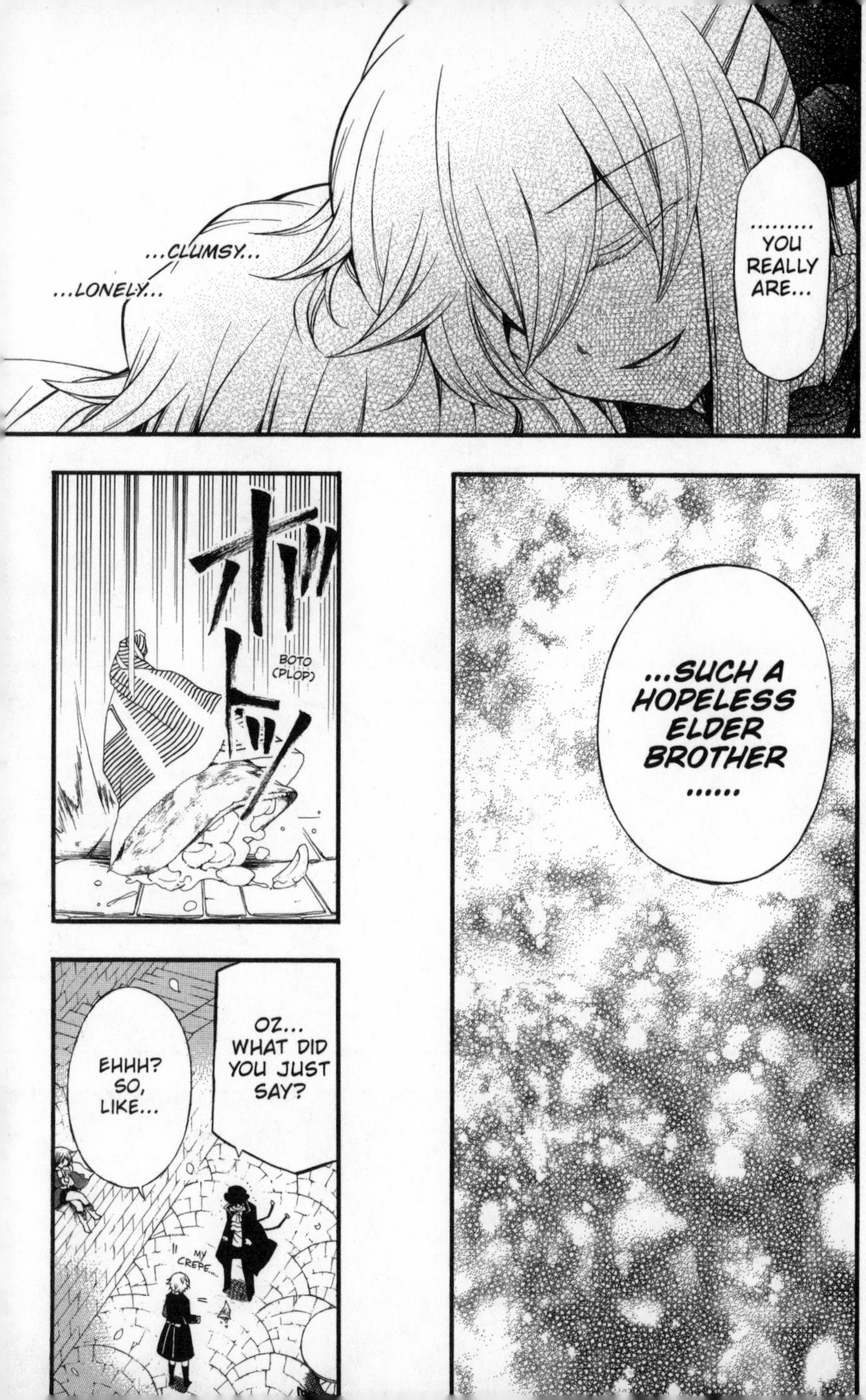
.... YOU REALLY ARE...
...CLUMSY...
...LONELY...
...SUCH A HOPELESS ELDER BROTHER ......
BOTO (PLOP)
OZ... WHAT DID YOU JUST SAY?
EHHH? SO, LIKE...
MY CREPE...

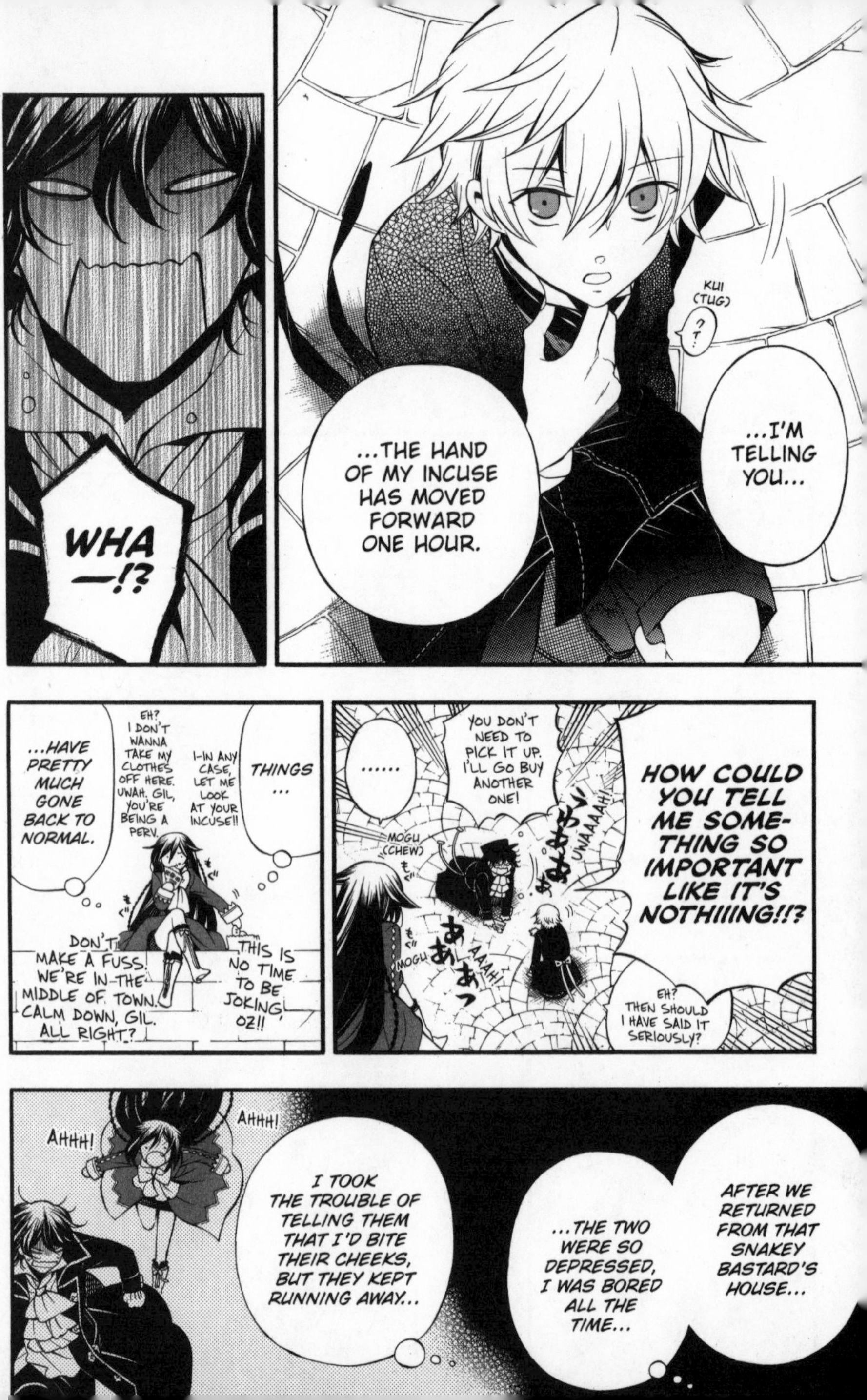
KUI (TUG)
?
...I'M TELLING YOU...
...THE HAND OF MY INCUSE HAS MOVED FORWARD ONE HOUR.
WHA—!?
HOW COULD YOU TELL ME SOME-THING SO IMPORTANT LIKE IT'S NOTHIIING!!?
YOU DON'T NEED TO PICK IT UP. I'LL GO BUY ANOTHER ONE!
......
UWAAAAH!
AAAH!
MOGU (CHEW)
MOGU
EH? THEN SHOULD I HAVE SAID IT SERIOUSLY?
THINGS ...
I-IN ANY CASE, LET ME LOOK AT YOUR INCUSE!!
EH? I DON'T WANNA TAKE MY CLOTHES OFF HERE. UWAH, GIL, YOU'RE BEING A PERV.
...HAVE PRETTY MUCH GONE BACK TO NORMAL.
THIS IS NO TIME TO BE JOKING, OZ!!
DON'T MAKE A FUSS. WE'RE IN THE MIDDLE OF TOWN. CALM DOWN, GIL. ALL RIGHT?
AFTER WE RETURNED FROM THAT SNAKEY BASTARD'S HOUSE...
...THE TWO WERE SO DEPRESSED, I WAS BORED ALL THE TIME...
I TOOK THE TROUBLE OF TELLING THEM THAT I'D BITE THEIR CHEEKS, BUT THEY KEPT RUNNING AWAY...
AHHH!
AHHH!

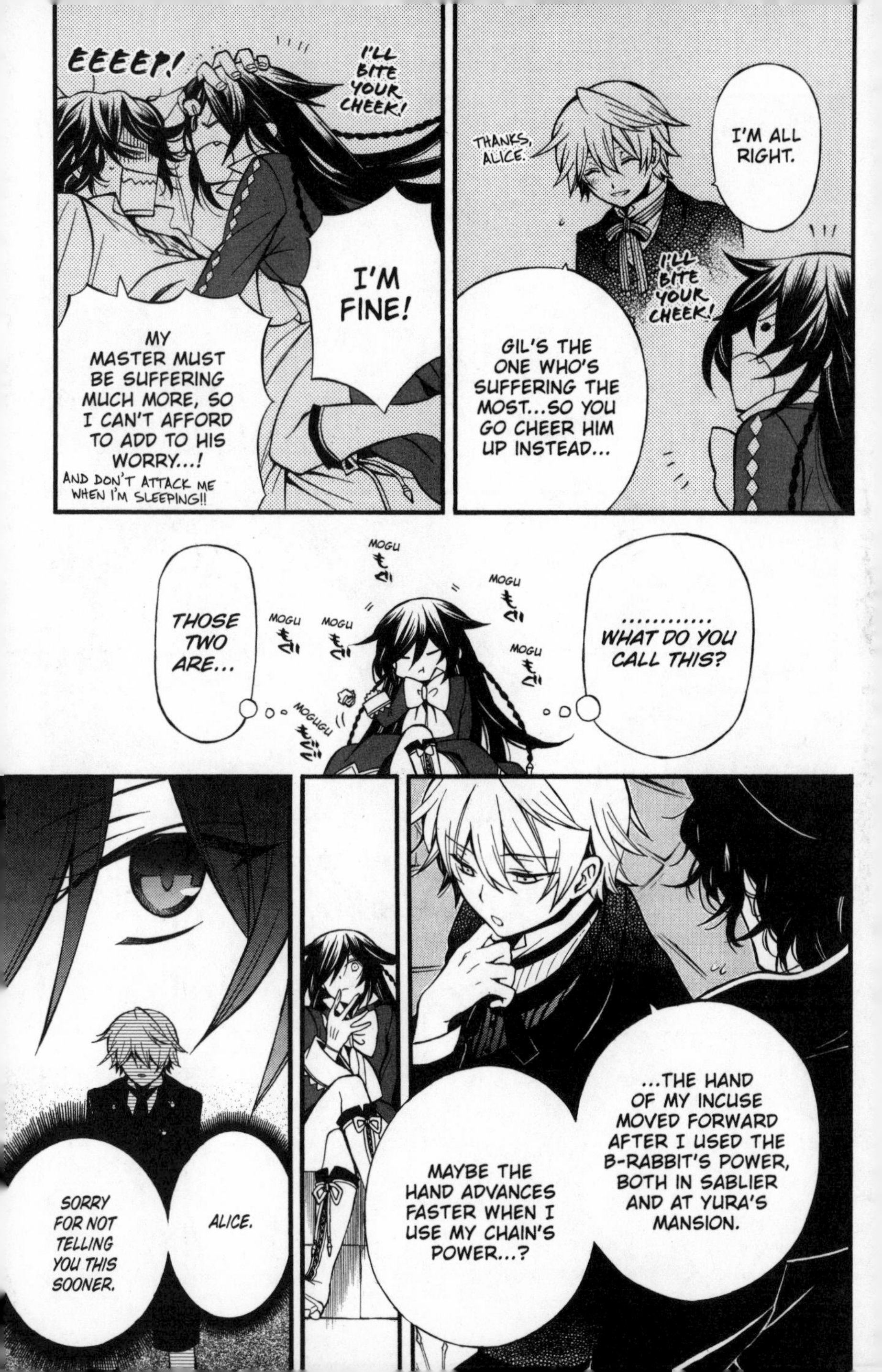
I'M ALL RIGHT.
THANKS, ALICE.
I'LL BITE YOUR CHEEK!
GIL'S THE ONE WHO'S SUFFERING THE MOST...SO YOU GO CHEER HIM UP INSTEAD...
I'LL BITE YOUR CHEEK!
EEEEP!
I'M FINE!
MY MASTER MUST BE SUFFERING MUCH MORE, SO I CAN'T AFFORD TO ADD TO HIS WORRY...!
AND DON'T ATTACK ME WHEN I'M SLEEPING!!
.... WHAT DO YOU CALL THIS?
MOGU
MOGU
MOGU
MOGU
MOGUGU
MOGU
THOSE TWO ARE...
...THE HAND OF MY INCUSE MOVED FORWARD AFTER I USED THE B-RABBIT'S POWER, BOTH IN SABLIER AND AT YURA'S MANSION.
MAYBE THE HAND ADVANCES FASTER WHEN I USE MY CHAIN'S POWER...?
ALICE.
SORRY FOR NOT TELLING YOU THIS SOONER.

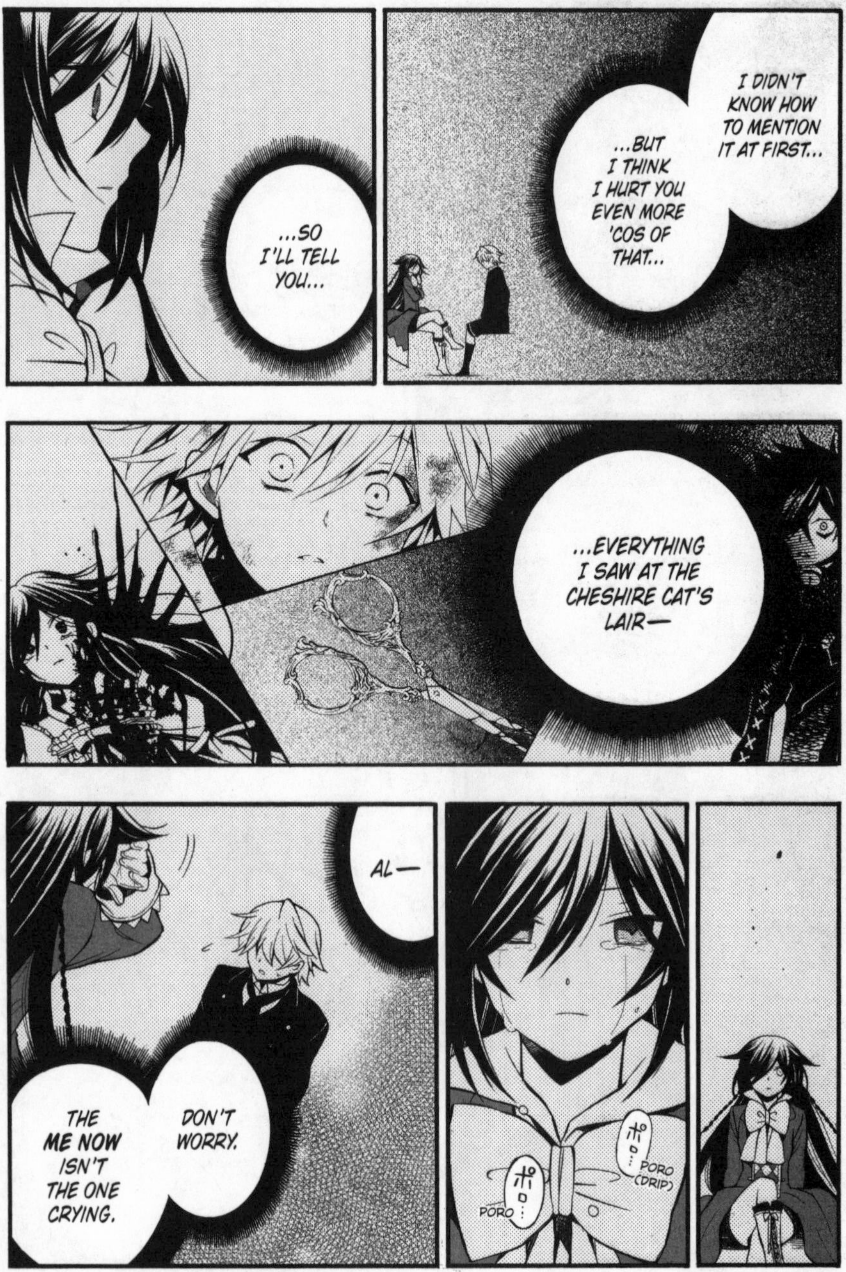
I DIDN'T KNOW HOW TO MENTION IT AT FIRST...
...BUT I THINK I HURT YOU EVEN MORE 'COS OF THAT...
...SO I'LL TELL YOU...
...EVERYTHING I SAW AT THE CHESHIRE CAT'S LAIR—
ポロ…
PORO (DRIP)
ポロ…
PORO
AL—
DON'T WORRY.
THE ME NOW ISN'T THE ONE CRYING.

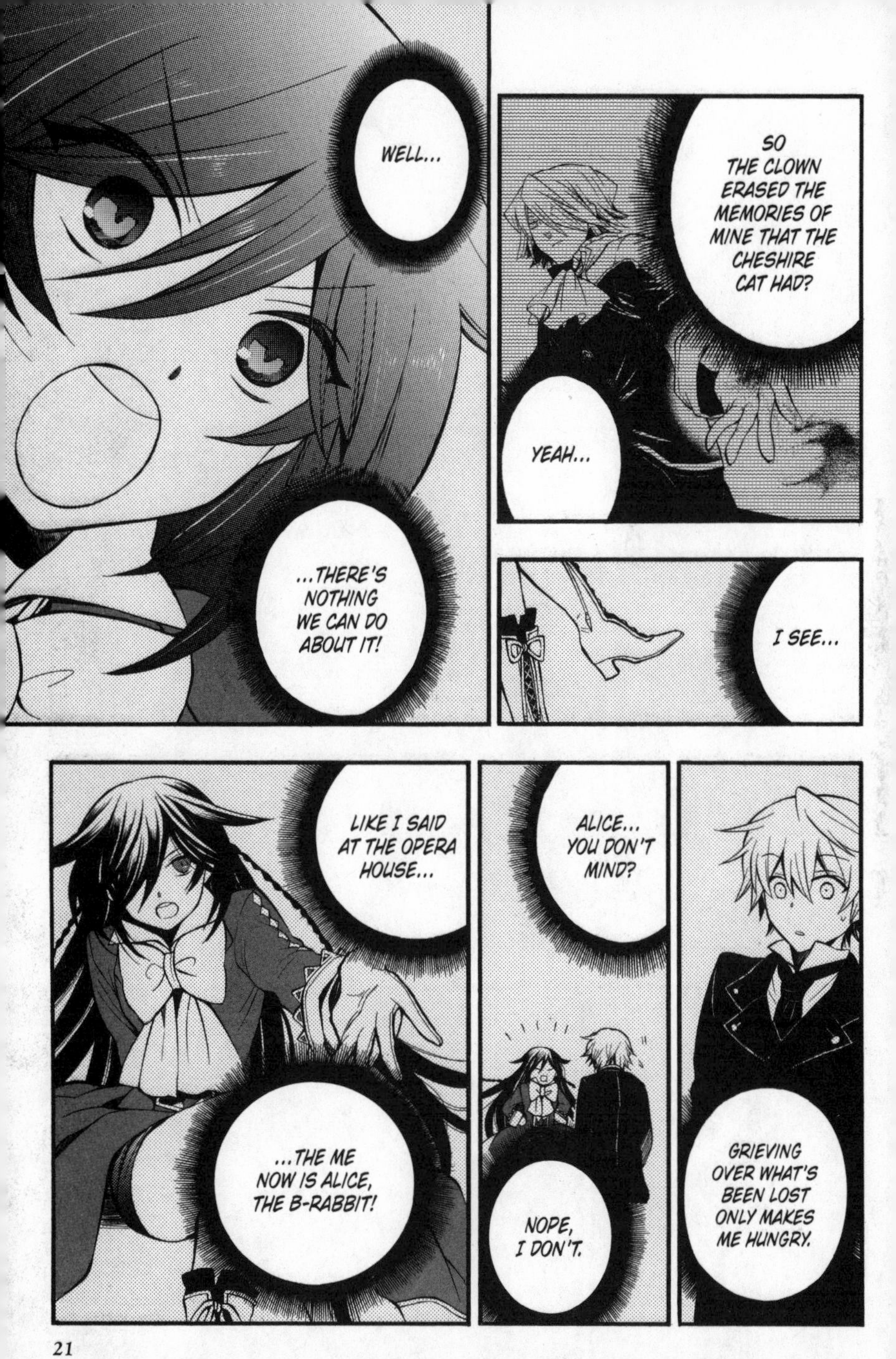
SO THE CLOWN ERASED THE MEMORIES OF MINE THAT THE CHESHIRE CAT HAD?
YEAH...
I SEE...
WELL...
...THERE'S NOTHING WE CAN DO ABOUT IT!
GRIEVING OVER WHAT'S BEEN LOST ONLY MAKES ME HUNGRY.
ALICE... YOU DON'T MIND?
NOPE, I DON'T.
LIKE I SAID AT THE OPERA HOUSE...
...THE ME NOW IS ALICE, THE B-RABBIT!

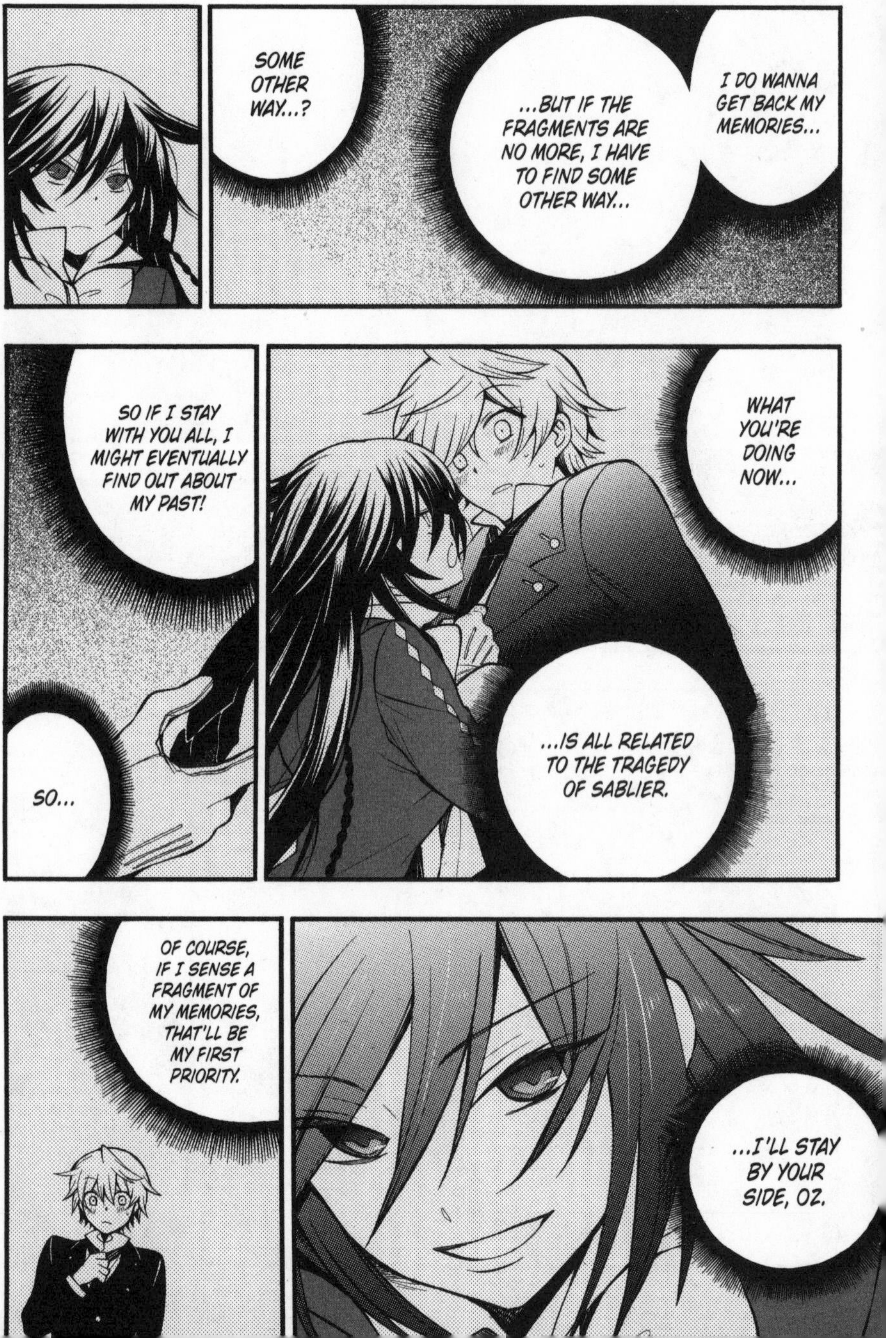
I DO WANNA GET BACK MY MEMORIES...
...BUT IF THE FRAGMENTS ARE NO MORE, I HAVE TO FIND SOME OTHER WAY...
SOME OTHER WAY...?
WHAT YOU'RE DOING NOW...
...IS ALL RELATED TO THE TRAGEDY OF SABLIER.
SO IF I STAY WITH YOU ALL, I MIGHT EVENTUALLY FIND OUT ABOUT MY PAST!
SO...
...I'LL STAY BY YOUR SIDE, OZ.
OF COURSE, IF I SENSE A FRAGMENT OF MY MEMORIES, THAT'LL BE MY FIRST PRIORITY.

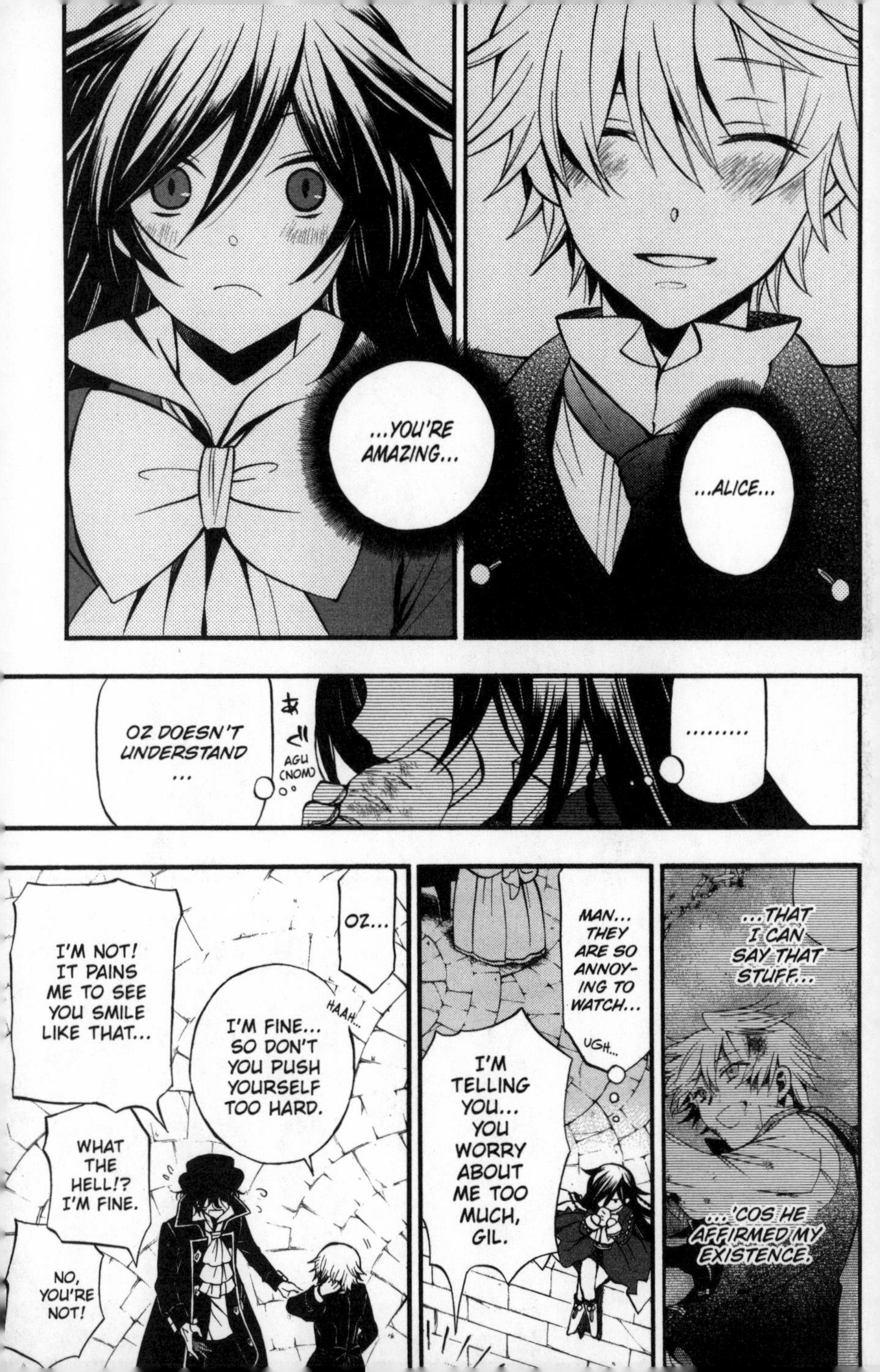
...ALICE...
...YOU'RE AMAZING...
....
あぐ
AGU (NOM)
OZ DOESN'T UNDERSTAND ...
...THAT I CAN SAY THAT STUFF...
...'COS HE AFFIRMED MY EXISTENCE.
MAN... THEY ARE SO ANNOY-ING TO WATCH...
UGH...
I'M TELLING YOU... YOU WORRY ABOUT ME TOO MUCH, GIL.
OZ...
HAAH...
I'M FINE... SO DON'T YOU PUSH YOURSELF TOO HARD.
I'M NOT! IT PAINS ME TO SEE YOU SMILE LIKE THAT...
WHAT THE HELL!? I'M FINE.
NO, YOU'RE NOT!

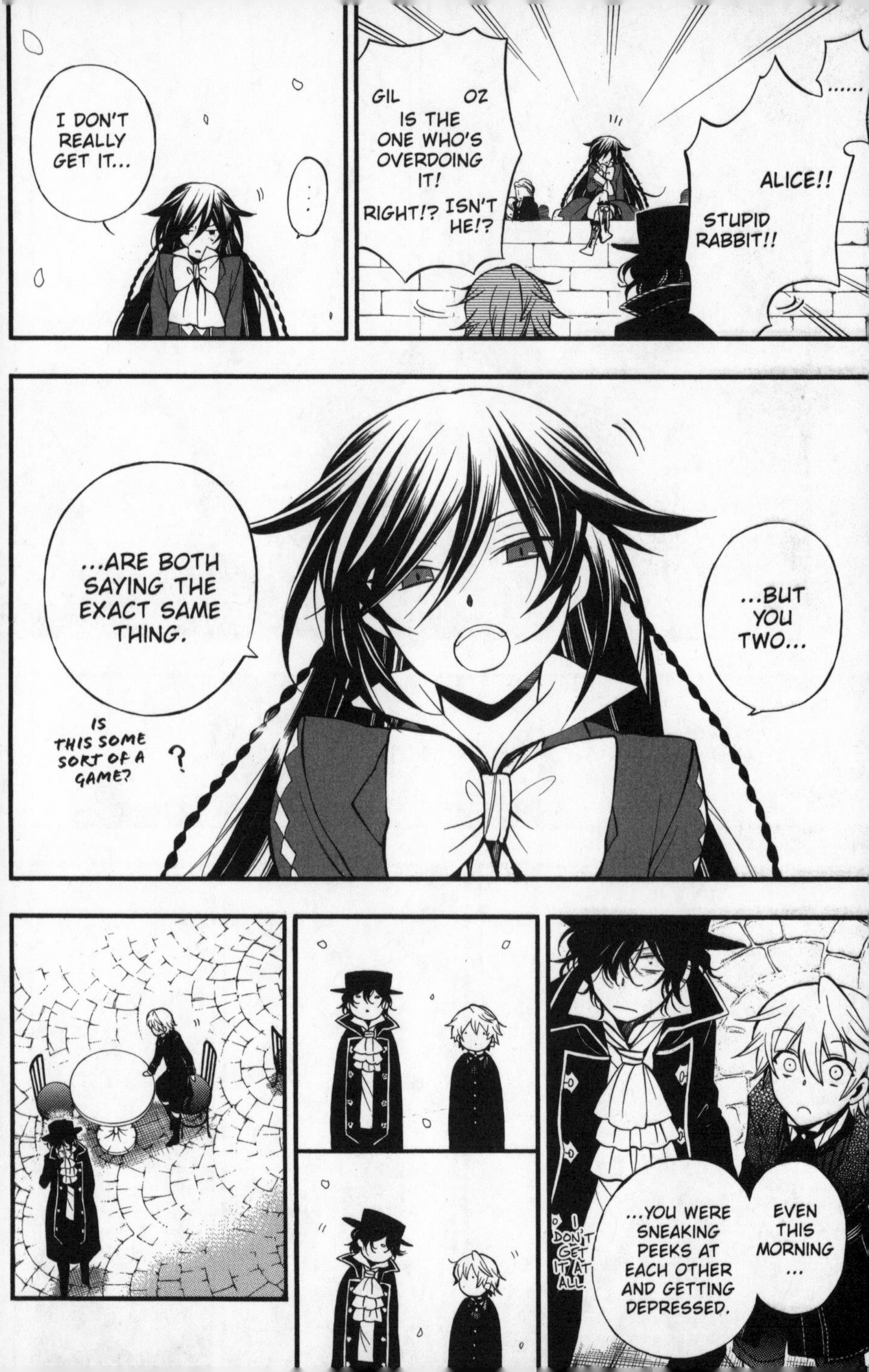
......
ALICE!!
STUPID RABBIT!!
GIL OZ
IS THE ONE WHO'S OVERDOING IT!
RIGHT!? ISN'T HE!?
I DON'T REALLY GET IT...
...
...BUT YOU TWO...
...ARE BOTH SAYING THE EXACT SAME THING.
IS THIS SOME SORT OF A GAME?
?
EVEN THIS MORNING ...
...YOU WERE SNEAKING PEEKS AT EACH OTHER AND GETTING DEPRESSED.
I DON'T GET IT AT ALL.

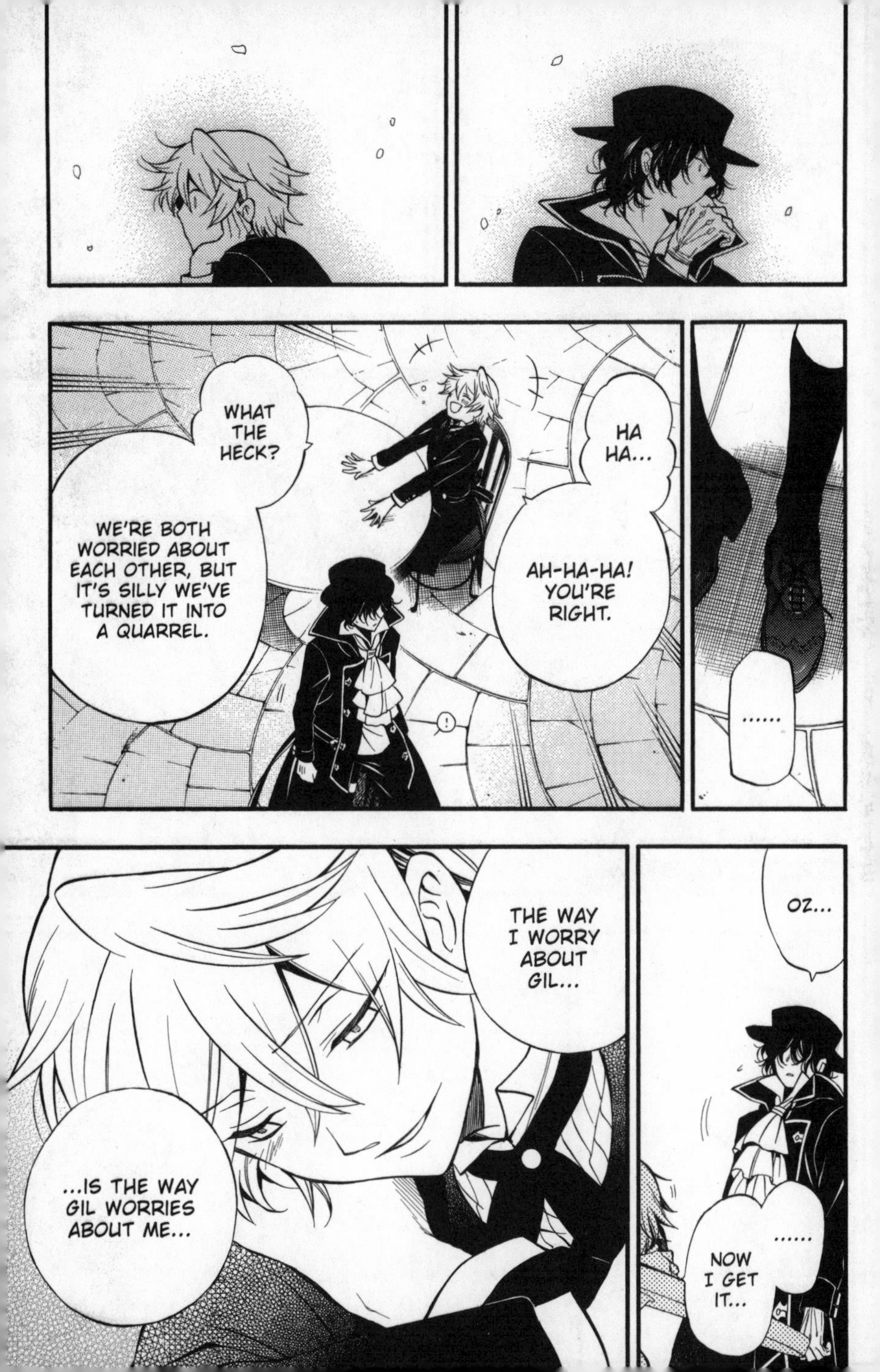
......
HA HA...
AH-HA-HA! YOU'RE RIGHT.
WHAT THE HECK?
WE'RE BOTH WORRIED ABOUT EACH OTHER, BUT IT'S SILLY WE'VE TURNED IT INTO A QUARREL.
OZ...
......
NOW I GET IT...
THE WAY I WORRY ABOUT GIL...
...IS THE WAY GIL WORRIES ABOUT ME...

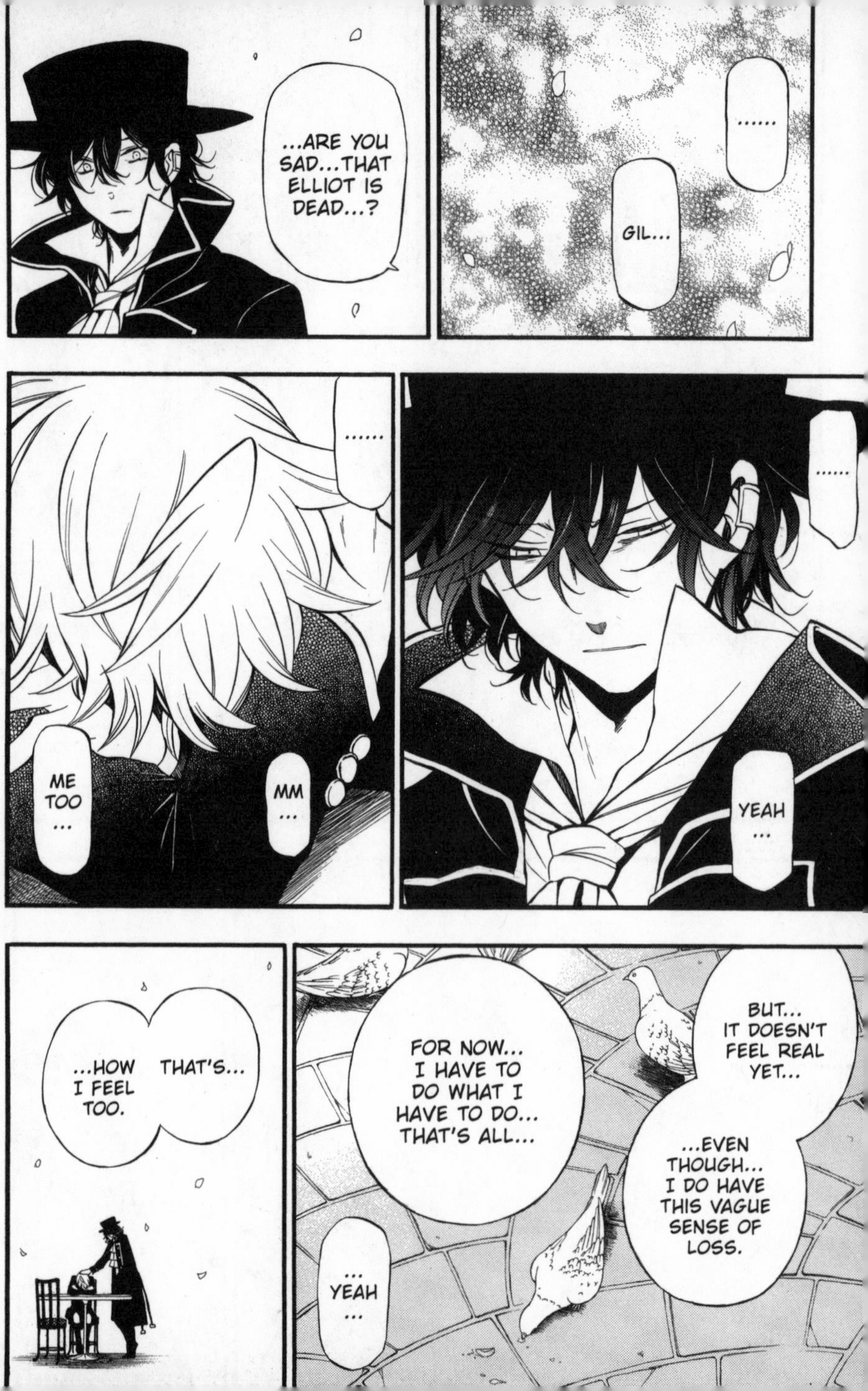
......
GIL...
...ARE YOU SAD...THAT ELLIOT IS DEAD...?
......
YEAH ...
......
MM ...
ME TOO ...
BUT... IT DOESN'T FEEL REAL YET...
...EVEN THOUGH... I DO HAVE THIS VAGUE SENSE OF LOSS.
FOR NOW... I HAVE TO DO WHAT I HAVE TO DO... THAT'S ALL...
... YEAH ...
THAT'S...
...HOW I FEEL TOO.

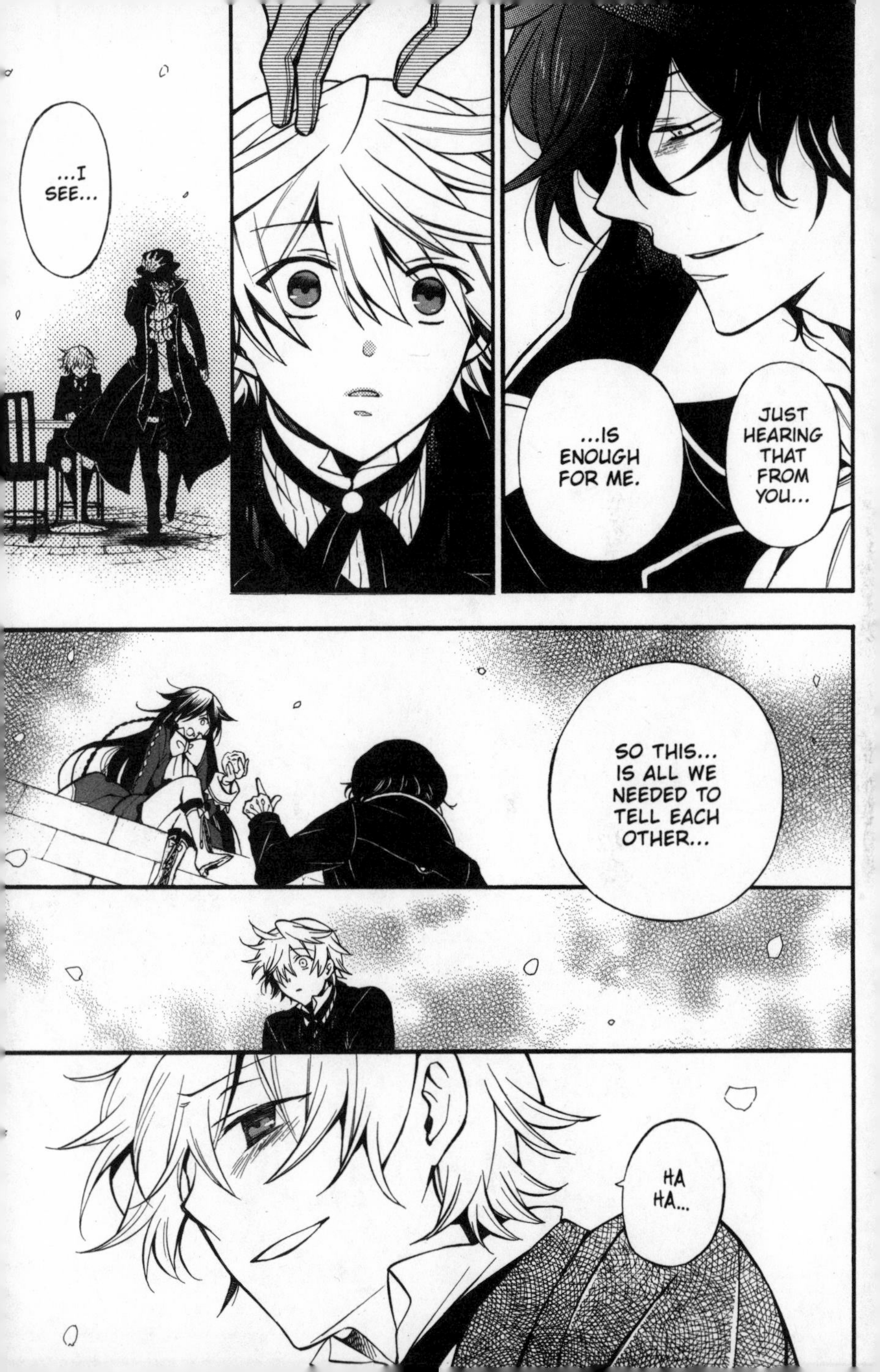
JUST HEARING THAT FROM YOU...
...IS ENOUGH FOR ME.
...I SEE...
SO THIS... IS ALL WE NEEDED TO TELL EACH OTHER...
HA HA...

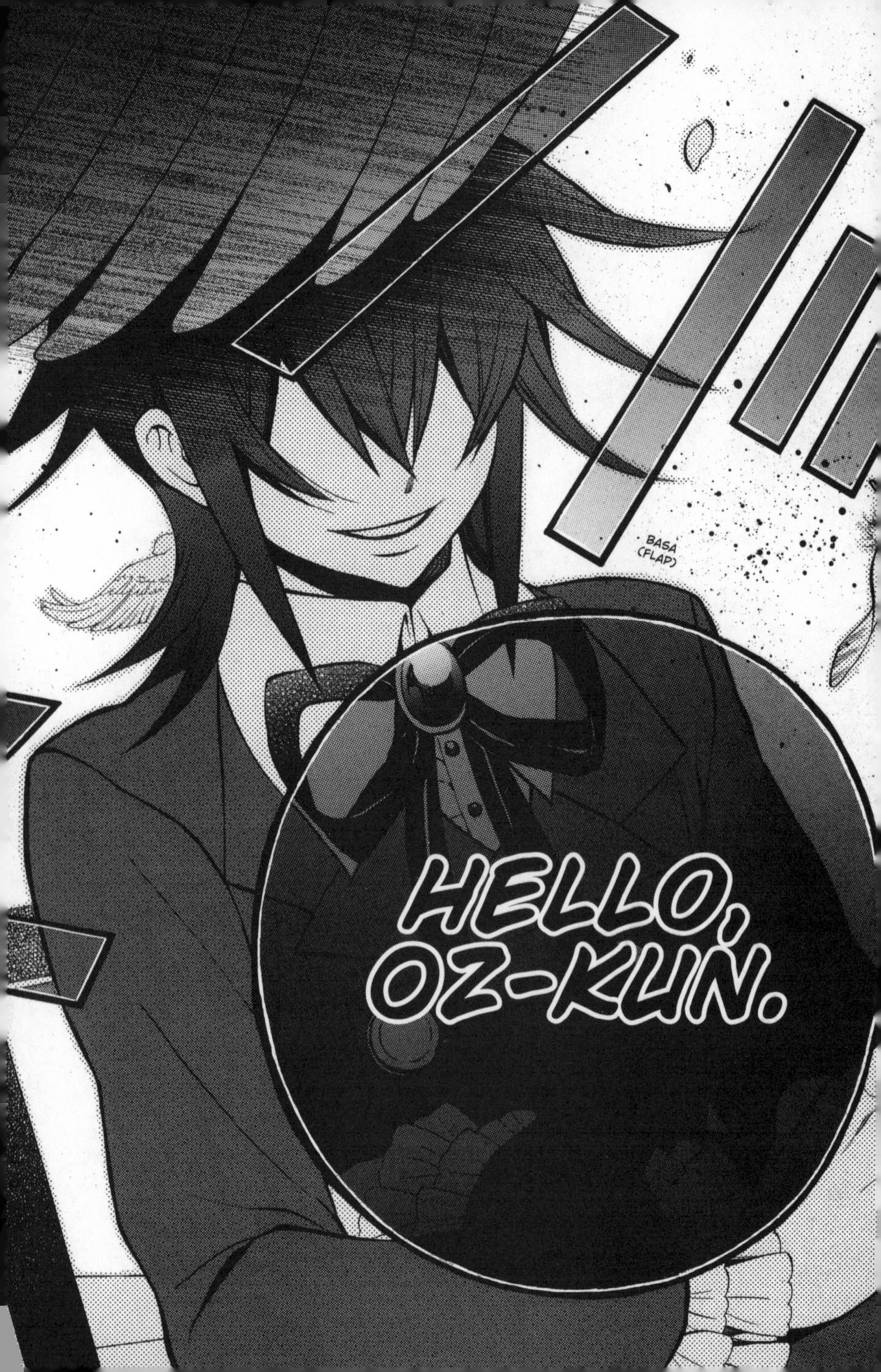
BASA (FLAP)
HELLO, OZ-KUN.

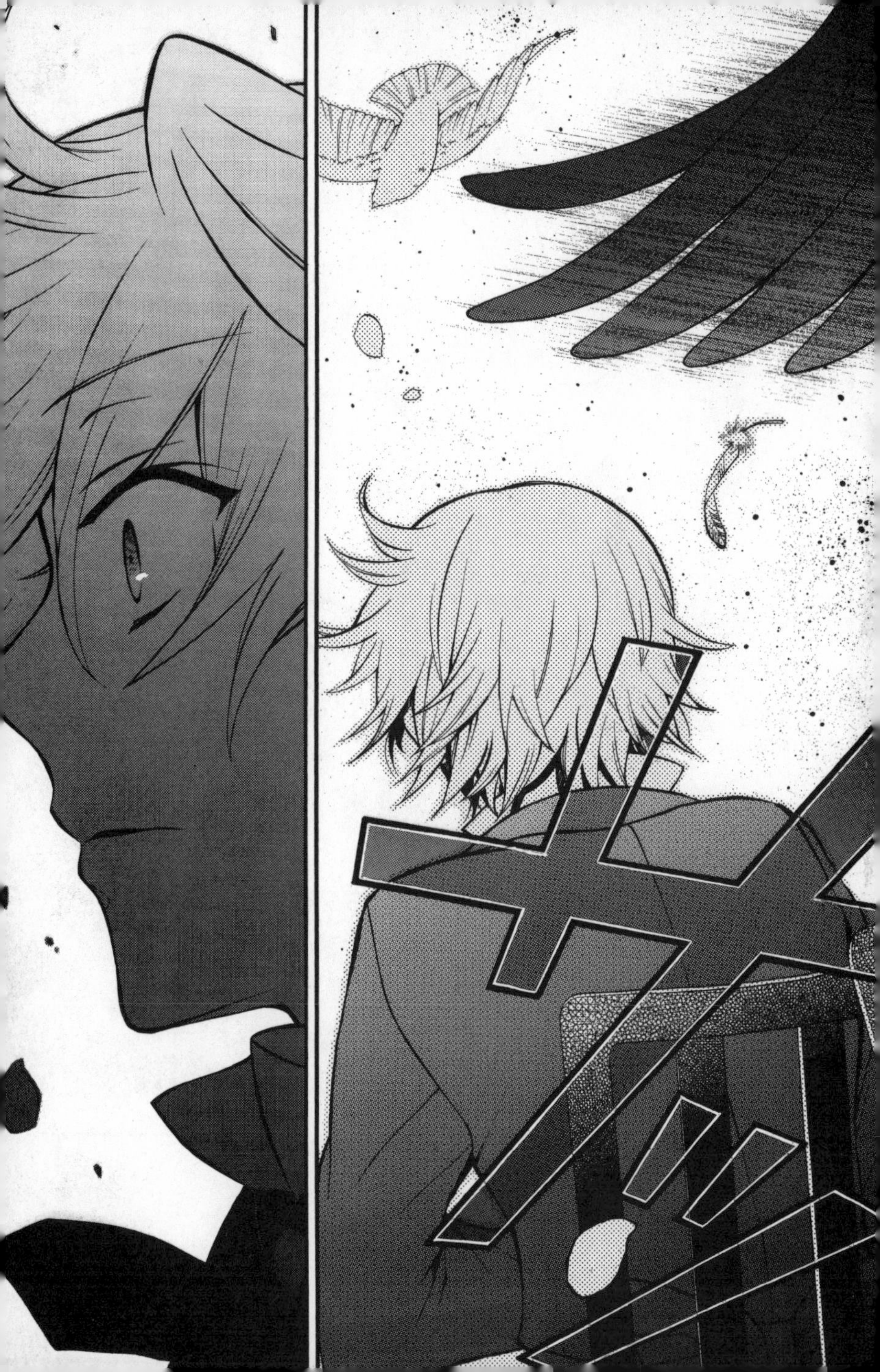

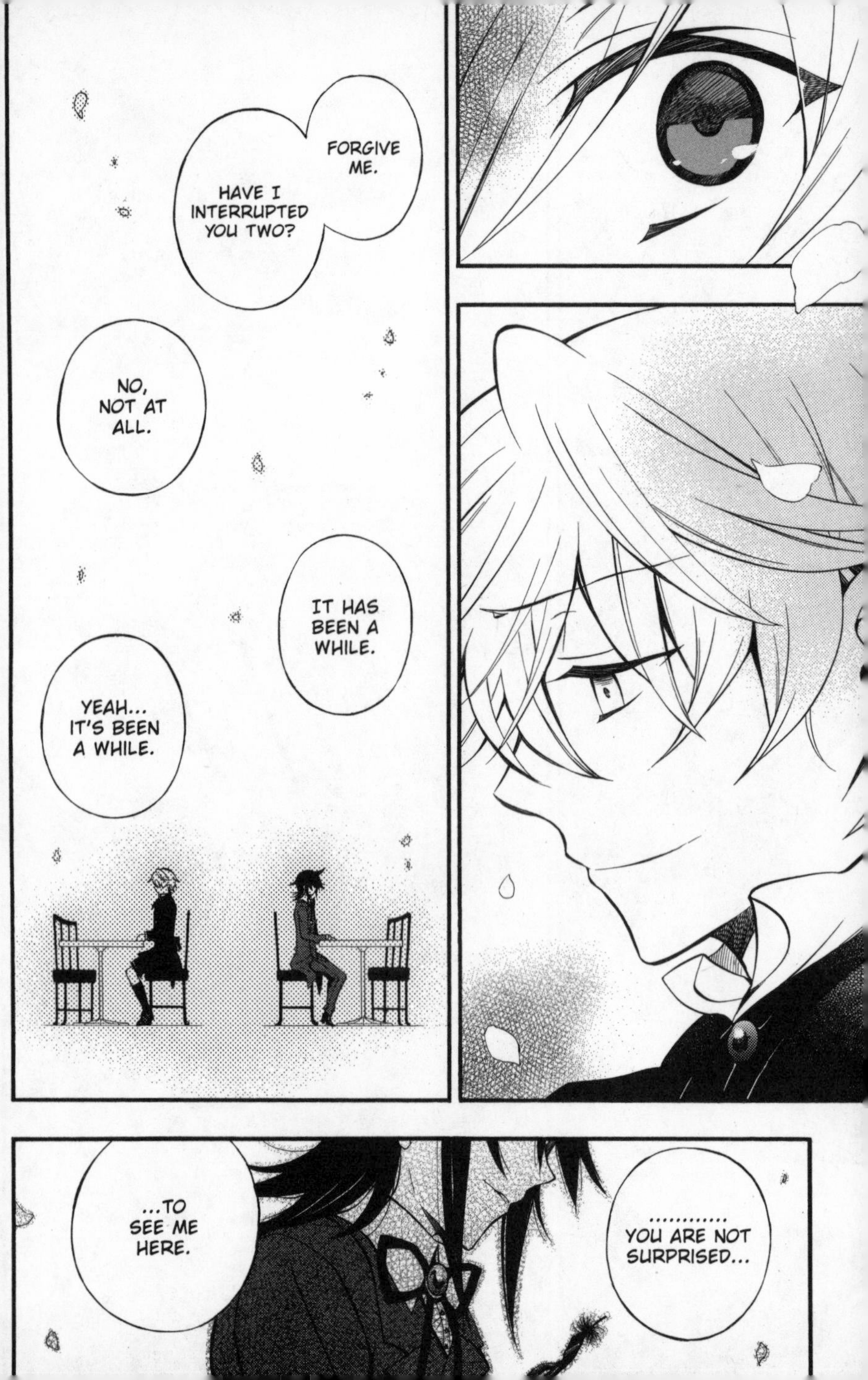
FORGIVE ME.
HAVE I INTERRUPTED YOU TWO?
NO, NOT AT ALL.
IT HAS BEEN A WHILE.
YEAH... IT'S BEEN A WHILE.
.... YOU ARE NOT SURPRISED...
...TO SEE ME HERE.

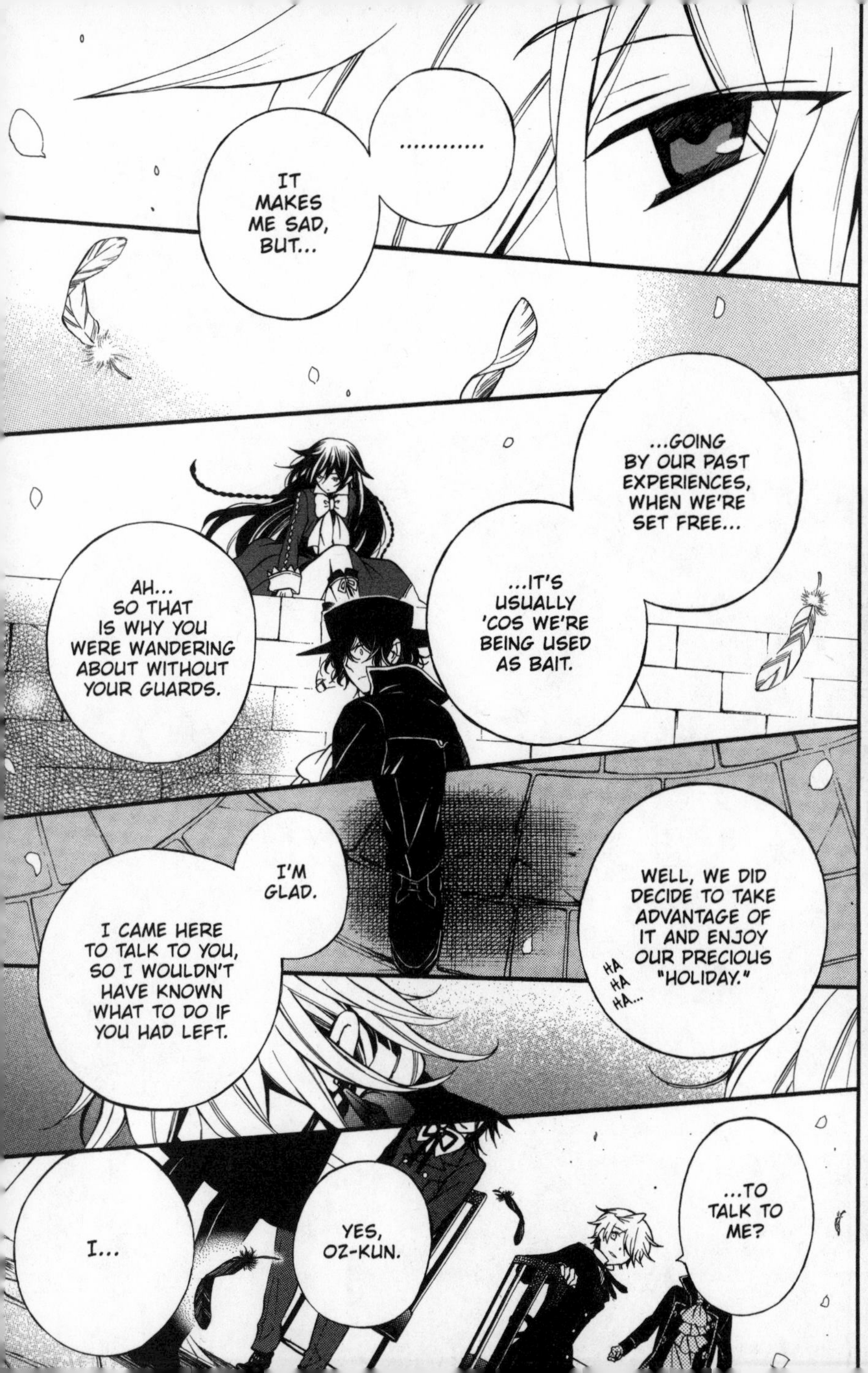
....
IT MAKES ME SAD, BUT...
...GOING BY OUR PAST EXPERIENCES, WHEN WE'RE SET FREE...
...IT'S USUALLY 'COS WE'RE BEING USED AS BAIT.
AH... SO THAT IS WHY YOU WERE WANDERING ABOUT WITHOUT YOUR GUARDS.
WELL, WE DID DECIDE TO TAKE ADVANTAGE OF IT AND ENJOY OUR PRECIOUS "HOLIDAY."
HA HA HA...
I'M GLAD.
I CAME HERE TO TALK TO YOU, SO I WOULDN'T HAVE KNOWN WHAT TO DO IF YOU HAD LEFT.
...TO TALK TO ME?
YES, OZ-KUN.
I...

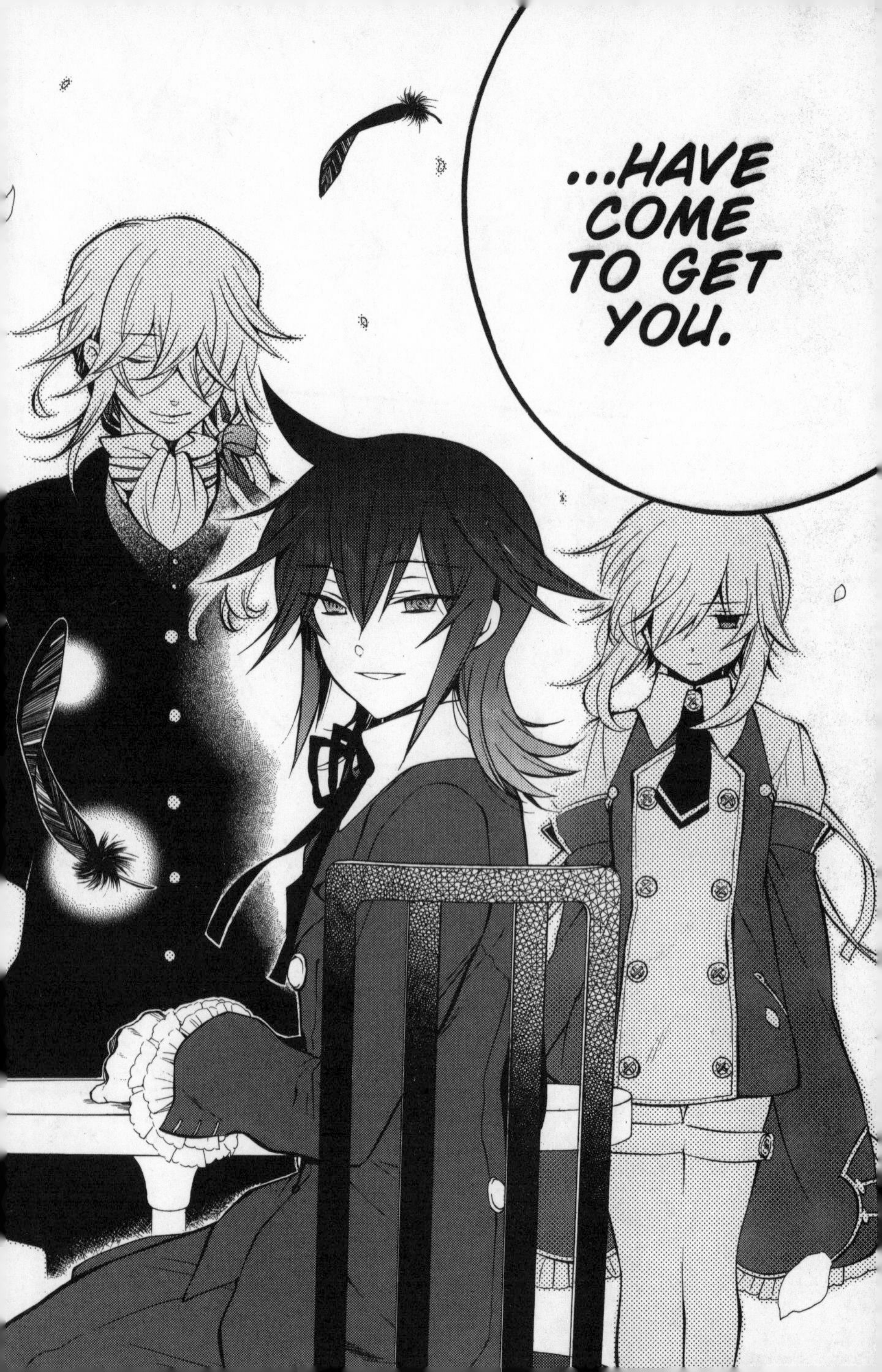
...HAVE COME TO GET YOU.

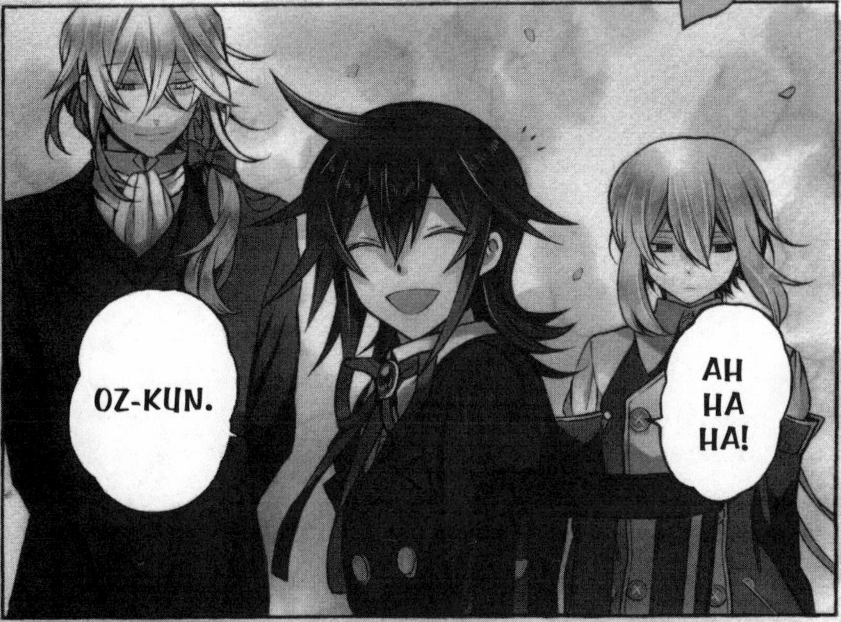
AH HA HA!
OZ-KUN.

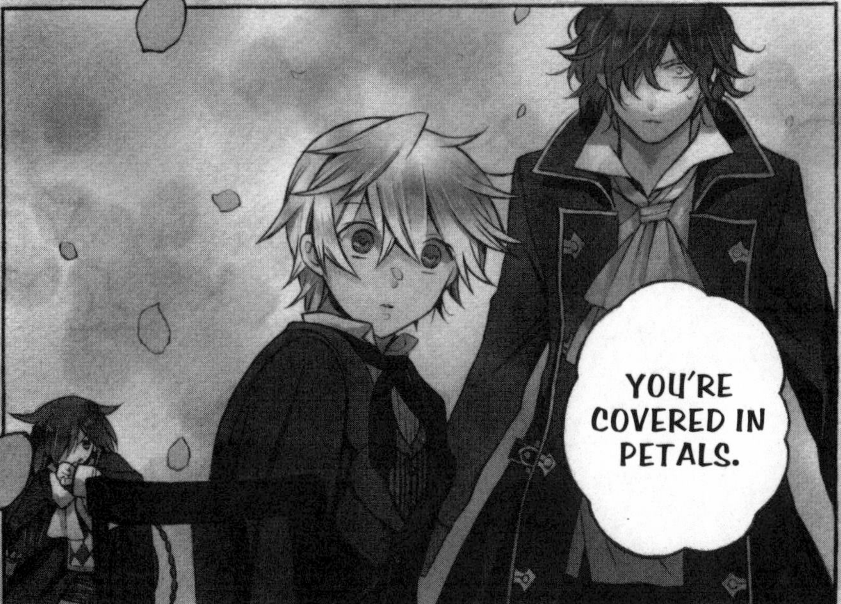
YOU'RE COVERED IN PETALS.

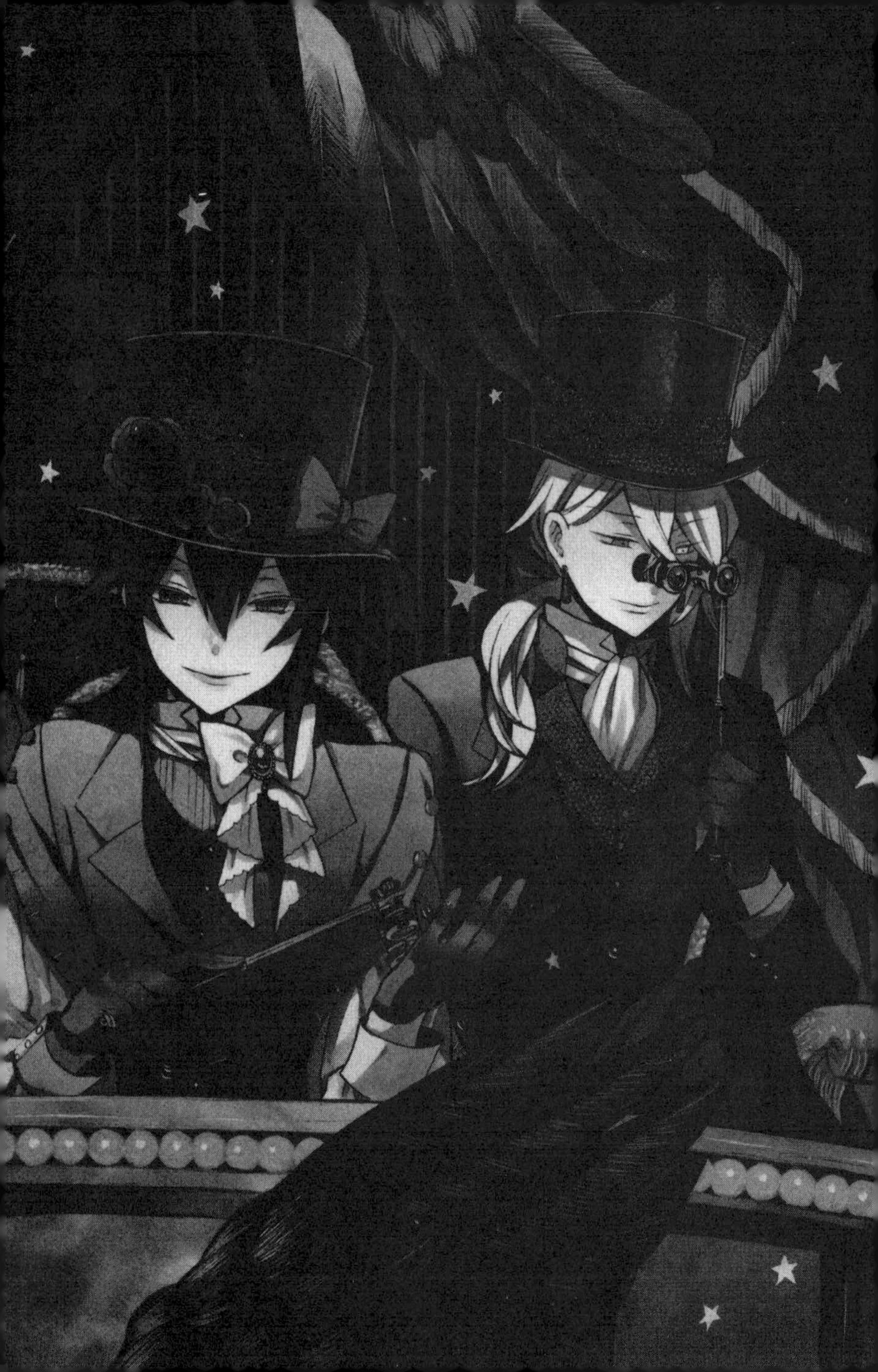

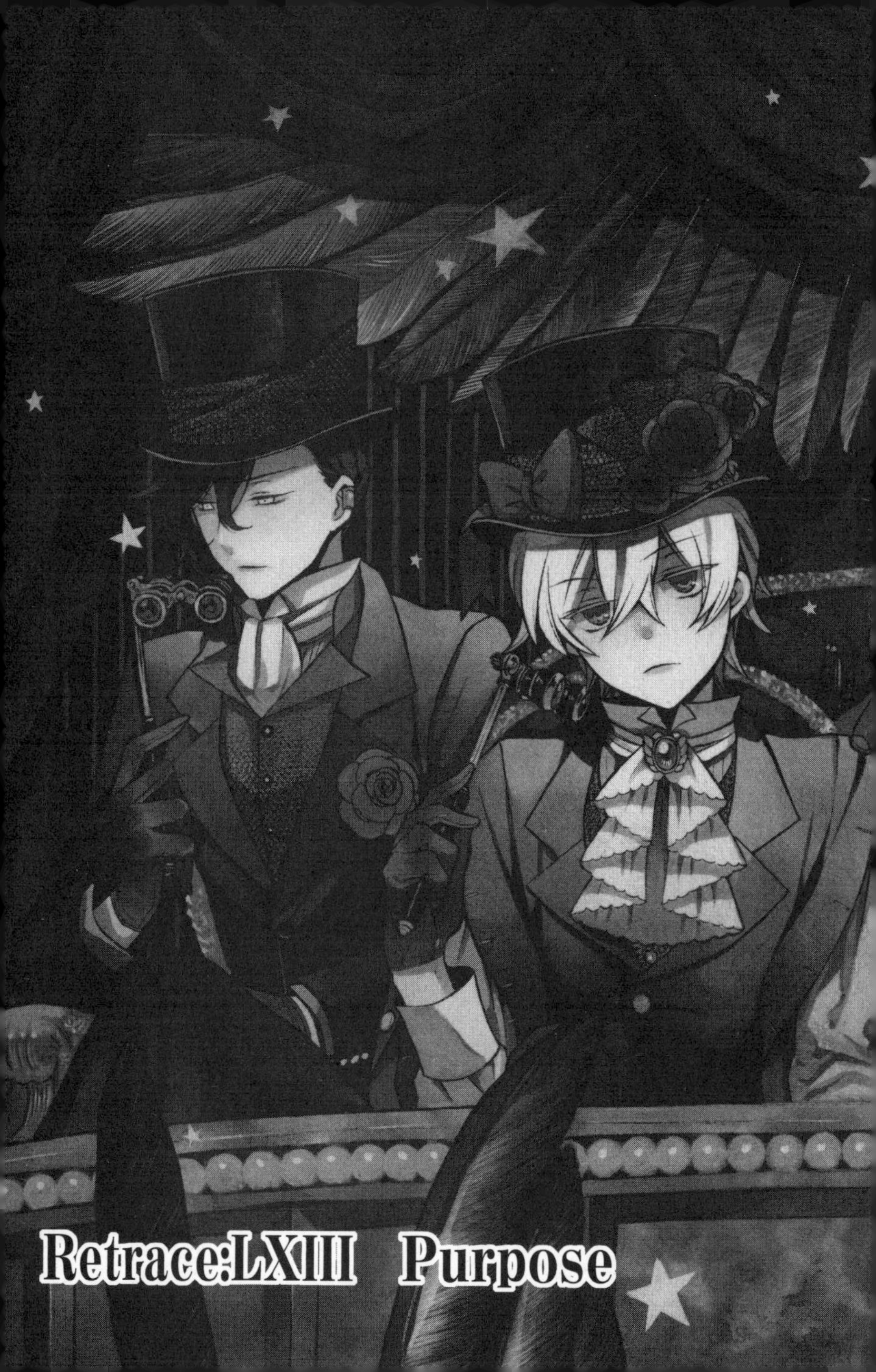
Retrace:LXIII Purpose

BONUS: TO EACH, THEIR OWN REVEIL

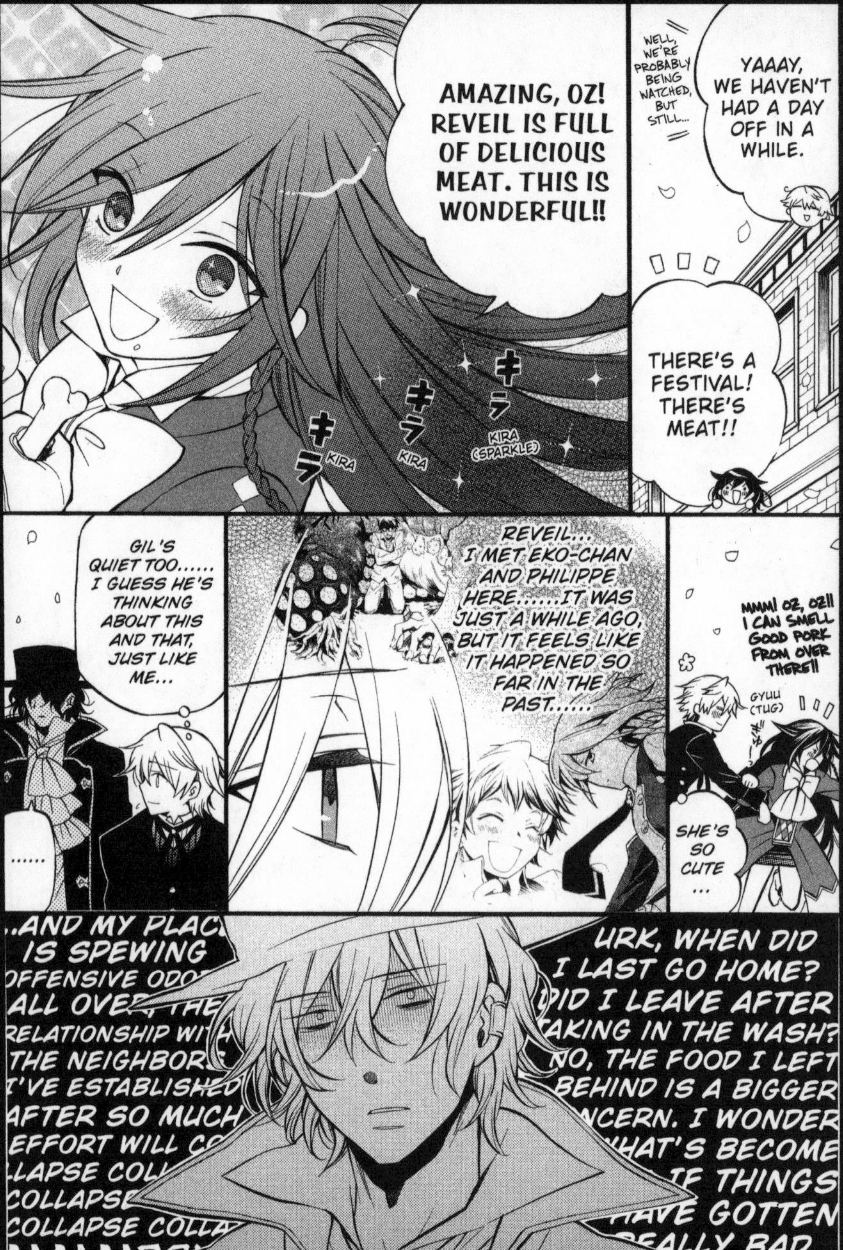
YAAAY, WE HAVEN'T HAD A DAY OFF IN A WHILE.
WELL, WE'RE PROBABLY BEING WATCHED, BUT STILL...
THERE'S A FESTIVAL! THERE'S MEAT!!
AMAZING, OZ! REVEIL IS FULL OF DELICIOUS MEAT. THIS IS WONDERFUL!!
KIRA (SPARKLE)
KIRA
KIRA
MMM! OZ, OZ!! I CAN SMELL GOOD PORK FROM OVER THERE!!
GYUU (TUG)
SHE'S SO CUTE ...
REVEIL... I MET EKO-CHAN AND PHILIPPE HERE......IT WAS JUST A WHILE AGO, BUT IT FEELS LIKE IT HAPPENED SO FAR IN THE PAST......
GIL'S QUIET TOO...... I GUESS HE'S THINKING ABOUT THIS AND THAT, JUST LIKE ME...
......
URK, WHEN DID I LAST GO HOME? DID I LEAVE AFTER TAKING IN THE WASH? NO, THE FOOD I LEFT BEHIND IS A BIGGER CONCERN. I WONDER WHAT'S BECOME ... IF THINGS HAVE GOTTEN REALLY BAD...
...AND MY PLACE IS SPEWING OFFENSIVE ODOR ALL OVER, THE RELATIONSHIP WITH THE NEIGHBORS I'VE ESTABLISHED AFTER SO MUCH EFFORT WILL COLLAPSE COLLAPSE COLLAPSE COLLA... AAAAAARGH

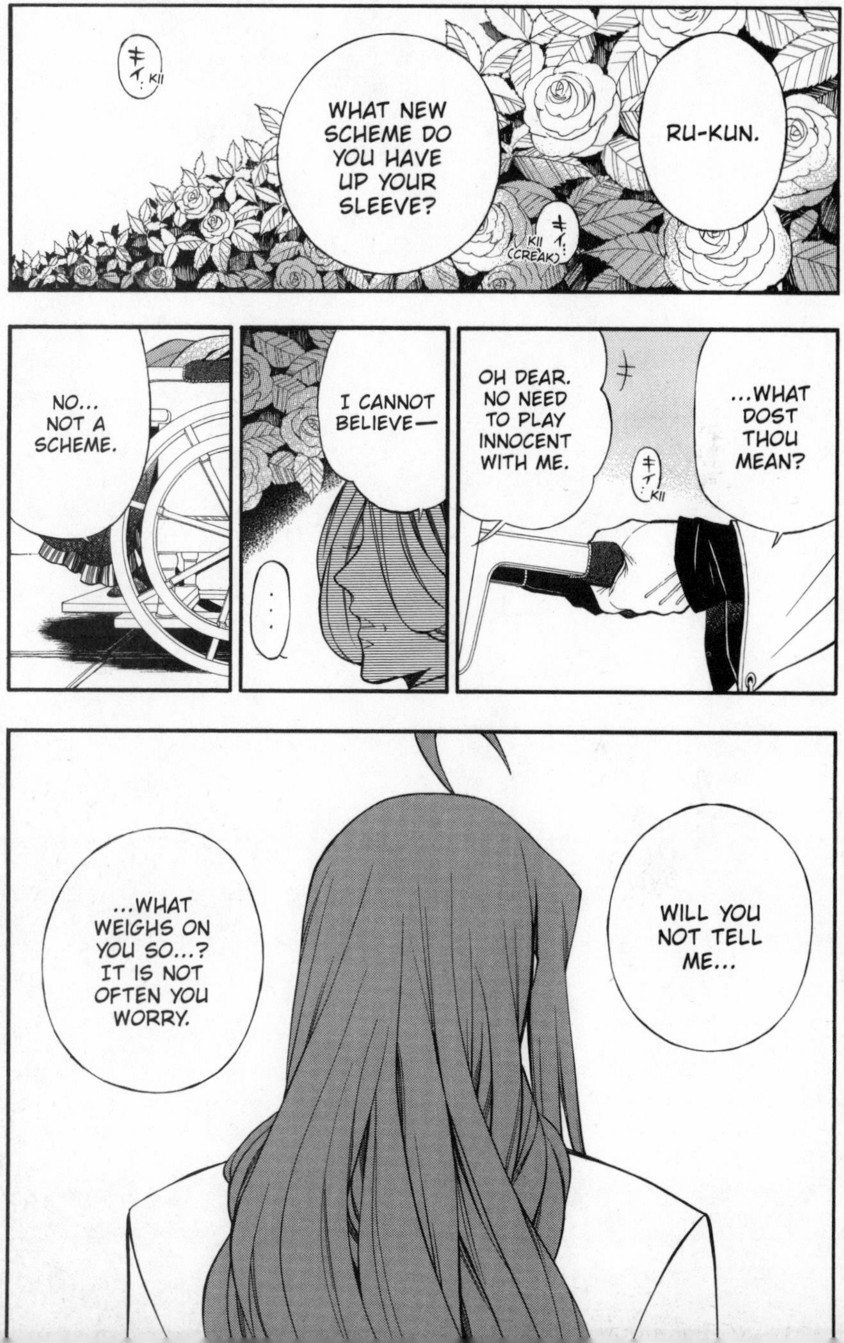
RU-KUN.
WHAT NEW SCHEME DO YOU HAVE UP YOUR SLEEVE?
キイ KII
キイ KII (CREAK)
...WHAT DOST THOU MEAN?
キ
OH DEAR. NO NEED TO PLAY INNOCENT WITH ME.
キイ KII
I CANNOT BELIEVE—
...
NO... NOT A SCHEME.
WILL YOU NOT TELL ME...
...WHAT WEIGHS ON YOU SO...? IT IS NOT OFTEN YOU WORRY.

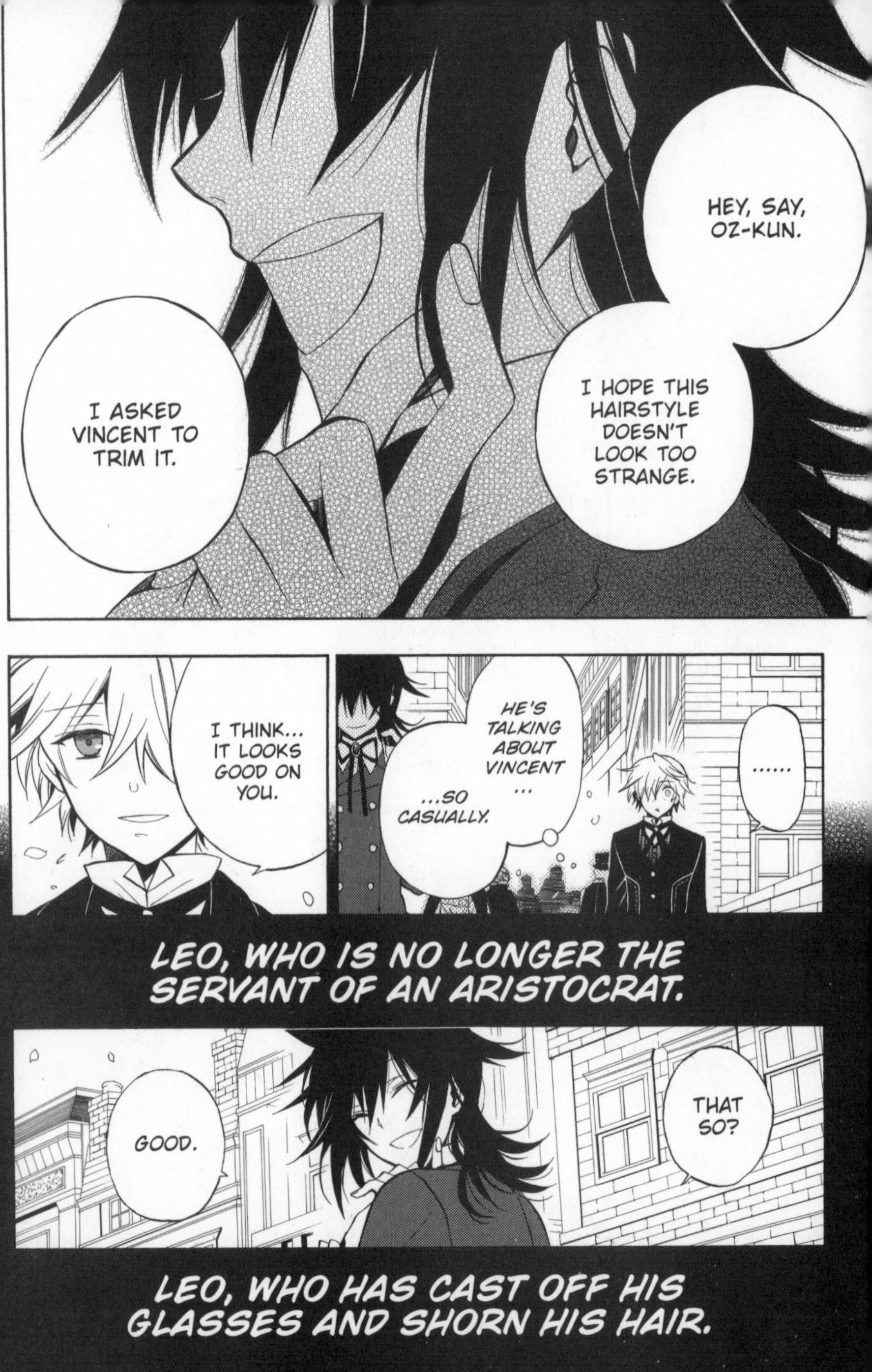
HEY, SAY, OZ-KUN.
I HOPE THIS HAIRSTYLE DOESN'T LOOK TOO STRANGE.
I ASKED VINCENT TO TRIM IT.
......
HE'S TALKING ABOUT VINCENT ... ...SO CASUALLY.
I THINK... IT LOOKS GOOD ON YOU.
LEO, WHO IS NO LONGER THE SERVANT OF AN ARISTOCRAT.
THAT SO?
GOOD.
LEO, WHO HAS CAST OFF HIS GLASSES AND SHORN HIS HAIR.

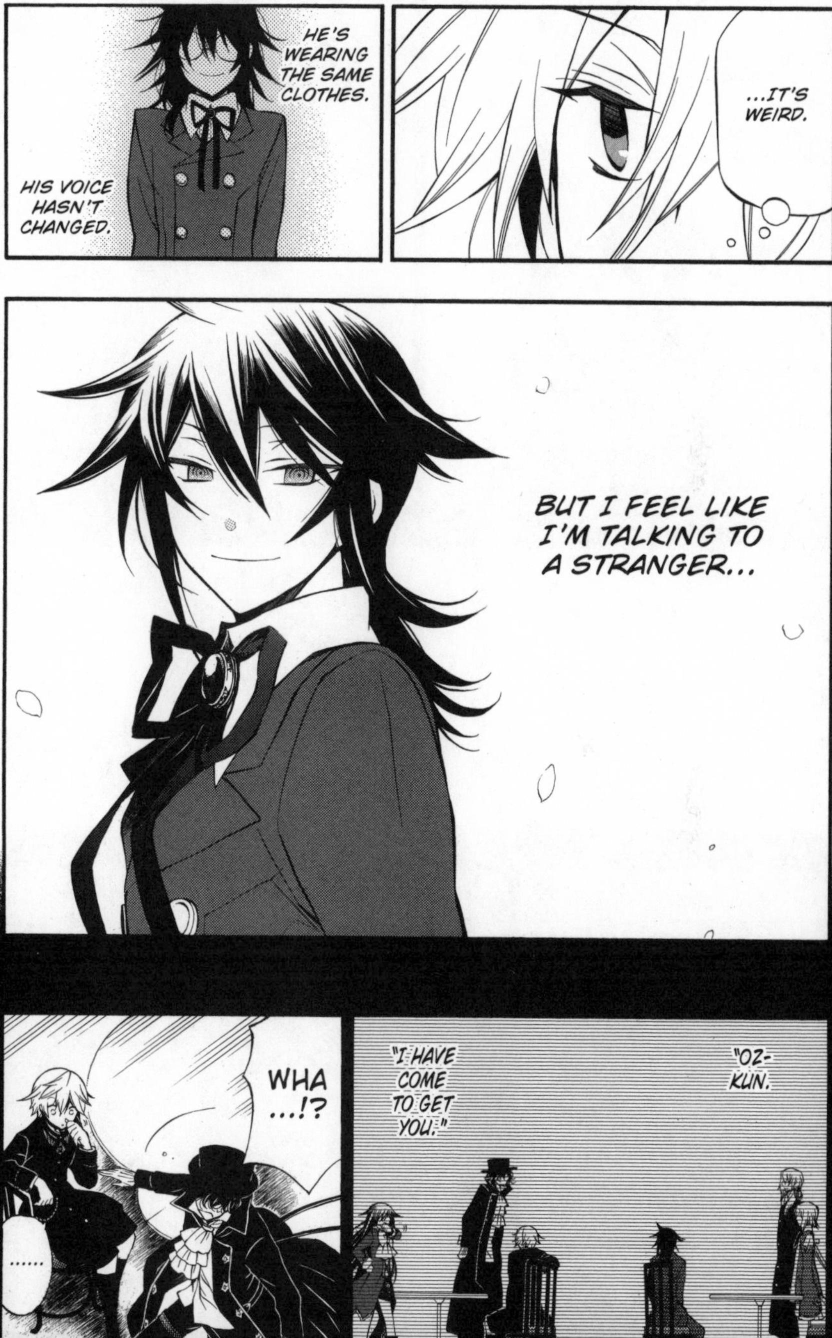
...IT'S WEIRD.
HE'S WEARING THE SAME CLOTHES.
HIS VOICE HASN'T CHANGED.
BUT I FEEL LIKE I'M TALKING TO A STRANGER...
"OZ-KUN.
"I HAVE COME TO GET YOU."
WHA ...!?
......

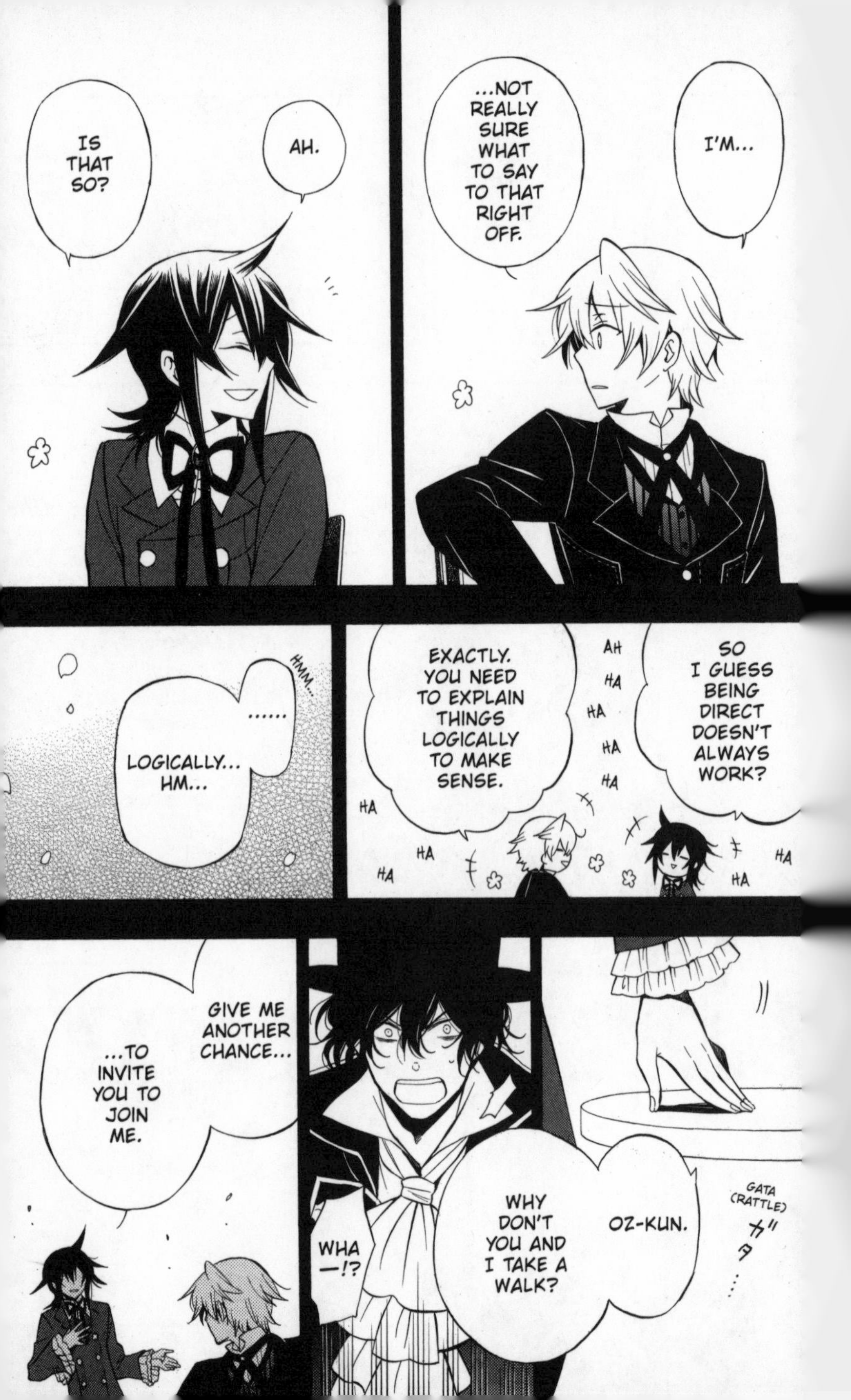
I'M...
...NOT REALLY SURE WHAT TO SAY TO THAT RIGHT OFF.
AH.
IS THAT SO?
SO I GUESS BEING DIRECT DOESN'T ALWAYS WORK?
AH HA HA HA HA
EXACTLY. YOU NEED TO EXPLAIN THINGS LOGICALLY TO MAKE SENSE.
HA HA HA HA HA HA
HMM...
......
LOGICALLY... HM...
GATA (RATTLE)
OZ-KUN.
WHY DON'T YOU AND I TAKE A WALK?
WHA—!?
GIVE ME ANOTHER CHANCE...
...TO INVITE YOU TO JOIN ME.

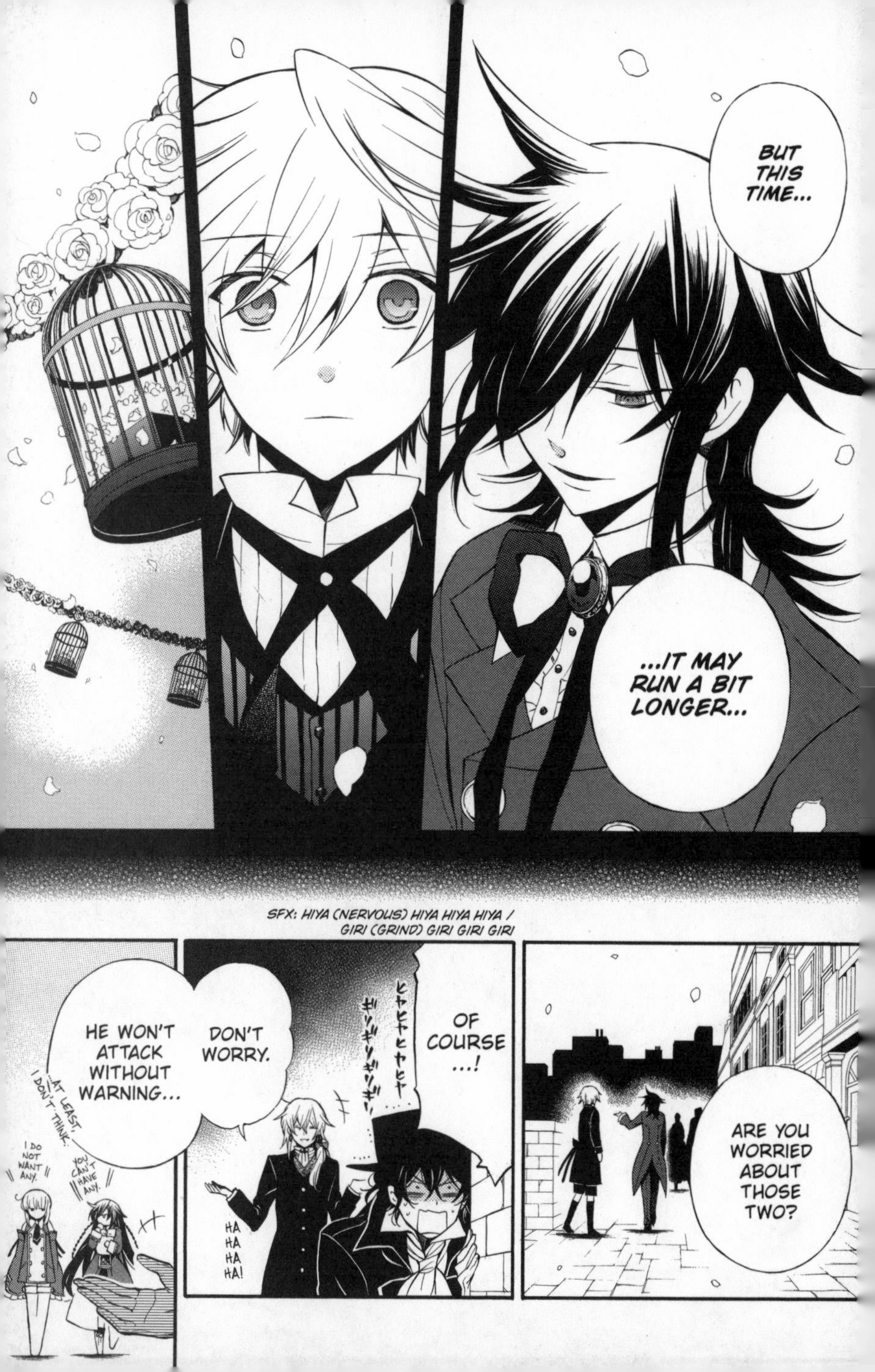
BUT THIS TIME...
...IT MAY RUN A BIT LONGER...
SFX: HIYA (NERVOUS) HIYA HIYA HIYA / GIRI (GRIND) GIRI GIRI GIRI
ARE YOU WORRIED ABOUT THOSE TWO?
OF COURSE ...!
...
HA HA HA HA HA!
DON'T WORRY.
HE WON'T ATTACK WITHOUT WARNING...
...AT LEAST, I DON'T THINK.
YOU CAN'T HAVE ANY.
I DO NOT WANT ANY.

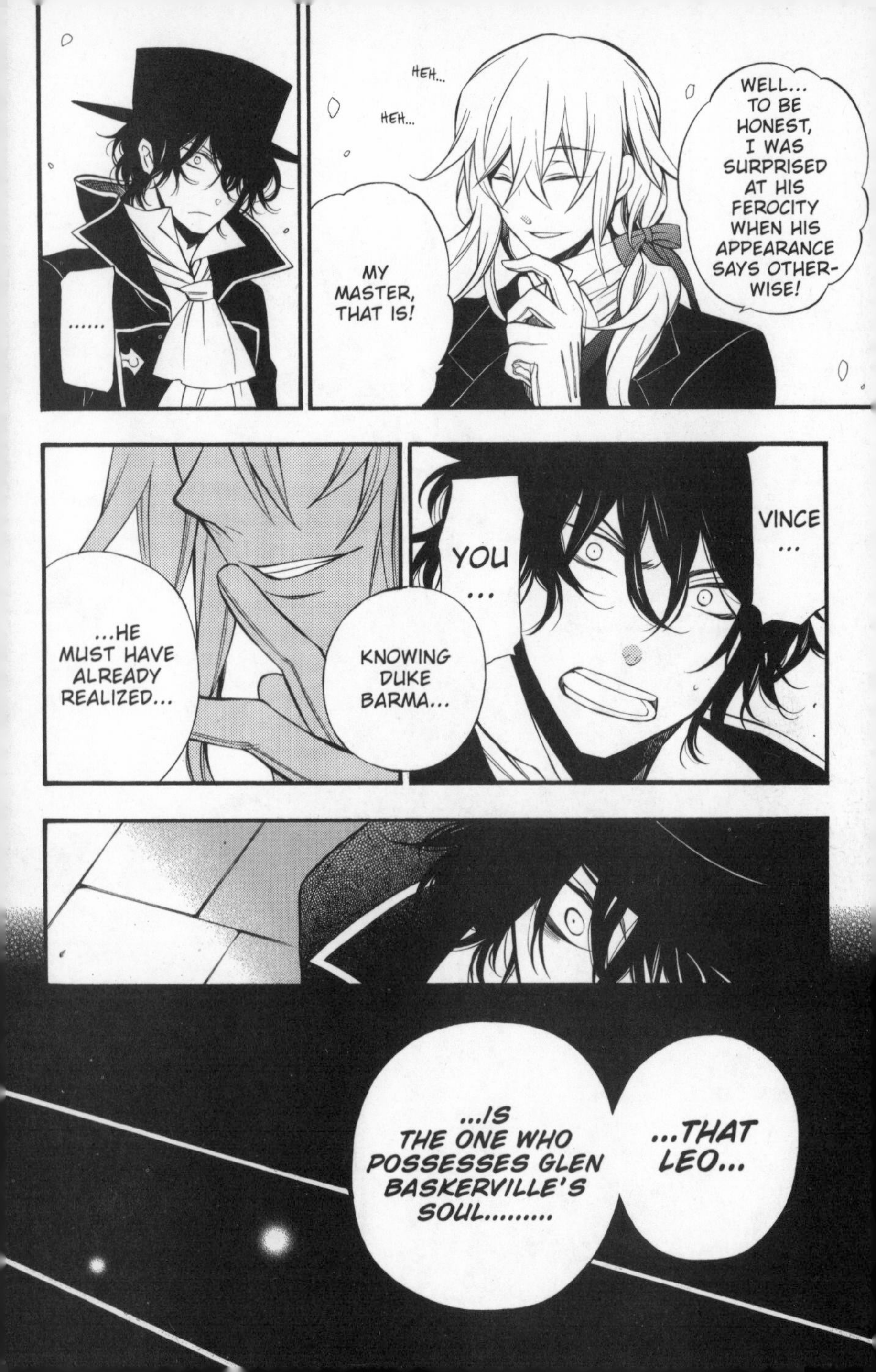
WELL... TO BE HONEST, I WAS SURPRISED AT HIS FEROCITY WHEN HIS APPEARANCE SAYS OTHERWISE!
HEH...
HEH...
MY MASTER, THAT IS!
......
VINCE ...
YOU ...
KNOWING DUKE BARMA...
...HE MUST HAVE ALREADY REALIZED...
...THAT LEO...
...IS THE ONE WHO POSSESSES GLEN BASKERVILLE'S SOUL.........

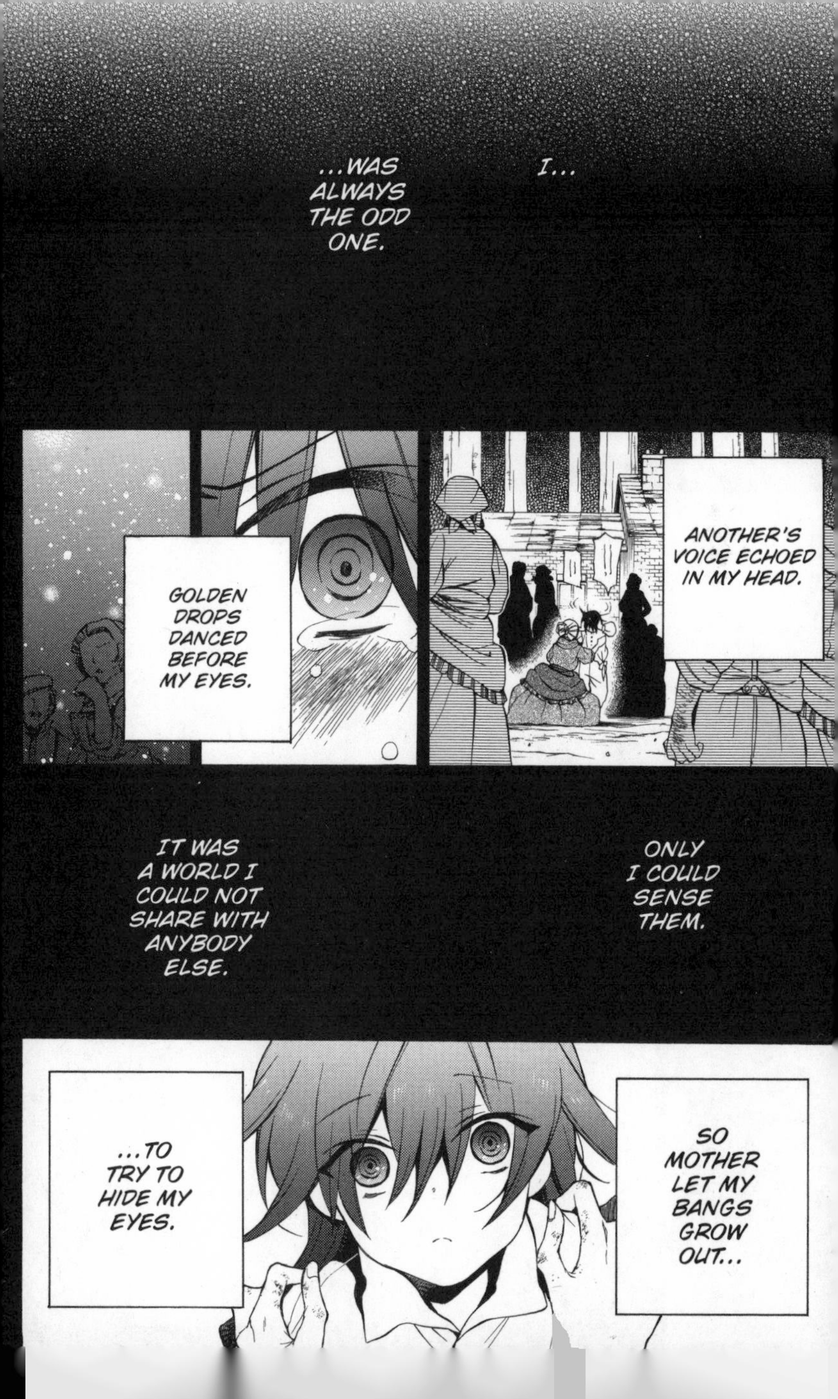
I...
...WAS ALWAYS THE ODD ONE.
ANOTHER'S VOICE ECHOED IN MY HEAD.
GOLDEN DROPS DANCED BEFORE MY EYES.
ONLY I COULD SENSE THEM.
IT WAS A WORLD I COULD NOT SHARE WITH ANYBODY ELSE.
SO MOTHER LET MY BANGS GROW OUT...
...TO TRY TO HIDE MY EYES.

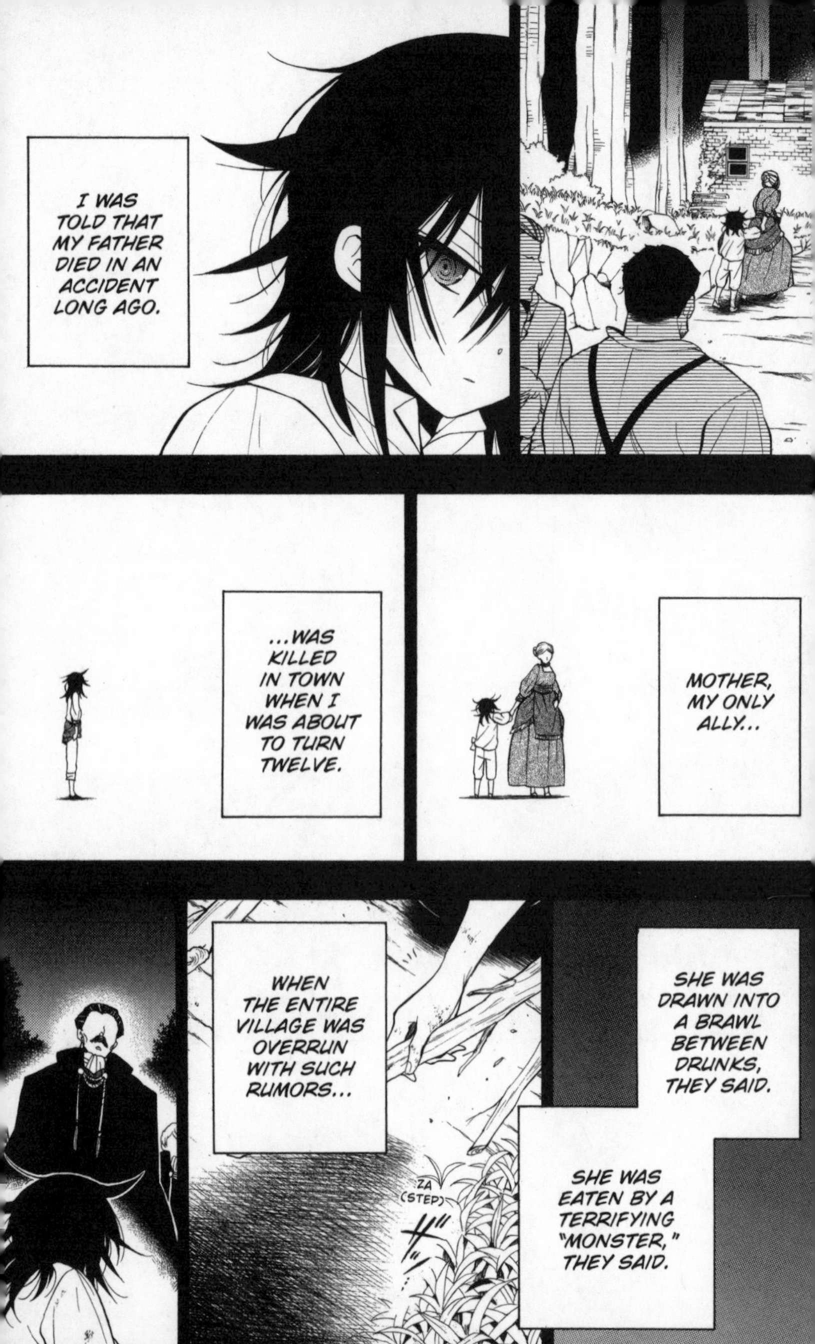
I WAS TOLD THAT MY FATHER DIED IN AN ACCIDENT LONG AGO.
MOTHER, MY ONLY ALLY...
...WAS KILLED IN TOWN WHEN I WAS ABOUT TO TURN TWELVE.
SHE WAS DRAWN INTO A BRAWL BETWEEN DRUNKS, THEY SAID.
SHE WAS EATEN BY A TERRIFYING "MONSTER," THEY SAID.
WHEN THE ENTIRE VILLAGE WAS OVERRUN WITH SUCH RUMORS...
ZA (STEP)

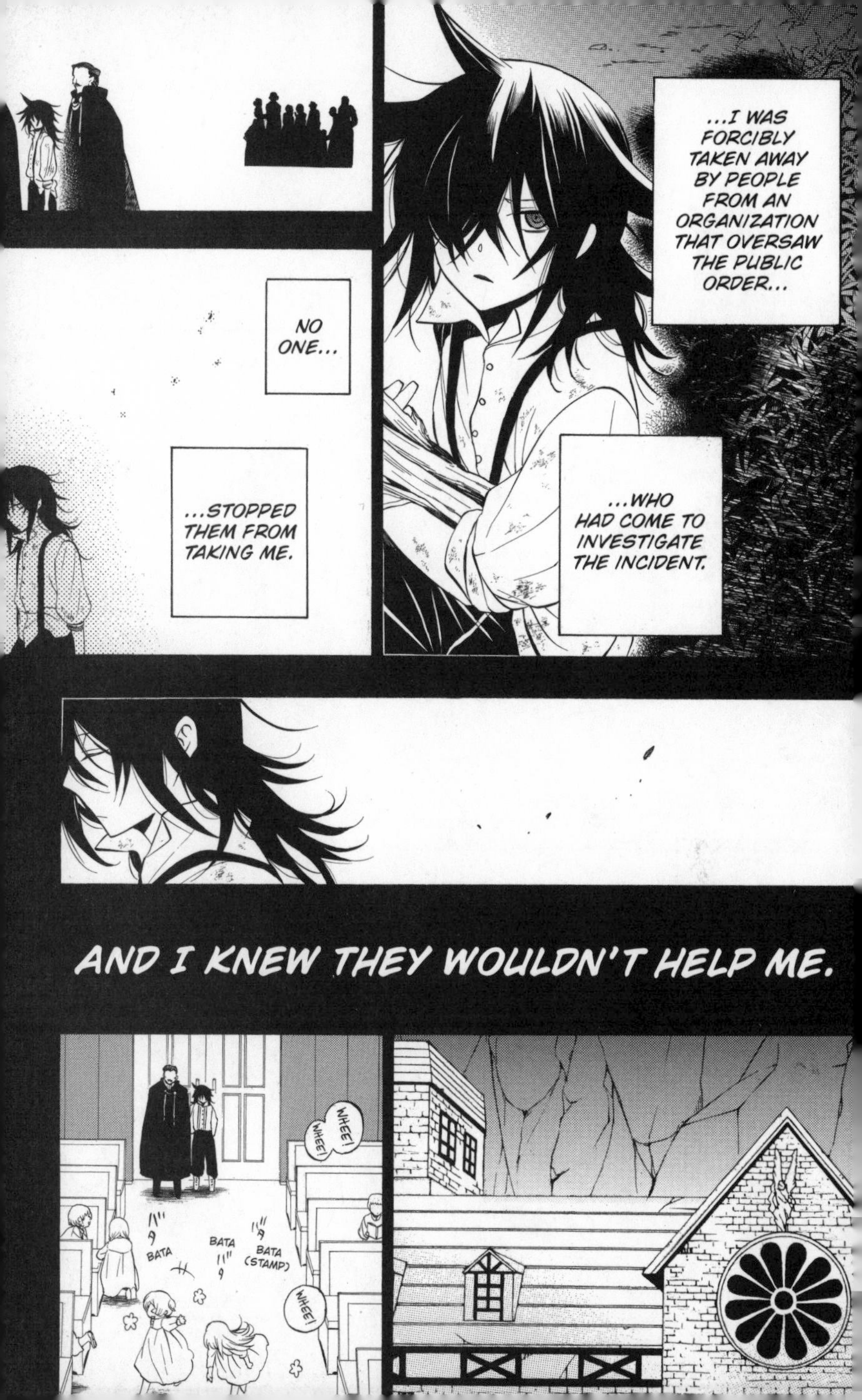
...I WAS FORCIBLY TAKEN AWAY BY PEOPLE FROM AN ORGANIZATION THAT OVERSAW THE PUBLIC ORDER...
...WHO HAD COME TO INVESTIGATE THE INCIDENT.
NO ONE...
...STOPPED THEM FROM TAKING ME.
AND I KNEW THEY WOULDN'T HELP ME.
WHEE! WHEE!
BATA (STAMP)
BATA
WHEE!

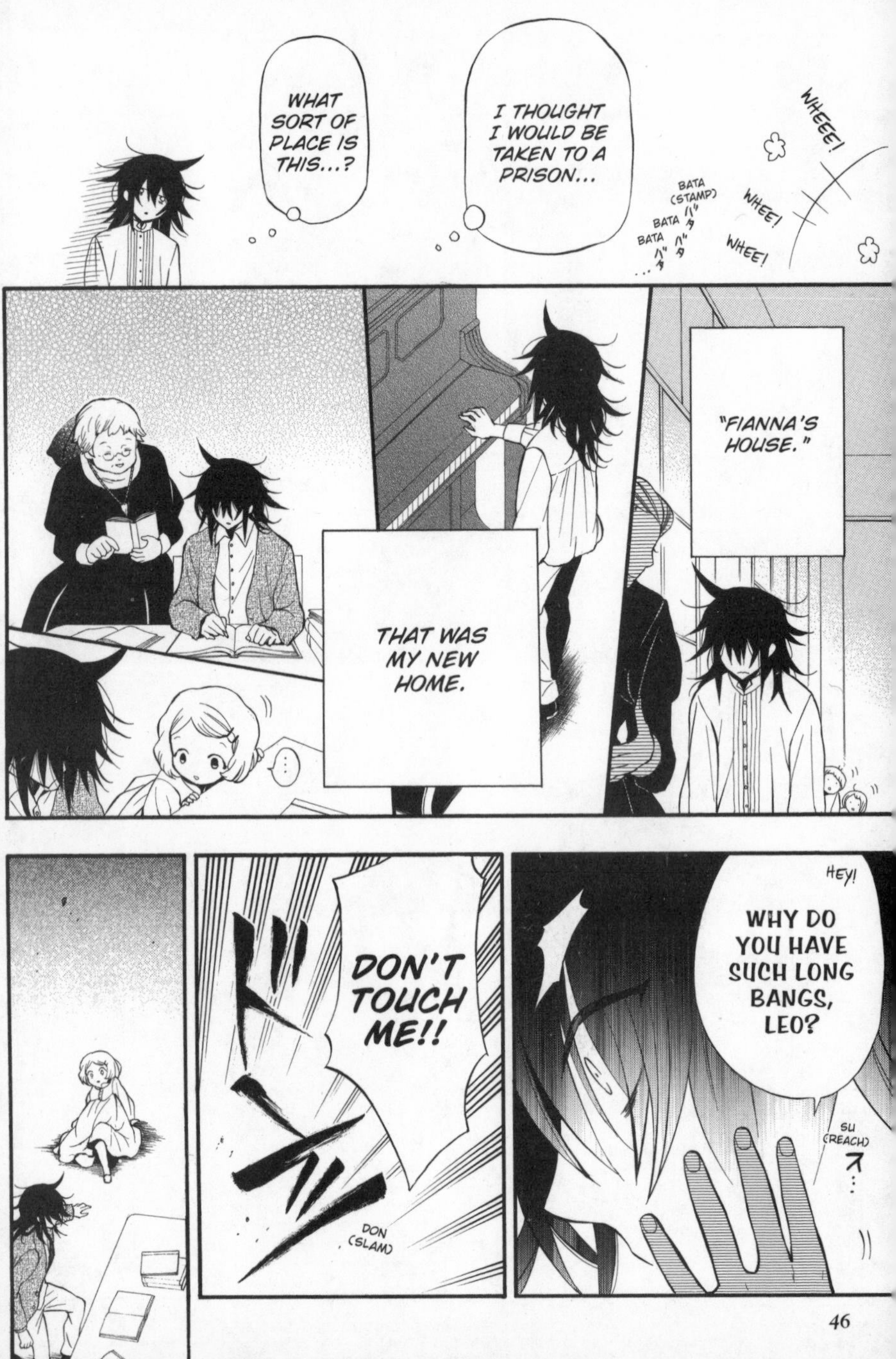
WHEEE!
WHEE!
WHEE!
BATA (STAMP) バタ
BATA バタ
BATA バタ ...
I THOUGHT I WOULD BE TAKEN TO A PRISON...
WHAT SORT OF PLACE IS THIS...?
"FIANNA'S HOUSE."
THAT WAS MY NEW HOME.
...
HEY!
WHY DO YOU HAVE SUCH LONG BANGS, LEO?
SU (REACH)
DON'T TOUCH ME!!
DON (SLAM)

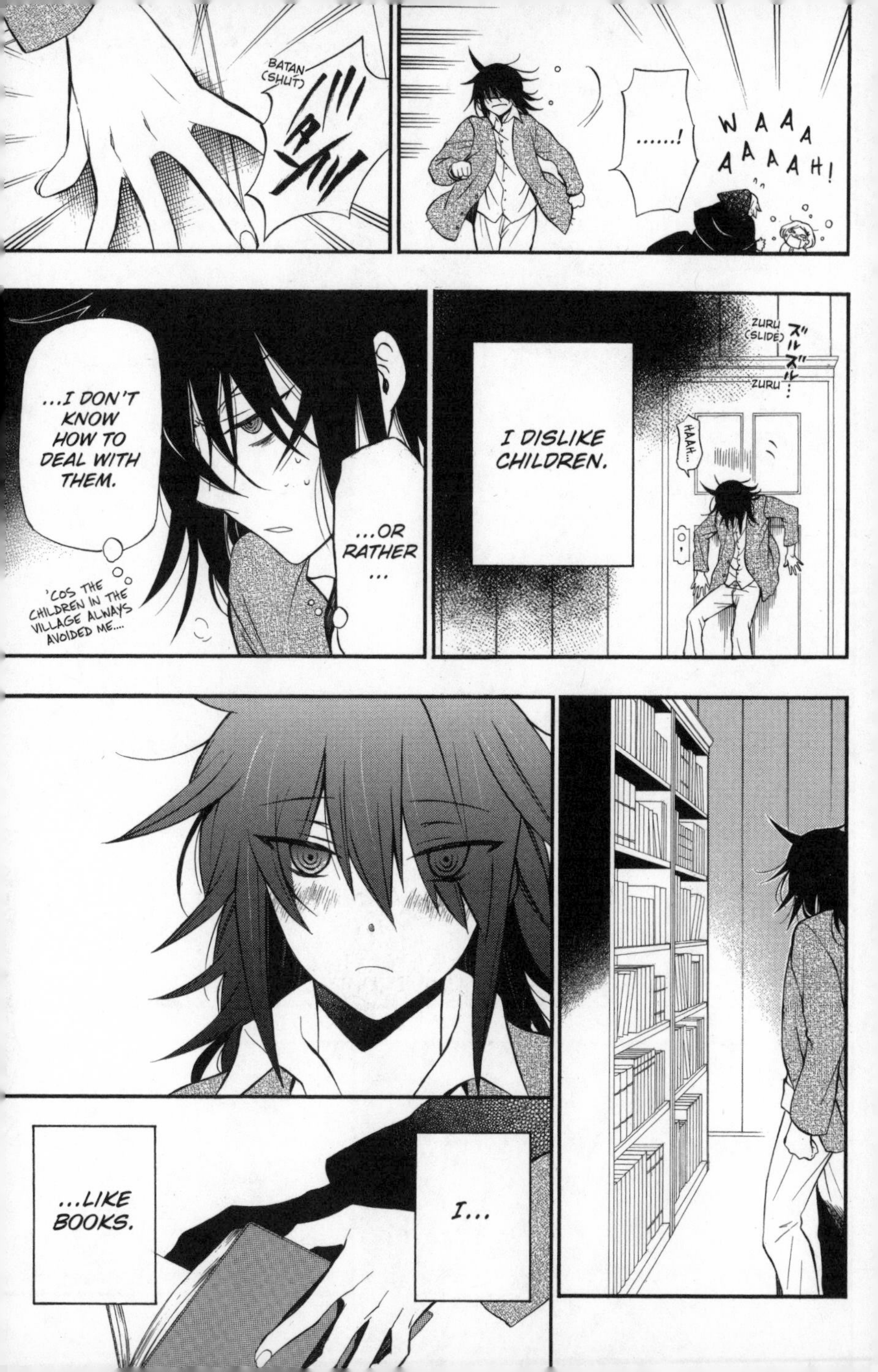
......!
WAAAAAAAH!
BATAN (SHUT)
ZURU (SLIDE)
ズルズル…
ZURU
HAAH...
I DISLIKE CHILDREN.
...OR RATHER ...
...I DON'T KNOW HOW TO DEAL WITH THEM.
'COS THE CHILDREN IN THE VILLAGE ALWAYS AVOIDED ME....
I...
...LIKE BOOKS.

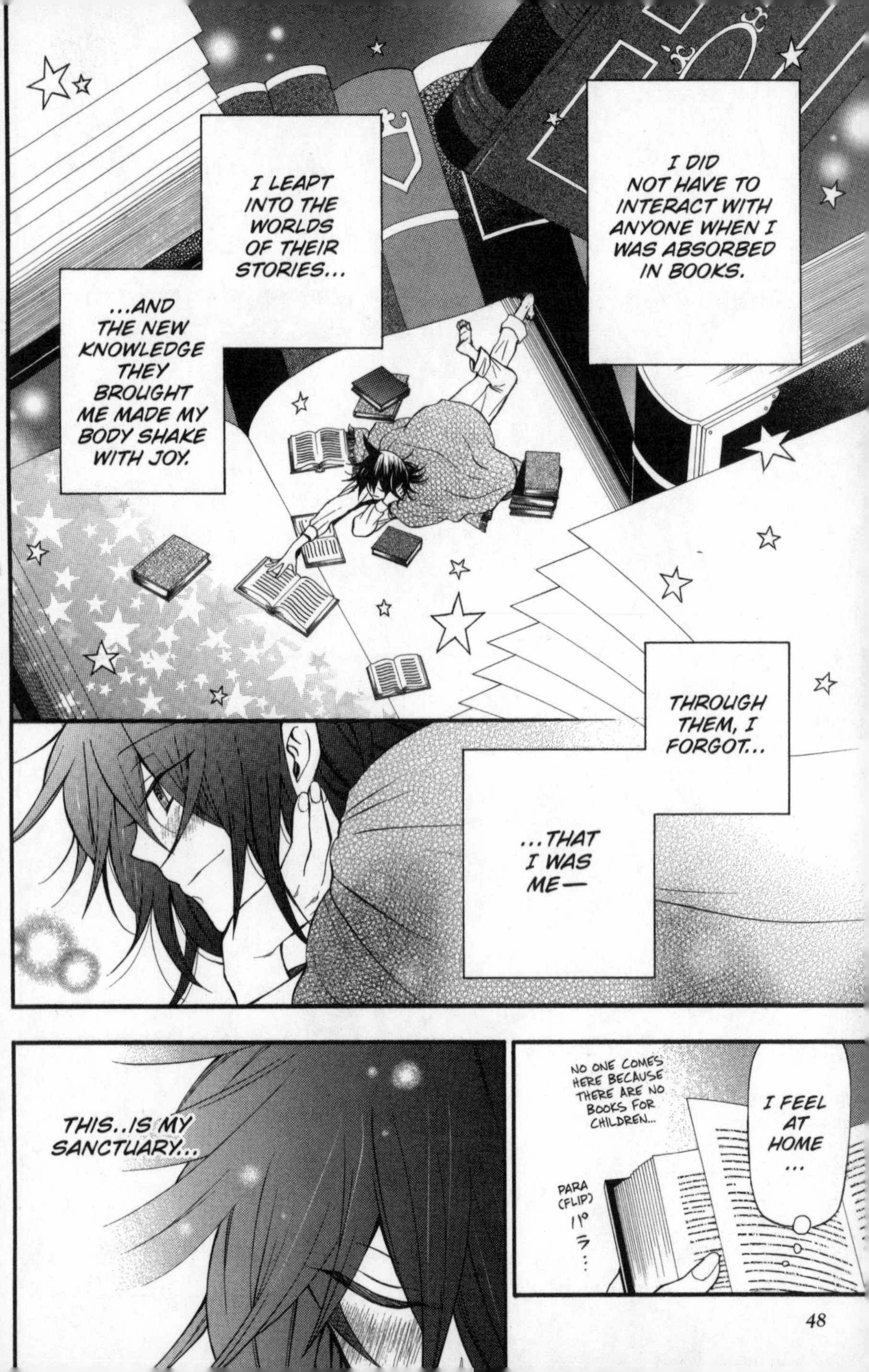

I DID NOT HAVE TO INTERACT WITH ANYONE WHEN I WAS ABSORBED IN BOOKS.
I LEAPT INTO THE WORLDS OF THEIR STORIES...
...AND THE NEW KNOWLEDGE THEY BROUGHT ME MADE MY BODY SHAKE WITH JOY.
THROUGH THEM, I FORGOT...
...THAT I WAS ME—
I FEEL AT HOME...
NO ONE COMES HERE BECAUSE THERE ARE NO BOOKS FOR CHILDREN...
PARA (FLIP)
パラ…
THIS..IS MY SANCTUARY...

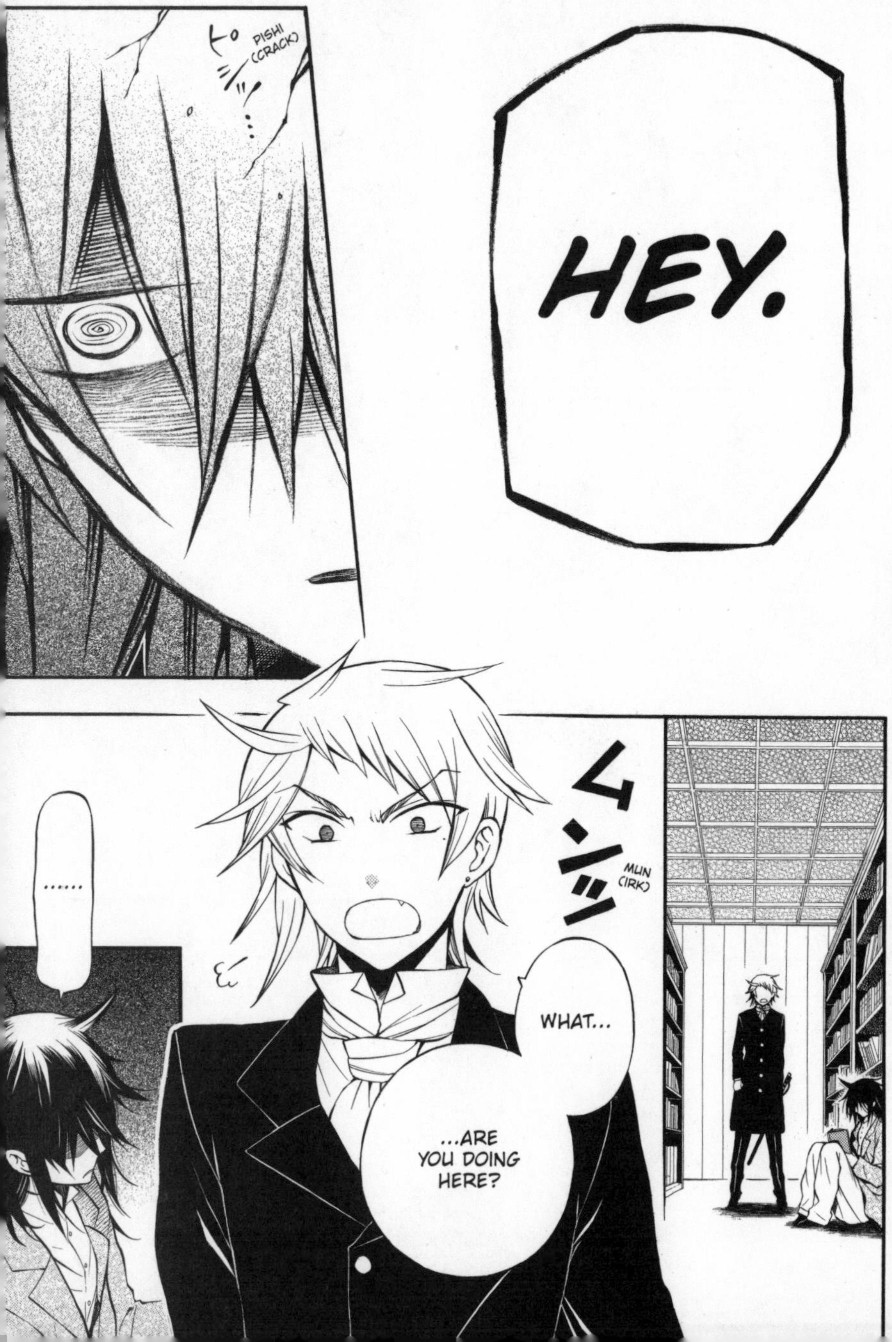
HEY.
PISHI (CRACK)
MUN (IRK)
WHAT...
...ARE YOU DOING HERE?
......

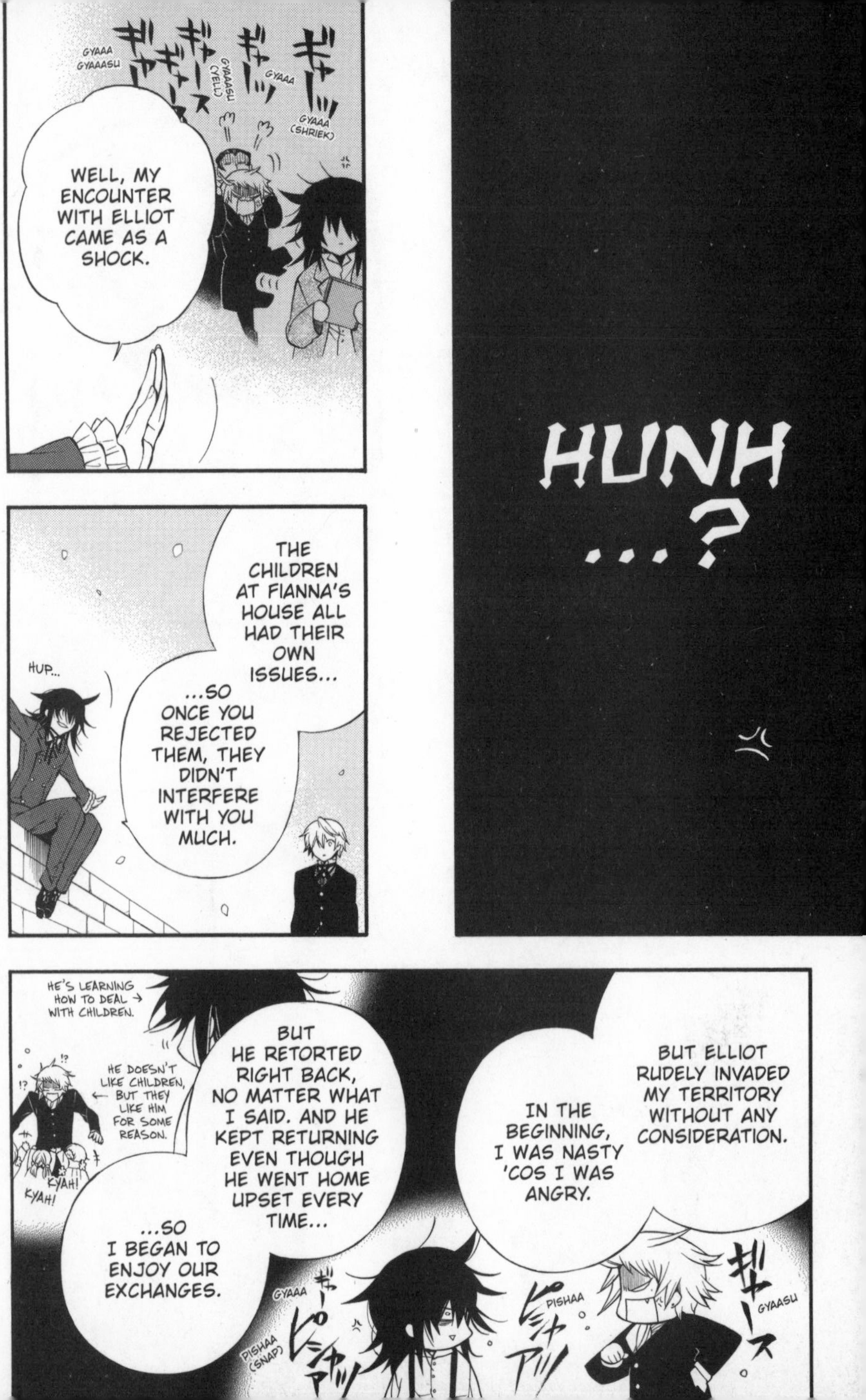
HUNH ...?
GYAAA (SHRIEK)
GYAAA
GYAAASU (YELL)
GYAAA GYAAASU
WELL, MY ENCOUNTER WITH ELLIOT CAME AS A SHOCK.
THE CHILDREN AT FIANNA'S HOUSE ALL HAD THEIR OWN ISSUES...
...SO ONCE YOU REJECTED THEM, THEY DIDN'T INTERFERE WITH YOU MUCH.
HUP...
BUT ELLIOT RUDELY INVADED MY TERRITORY WITHOUT ANY CONSIDERATION.
IN THE BEGINNING, I WAS NASTY 'COS I WAS ANGRY.
BUT HE RETORTED RIGHT BACK, NO MATTER WHAT I SAID. AND HE KEPT RETURNING EVEN THOUGH HE WENT HOME UPSET EVERY TIME...
...SO I BEGAN TO ENJOY OUR EXCHANGES.
HE'S LEARNING HOW TO DEAL WITH CHILDREN.
HE DOESN'T LIKE CHILDREN, BUT THEY LIKE HIM FOR SOME REASON.
KYAH!
KYAH!
GYAASU
PISHAA
GYAAA
PISHAA (SNAP)

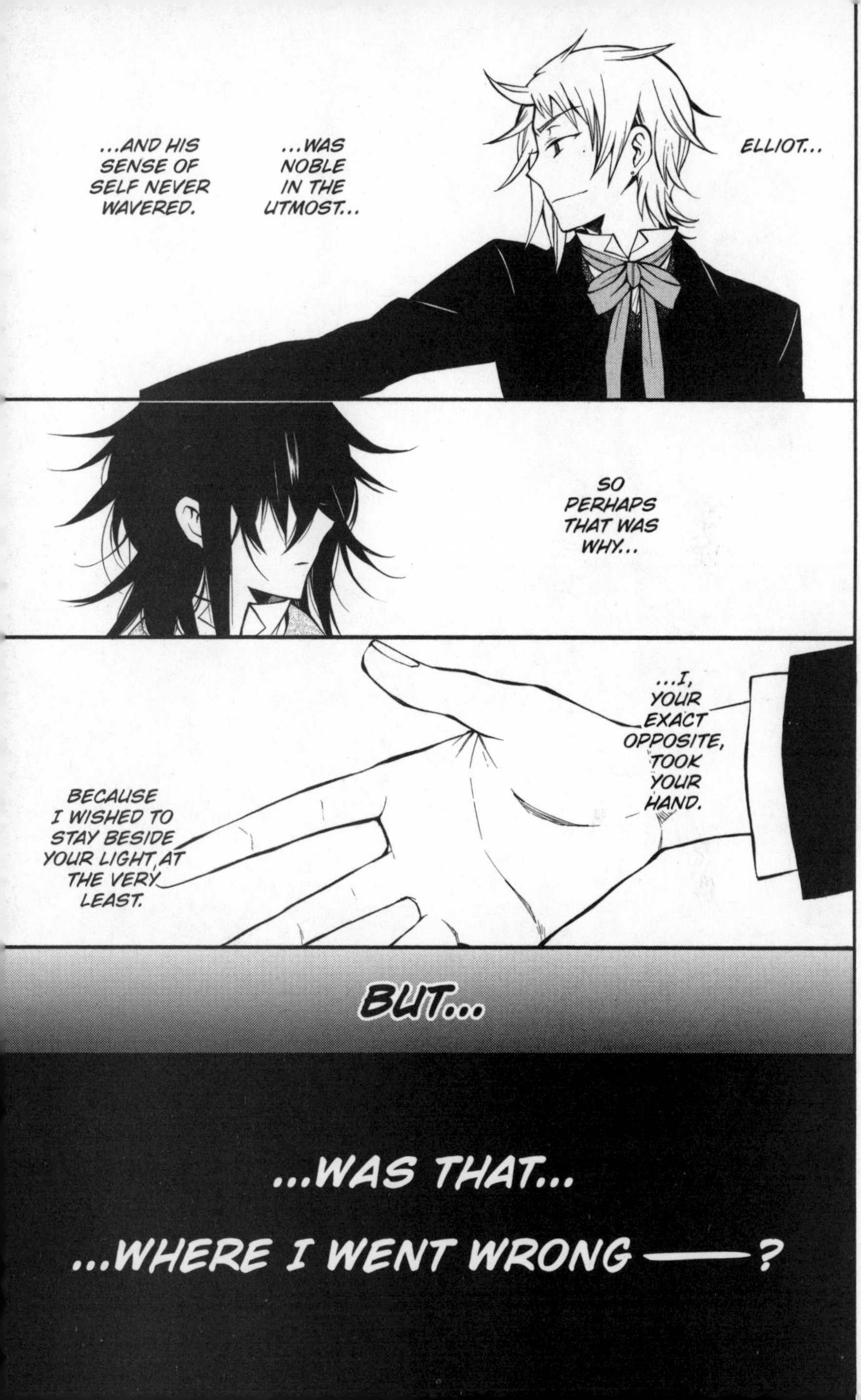
ELLIOT...
...WAS NOBLE IN THE UTMOST...
...AND HIS SENSE OF SELF NEVER WAVERED.
SO PERHAPS THAT WAS WHY...
...I, YOUR EXACT OPPOSITE, TOOK YOUR HAND.
BECAUSE I WISHED TO STAY BESIDE YOUR LIGHT, AT THE VERY LEAST.
BUT...
...WAS THAT...
...WHERE I WENT WRONG——?

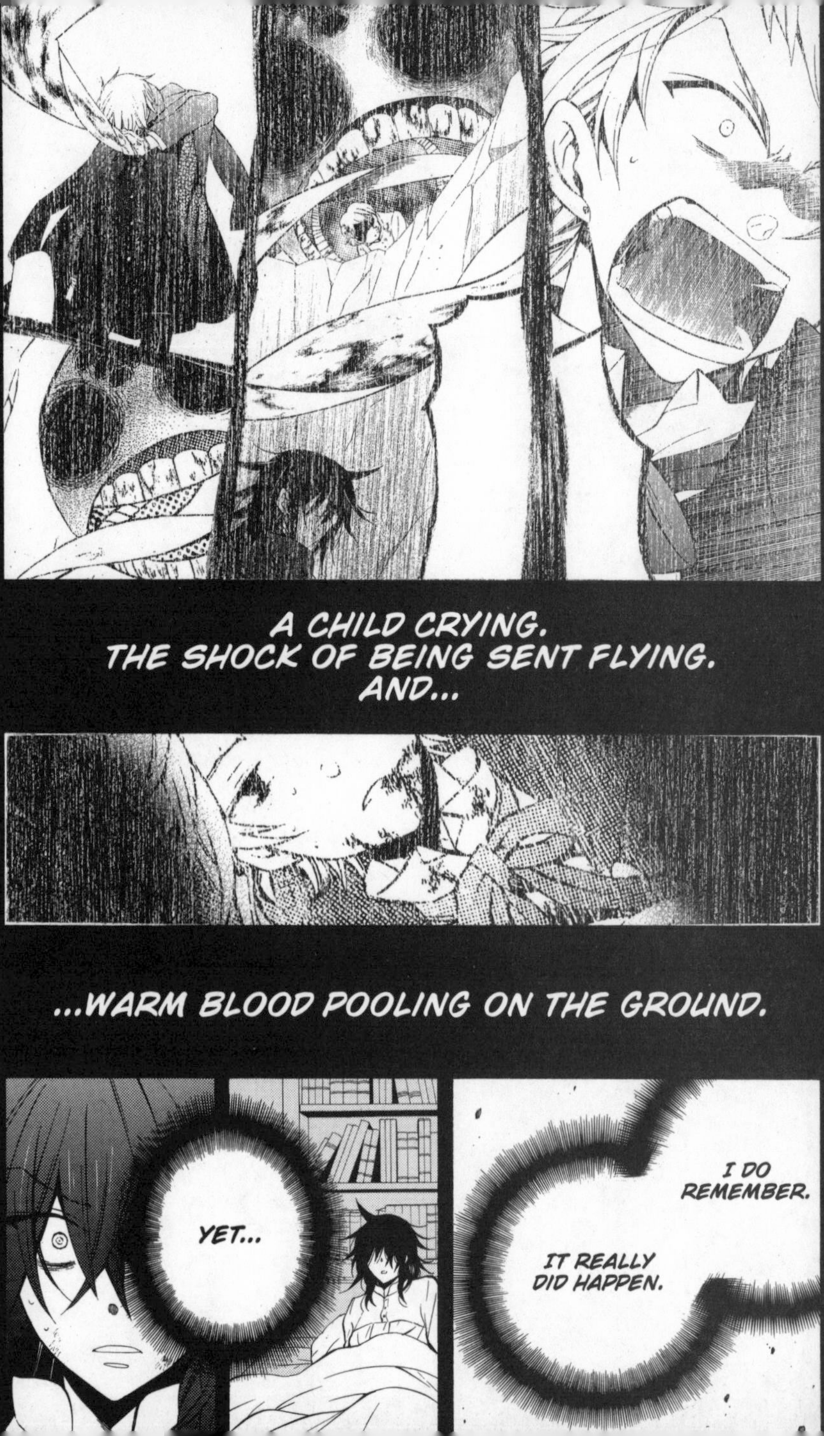
A CHILD CRYING.
THE SHOCK OF BEING SENT FLYING.
AND...
...WARM BLOOD POOLING ON THE GROUND.
I DO REMEMBER.
IT REALLY DID HAPPEN.
YET...

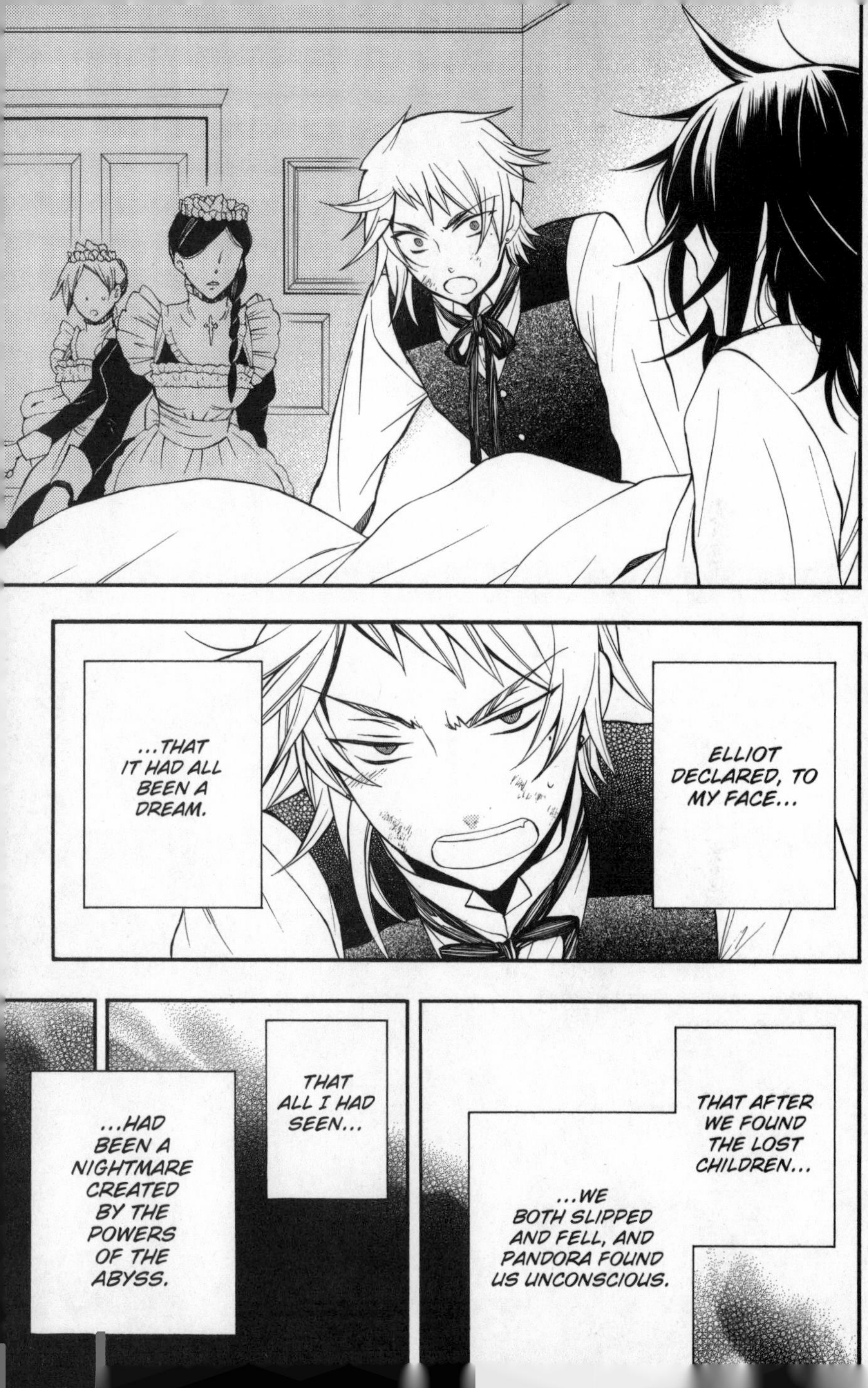
ELLIOT DECLARED, TO MY FACE...
...THAT IT HAD ALL BEEN A DREAM.
THAT AFTER WE FOUND THE LOST CHILDREN...
...WE BOTH SLIPPED AND FELL, AND PANDORA FOUND US UNCONSCIOUS.
THAT ALL I HAD SEEN...
...HAD BEEN A NIGHTMARE CREATED BY THE POWERS OF THE ABYSS.

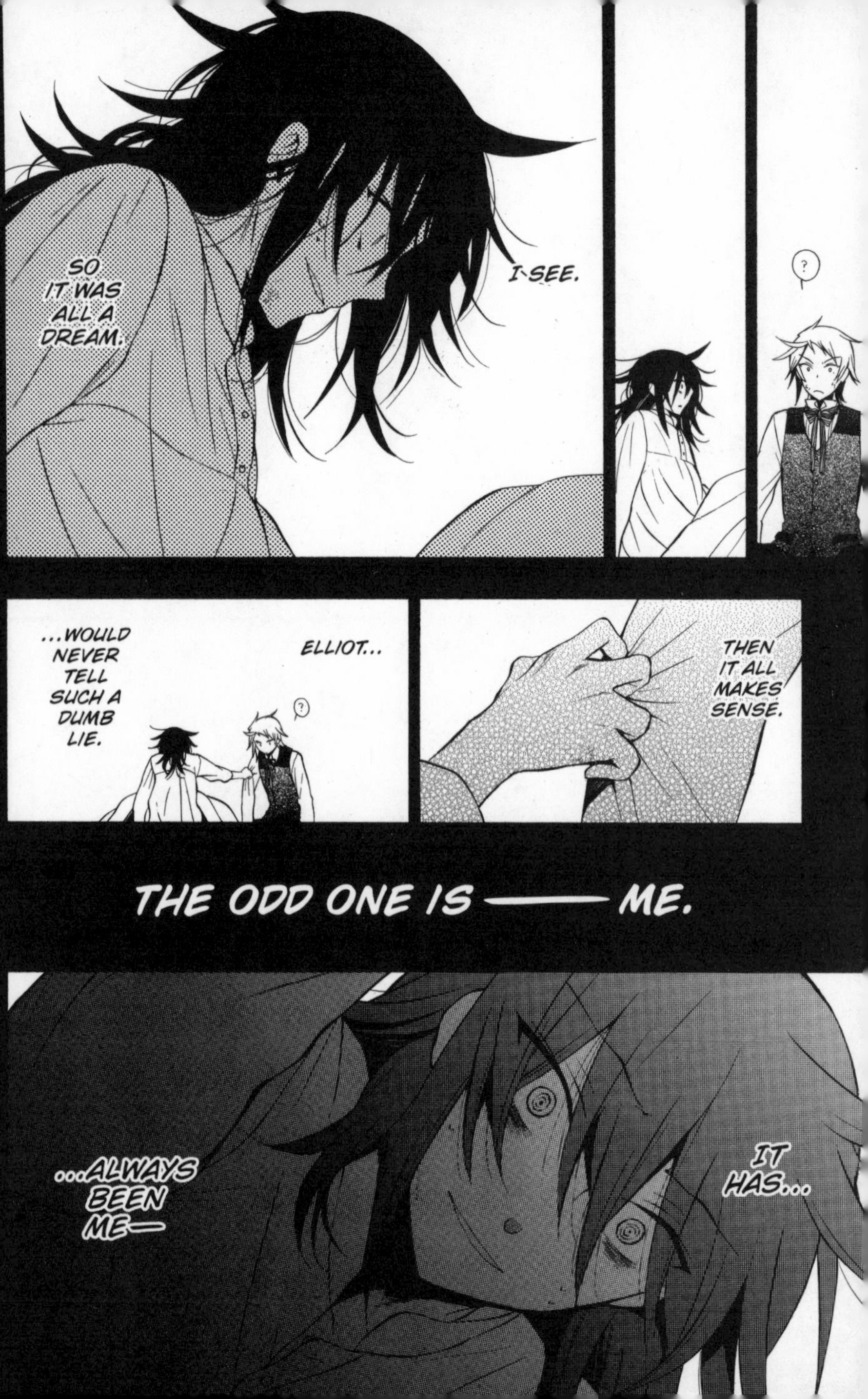
?
I SEE.
SO IT WAS ALL A DREAM.
THEN IT ALL MAKES SENSE.
ELLIOT...
?
...WOULD NEVER TELL SUCH A DUMB LIE.
THE ODD ONE IS —— ME.
IT HAS...
...ALWAYS BEEN ME—

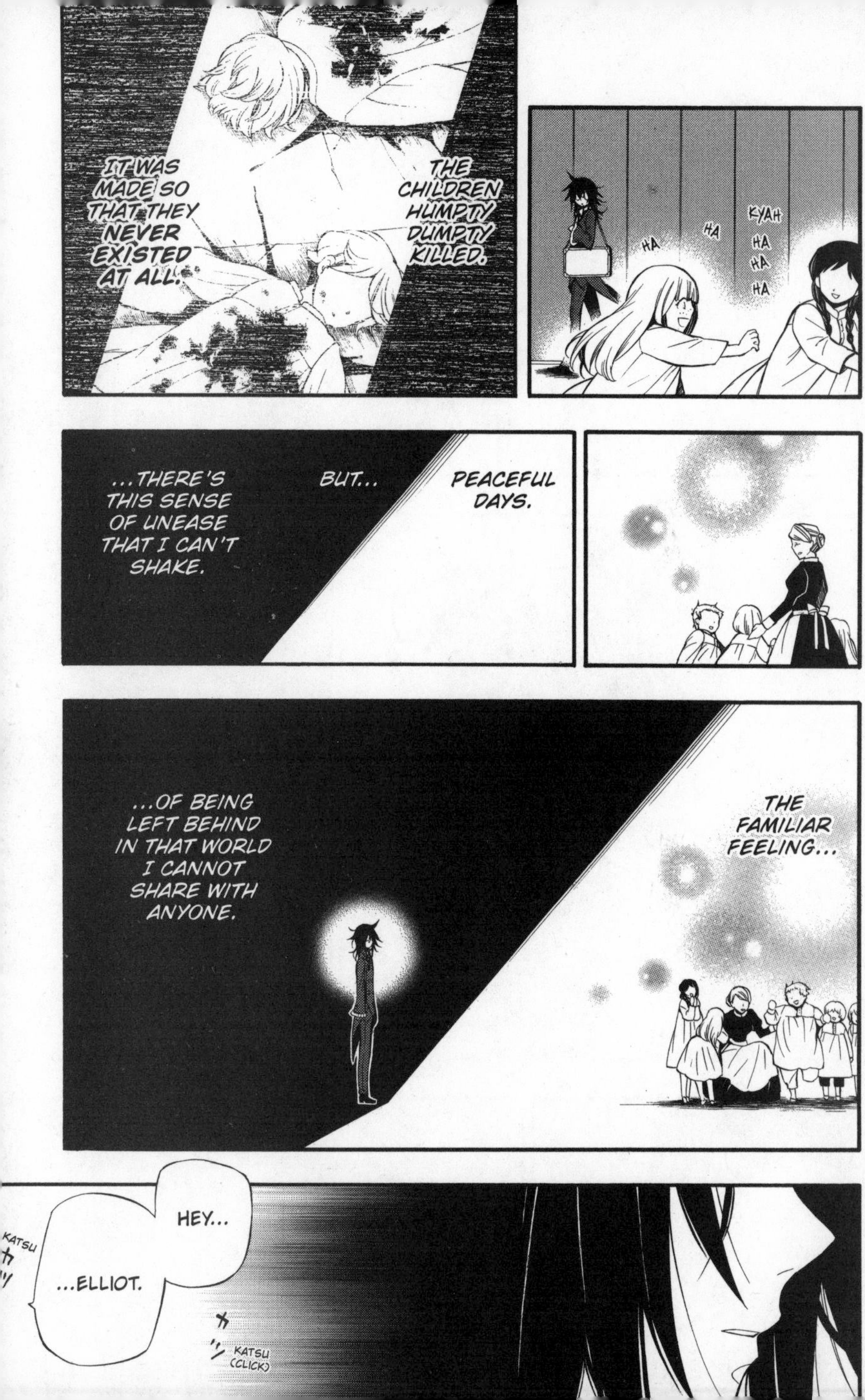
KYAH HA HA HA
HA
HA
THE CHILDREN HUMPTY DUMPTY KILLED.
IT WAS MADE SO THAT THEY NEVER EXISTED AT ALL.
PEACEFUL DAYS.
BUT...
...THERE'S THIS SENSE OF UNEASE THAT I CAN'T SHAKE.
THE FAMILIAR FEELING...
...OF BEING LEFT BEHIND IN THAT WORLD I CANNOT SHARE WITH ANYONE.
HEY...
...ELLIOT.
KATSU (CLICK)
KATSU

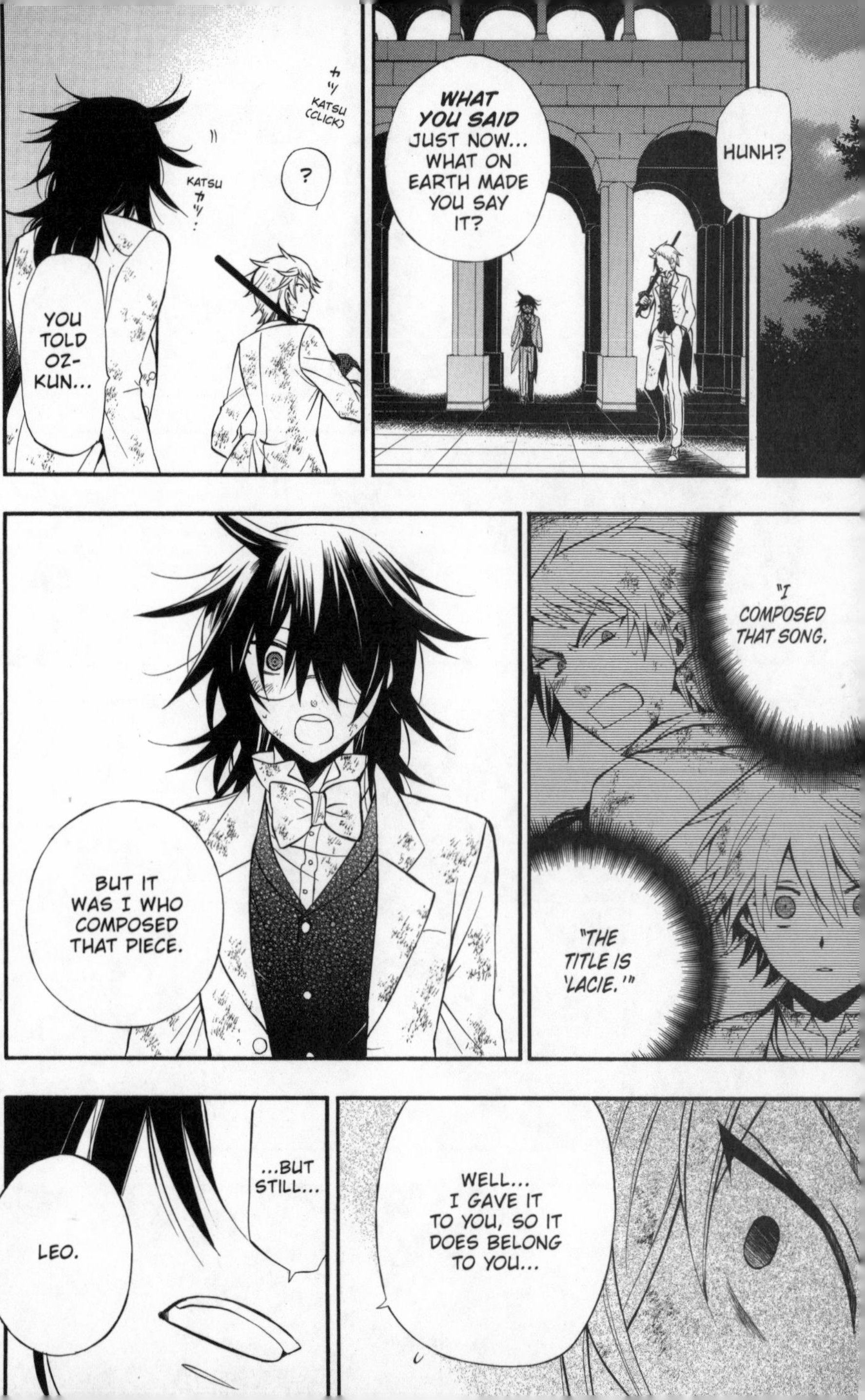
WHAT YOU SAID JUST NOW... WHAT ON EARTH MADE YOU SAY IT?
HUNH?
KATSU (CLICK)
?
KATSU
YOU TOLD OZ-KUN...
"I COMPOSED THAT SONG.
"THE TITLE IS 'LACIE.'"
BUT IT WAS I WHO COMPOSED THAT PIECE.
WELL... I GAVE IT TO YOU, SO IT DOES BELONG TO YOU...
...BUT STILL...
LEO.

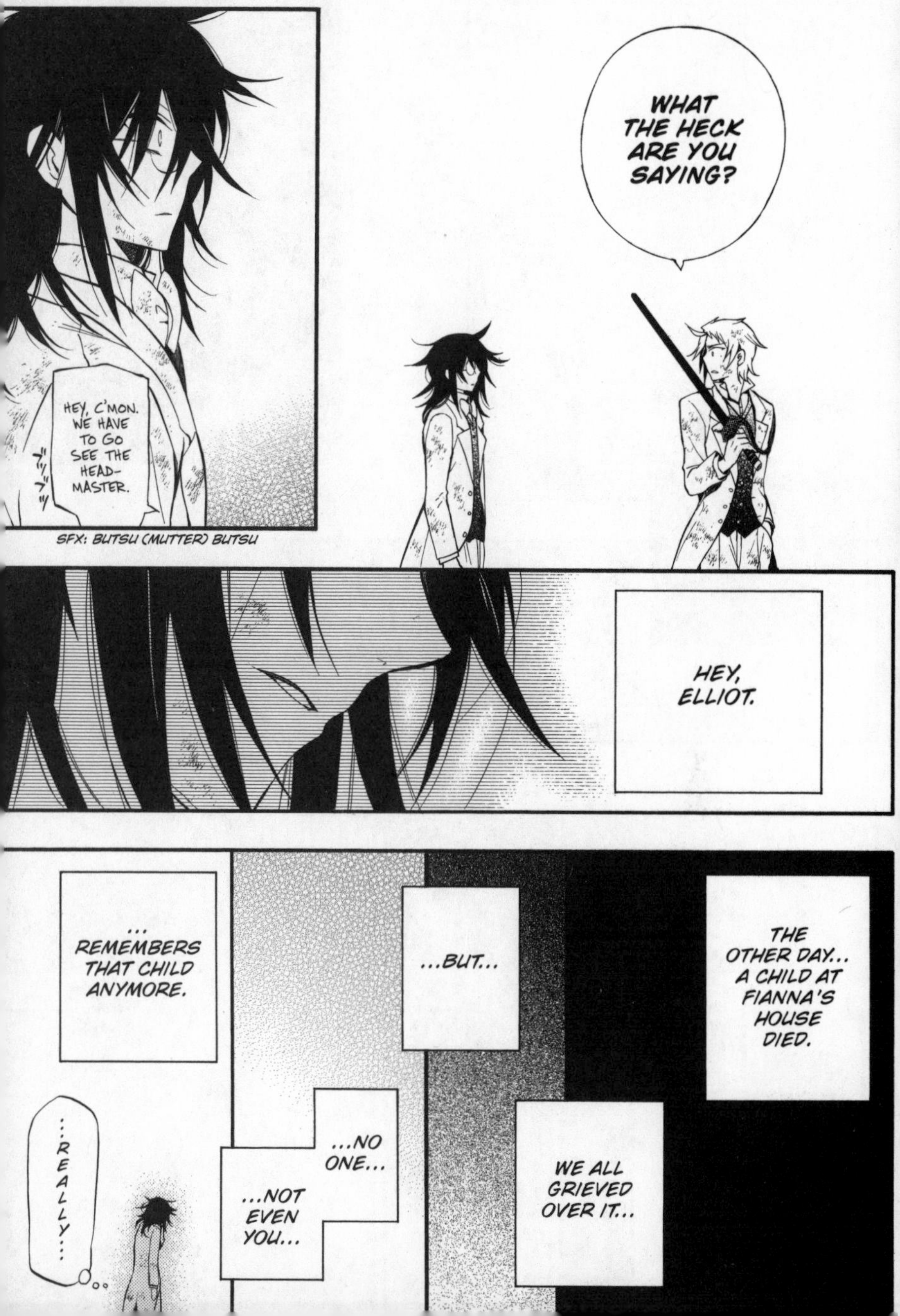
WHAT THE HECK ARE YOU SAYING?
HEY, C'MON. WE HAVE TO GO SEE THE HEAD-MASTER.
SFX: BUTSU (MUTTER) BUTSU
HEY, ELLIOT.
THE OTHER DAY... A CHILD AT FIANNA'S HOUSE DIED.
WE ALL GRIEVED OVER IT...
...BUT...
...NO ONE...
...NOT EVEN YOU...
...REMEMBERS THAT CHILD ANYMORE.
...REALLY...

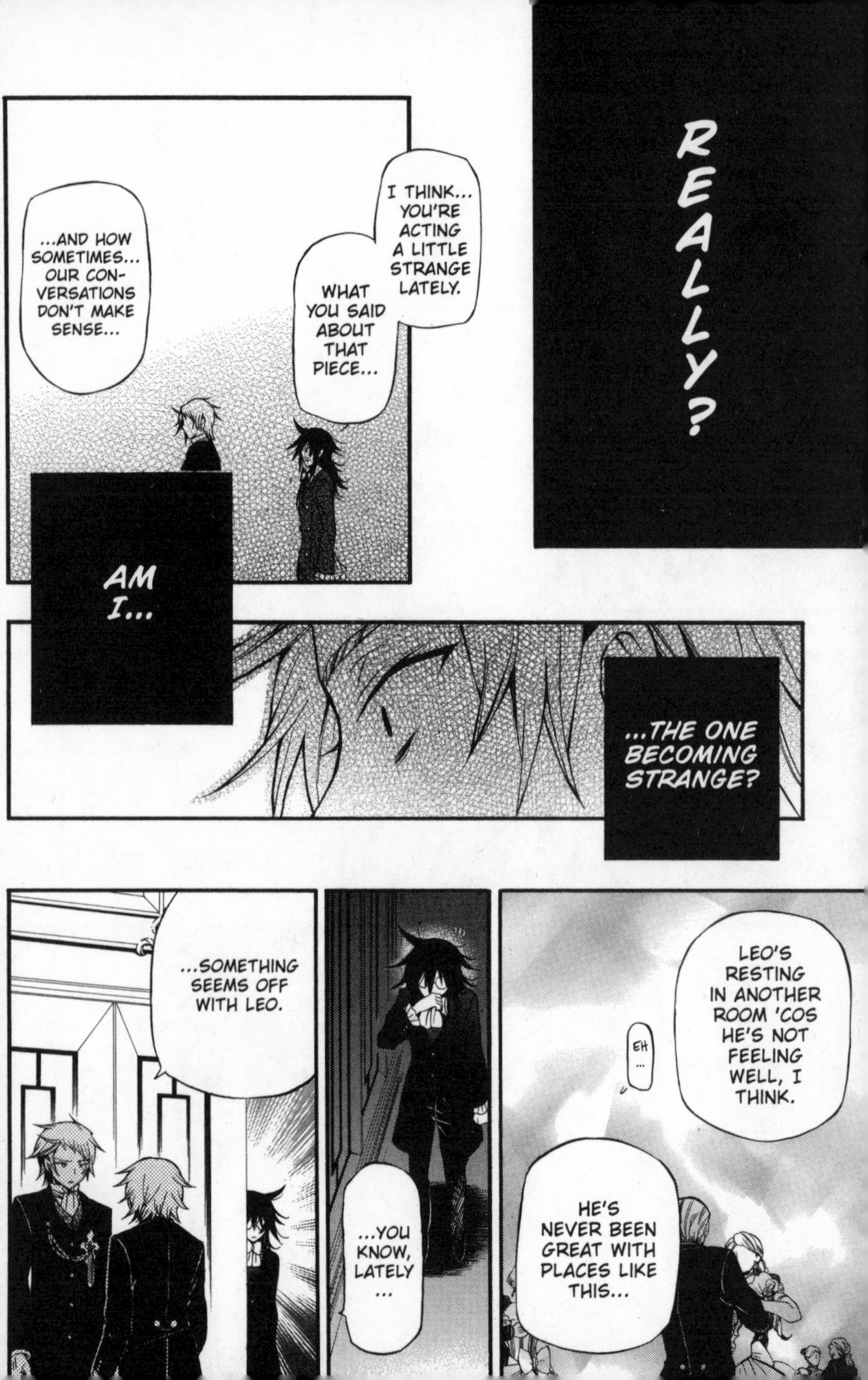
REALLY?
I THINK... YOU'RE ACTING A LITTLE STRANGE LATELY.
WHAT YOU SAID ABOUT THAT PIECE...
...AND HOW SOMETIMES... OUR CON-VERSATIONS DON'T MAKE SENSE...
AM I...
...THE ONE BECOMING STRANGE?
LEO'S RESTING IN ANOTHER ROOM 'COS HE'S NOT FEELING WELL, I THINK.
EH...
HE'S NEVER BEEN GREAT WITH PLACES LIKE THIS...
...YOU KNOW, LATELY...
...SOMETHING SEEMS OFF WITH LEO.

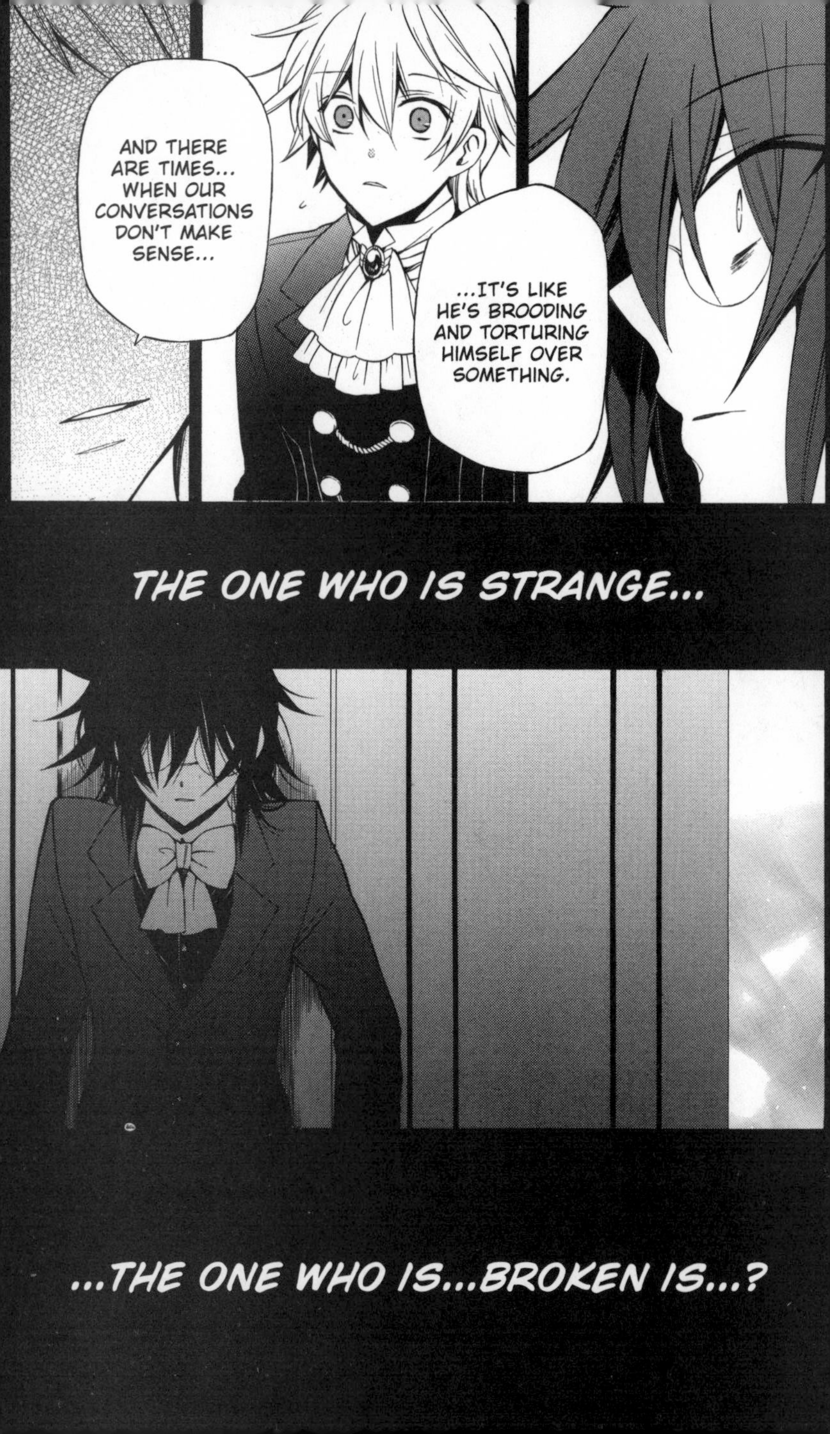
...IT'S LIKE HE'S BROODING AND TORTURING HIMSELF OVER SOMETHING.
AND THERE ARE TIMES... WHEN OUR CONVERSATIONS DON'T MAKE SENSE...
THE ONE WHO IS STRANGE...
...THE ONE WHO IS...BROKEN IS...?

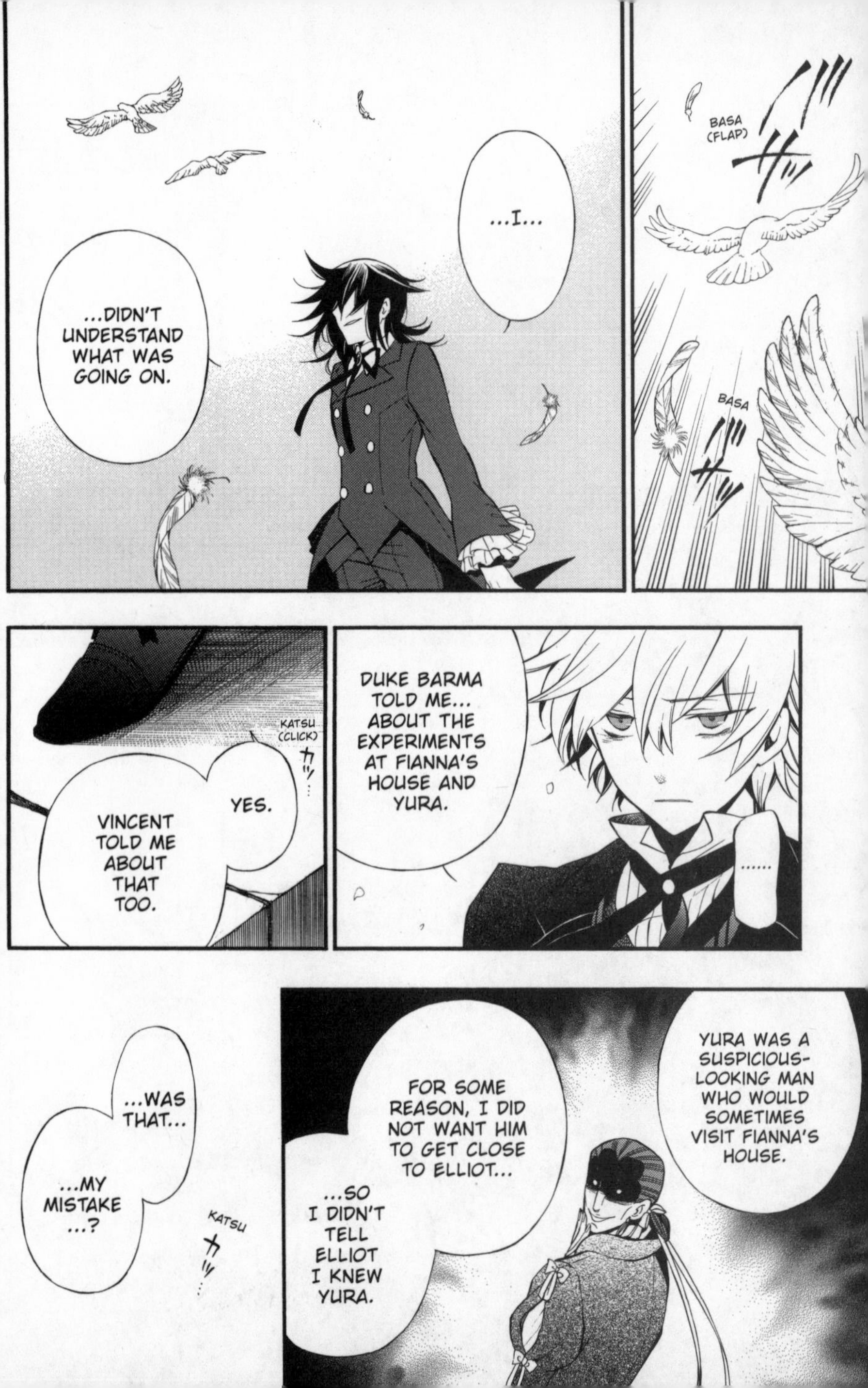
BASA (FLAP)
BASA
...I...
...DIDN'T UNDERSTAND WHAT WAS GOING ON.
DUKE BARMA TOLD ME... ABOUT THE EXPERIMENTS AT FIANNA'S HOUSE AND YURA.
......
KATSU (CLICK)
YES.
VINCENT TOLD ME ABOUT THAT TOO.
YURA WAS A SUSPICIOUS-LOOKING MAN WHO WOULD SOMETIMES VISIT FIANNA'S HOUSE.
FOR SOME REASON, I DID NOT WANT HIM TO GET CLOSE TO ELLIOT...
...SO I DIDN'T TELL ELLIOT I KNEW YURA.
KATSU
...WAS THAT...
...MY MISTAKE ...?

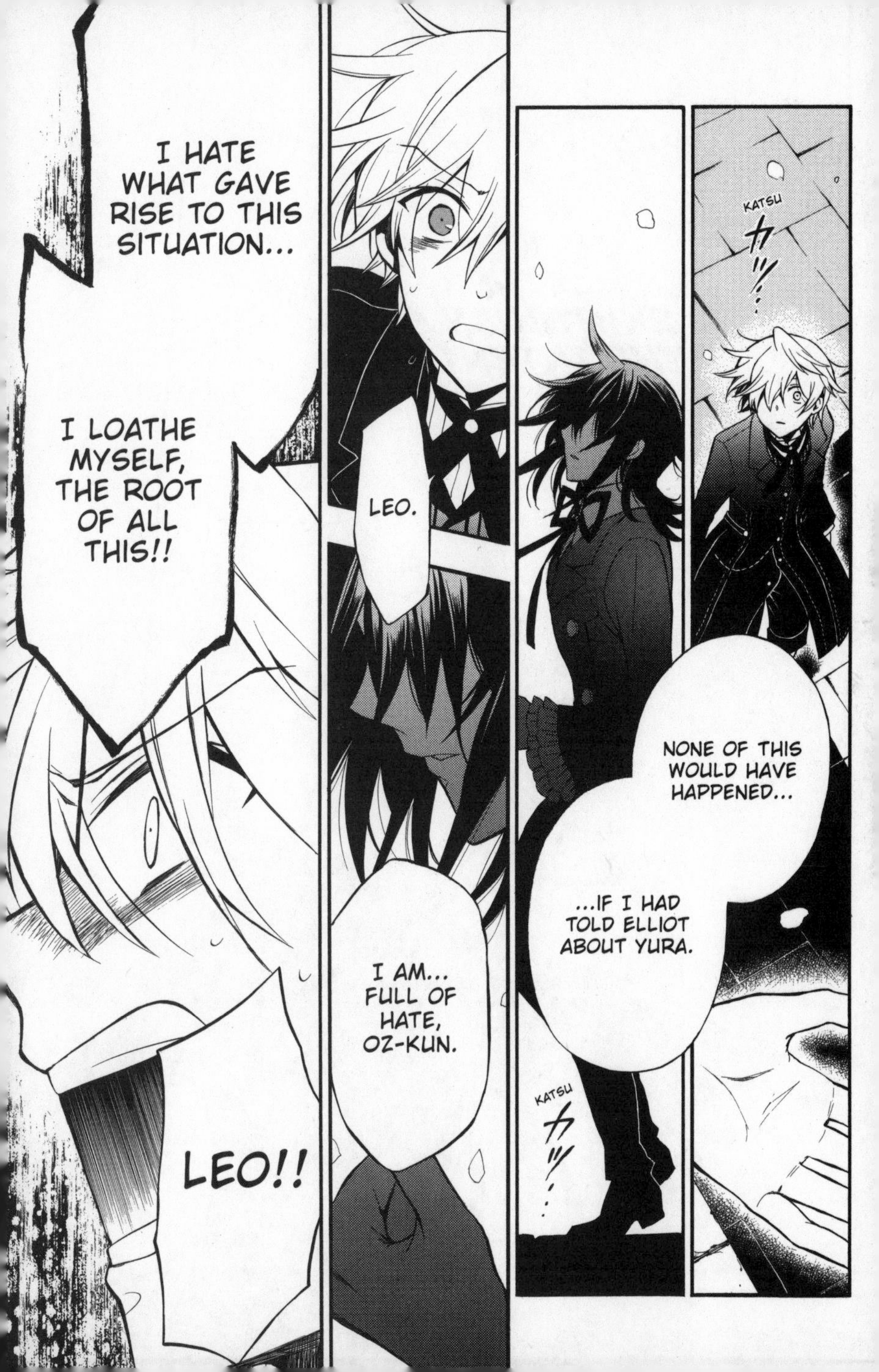
KATSU
NONE OF THIS WOULD HAVE HAPPENED...
...IF I HAD TOLD ELLIOT ABOUT YURA.
KATSU
LEO.
I AM... FULL OF HATE, OZ-KUN.
I HATE WHAT GAVE RISE TO THIS SITUATION...
I LOATHE MYSELF, THE ROOT OF ALL THIS!!
LEO!!

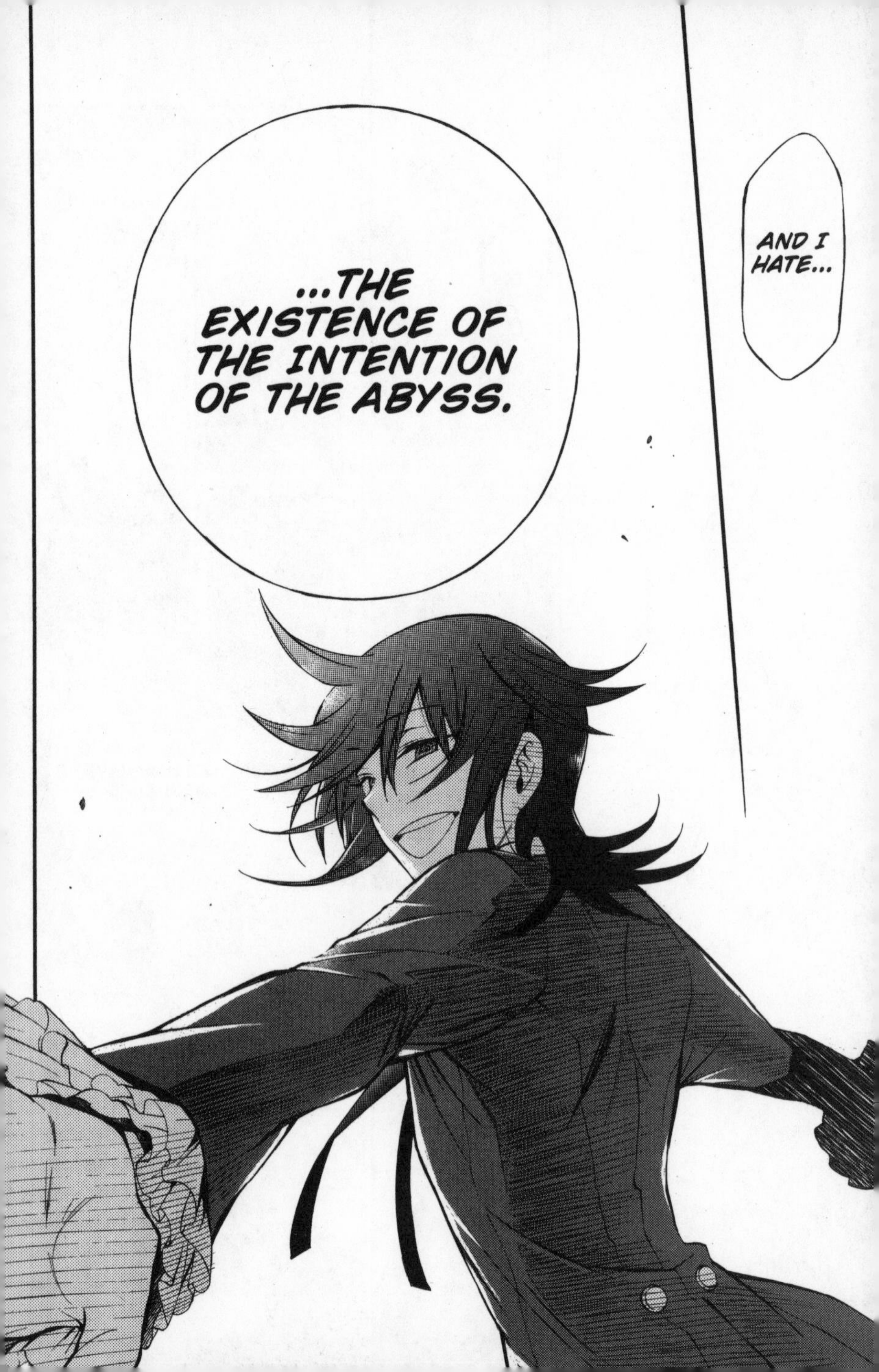
AND I HATE...
...THE EXISTENCE OF THE INTENTION OF THE ABYSS.

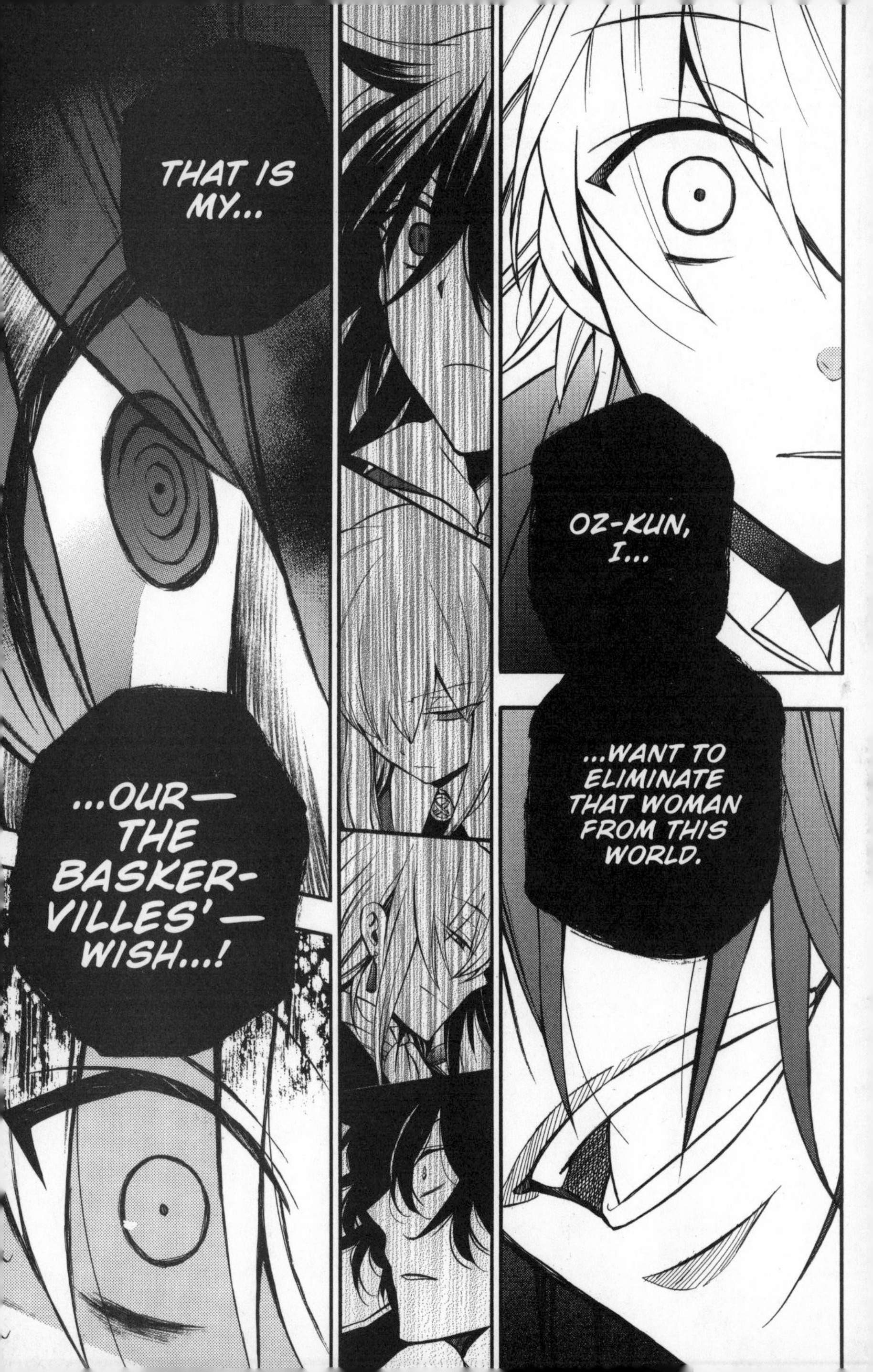
OZ-KUN, I...
...WANT TO ELIMINATE THAT WOMAN FROM THIS WORLD.
THAT IS MY...
...OUR—THE BASKER-VILLES'—WISH...!

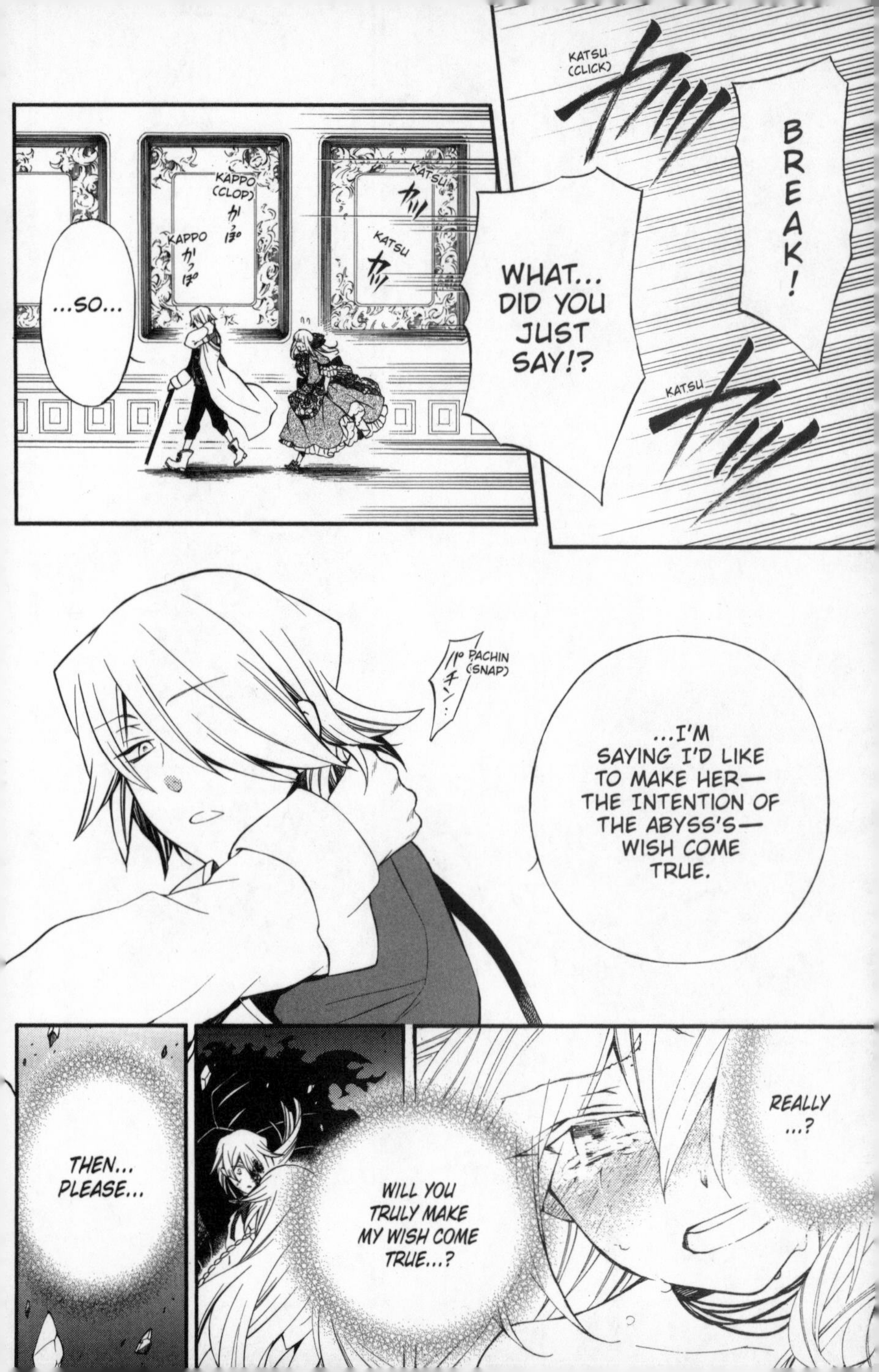
KATSU (CLICK)
BREAK!
WHAT... DID YOU JUST SAY!?
KATSU
KATSU
KATSU
KAPPO (CLOP)
KAPPO
...SO...
PACHIN (SNAP)
...I'M SAYING I'D LIKE TO MAKE HER— THE INTENTION OF THE ABYSS'S— WISH COME TRUE.
REALLY ...?
WILL YOU TRULY MAKE MY WISH COME TRUE...?
THEN... PLEASE...

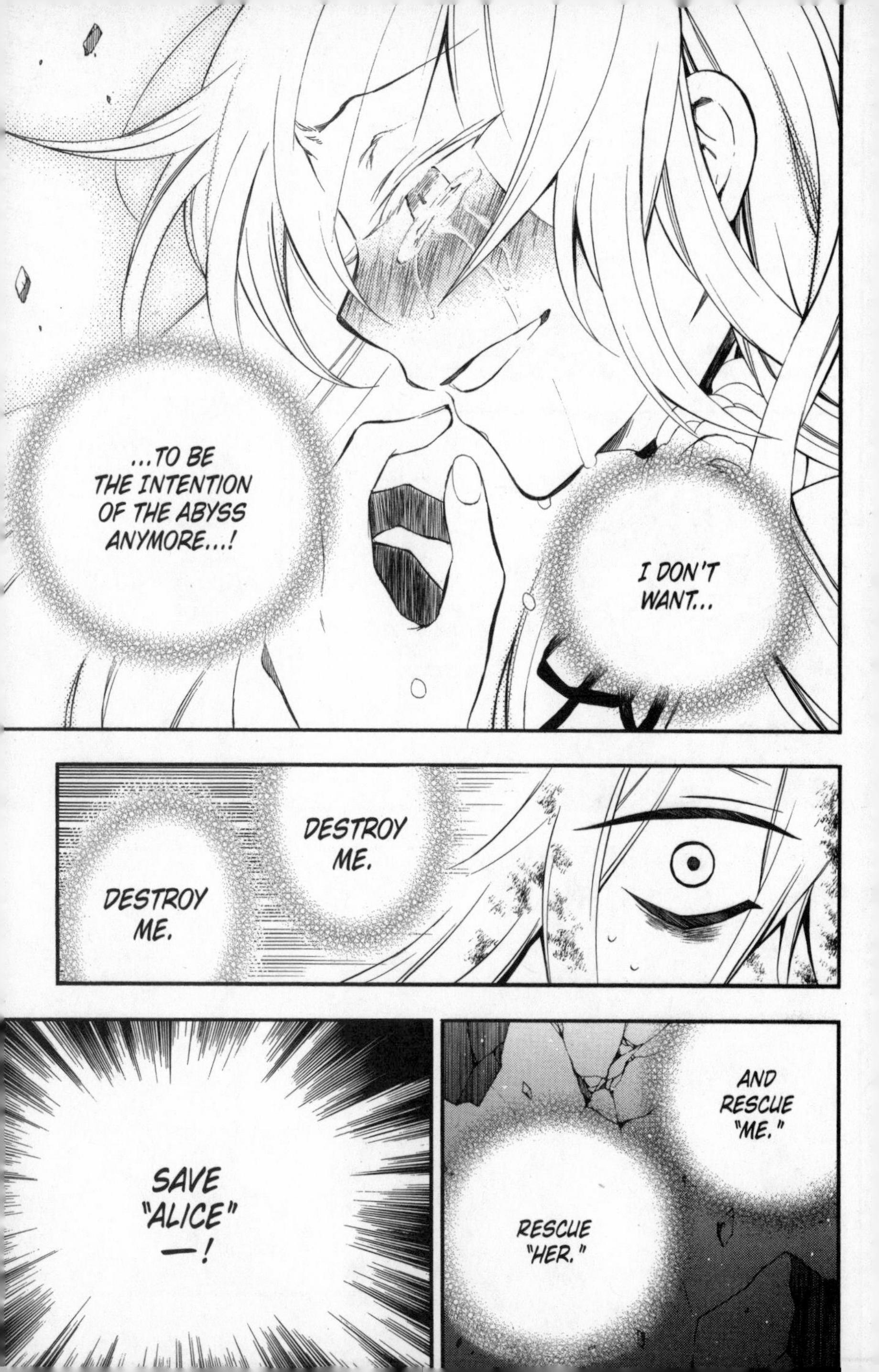
I DON'T WANT...
...TO BE THE INTENTION OF THE ABYSS ANYMORE...!
DESTROY ME.
DESTROY ME.
AND RESCUE "ME."
RESCUE "HER."
SAVE "ALICE" —!

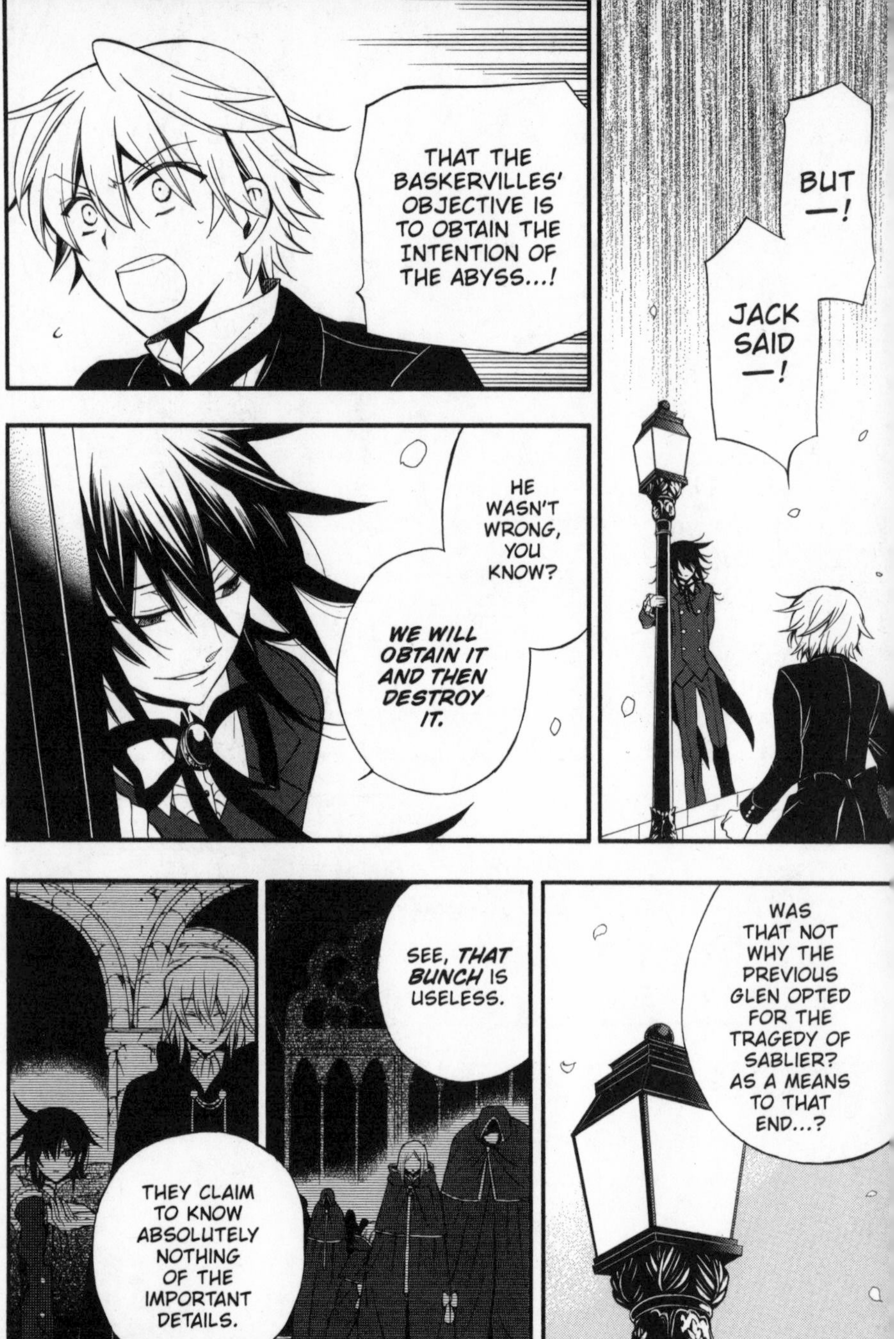
BUT—!
JACK SAID—!
THAT THE BASKERVILLES' OBJECTIVE IS TO OBTAIN THE INTENTION OF THE ABYSS...!
HE WASN'T WRONG, YOU KNOW?
WE WILL OBTAIN IT AND THEN DESTROY IT.
WAS THAT NOT WHY THE PREVIOUS GLEN OPTED FOR THE TRAGEDY OF SABLIER? AS A MEANS TO THAT END...?
SEE, *THAT BUNCH* IS USELESS.
THEY CLAIM TO KNOW ABSOLUTELY NOTHING OF THE IMPORTANT DETAILS.

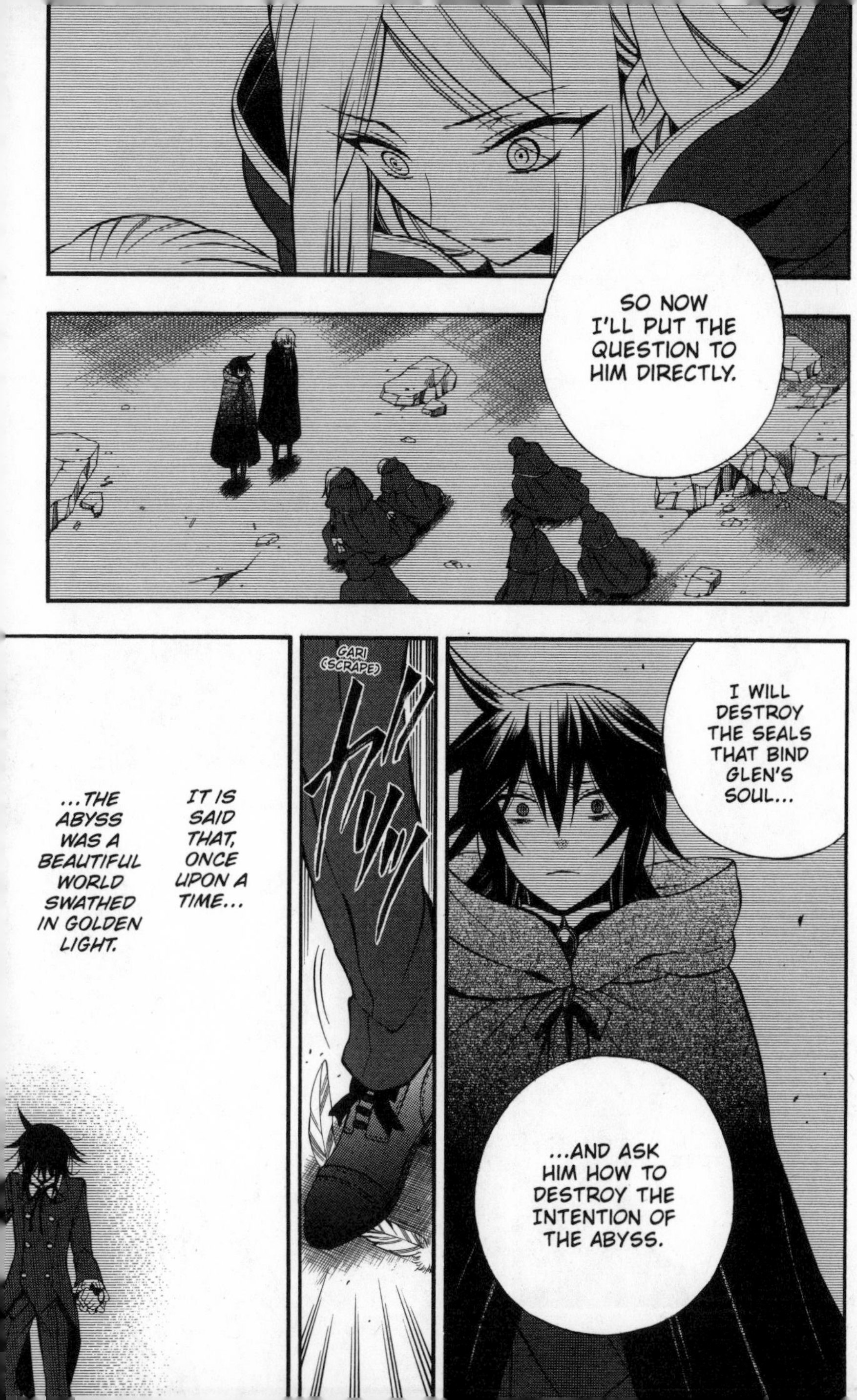
SO NOW I'LL PUT THE QUESTION TO HIM DIRECTLY.
I WILL DESTROY THE SEALS THAT BIND GLEN'S SOUL...
...AND ASK HIM HOW TO DESTROY THE INTENTION OF THE ABYSS.
GARI (SCRAPE)
IT IS SAID THAT, ONCE UPON A TIME...
...THE ABYSS WAS A BEAUTIFUL WORLD SWATHED IN GOLDEN LIGHT.

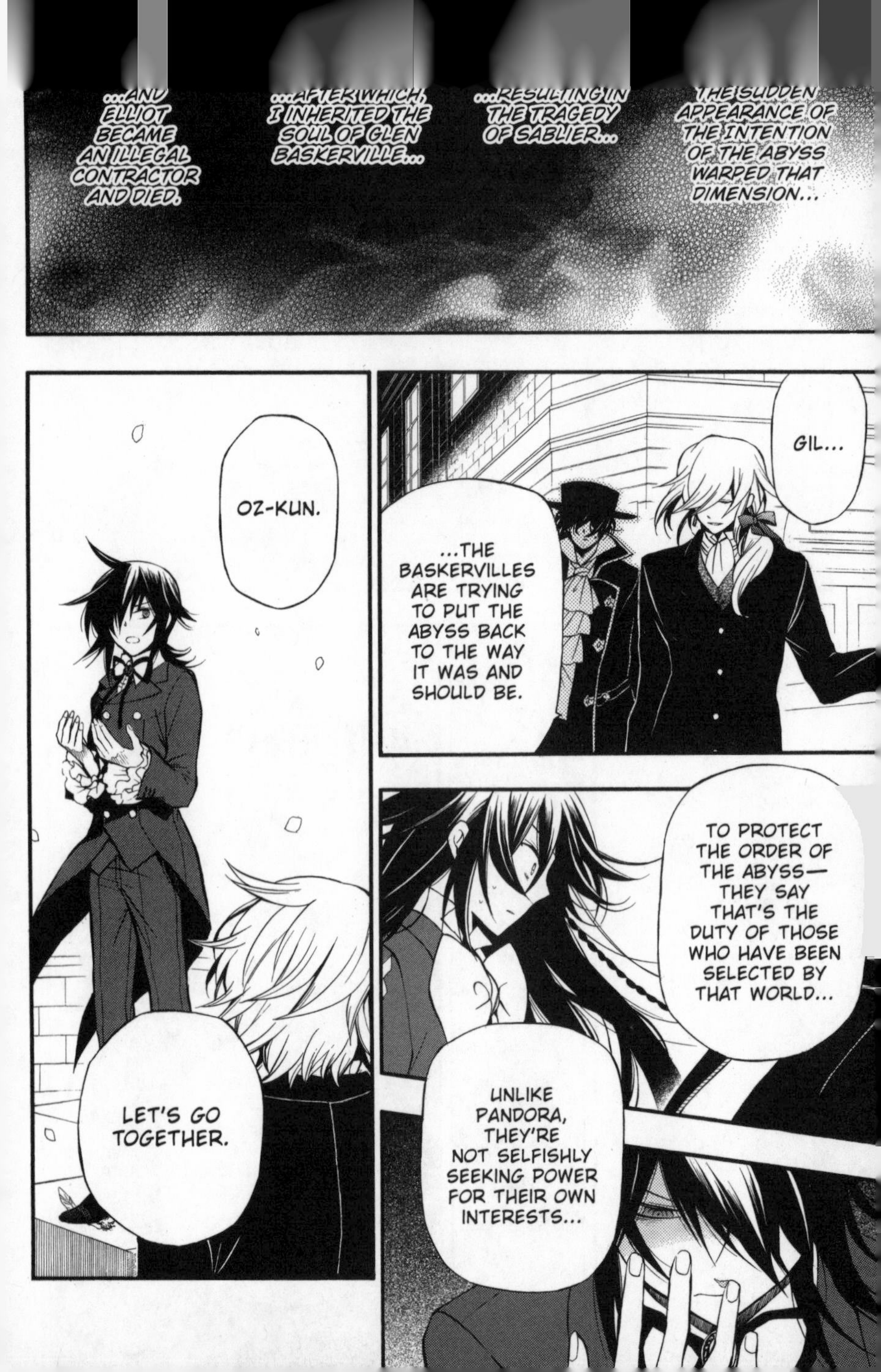
THE SUDDEN APPEARANCE OF THE INTENTION OF THE ABYSS WARPED THAT DIMENSION...
...RESULTING IN THE TRAGEDY OF SABLIER...
...AFTER WHICH, I INHERITED THE SOUL OF GLEN BASKERVILLE...
...AND ELLIOT BECAME AN ILLEGAL CONTRACTOR AND DIED.
GIL...
...THE BASKERVILLES ARE TRYING TO PUT THE ABYSS BACK TO THE WAY IT WAS AND SHOULD BE.
TO PROTECT THE ORDER OF THE ABYSS—THEY SAY THAT'S THE DUTY OF THOSE WHO HAVE BEEN SELECTED BY THAT WORLD...
UNLIKE PANDORA, THEY'RE NOT SELFISHLY SEEKING POWER FOR THEIR OWN INTERESTS...
OZ-KUN.
LET'S GO TOGETHER.

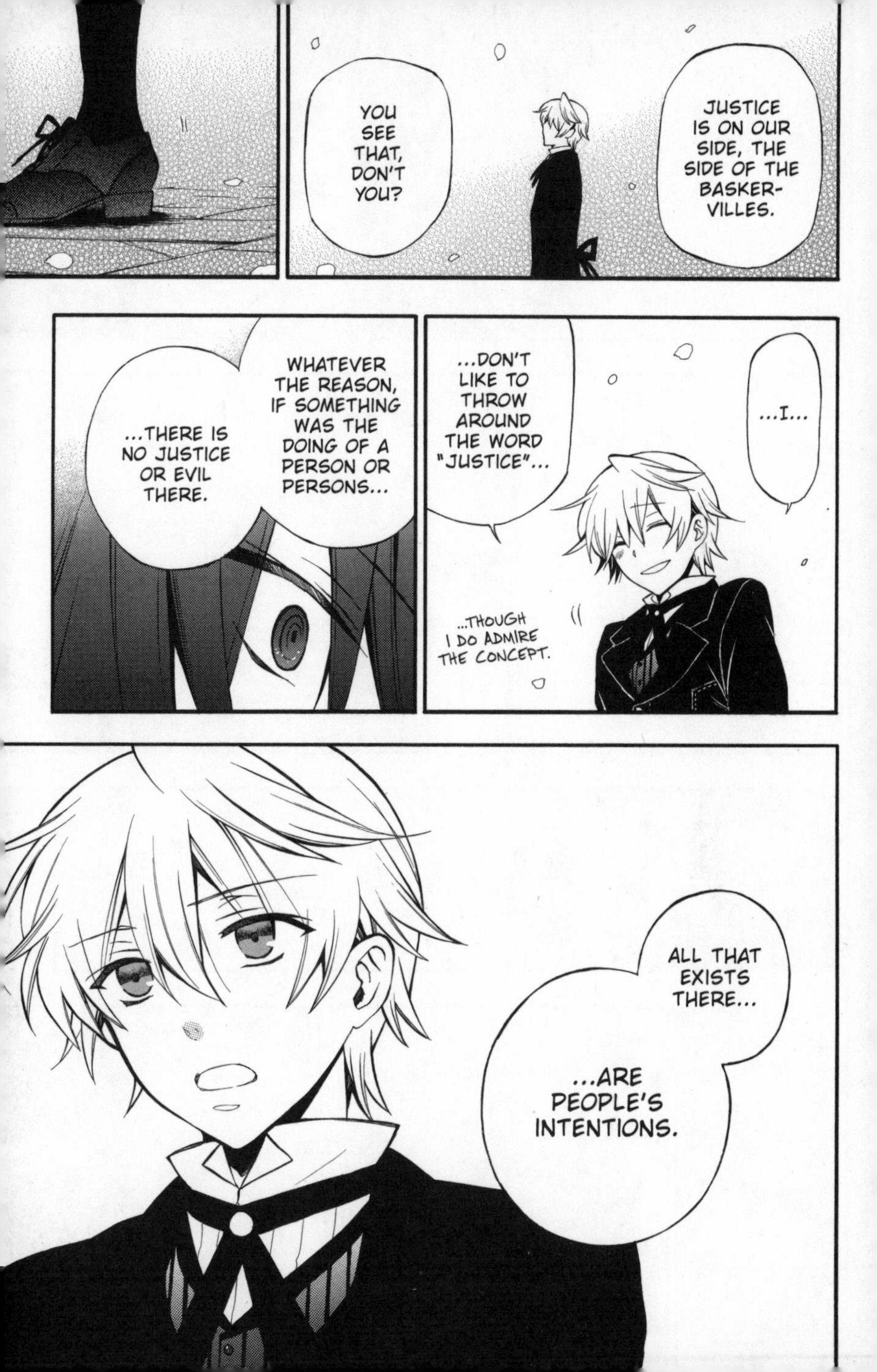
JUSTICE IS ON OUR SIDE, THE SIDE OF THE BASKER-VILLES.
YOU SEE THAT, DON'T YOU?
...I...
...DON'T LIKE TO THROW AROUND THE WORD "JUSTICE"...
...THOUGH I DO ADMIRE THE CONCEPT.
WHATEVER THE REASON, IF SOMETHING WAS THE DOING OF A PERSON OR PERSONS...
...THERE IS NO JUSTICE OR EVIL THERE.
ALL THAT EXISTS THERE...
...ARE PEOPLE'S INTENTIONS.

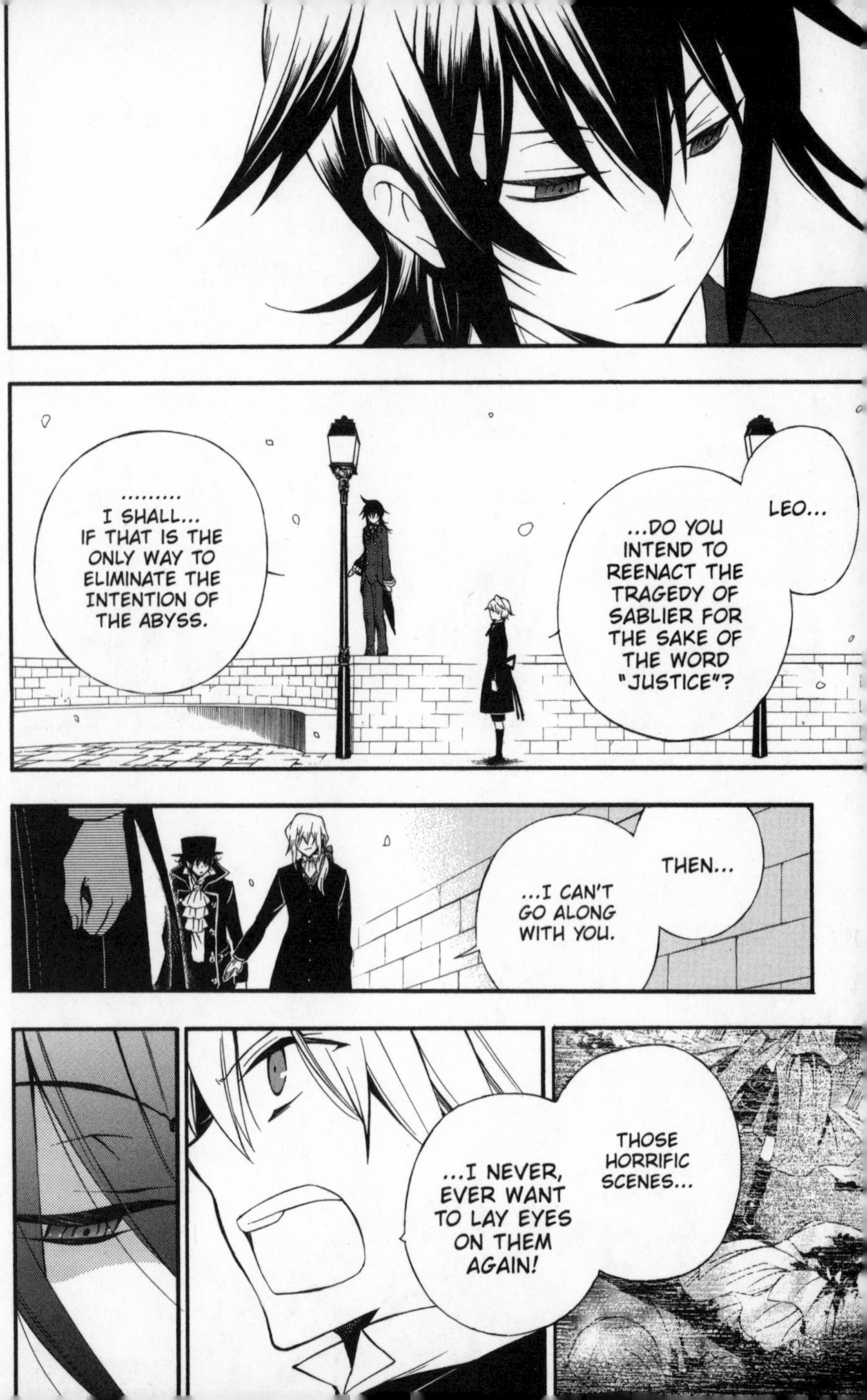
LEO...
...DO YOU INTEND TO REENACT THE TRAGEDY OF SABLIER FOR THE SAKE OF THE WORD "JUSTICE"?
.... I SHALL... IF THAT IS THE ONLY WAY TO ELIMINATE THE INTENTION OF THE ABYSS.
THEN...
...I CAN'T GO ALONG WITH YOU.
THOSE HORRIFIC SCENES...
...I NEVER, EVER WANT TO LAY EYES ON THEM AGAIN!

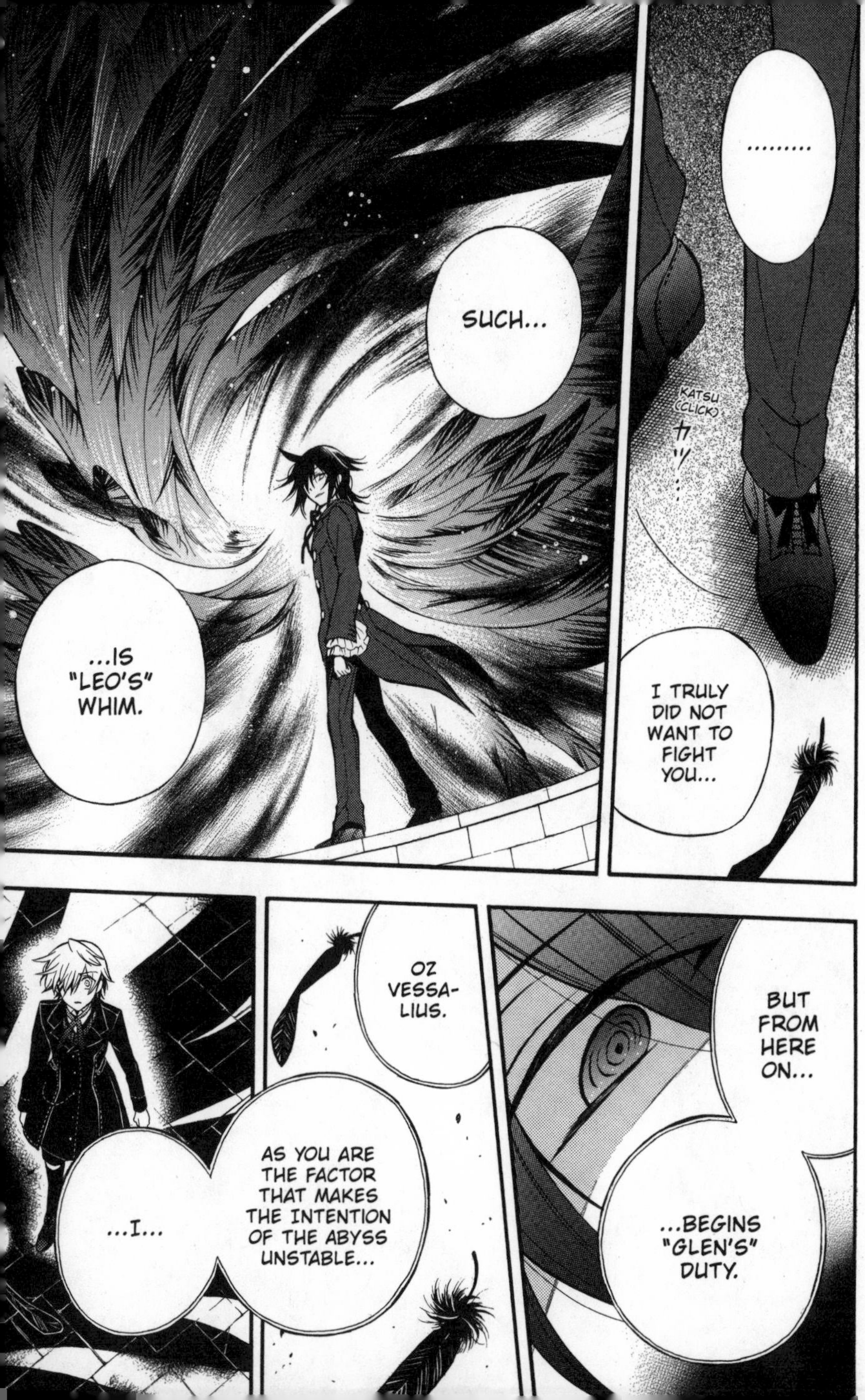
....
KATSU (CLICK)
カツ…
I TRULY DID NOT WANT TO FIGHT YOU...
SUCH...
...IS "LEO'S" WHIM.
BUT FROM HERE ON...
...BEGINS "GLEN'S" DUTY.
OZ VESSA-LIUS.
AS YOU ARE THE FACTOR THAT MAKES THE INTENTION OF THE ABYSS UNSTABLE...
...I...

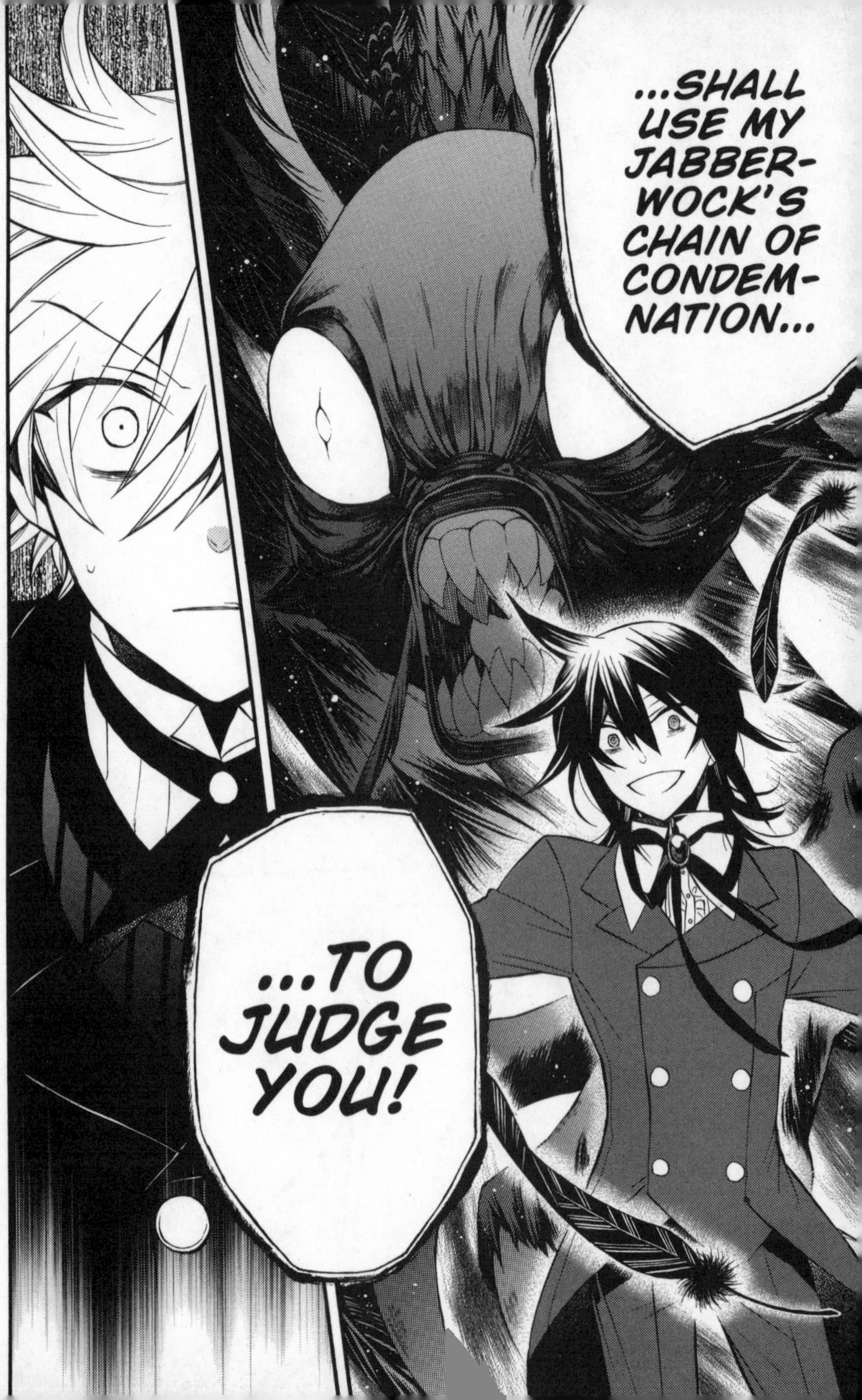
...SHALL USE MY JABBER-WOCK'S CHAIN OF CONDEM-NATION...
...TO JUDGE YOU!

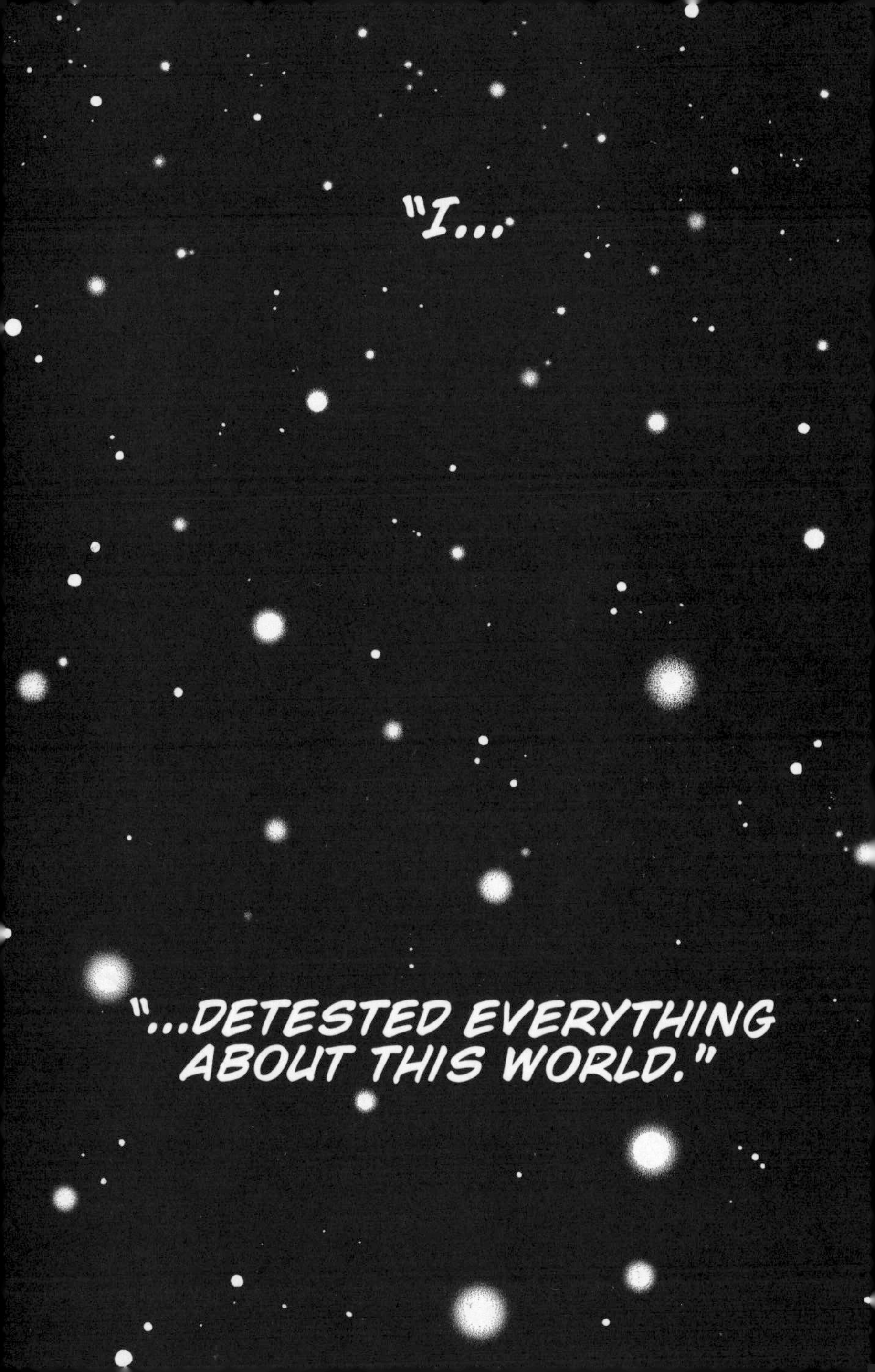
"I..."
"...DETESTED EVERYTHING ABOUT THIS WORLD."

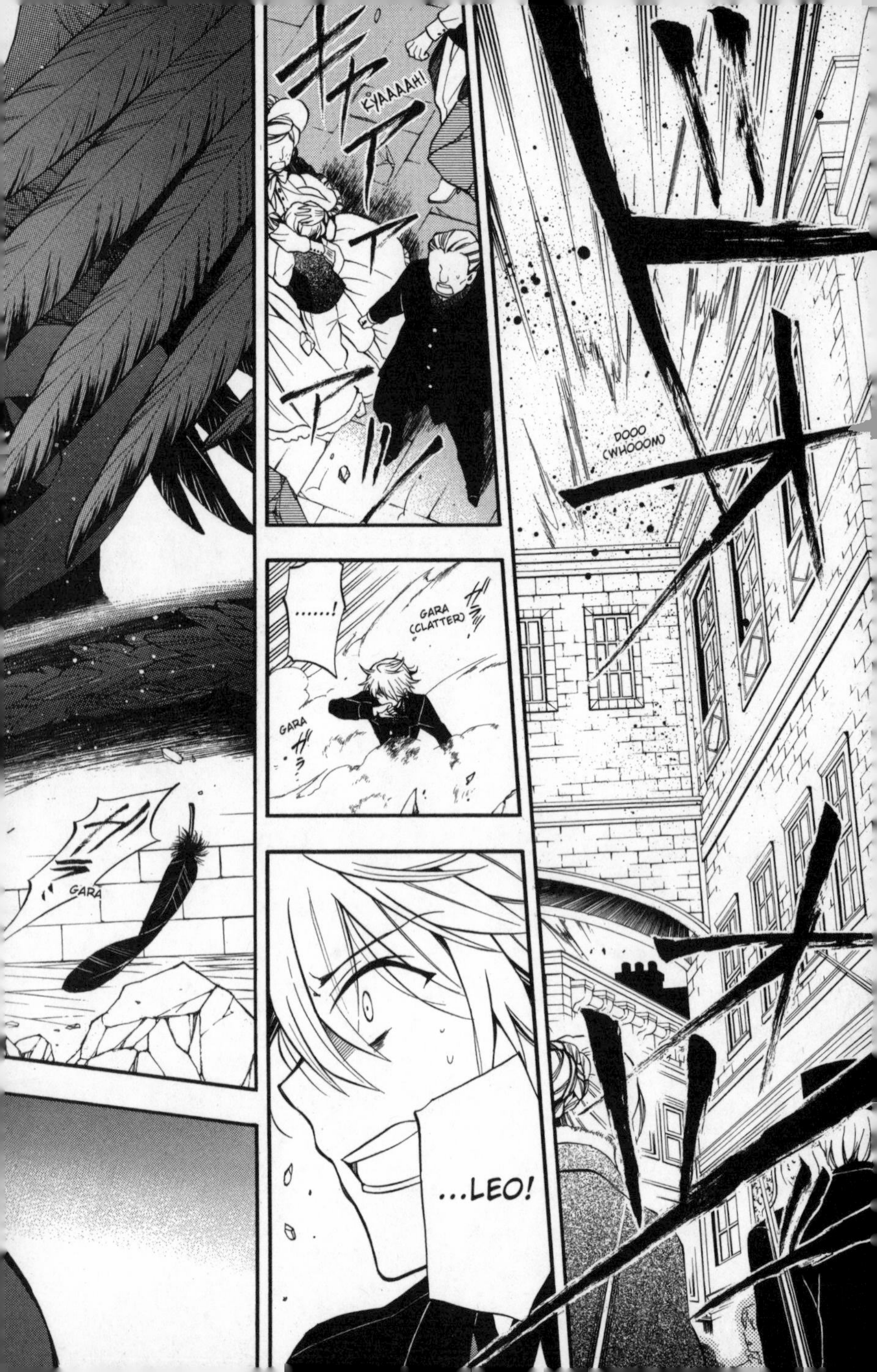
DOOO (WHOOOM)
KYAAAAH!
......!
GARA (CLATTER)
GARA
...LEO!
GARA

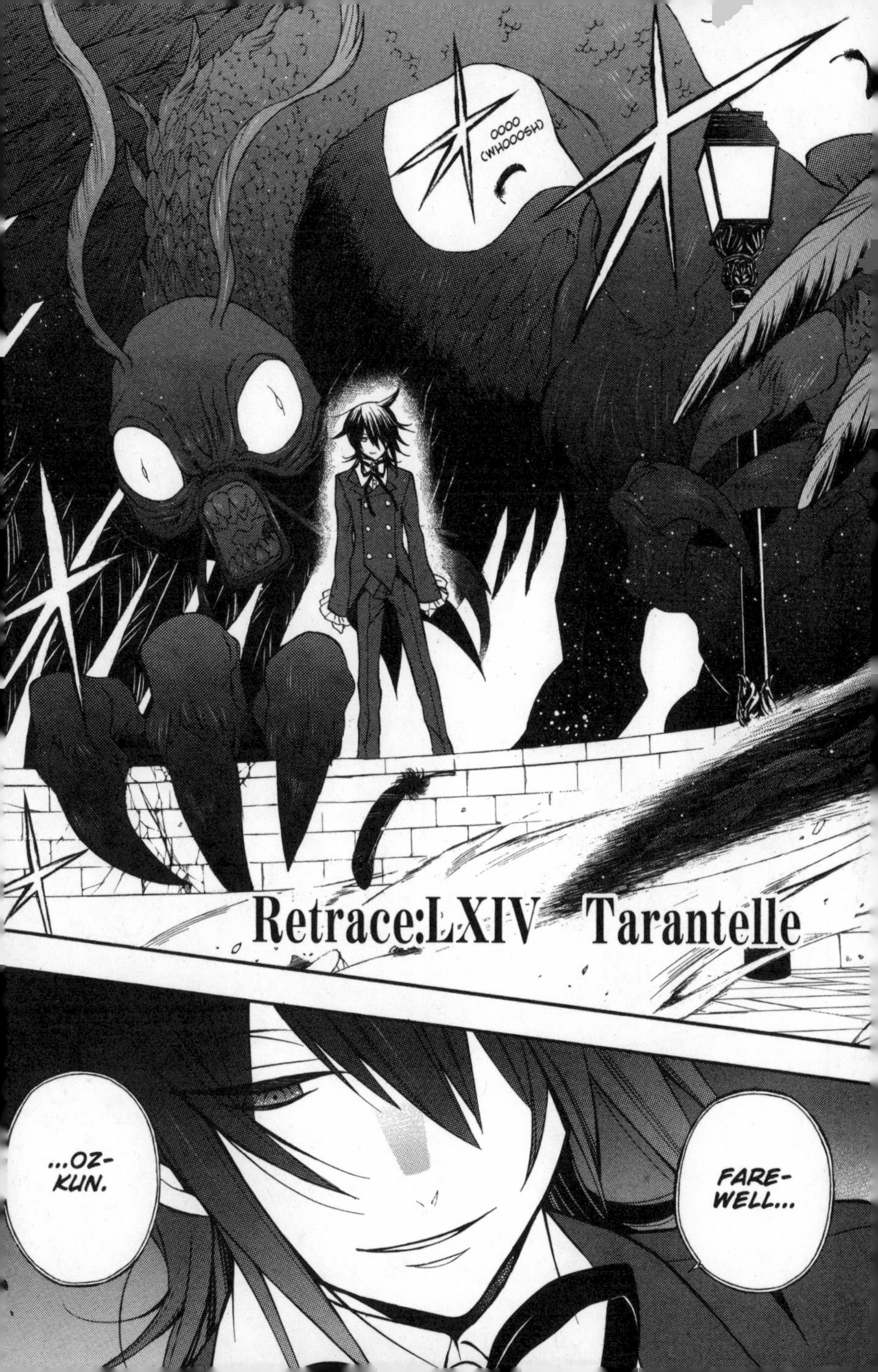
OOOO (WHOOOSH)
Retrace:LXIV Tarantelle
FARE-WELL...
...OZ-KUN.

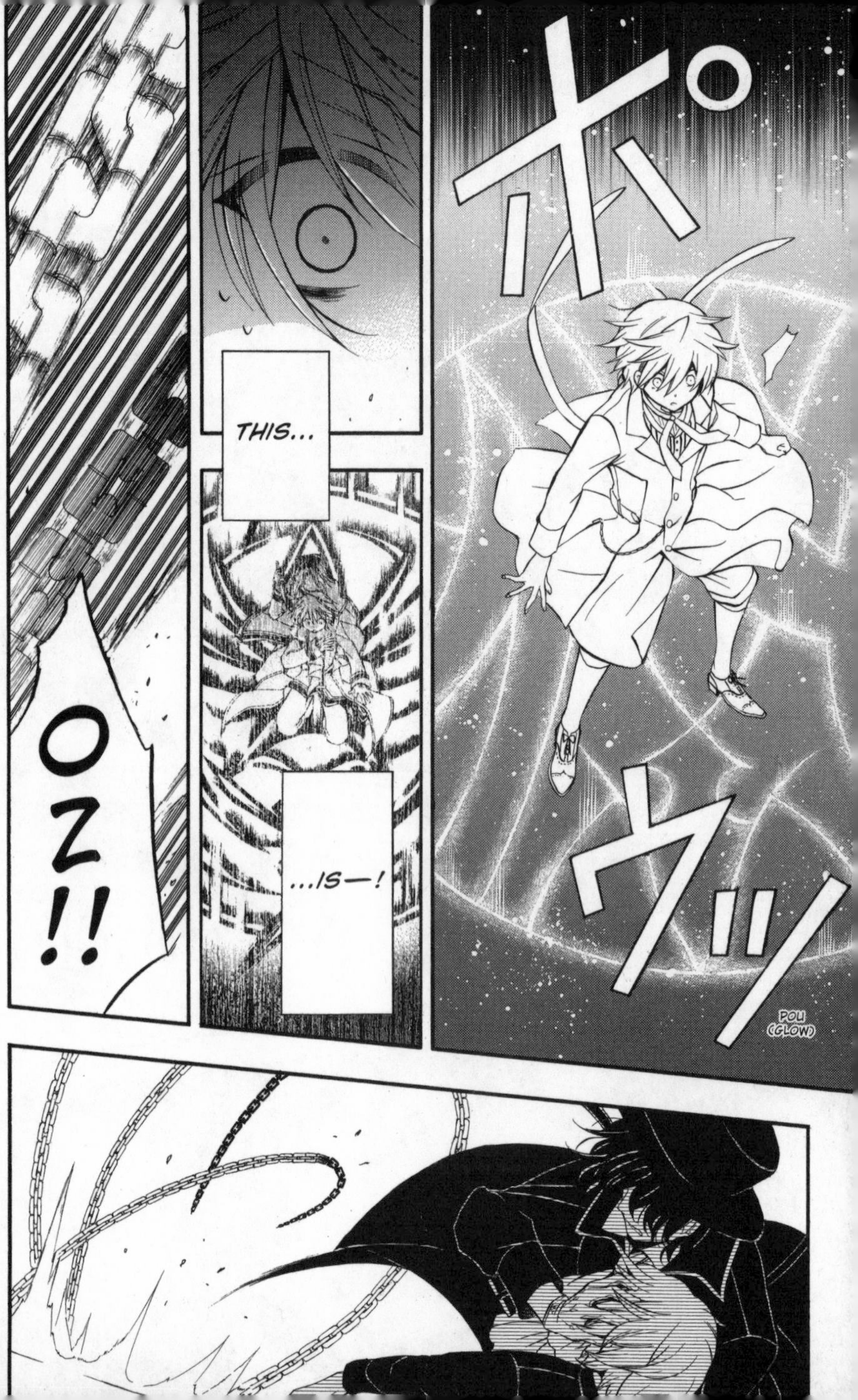
ポウッ
POU
(GLOW)
THIS...
...IS—!
OZ!!

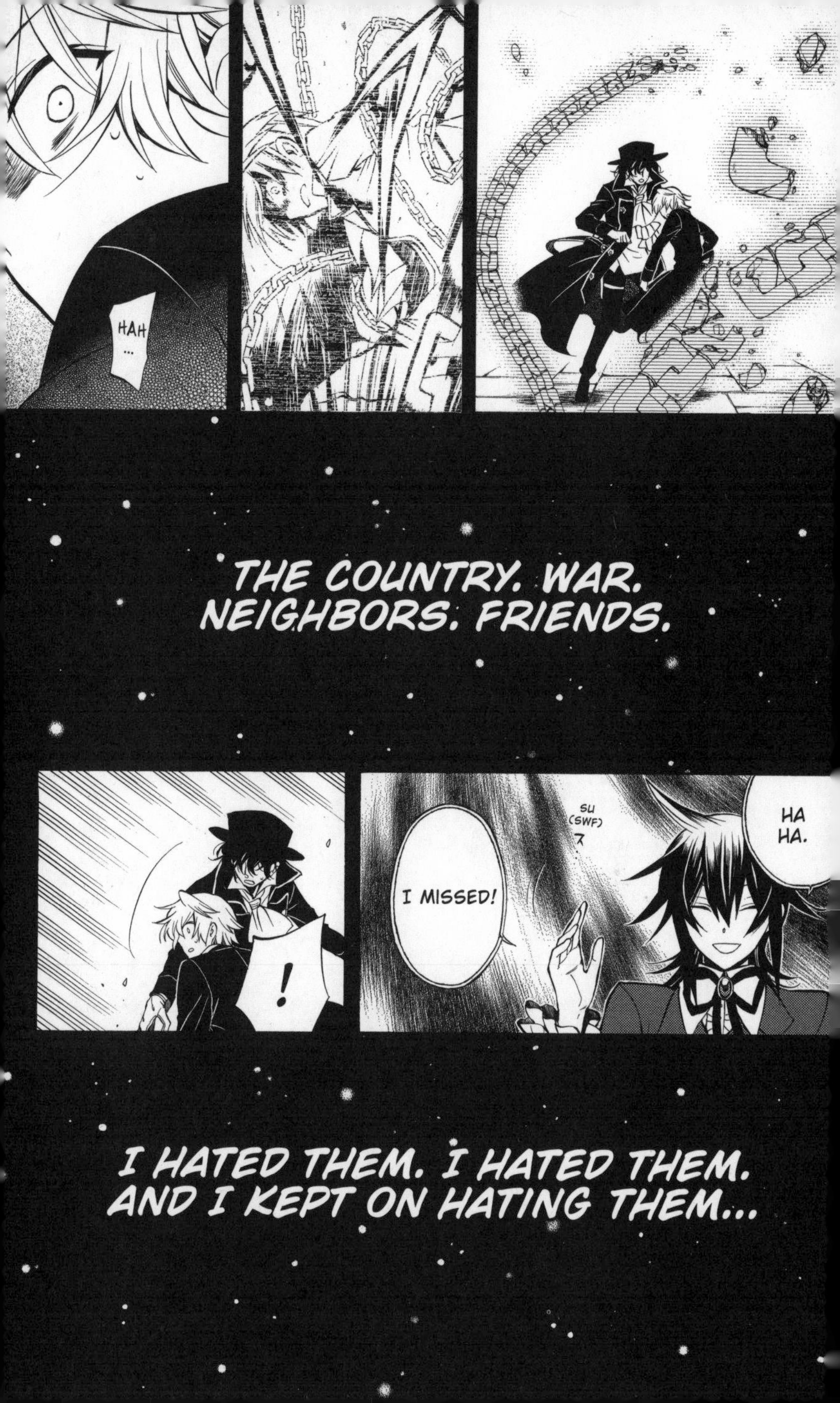
HAH ...
THE COUNTRY. WAR. NEIGHBORS. FRIENDS.
HA HA.
SU (SWF)
I MISSED!
!
I HATED THEM. I HATED THEM. AND I KEPT ON HATING THEM...

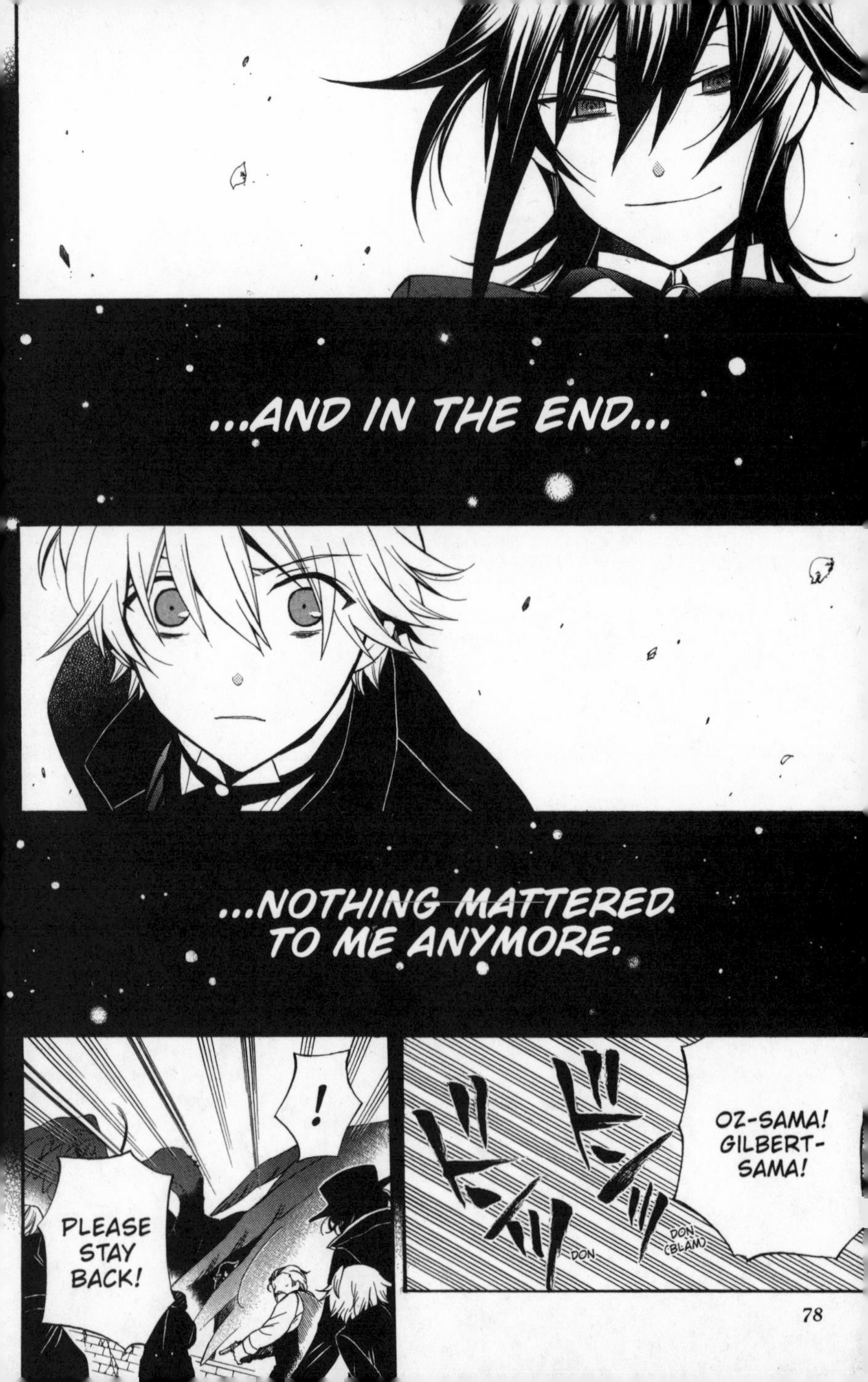
...AND IN THE END...
...NOTHING MATTERED TO ME ANYMORE.
OZ-SAMA! GILBERT-SAMA!
DON
DON (BLAM)
!
PLEASE STAY BACK!

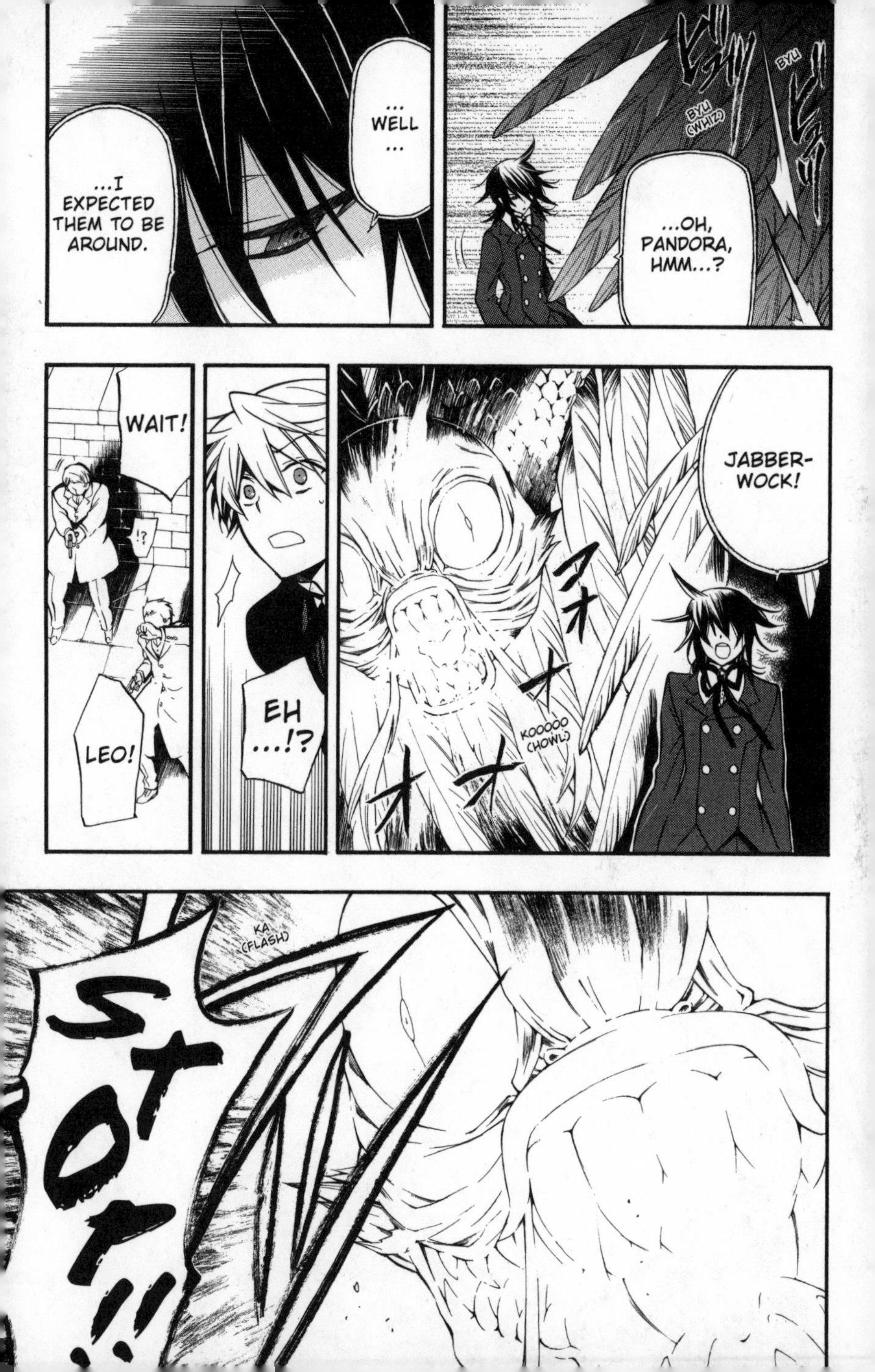
BYU (WHIZ)
BYU
...OH, PANDORA, HMM...?
... WELL ...
...I EXPECTED THEM TO BE AROUND.
JABBER-WOCK!
KOOOOO (HOWL)
EH ...!?
WAIT!
!?
LEO!
KA (FLASH)
STOP!!!

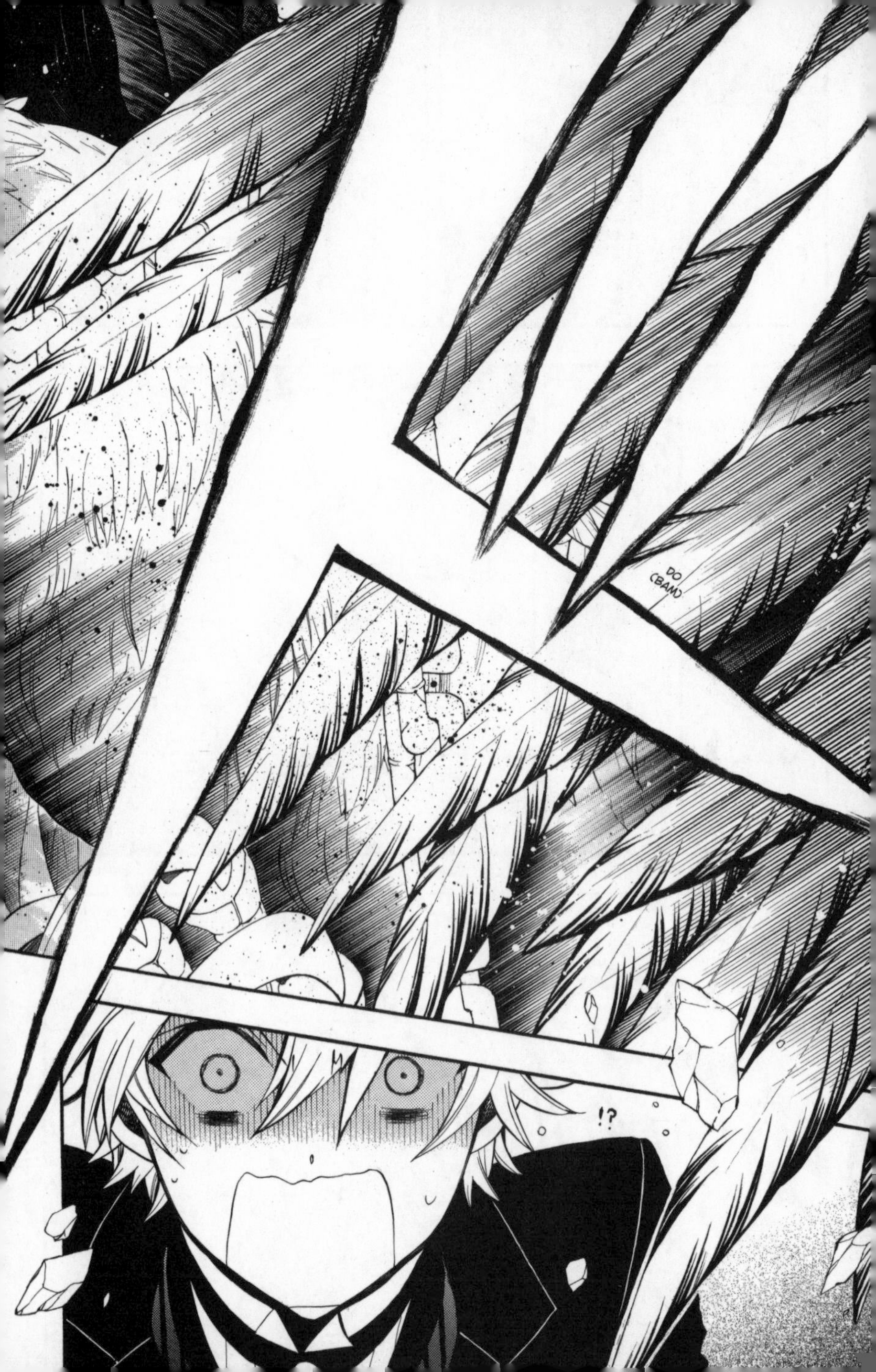
DO
(BAM)
!?

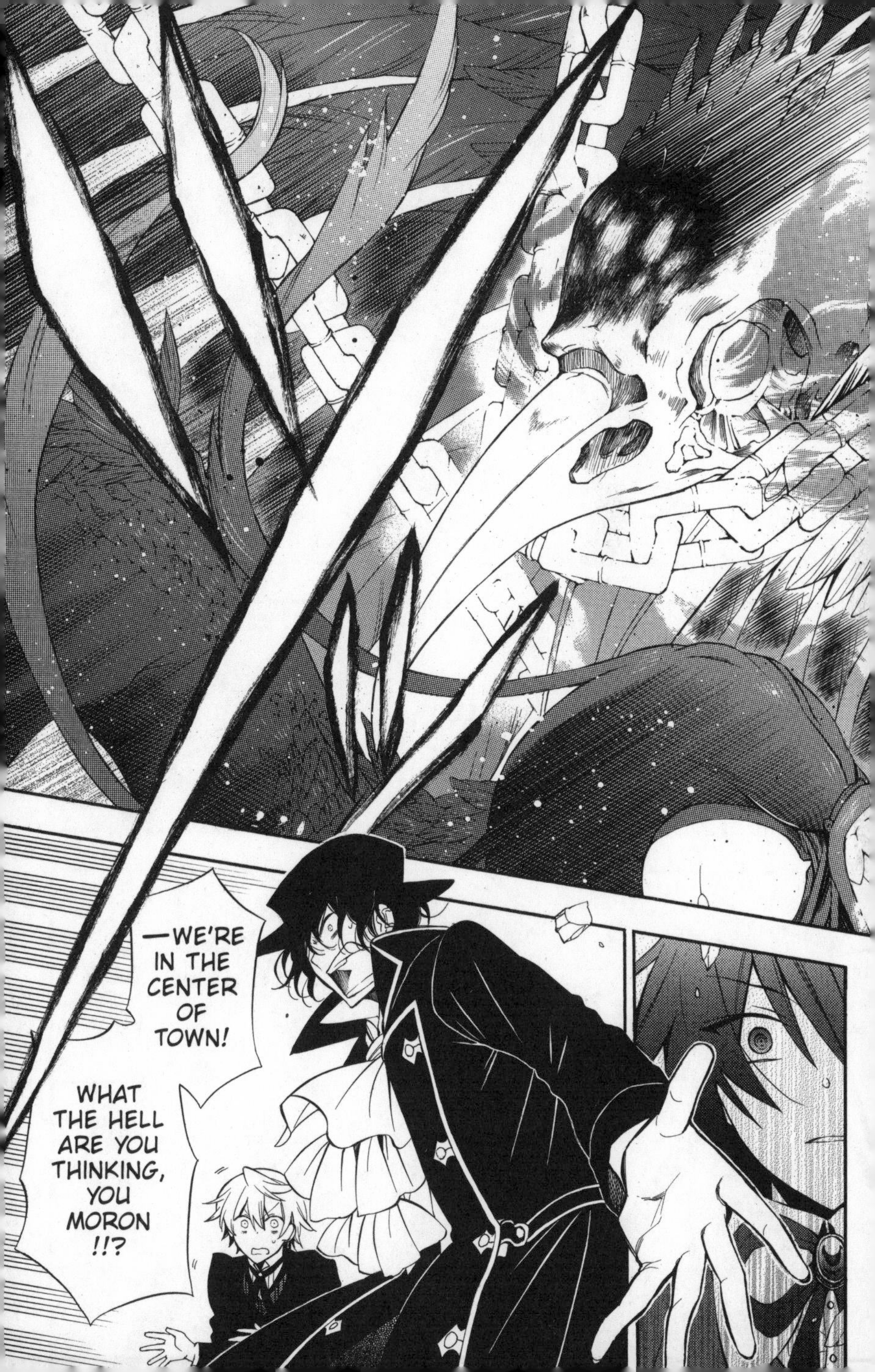
—WE'RE IN THE CENTER OF TOWN!
WHAT THE HELL ARE YOU THINKING, YOU MORON !!?

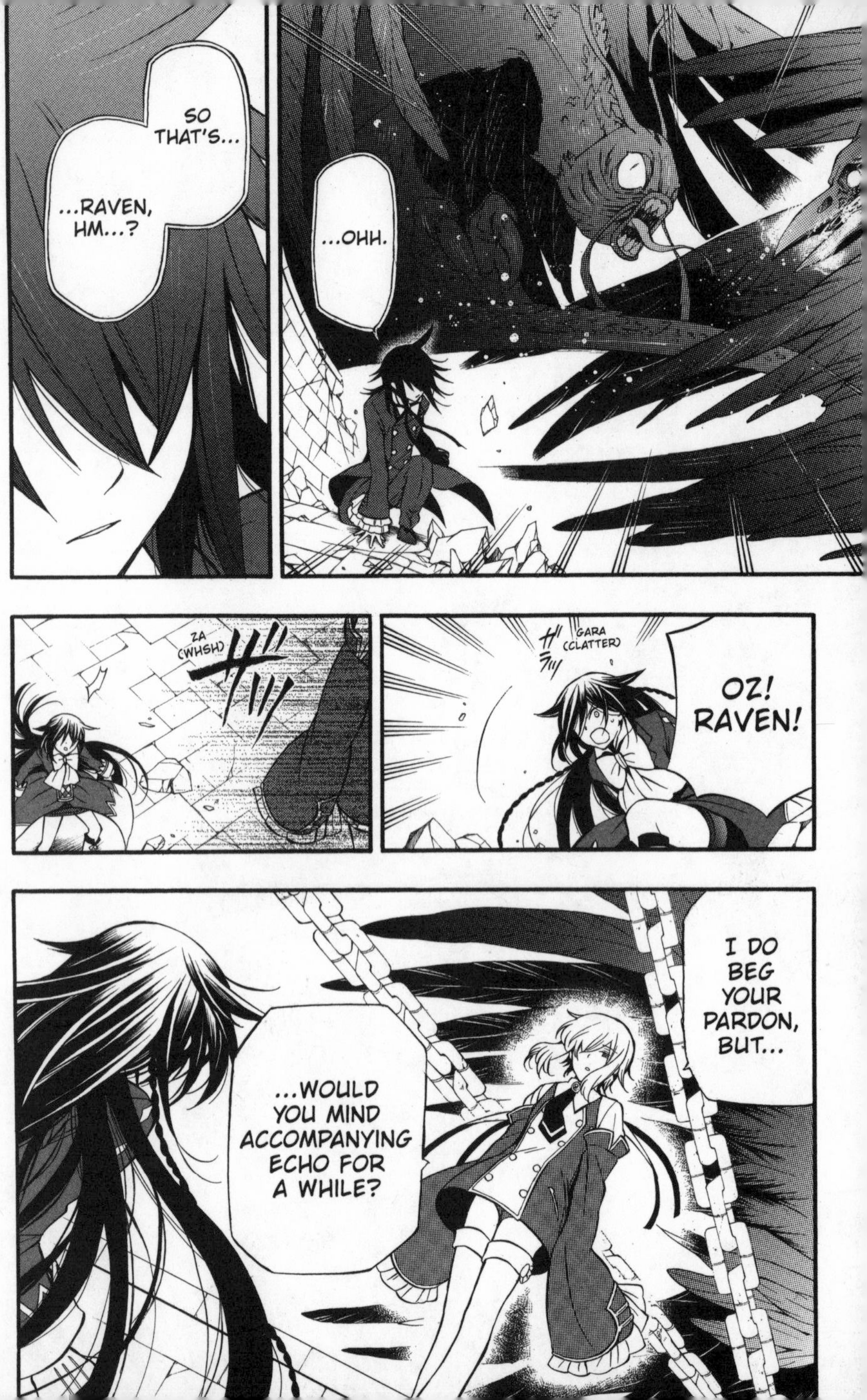
...OHH.
SO THAT'S...
...RAVEN, HM...?
GARA (CLATTER)
OZ! RAVEN!
ZA (WHSH)
I DO BEG YOUR PARDON, BUT...
...WOULD YOU MIND ACCOMPANYING ECHO FOR A WHILE?

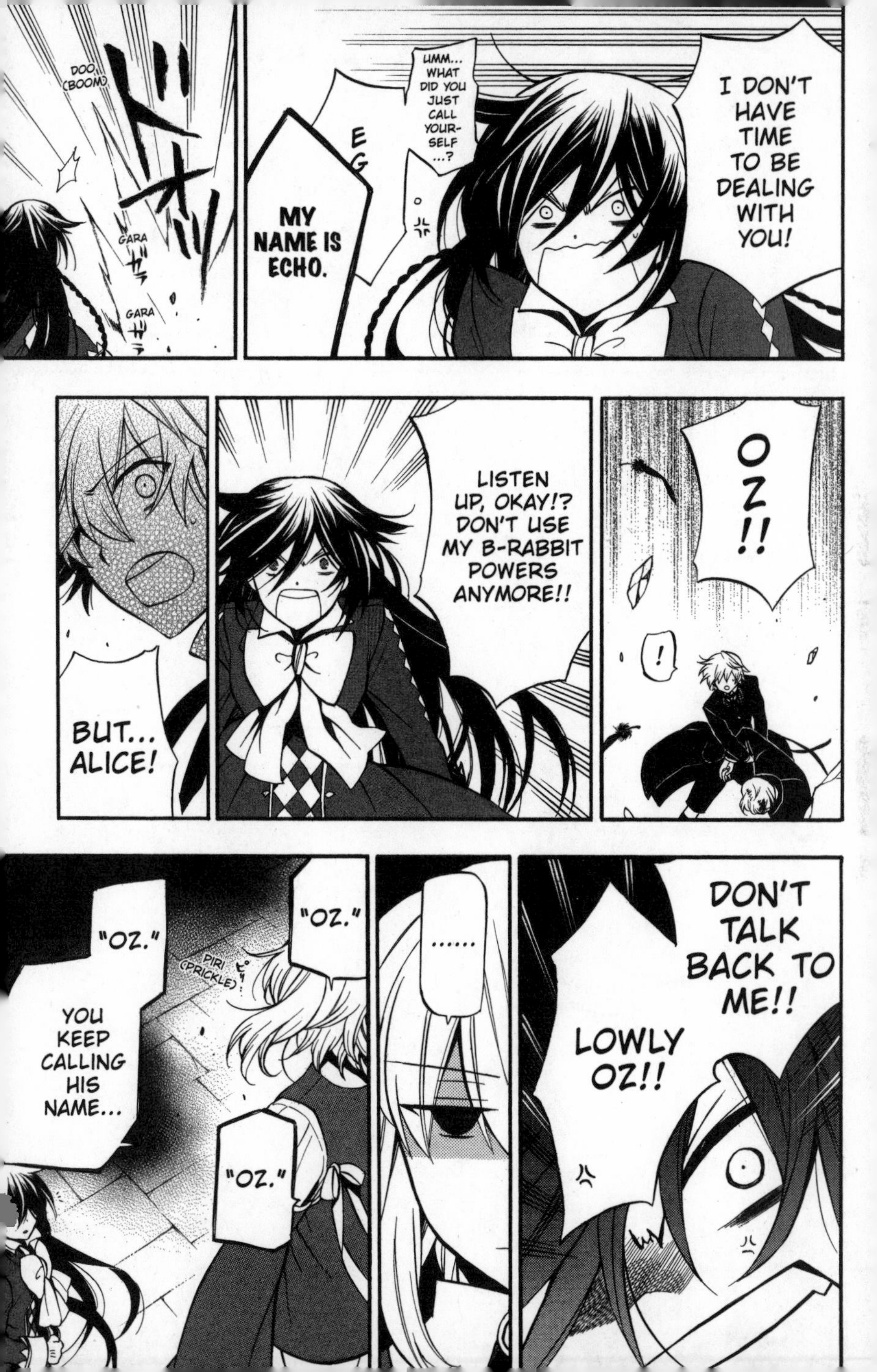
I DON'T HAVE TIME TO BE DEALING WITH YOU!
UMM... WHAT DID YOU JUST CALL YOUR-SELF ...?
MY NAME IS ECHO.
DOO (BOOM)
GARA
GARA
OZ!!
!
LISTEN UP, OKAY!? DON'T USE MY B-RABBIT POWERS ANYMORE!!
BUT... ALICE!
DON'T TALK BACK TO ME!!
LOWLY OZ!!
......
"OZ."
"OZ."
PIRI (PRICKLE)
YOU KEEP CALLING HIS NAME...
"OZ."

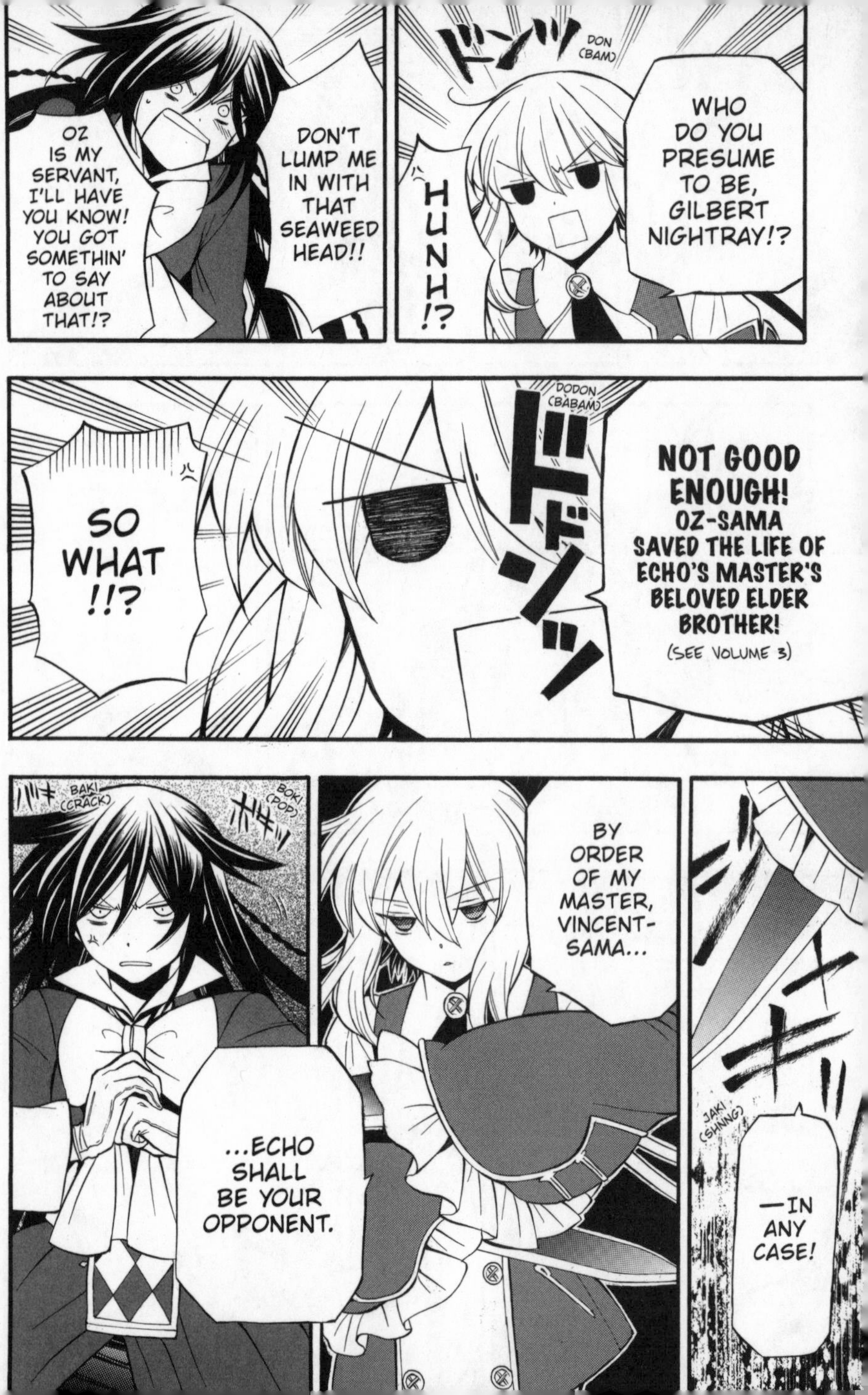
DON (BAM)
WHO DO YOU PRESUME TO BE, GILBERT NIGHTRAY!?
HUNH!?
DON'T LUMP ME IN WITH THAT SEAWEED HEAD!!
OZ IS MY SERVANT, I'LL HAVE YOU KNOW! YOU GOT SOMETHIN' TO SAY ABOUT THAT!?
DODON (BABAM)
NOT GOOD ENOUGH! OZ-SAMA SAVED THE LIFE OF ECHO'S MASTER'S BELOVED ELDER BROTHER!
(SEE VOLUME 3)
SO WHAT!!?
JAKI (SHNNG)
—IN ANY CASE!
BY ORDER OF MY MASTER, VINCENT-SAMA...
...ECHO SHALL BE YOUR OPPONENT.
BOKI (POP)
BAKI (CRACK)

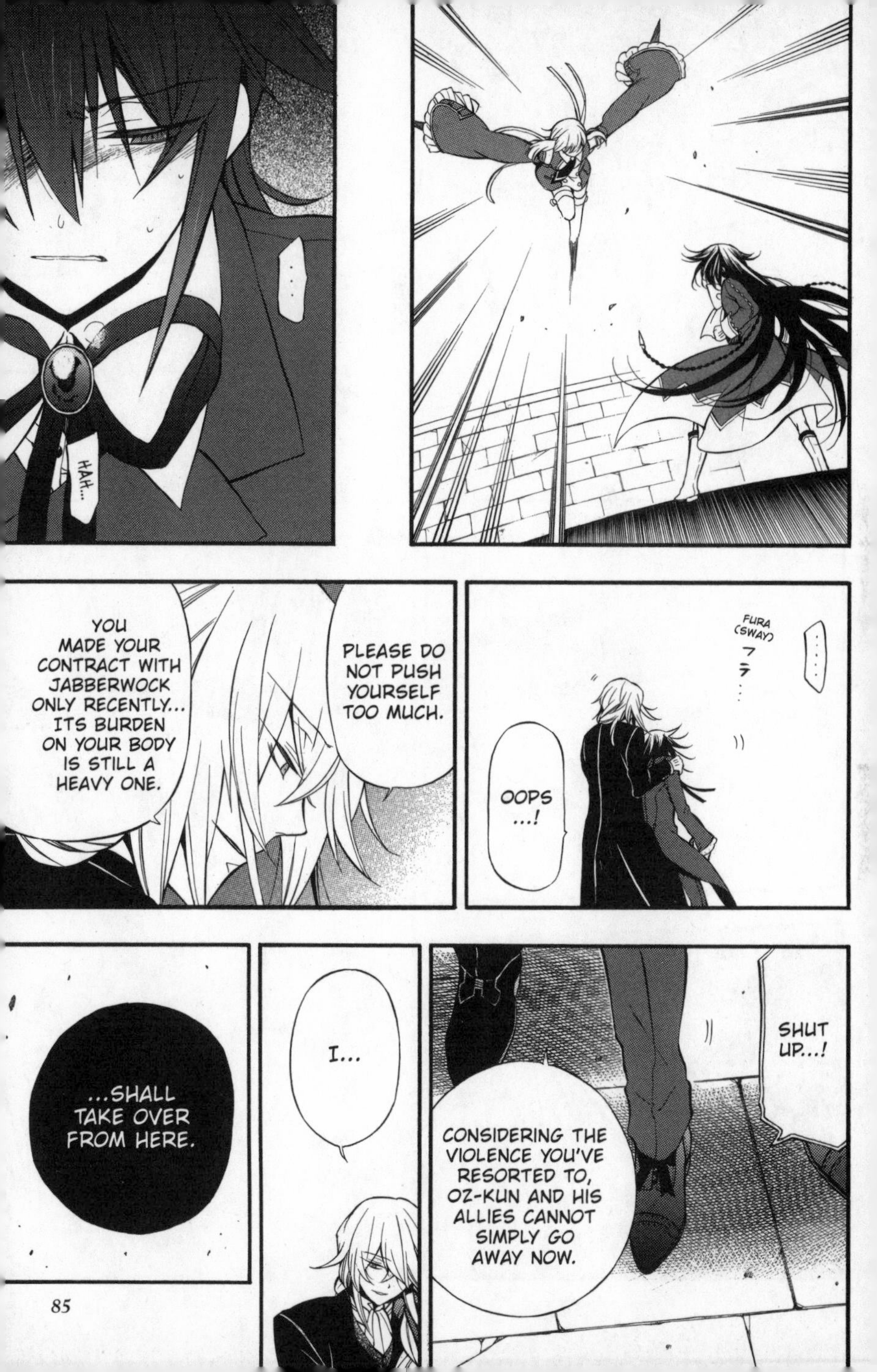
...
HAH...
FURA (SWAY)
フラ…
.....
OOPS ...!
PLEASE DO NOT PUSH YOURSELF TOO MUCH.
YOU MADE YOUR CONTRACT WITH JABBERWOCK ONLY RECENTLY... ITS BURDEN ON YOUR BODY IS STILL A HEAVY ONE.
SHUT UP...!
CONSIDERING THE VIOLENCE YOU'VE RESORTED TO, OZ-KUN AND HIS ALLIES CANNOT SIMPLY GO AWAY NOW.
I...
...SHALL TAKE OVER FROM HERE.

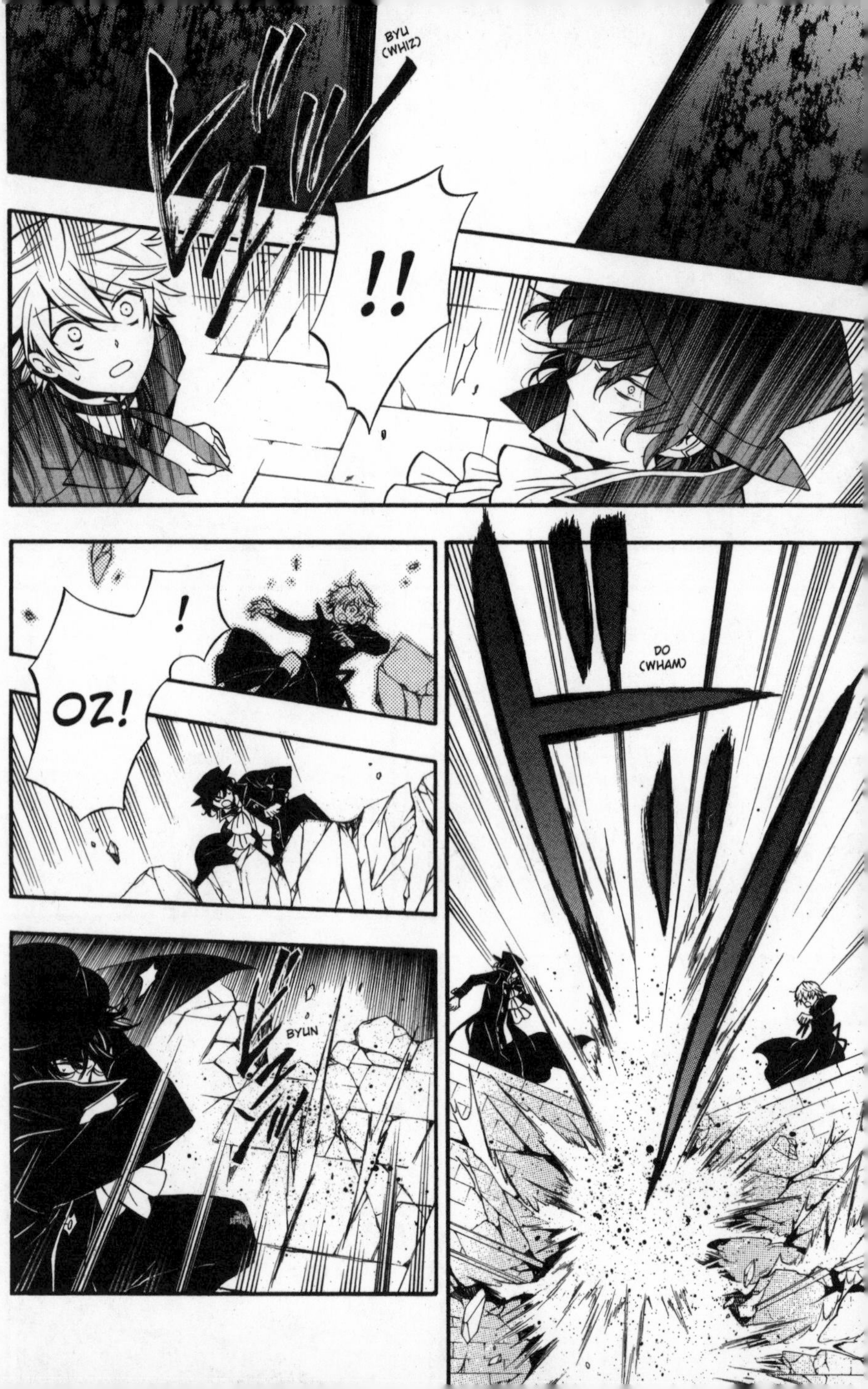

BYU (WHIZ)
!!
DO (WHAM)
!
OZ!
BYUN

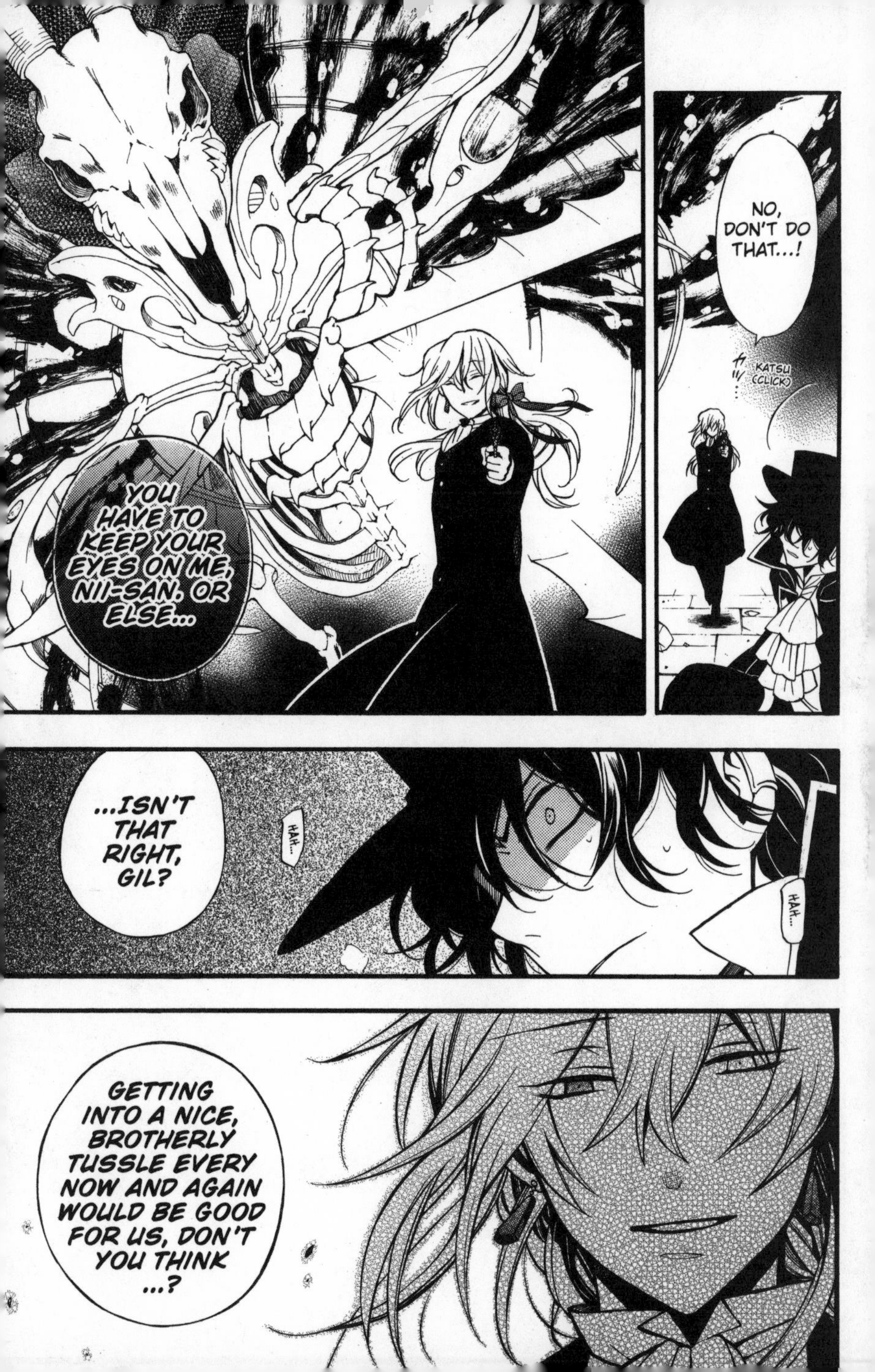
NO, DON'T DO THAT...!
KATSU (CLICK)
YOU HAVE TO KEEP YOUR EYES ON ME, NII-SAN. OR ELSE...
HAH...
...ISN'T THAT RIGHT, GIL?
HAH...
GETTING INTO A NICE, BROTHERLY TUSSLE EVERY NOW AND AGAIN WOULD BE GOOD FOR US, DON'T YOU THINK ...?

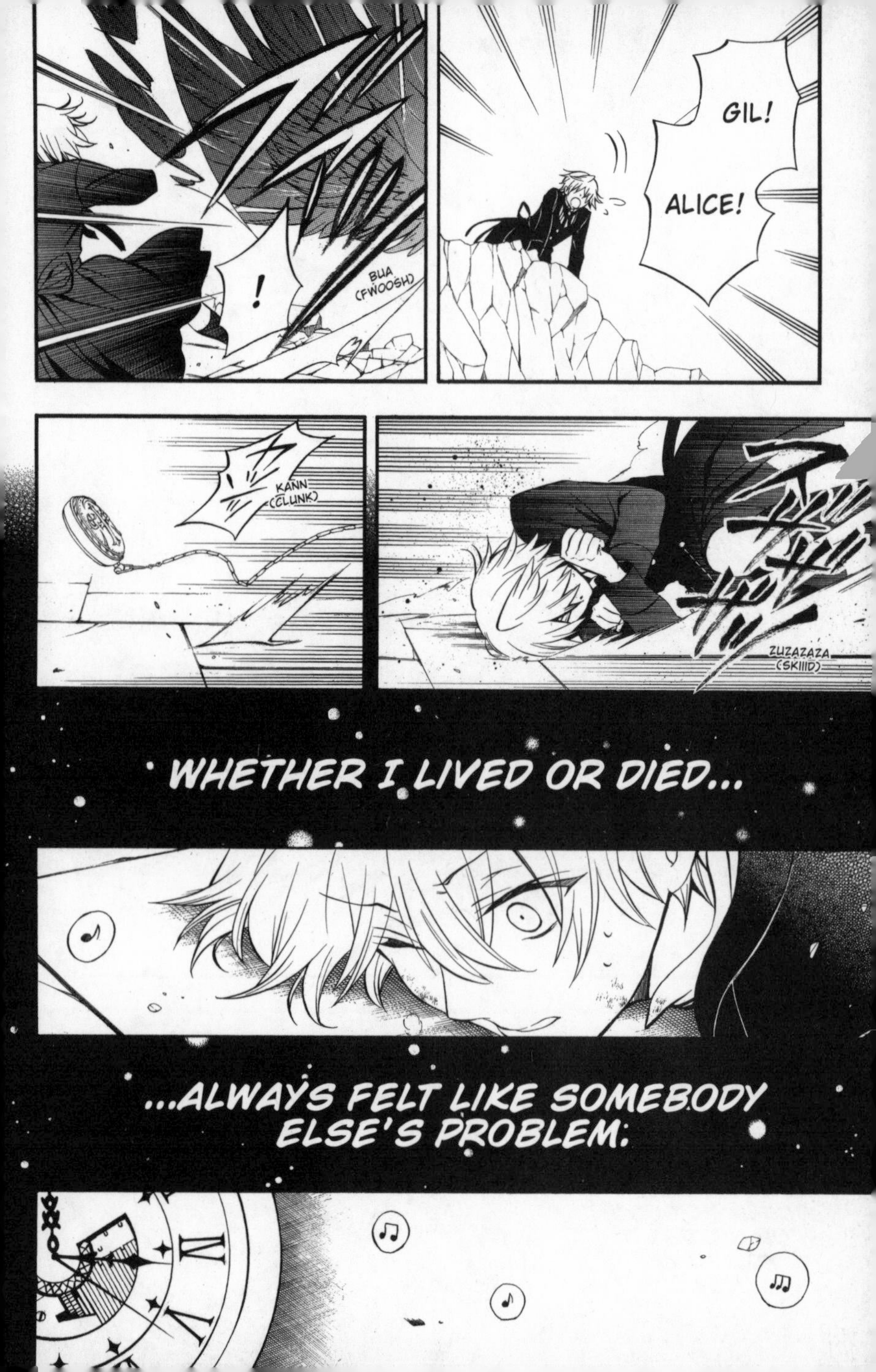
GIL!
ALICE!
BUA (FWOOSH)
!
ZUZAZAZA (SKIIID)
KANN (CLUNK)
WHETHER I LIVED OR DIED...
...ALWAYS FELT LIKE SOMEBODY ELSE'S PROBLEM.

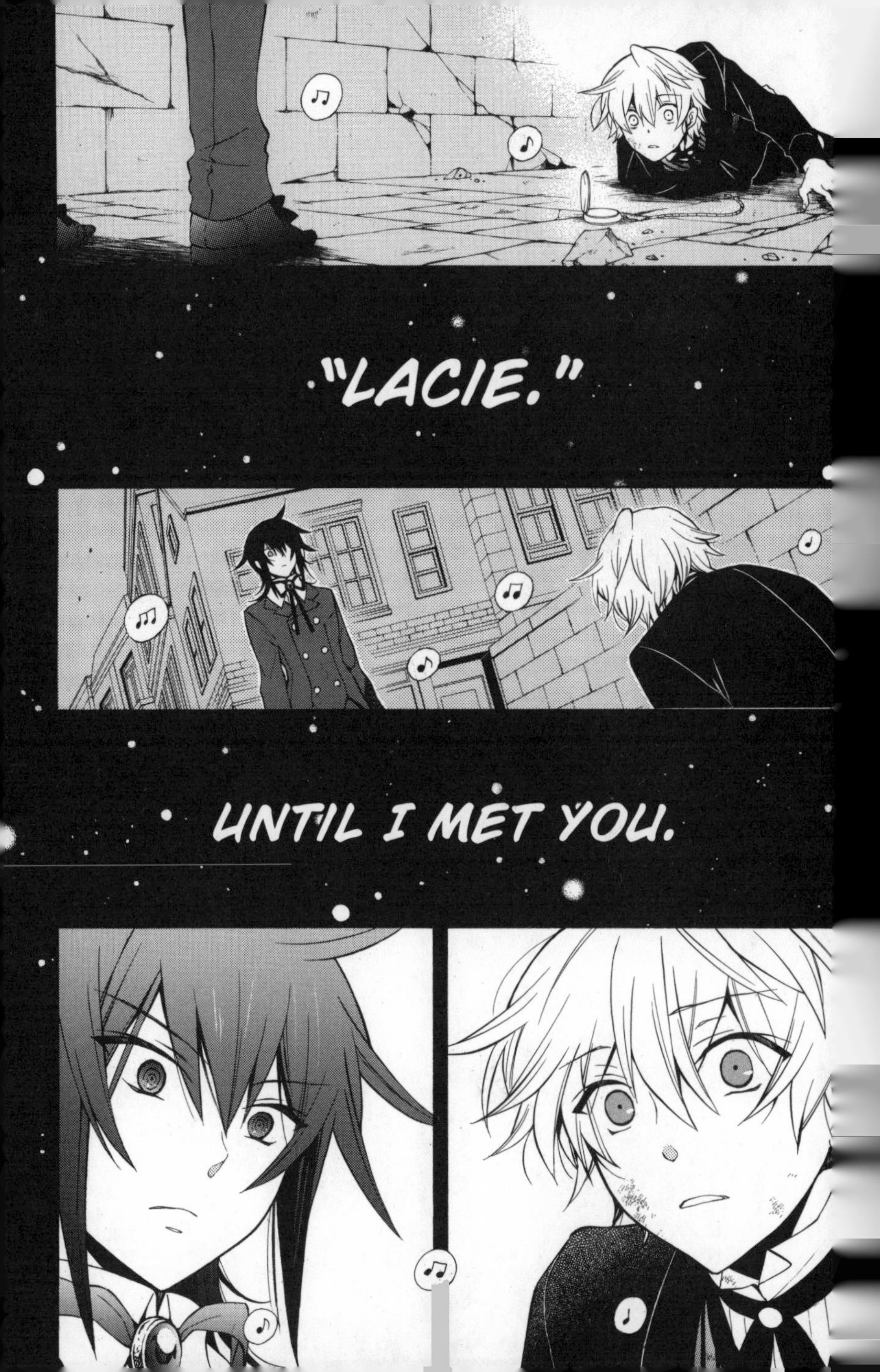
"LACIE."
UNTIL I MET YOU.

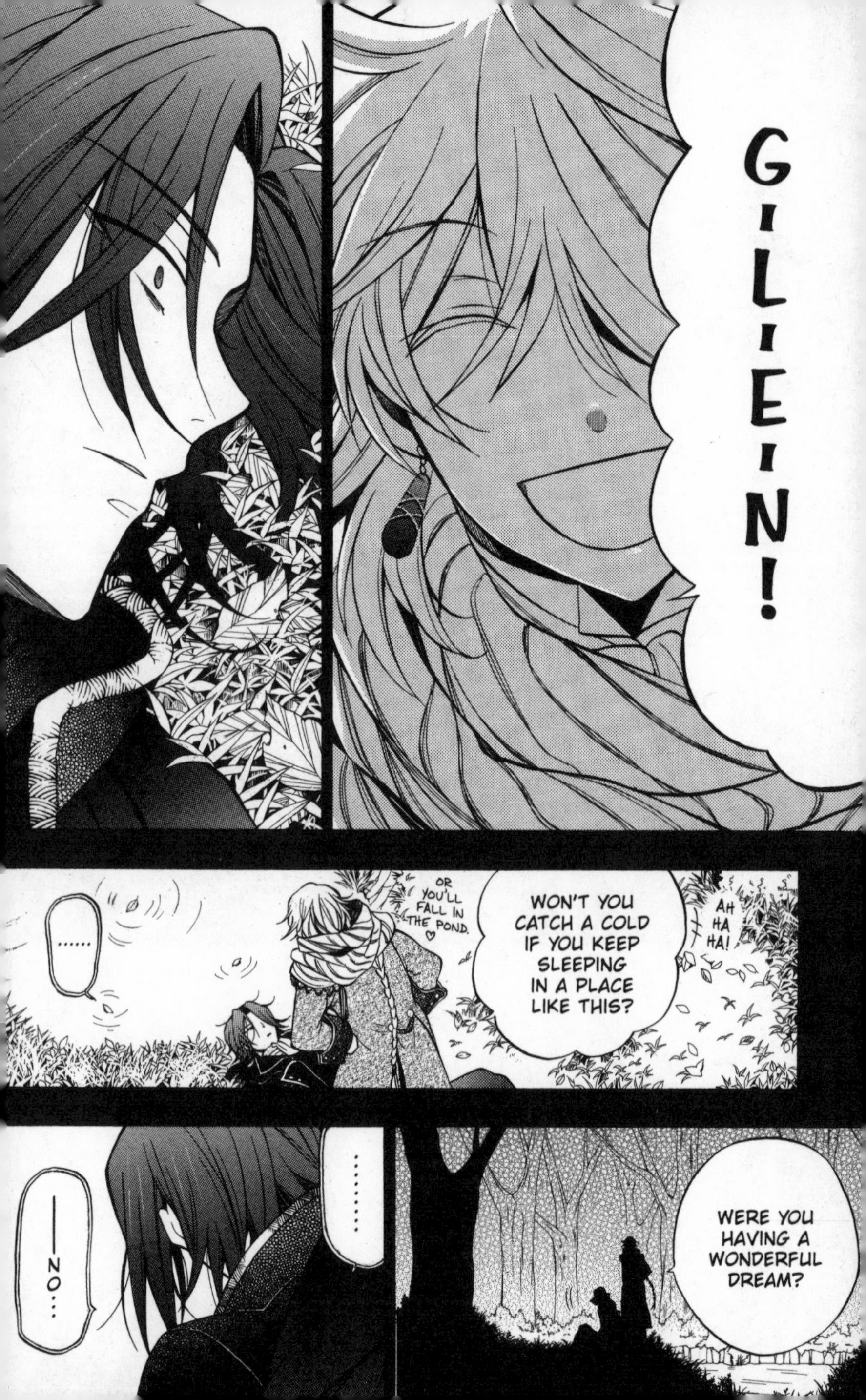
GILIEN!
AH HA HA!
WON'T YOU CATCH A COLD IF YOU KEEP SLEEPING IN A PLACE LIKE THIS?
OR YOU'LL FALL IN THE POND. ♡
......
WERE YOU HAVING A WONDERFUL DREAM?
......
——NO...

OH?
I THOUGHT I FELT A CHILL IN THE AIR.
SO IT'S SNOWING, IS IT?
SNOW MAKES ME HAPPY.
EVERY TIME IT SNOWS...

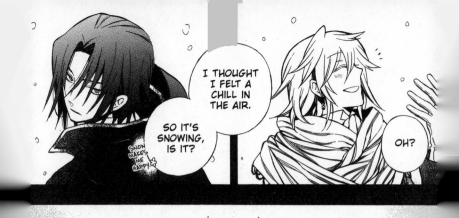

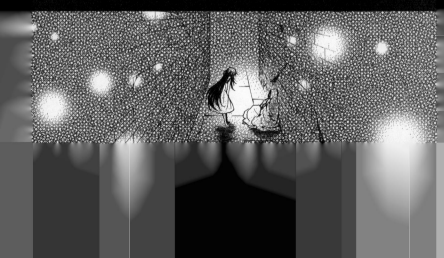

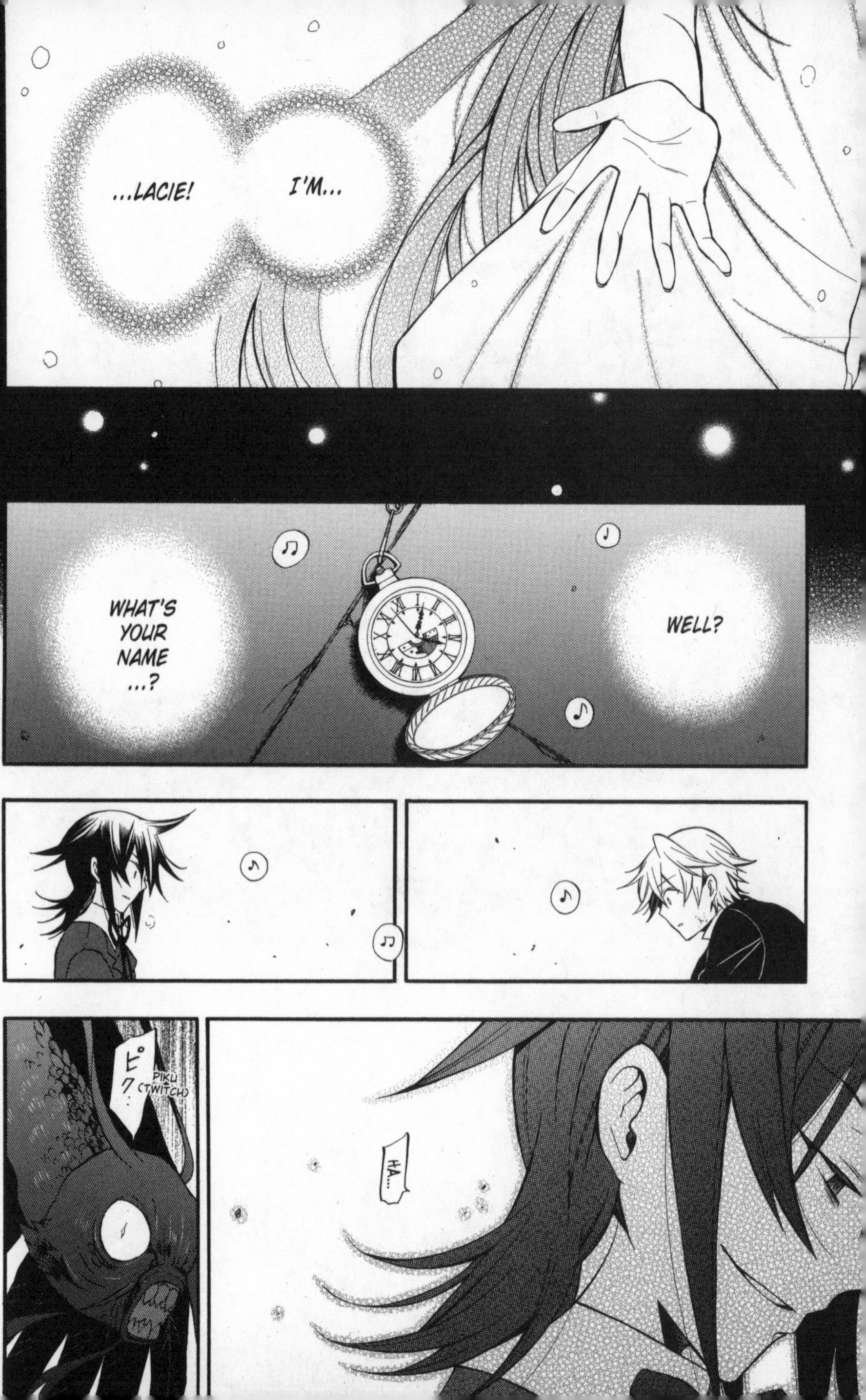
I'M...
...LACIE!
WELL?
WHAT'S YOUR NAME ...?
HA...
ピク
PIKU (TWITCH)

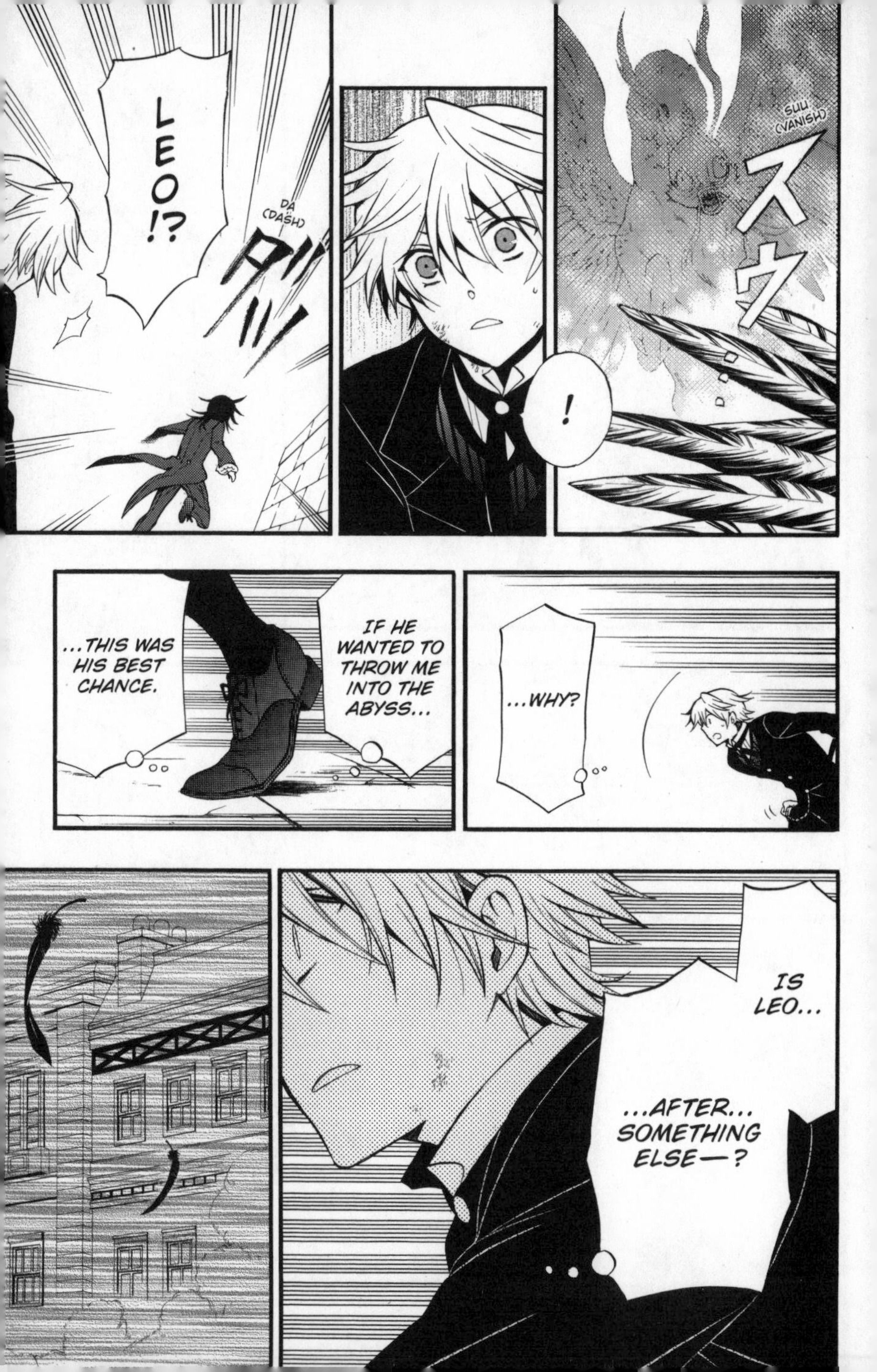
SUU (VANISH)
スウ
!
LEO!?
DA (DASH)
ダッ
...WHY?
IF HE WANTED TO THROW ME INTO THE ABYSS...
...THIS WAS HIS BEST CHANCE.
IS LEO...
...AFTER... SOMETHING ELSE—?

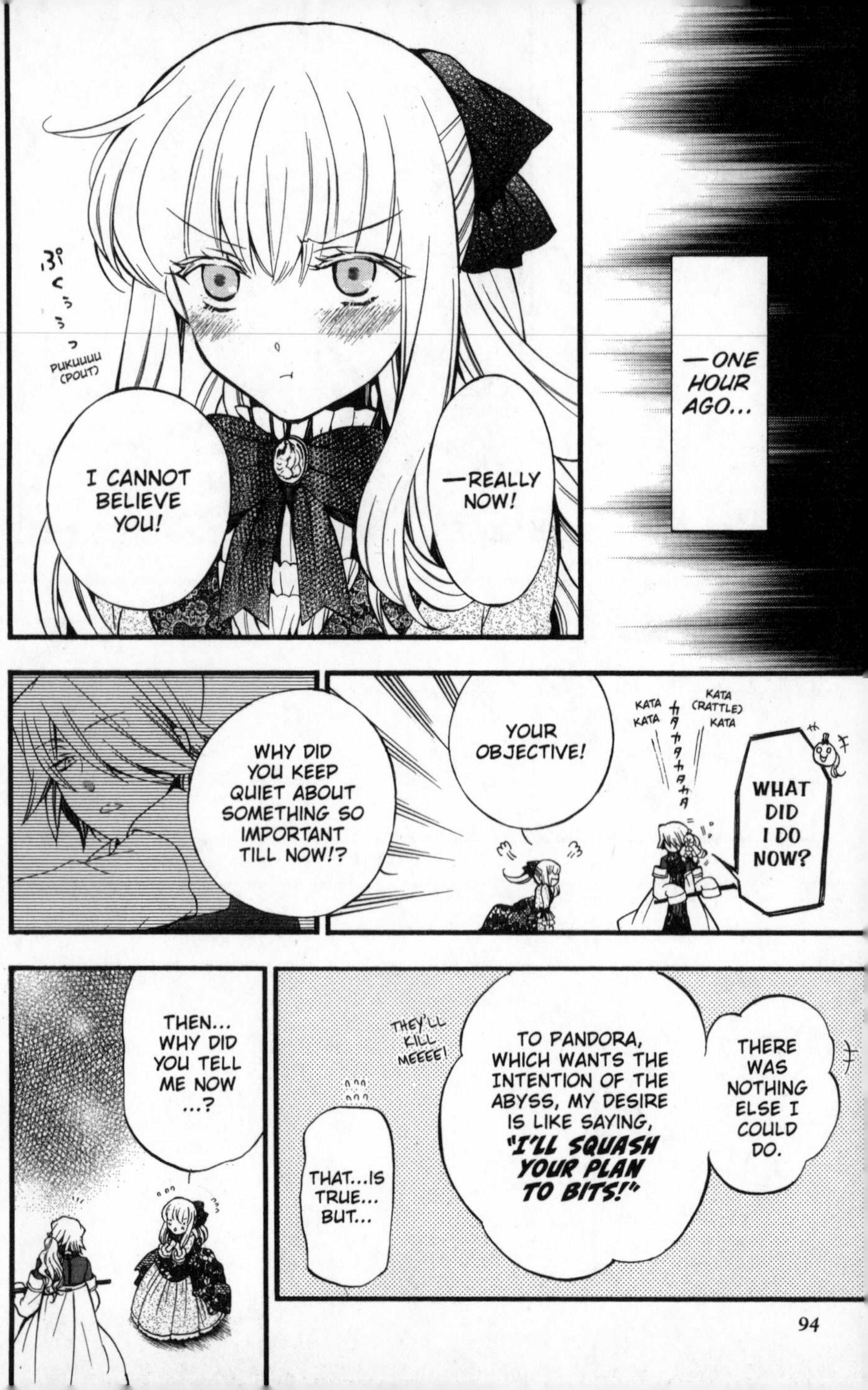
—ONE HOUR AGO...
—REALLY NOW!
I CANNOT BELIEVE YOU!
ぷくううっ
PUKUUUU (POUT)
WHAT DID I DO NOW?
KATA KATA
カタカタカタカタ
KATA (RATTLE) KATA
YOUR OBJECTIVE!
WHY DID YOU KEEP QUIET ABOUT SOMETHING SO IMPORTANT TILL NOW!?
THERE WAS NOTHING ELSE I COULD DO.
TO PANDORA, WHICH WANTS THE INTENTION OF THE ABYSS, MY DESIRE IS LIKE SAYING, *"I'LL SQUASH YOUR PLAN TO BITS!"*
THEY'LL KILL MEEEE!
THAT...IS TRUE... BUT...
THEN... WHY DID YOU TELL ME NOW ...?

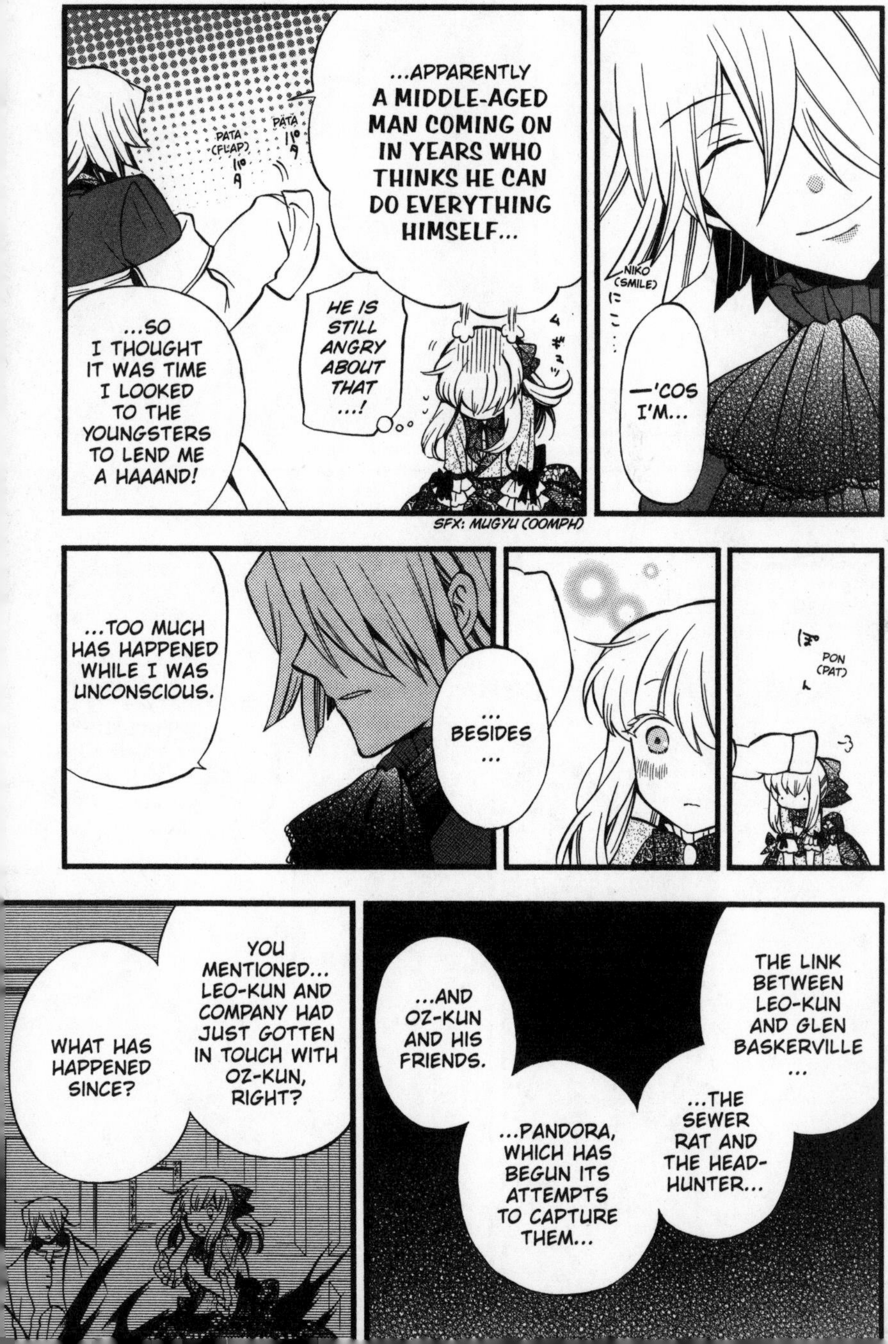
NIKO (SMILE)
—'COS I'M...
...APPARENTLY A MIDDLE-AGED MAN COMING ON IN YEARS WHO THINKS HE CAN DO EVERYTHING HIMSELF...
PATA PATA (FLAP)
HE IS STILL ANGRY ABOUT THAT ...!
...SO I THOUGHT IT WAS TIME I LOOKED TO THE YOUNGSTERS TO LEND ME A HAAAND!
SFX: MUGYU (OOMPH)
PON (PAT)
... BESIDES ...
...TOO MUCH HAS HAPPENED WHILE I WAS UNCONSCIOUS.
THE LINK BETWEEN LEO-KUN AND GLEN BASKERVILLE ...
...THE SEWER RAT AND THE HEAD-HUNTER...
...PANDORA, WHICH HAS BEGUN ITS ATTEMPTS TO CAPTURE THEM...
...AND OZ-KUN AND HIS FRIENDS.
YOU MENTIONED... LEO-KUN AND COMPANY HAD JUST GOTTEN IN TOUCH WITH OZ-KUN, RIGHT?
WHAT HAS HAPPENED SINCE?

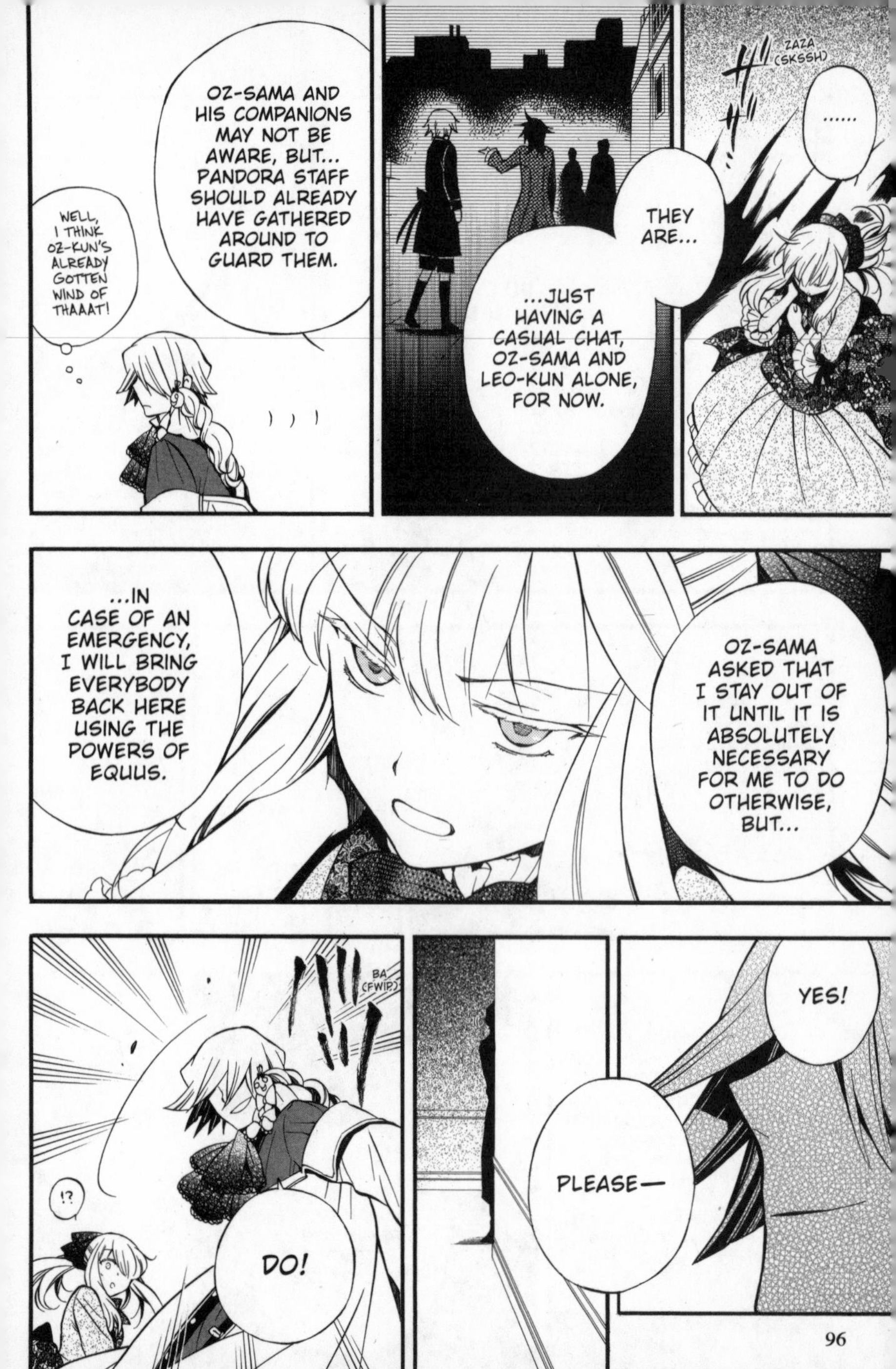
ZAZA (SKSSH)
......
THEY ARE...
...JUST HAVING A CASUAL CHAT, OZ-SAMA AND LEO-KUN ALONE, FOR NOW.
OZ-SAMA AND HIS COMPANIONS MAY NOT BE AWARE, BUT... PANDORA STAFF SHOULD ALREADY HAVE GATHERED AROUND TO GUARD THEM.
WELL, I THINK OZ-KUN'S ALREADY GOTTEN WIND OF THAAAT!
OZ-SAMA ASKED THAT I STAY OUT OF IT UNTIL IT IS ABSOLUTELY NECESSARY FOR ME TO DO OTHERWISE, BUT...
...IN CASE OF AN EMERGENCY, I WILL BRING EVERYBODY BACK HERE USING THE POWERS OF EQUUS.
YES!
PLEASE—
BA (FWIP)
DO!
!?

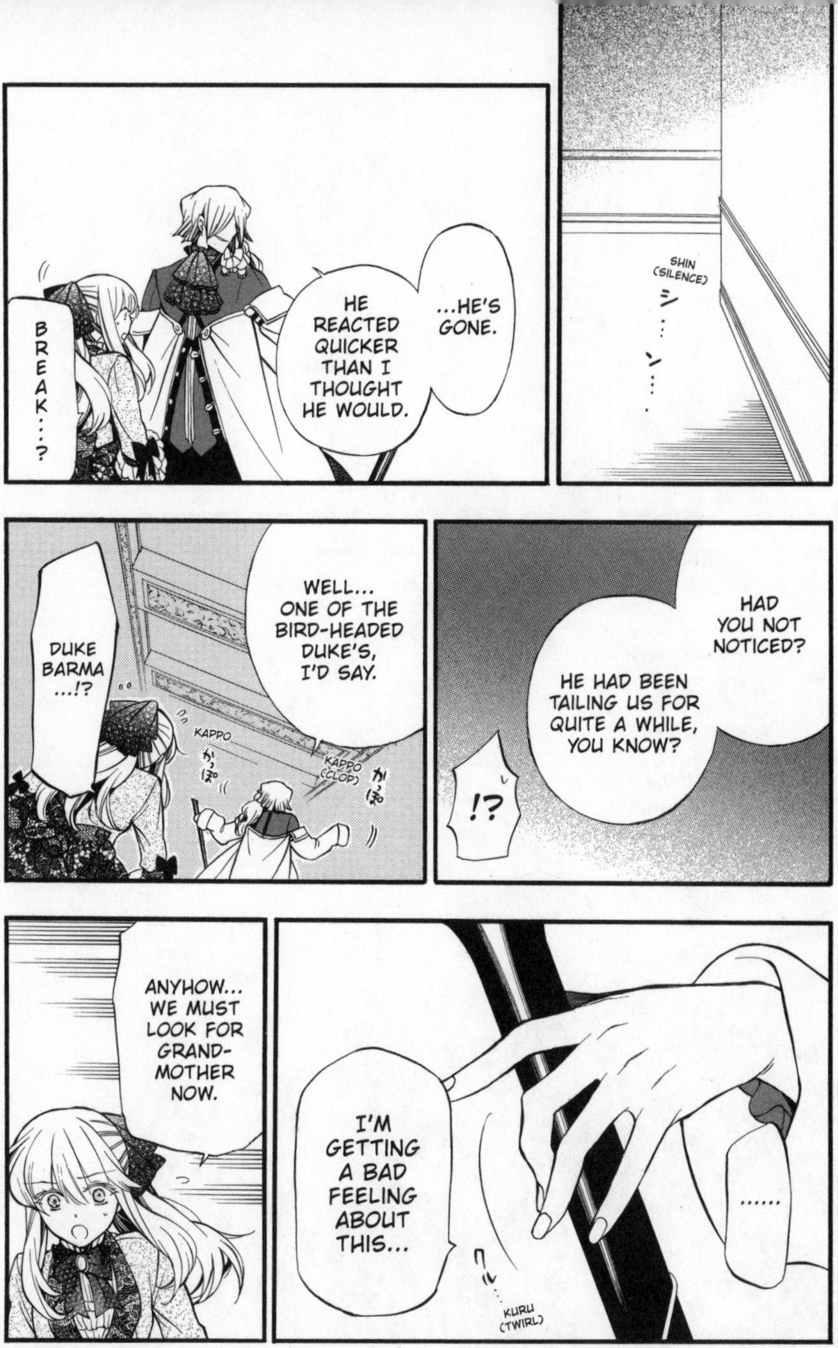
SHIN (SILENCE)
シ…ン…
...HE'S GONE.
HE REACTED QUICKER THAN I THOUGHT HE WOULD.
BREAK...?
HAD YOU NOT NOTICED?
HE HAD BEEN TAILING US FOR QUITE A WHILE, YOU KNOW?
!?
WELL... ONE OF THE BIRD-HEADED DUKE'S, I'D SAY.
KAPPO (CLOP)
かっぽ
KAPPO
かっぽ
DUKE BARMA ...!?
......
I'M GETTING A BAD FEELING ABOUT THIS...
クル…
KURU (TWIRL)
ANYHOW... WE MUST LOOK FOR GRAND-MOTHER NOW.

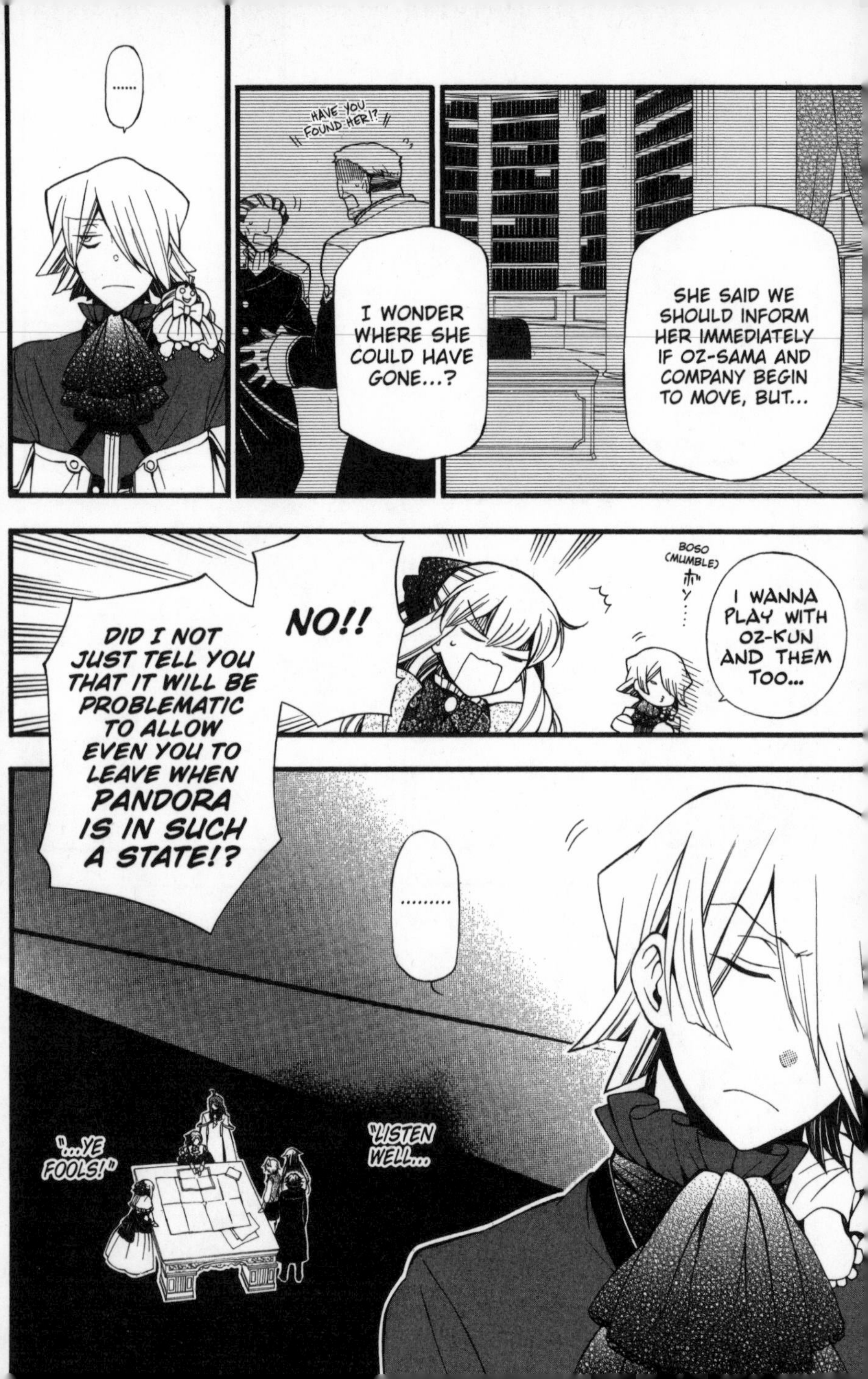
SHE SAID WE SHOULD INFORM HER IMMEDIATELY IF OZ-SAMA AND COMPANY BEGIN TO MOVE, BUT...
HAVE YOU FOUND HER!?
I WONDER WHERE SHE COULD HAVE GONE...?
......
BOSO (MUMBLE)
I WANNA PLAY WITH OZ-KUN AND THEM TOO...
NO!!
DID I NOT JUST TELL YOU THAT IT WILL BE PROBLEMATIC TO ALLOW EVEN YOU TO LEAVE WHEN PANDORA IS IN SUCH A STATE!?
....
"LISTEN WELL...
"...YE FOOLS!"

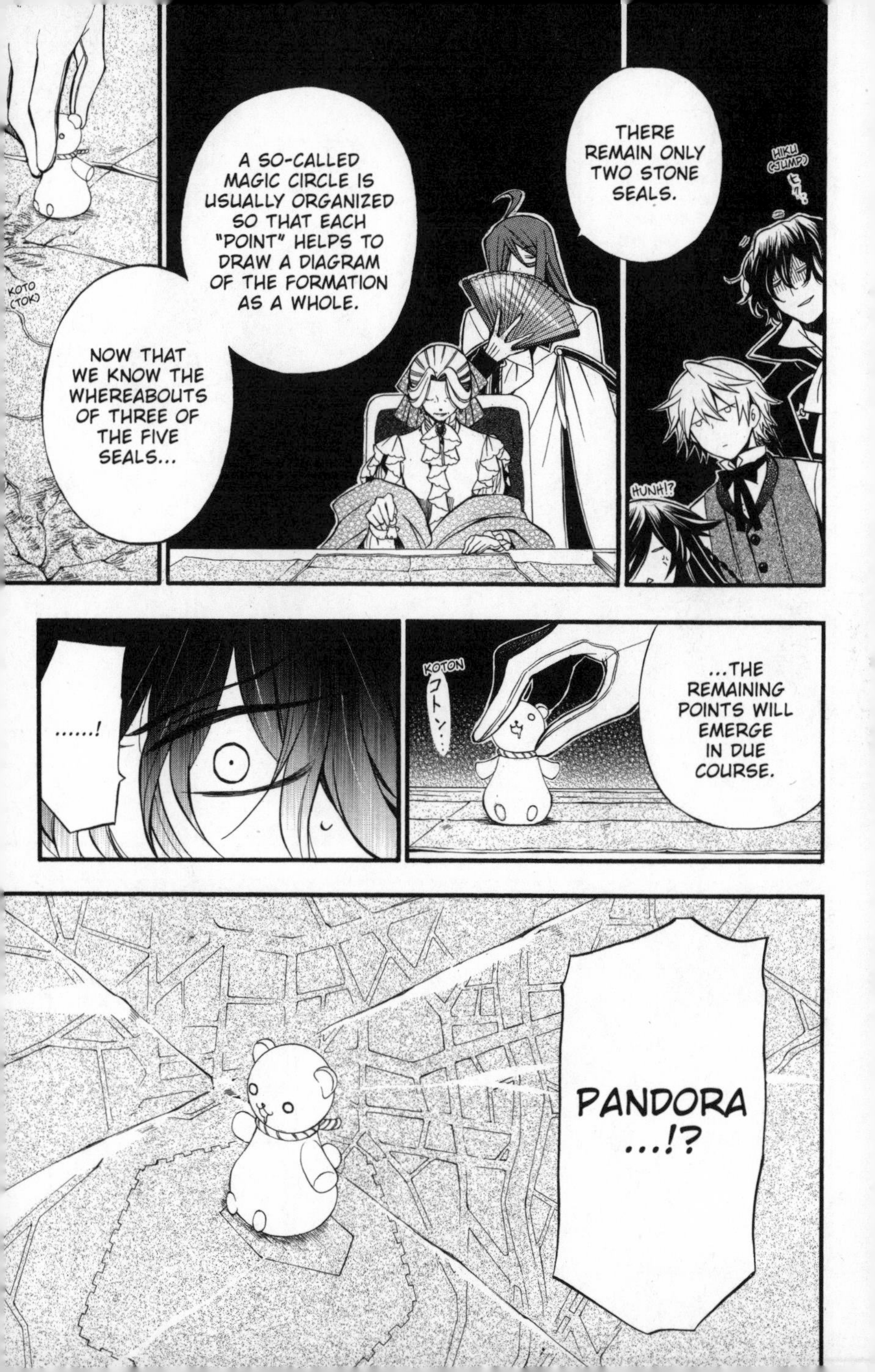
THERE REMAIN ONLY TWO STONE SEALS.
HIKU (JUMP)
HUNH!?
A SO-CALLED MAGIC CIRCLE IS USUALLY ORGANIZED SO THAT EACH "POINT" HELPS TO DRAW A DIAGRAM OF THE FORMATION AS A WHOLE.
NOW THAT WE KNOW THE WHEREABOUTS OF THREE OF THE FIVE SEALS...
KOTO (TOK)
KOTON
コトン…
...THE REMAINING POINTS WILL EMERGE IN DUE COURSE.
......!
PANDORA ...!?

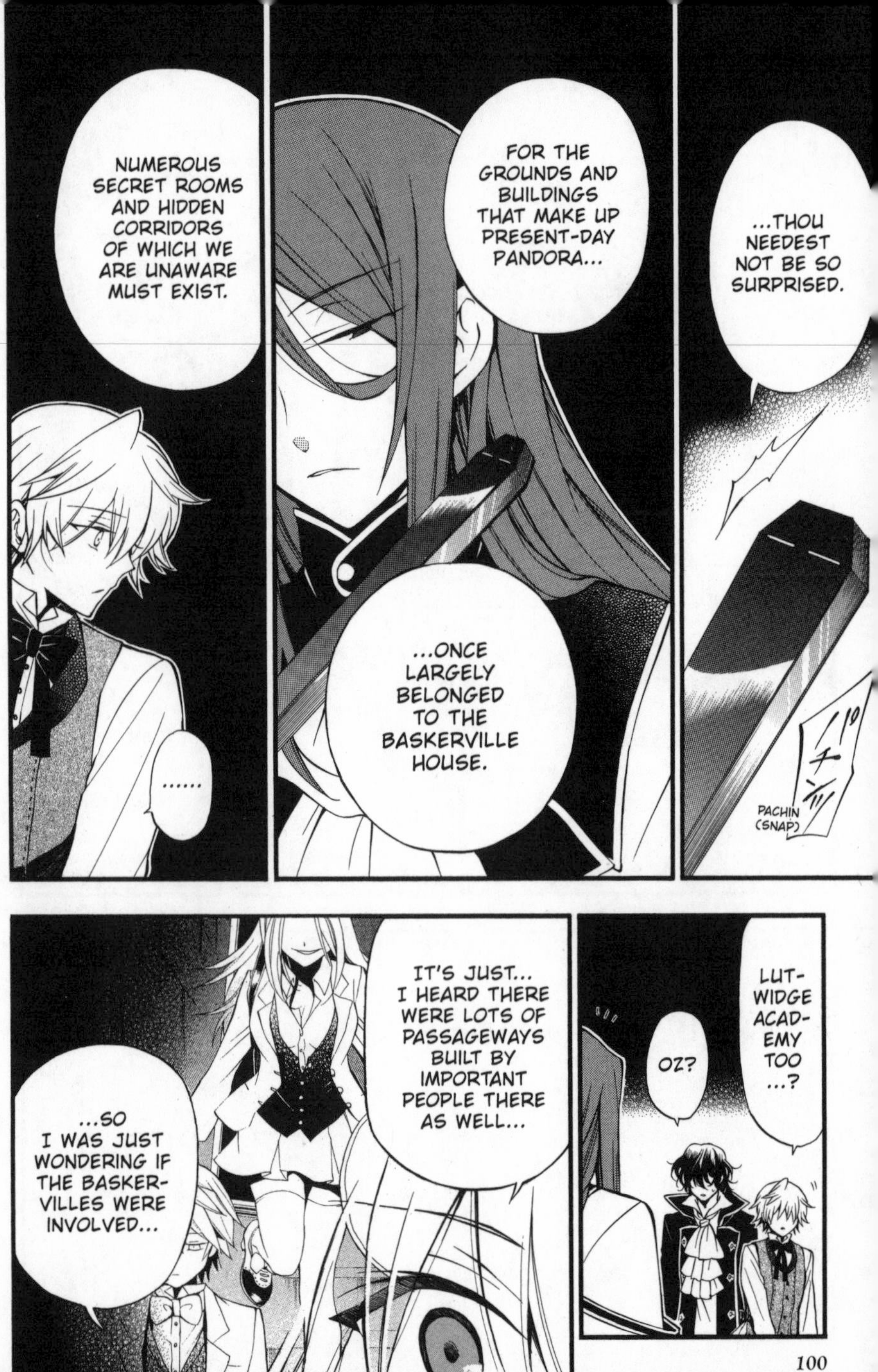
...THOU NEEDEST NOT BE SO SURPRISED.
PACHIN (SNAP)
FOR THE GROUNDS AND BUILDINGS THAT MAKE UP PRESENT-DAY PANDORA...
...ONCE LARGELY BELONGED TO THE BASKERVILLE HOUSE.
NUMEROUS SECRET ROOMS AND HIDDEN CORRIDORS OF WHICH WE ARE UNAWARE MUST EXIST.
......
LUT-WIDGE ACAD-EMY TOO ...?
OZ?
IT'S JUST... I HEARD THERE WERE LOTS OF PASSAGEWAYS BUILT BY IMPORTANT PEOPLE THERE AS WELL...
...SO I WAS JUST WONDERING IF THE BASKER-VILLES WERE INVOLVED...

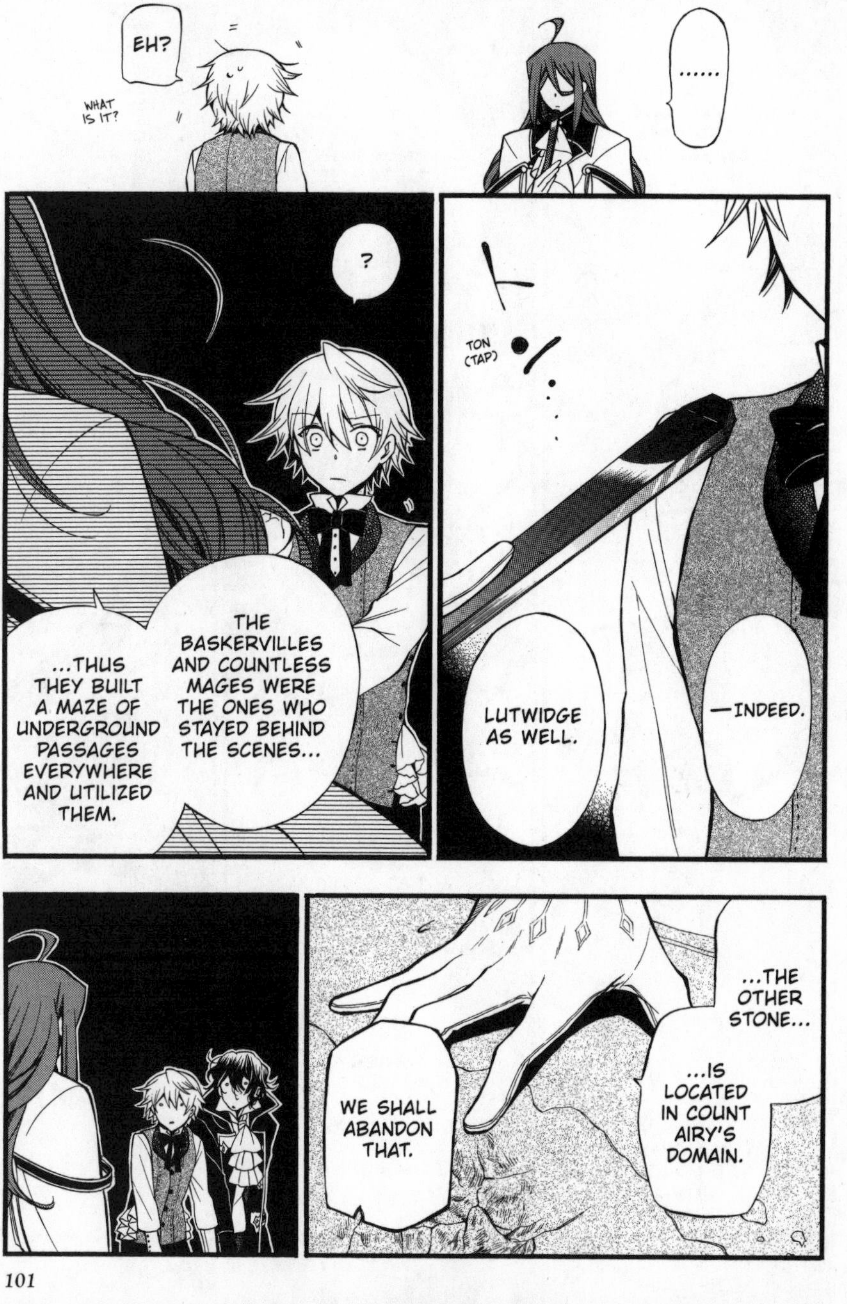
......
EH?
WHAT IS IT?
TON (TAP)
—INDEED.
LUTWIDGE AS WELL.
?
THE BASKERVILLES AND COUNTLESS MAGES WERE THE ONES WHO STAYED BEHIND THE SCENES...
...THUS THEY BUILT A MAZE OF UNDERGROUND PASSAGES EVERYWHERE AND UTILIZED THEM.
...THE OTHER STONE...
...IS LOCATED IN COUNT AIRY'S DOMAIN.
WE SHALL ABANDON THAT.

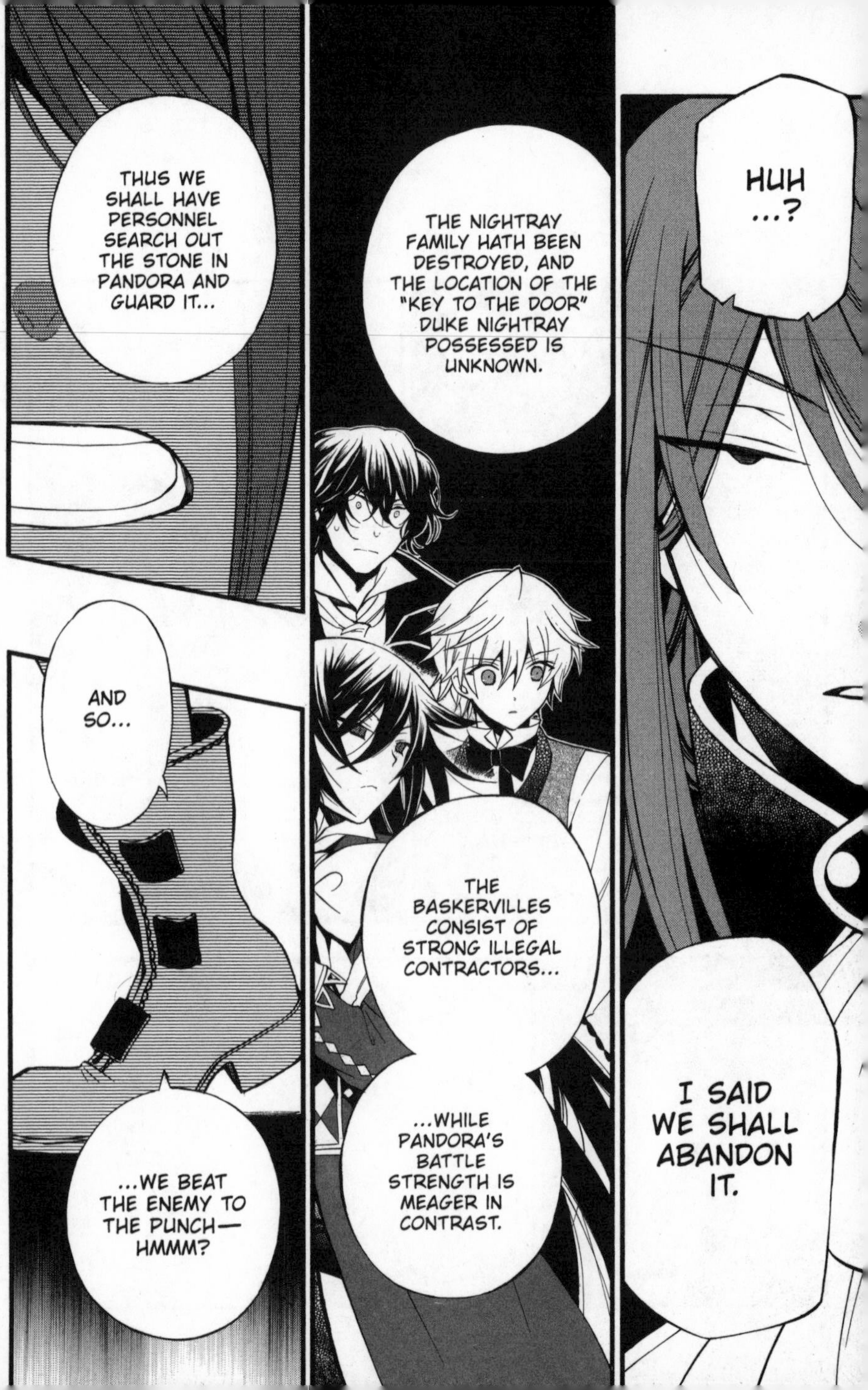
HUH ...?
I SAID WE SHALL ABANDON IT.
THE NIGHTRAY FAMILY HATH BEEN DESTROYED, AND THE LOCATION OF THE "KEY TO THE DOOR" DUKE NIGHTRAY POSSESSED IS UNKNOWN.
THE BASKERVILLES CONSIST OF STRONG ILLEGAL CONTRACTORS...
...WHILE PANDORA'S BATTLE STRENGTH IS MEAGER IN CONTRAST.
THUS WE SHALL HAVE PERSONNEL SEARCH OUT THE STONE IN PANDORA AND GUARD IT...
AND SO...
...WE BEAT THE ENEMY TO THE PUNCH— HMMM?

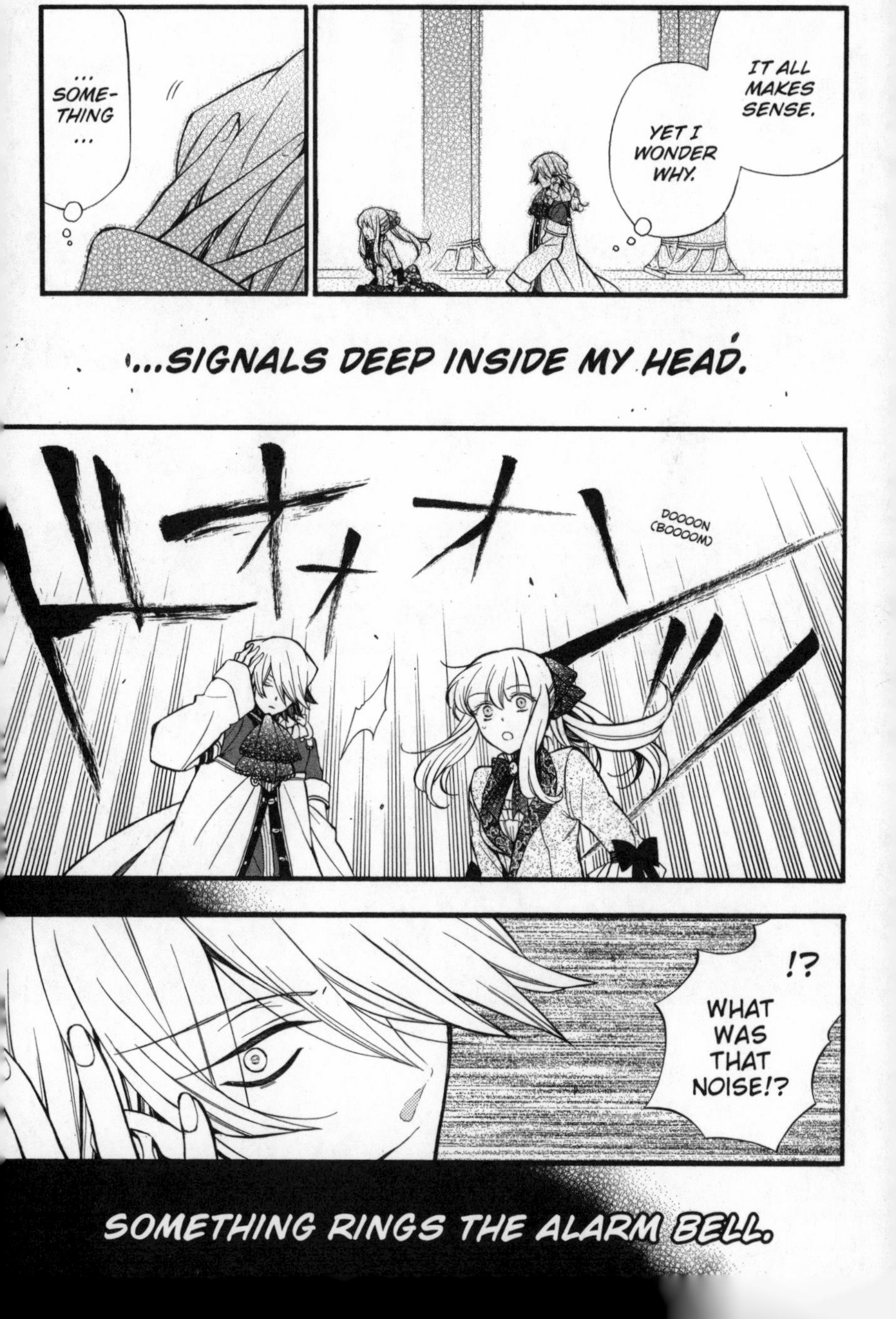
IT ALL MAKES SENSE.
YET I WONDER WHY.
...SOMETHING-...
...SIGNALS DEEP INSIDE MY HEAD.
DOOOON (BOOOOM)
!?
WHAT WAS THAT NOISE!?
SOMETHING RINGS THE ALARM BELL.

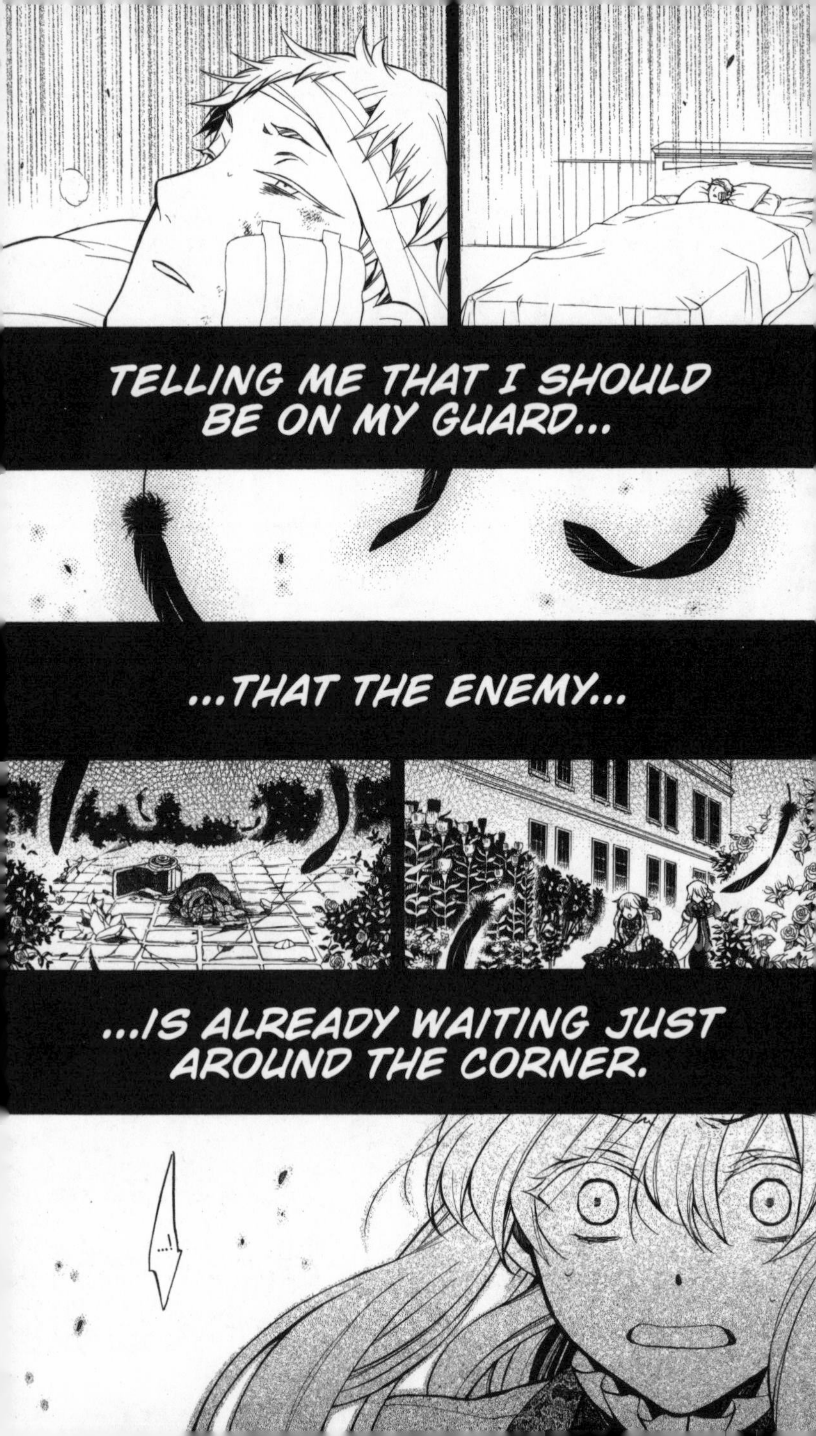
TELLING ME THAT I SHOULD BE ON MY GUARD...
...THAT THE ENEMY...
...IS ALREADY WAITING JUST AROUND THE CORNER.
...!

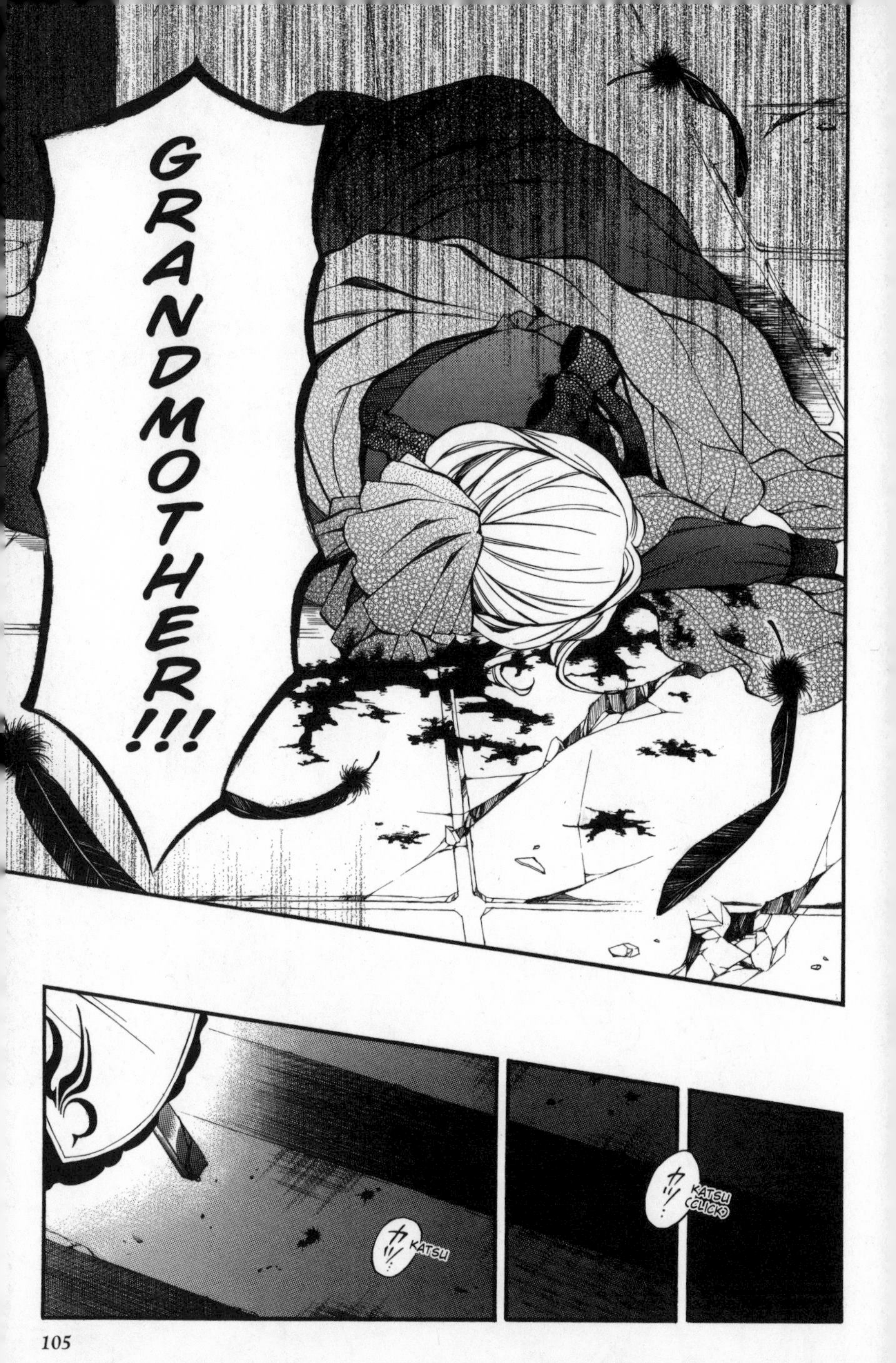
GRANDMOTHER!!!
カッ
KATSU (CLICK)
カッ!!
KATSU

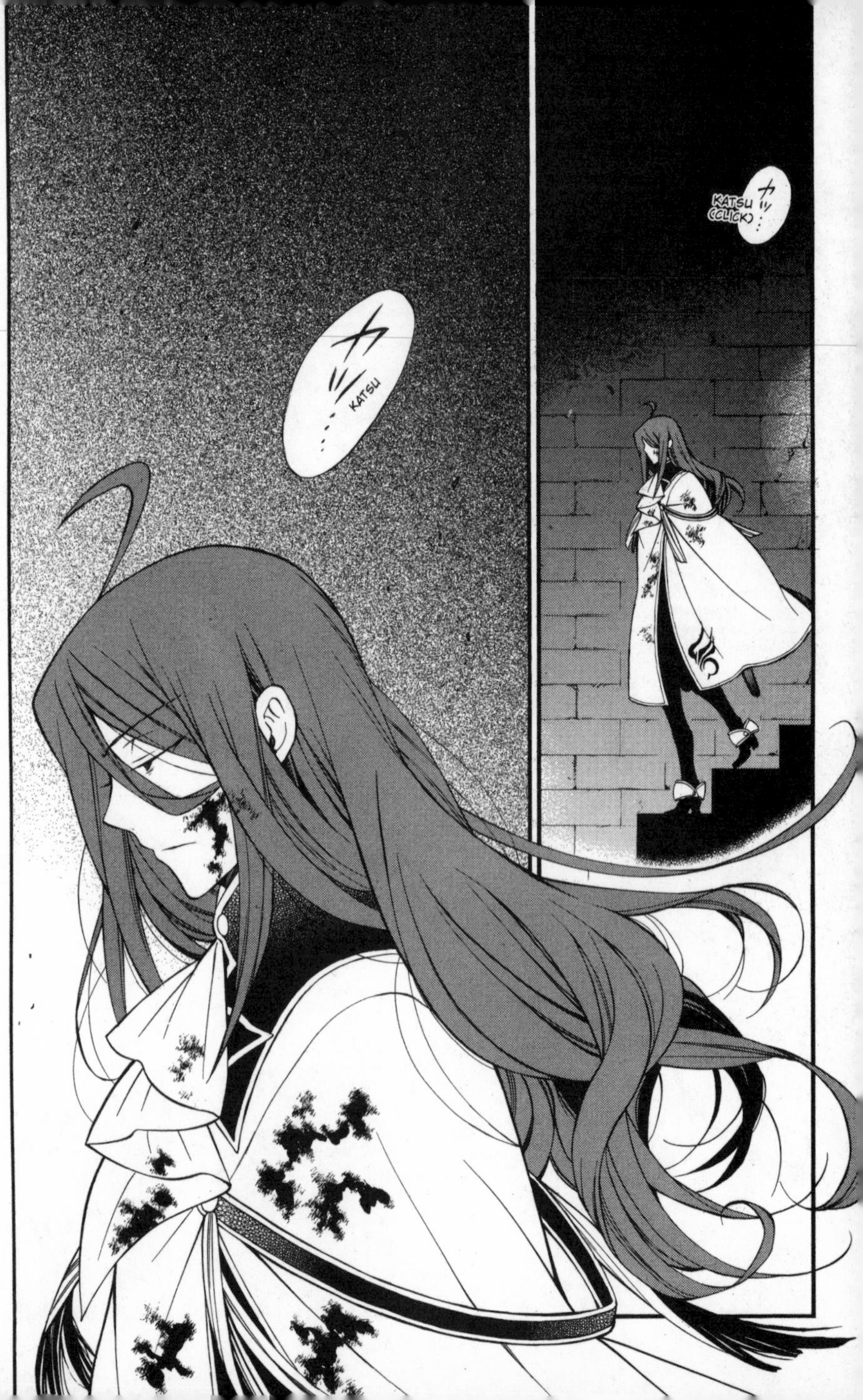
カッ…
KATSU (CLICK)
カッ…
KATSU

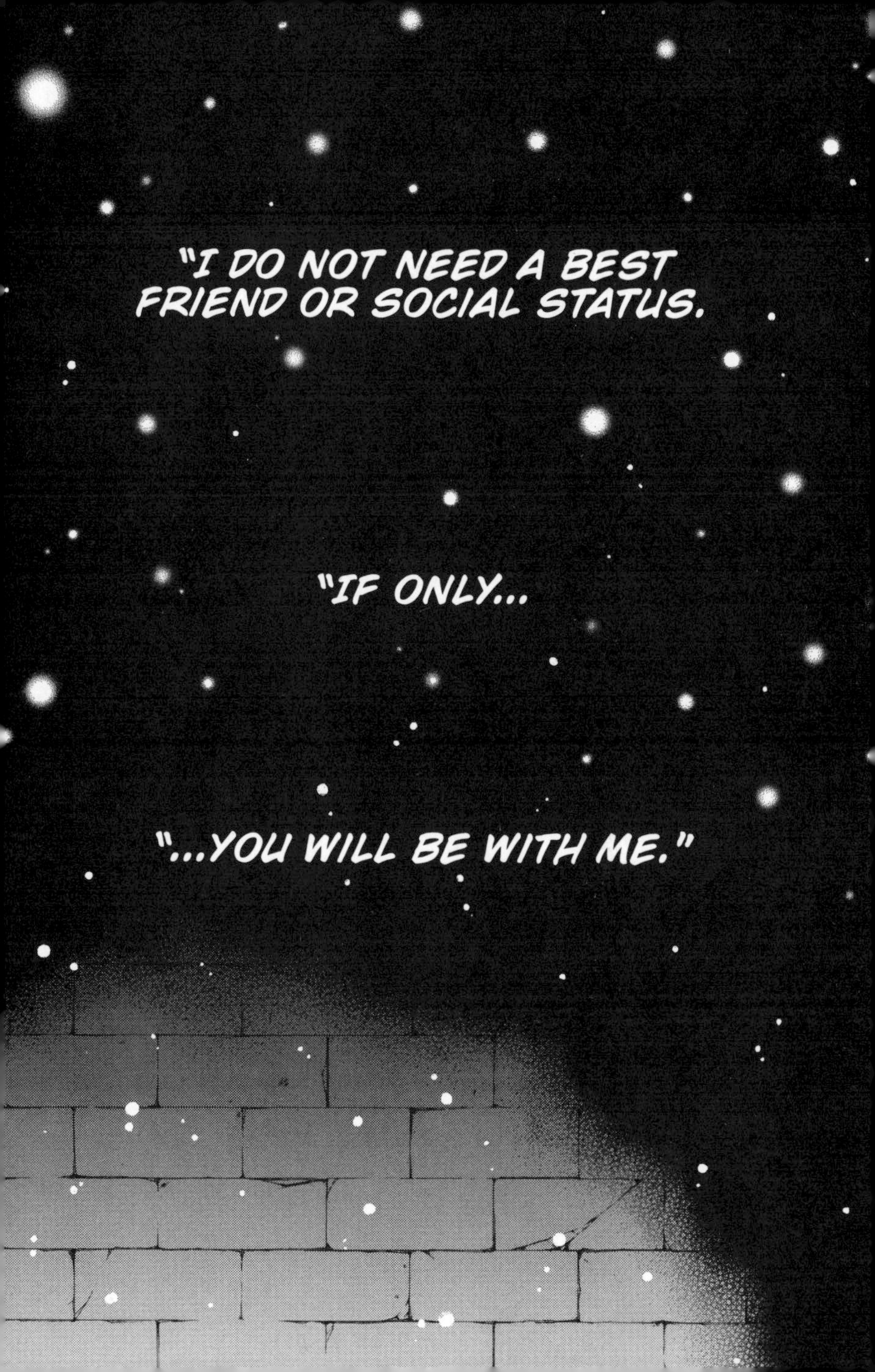
"I DO NOT NEED A BEST FRIEND OR SOCIAL STATUS.
"IF ONLY...
"...YOU WILL BE WITH ME."

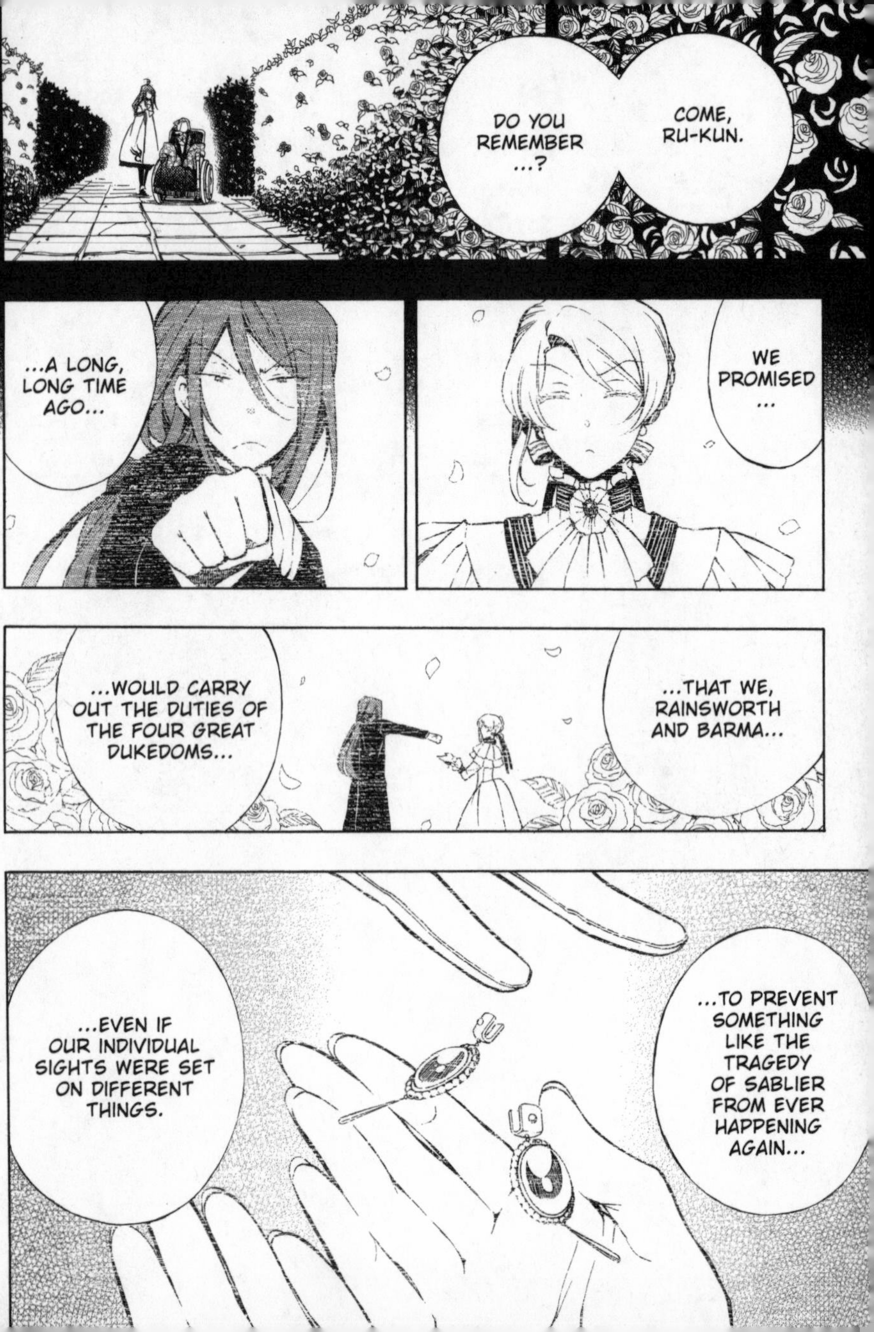
COME, RU-KUN.
DO YOU REMEMBER ...?
WE PROMISED ...
...A LONG, LONG TIME AGO...
...THAT WE, RAINSWORTH AND BARMA...
...WOULD CARRY OUT THE DUTIES OF THE FOUR GREAT DUKEDOMS...
...TO PREVENT SOMETHING LIKE THE TRAGEDY OF SABLIER FROM EVER HAPPENING AGAIN...
...EVEN IF OUR INDIVIDUAL SIGHTS WERE SET ON DIFFERENT THINGS.

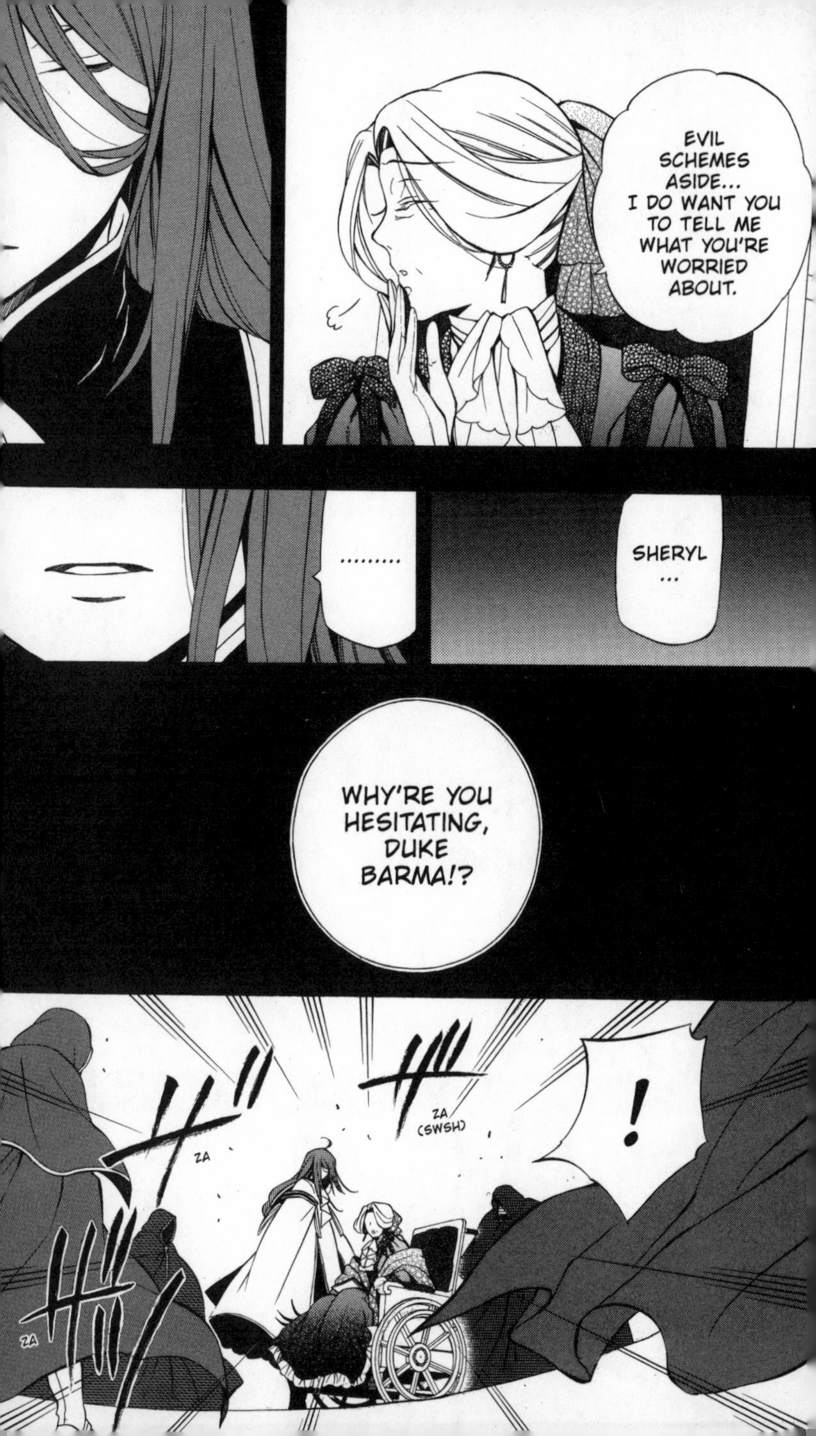
EVIL SCHEMES ASIDE... I DO WANT YOU TO TELL ME WHAT YOU'RE WORRIED ABOUT.
SHERYL ...
....
WHY'RE YOU HESITATING, DUKE BARMA!?
!
ZA (SWSH)
ZA
ZA

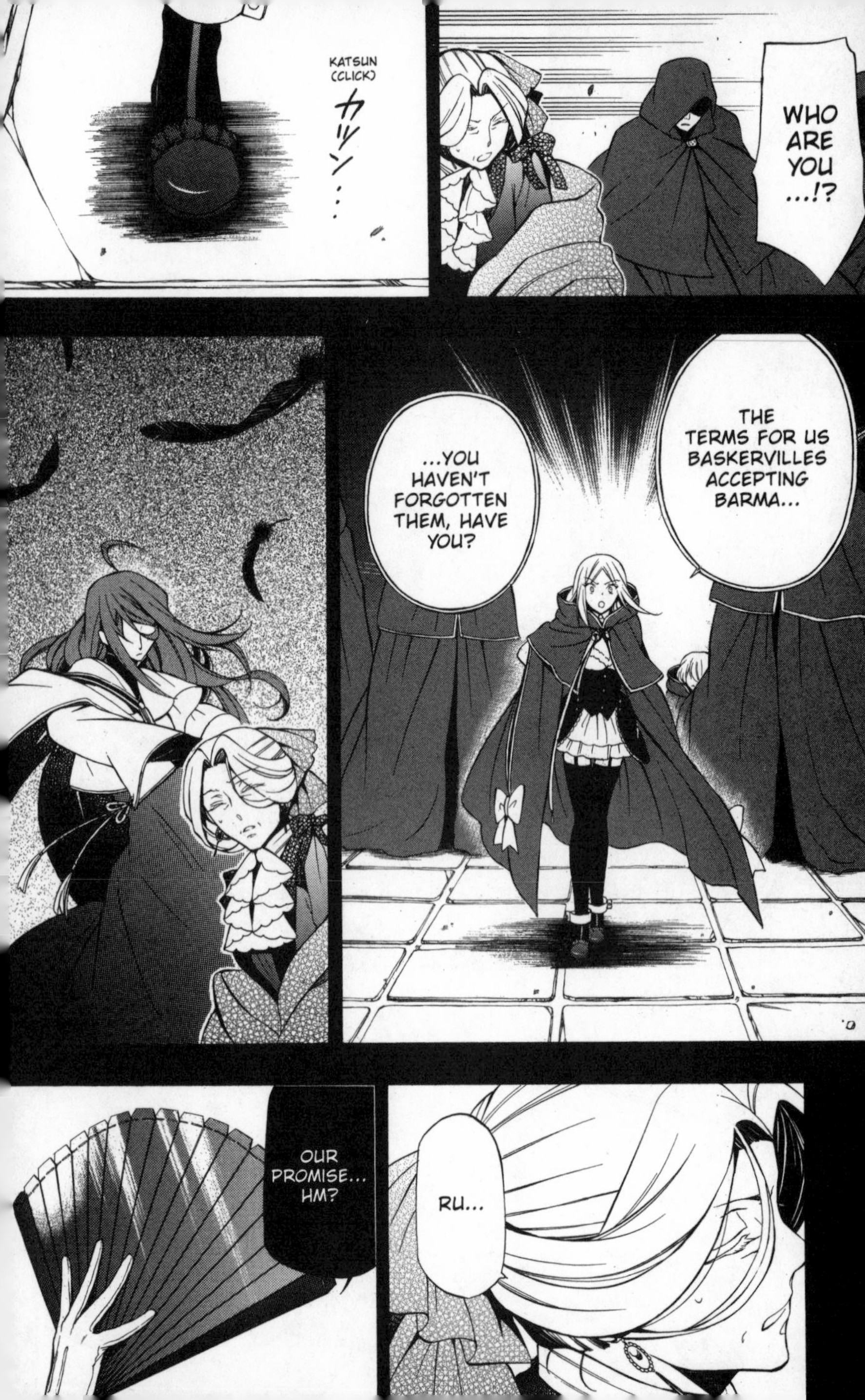
WHO ARE YOU ...!?
KATSUN (CLICK)
カツン‥
THE TERMS FOR US BASKERVILLES ACCEPTING BARMA...
...YOU HAVEN'T FORGOTTEN THEM, HAVE YOU?
RU...
OUR PROMISE... HM?

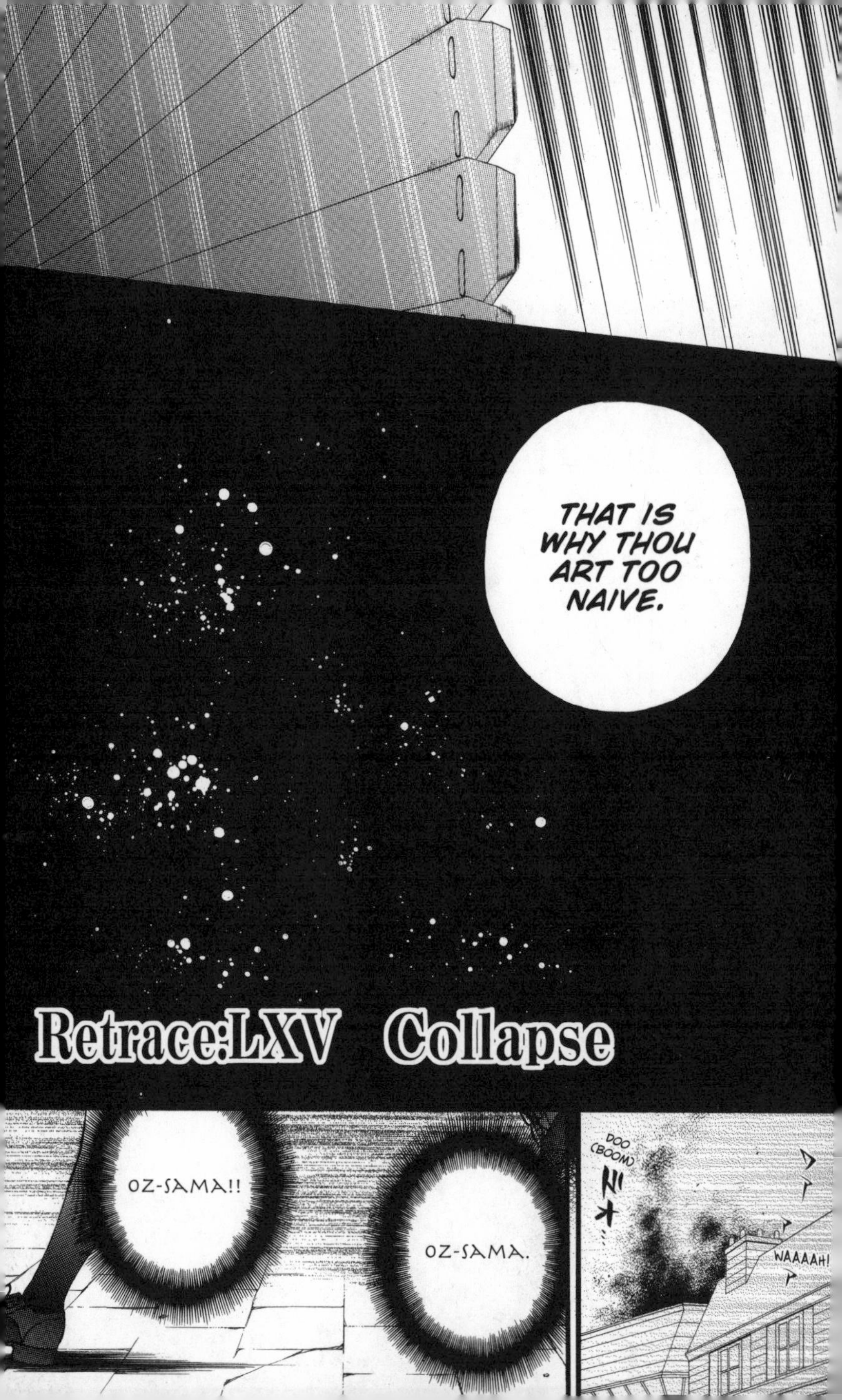
THAT IS WHY THOU ART TOO NAIVE.
Retrace:LXV Collapse
DOO (BOOM)
WAAAAH!
OZ-SAMA!!
OZ-SAMA.

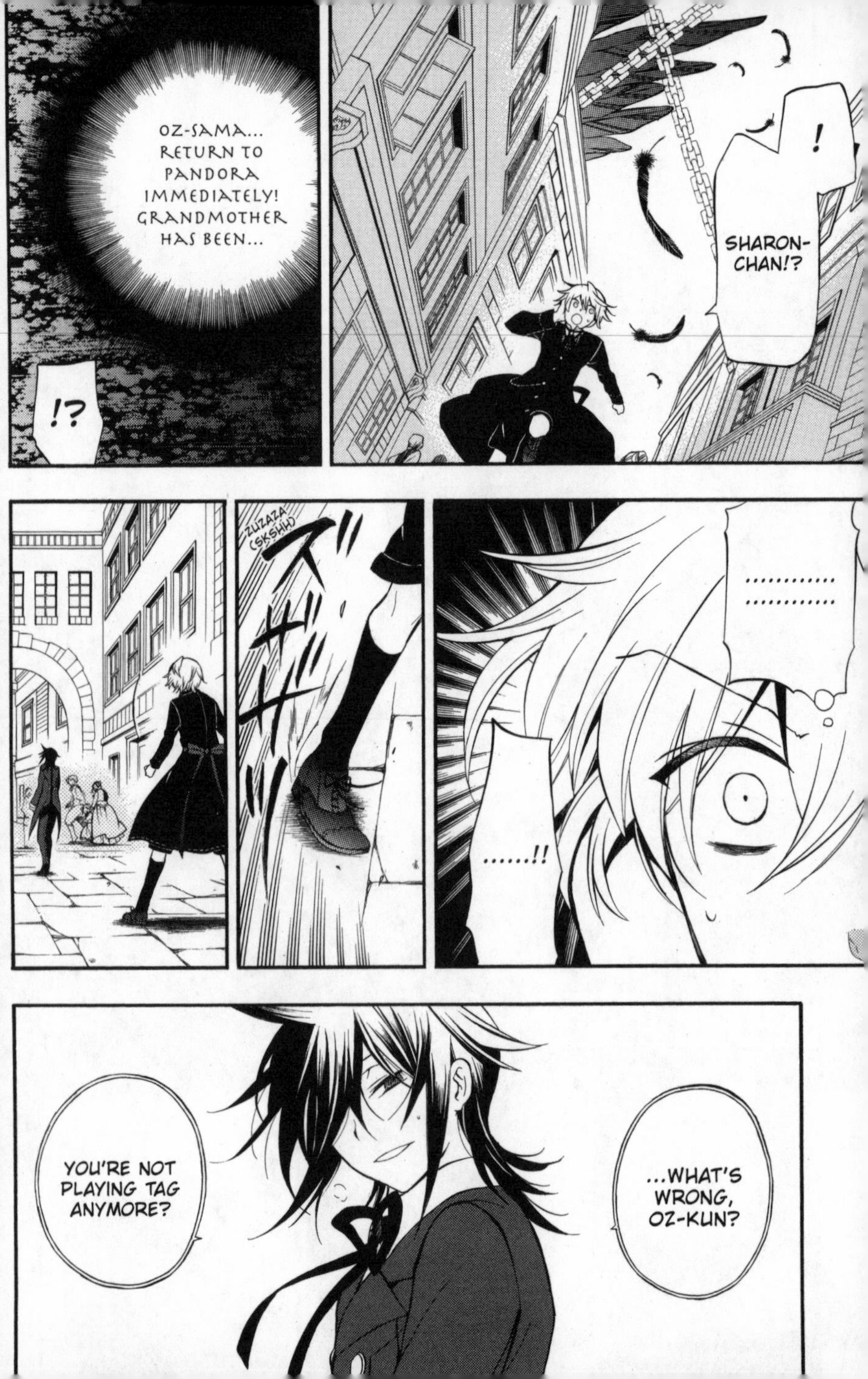
!
SHARON-CHAN!?
OZ-SAMA... RETURN TO PANDORA IMMEDIATELY! GRANDMOTHER HAS BEEN...
!?
....
......!!
ZUZAZA (SKSHH)
...WHAT'S WRONG, OZ-KUN?
YOU'RE NOT PLAYING TAG ANYMORE?

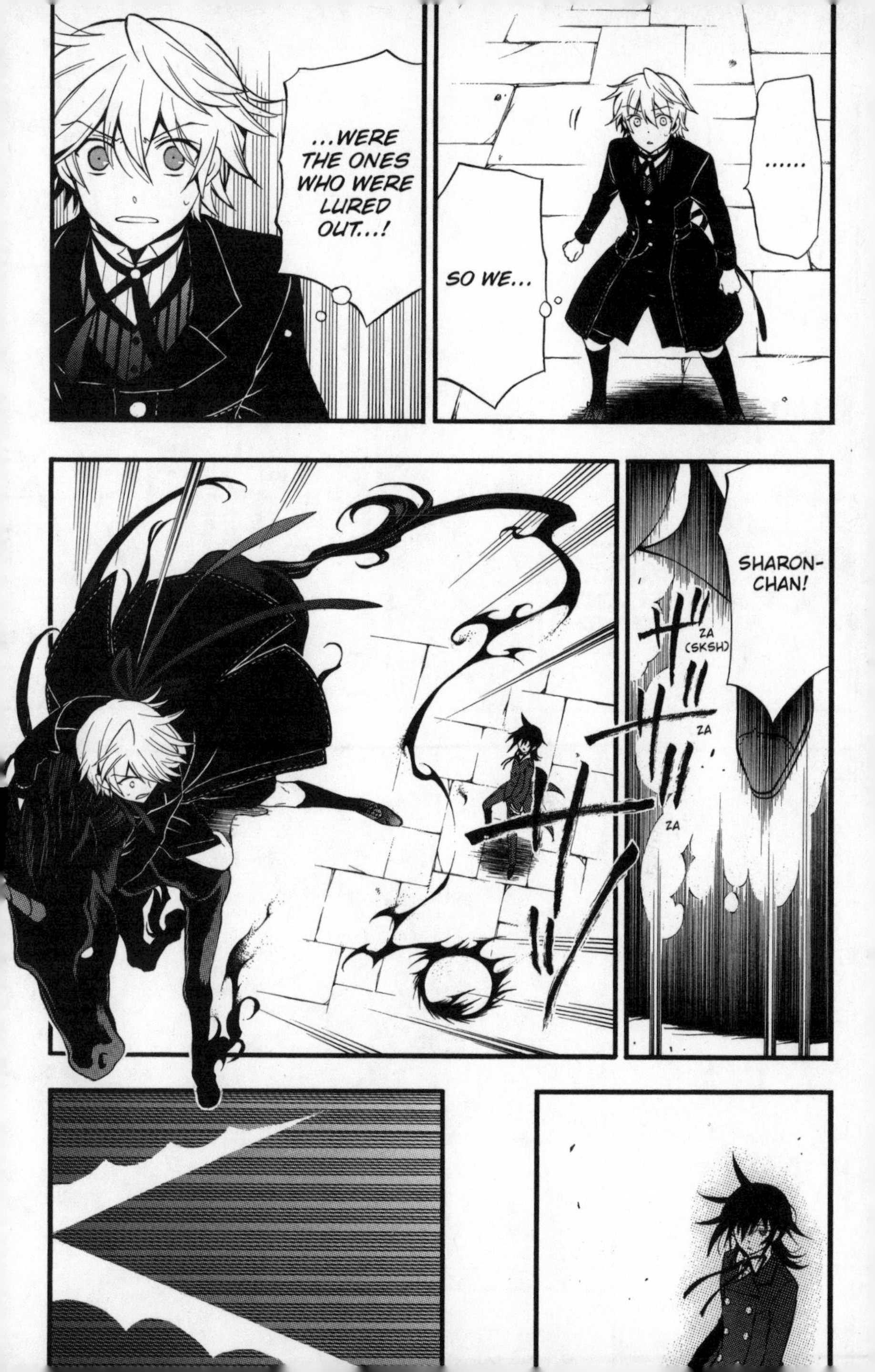
......
SO WE...
...WERE THE ONES WHO WERE LURED OUT...!
SHARON-CHAN!
ZA (SKSH)
ZA
ZA

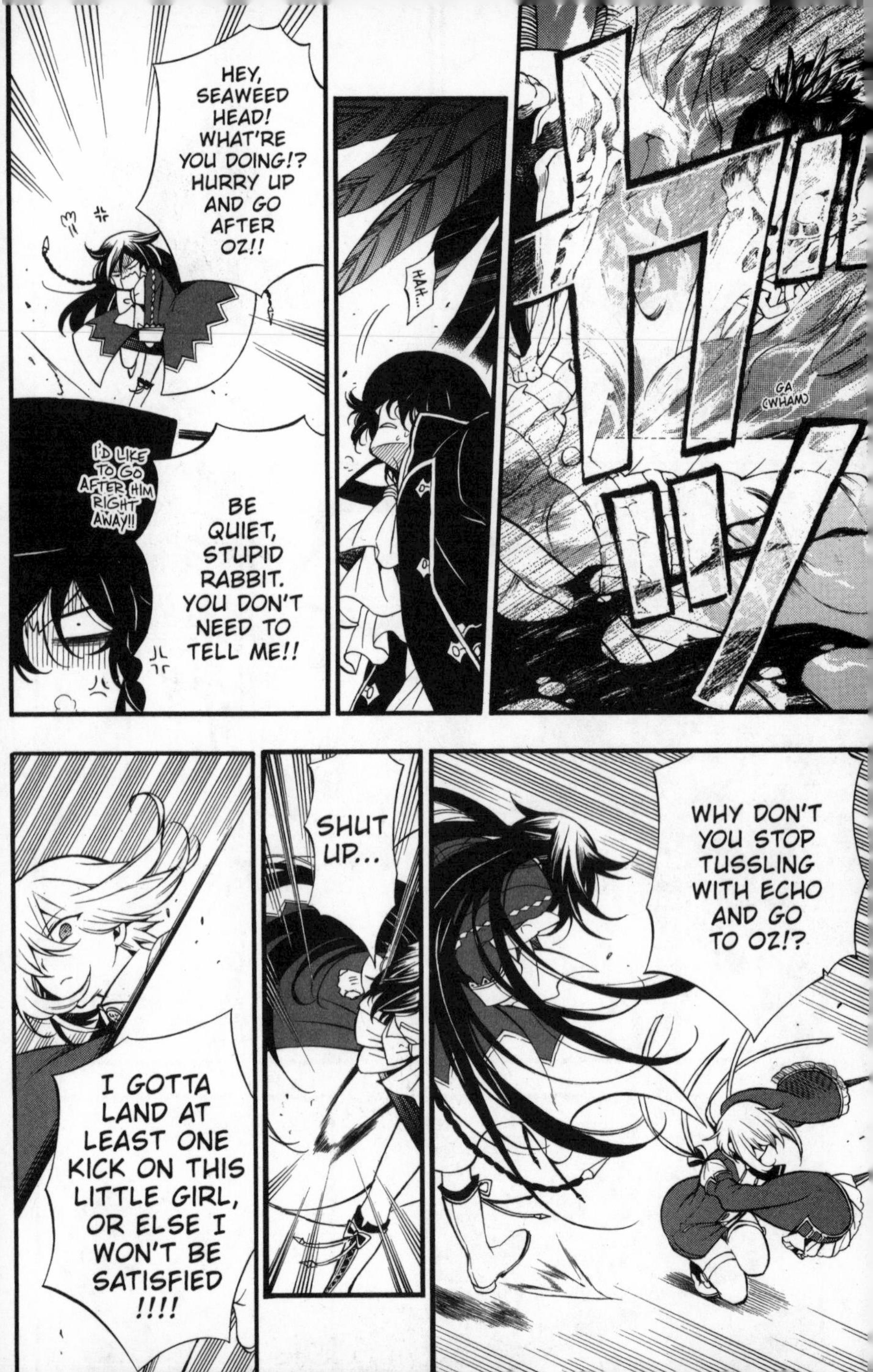
GA (WHAM)
HAH...
HEY, SEAWEED HEAD! WHAT'RE YOU DOING!? HURRY UP AND GO AFTER OZ!!
BE QUIET, STUPID RABBIT. YOU DON'T NEED TO TELL ME!!
I'D LIKE TO GO AFTER HIM RIGHT AWAY!!
WHY DON'T YOU STOP TUSSLING WITH ECHO AND GO TO OZ!?
SHUT UP...
I GOTTA LAND AT LEAST ONE KICK ON THIS LITTLE GIRL, OR ELSE I WON'T BE SATISFIED !!!!

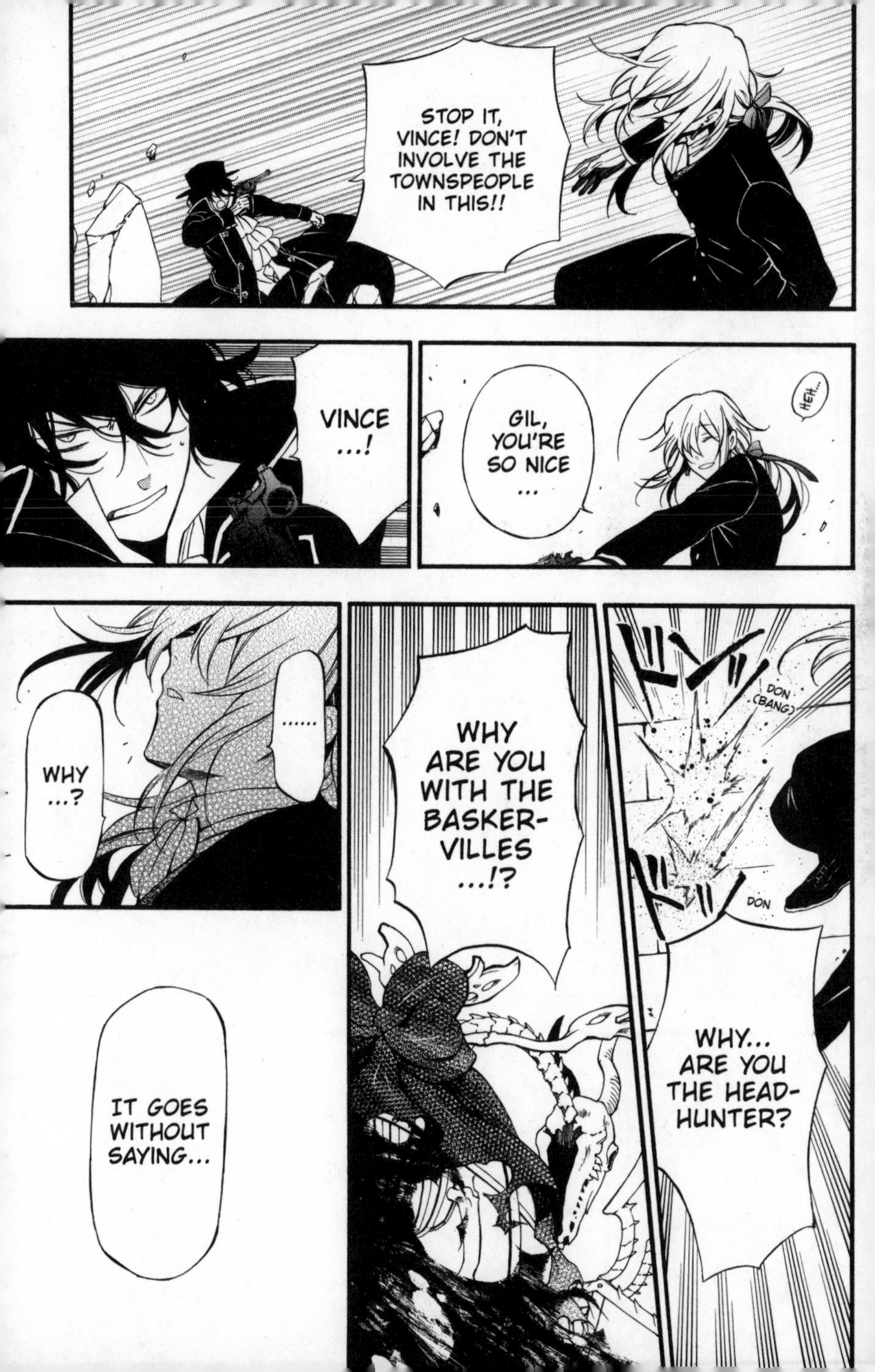
STOP IT, VINCE! DON'T INVOLVE THE TOWNSPEOPLE IN THIS!!
HEH...
GIL, YOU'RE SO NICE ...
VINCE ...!
DON (BANG)
DON
WHY... ARE YOU THE HEAD-HUNTER?
WHY ARE YOU WITH THE BASKER-VILLES ...!?
......
WHY ...?
IT GOES WITHOUT SAYING...

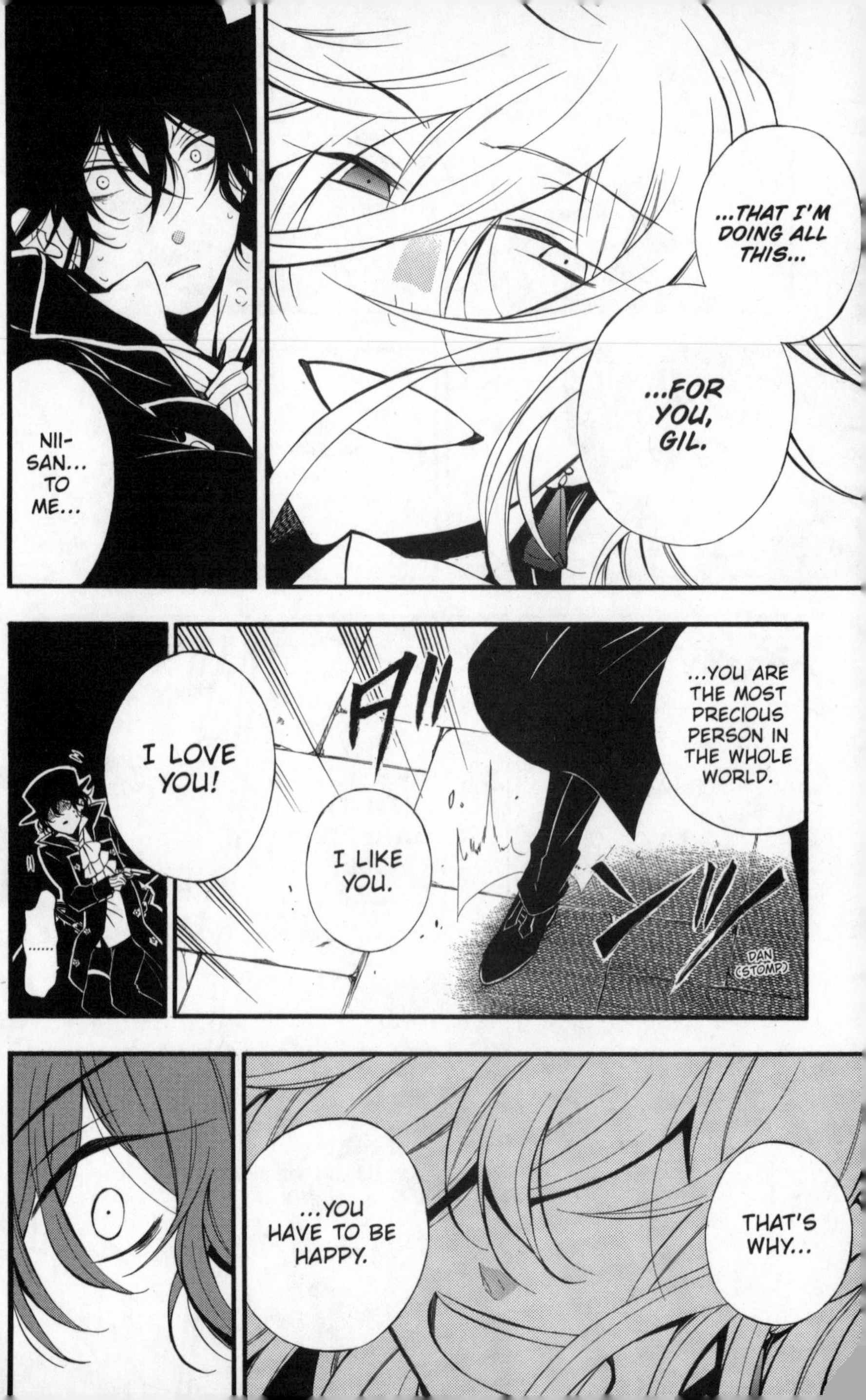
...THAT I'M DOING ALL THIS...
...FOR YOU, GIL.
NII-SAN... TO ME...
...YOU ARE THE MOST PRECIOUS PERSON IN THE WHOLE WORLD.
DAN (STOMP)
I LIKE YOU.
I LOVE YOU!
......
THAT'S WHY...
...YOU HAVE TO BE HAPPY.

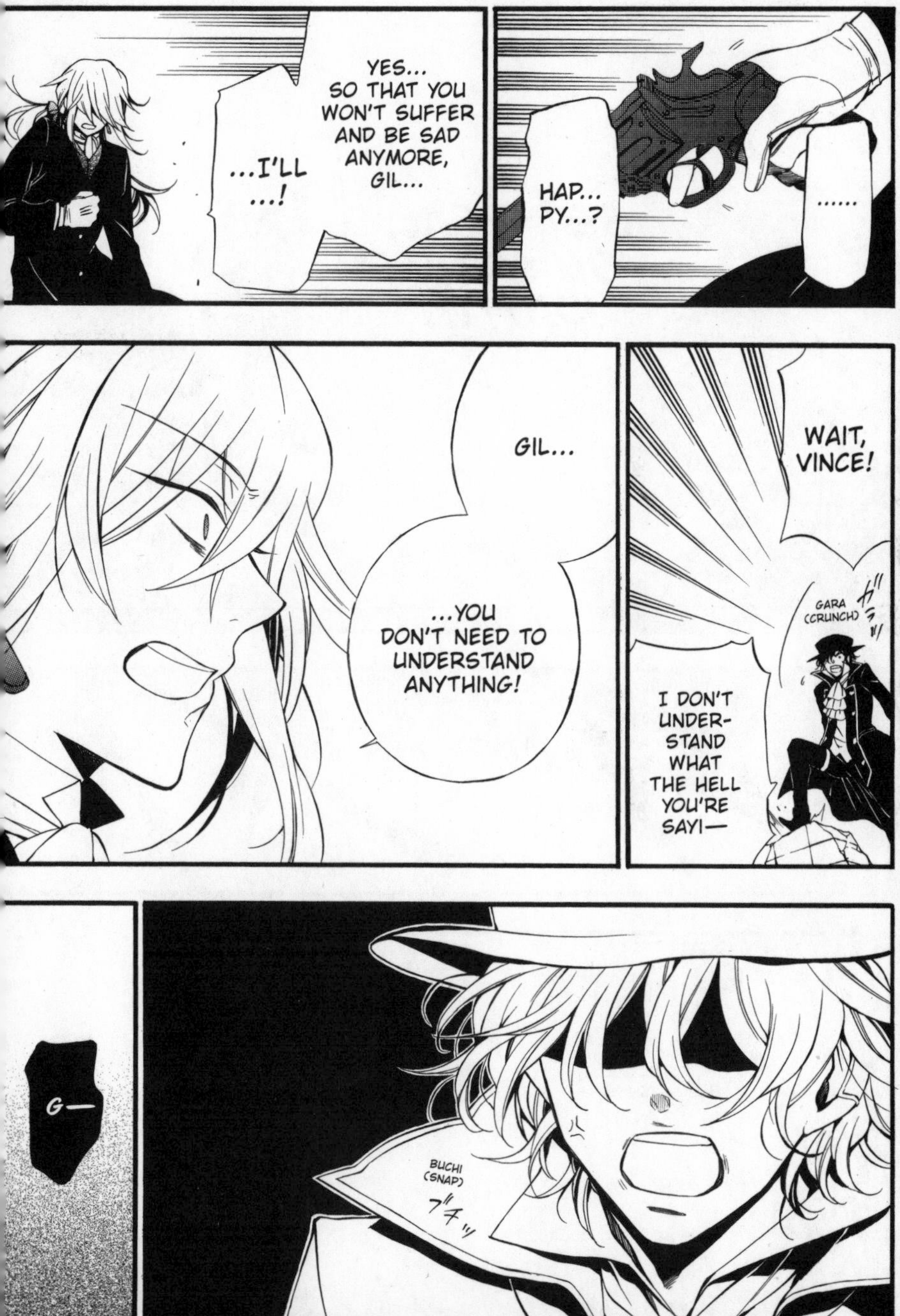
......
HAP... PY...?
YES... SO THAT YOU WON'T SUFFER AND BE SAD ANYMORE, GIL...
...I'LL ...!
WAIT, VINCE!
GARA (CRUNCH)
I DON'T UNDER-STAND WHAT THE HELL YOU'RE SAYI—
GIL...
...YOU DON'T NEED TO UNDERSTAND ANYTHING!
BUCHI (SNAP)
G—

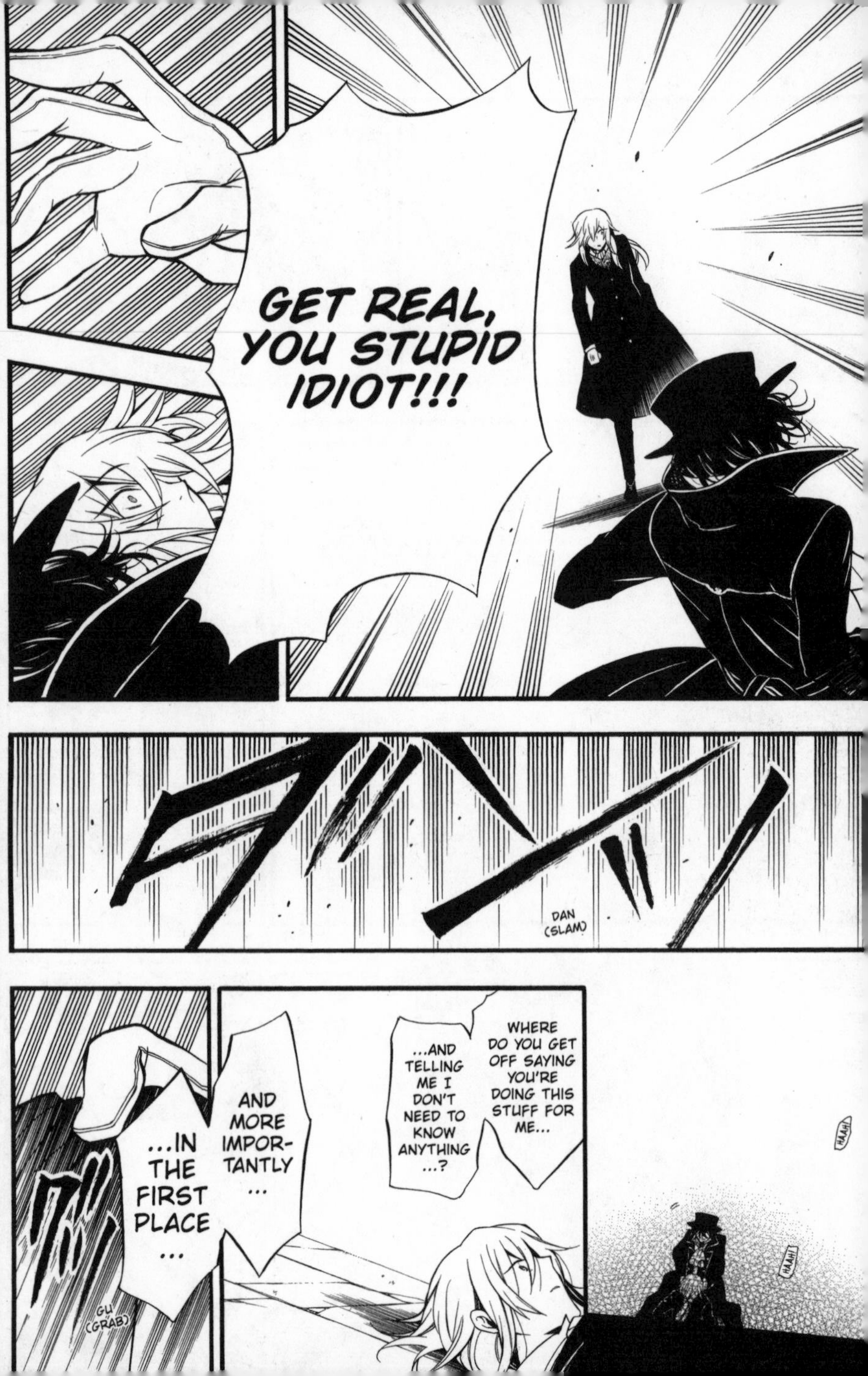
GET REAL, YOU STUPID IDIOT!!!
DAN (SLAM)
HAAH
WHERE DO YOU GET OFF SAYING YOU'RE DOING THIS STUFF FOR ME...
...AND TELLING ME I DON'T NEED TO KNOW ANYTHING ...?
HAAH
AND MORE IMPORTANTLY ...
...IN THE FIRST PLACE ...
GU (GRAB)

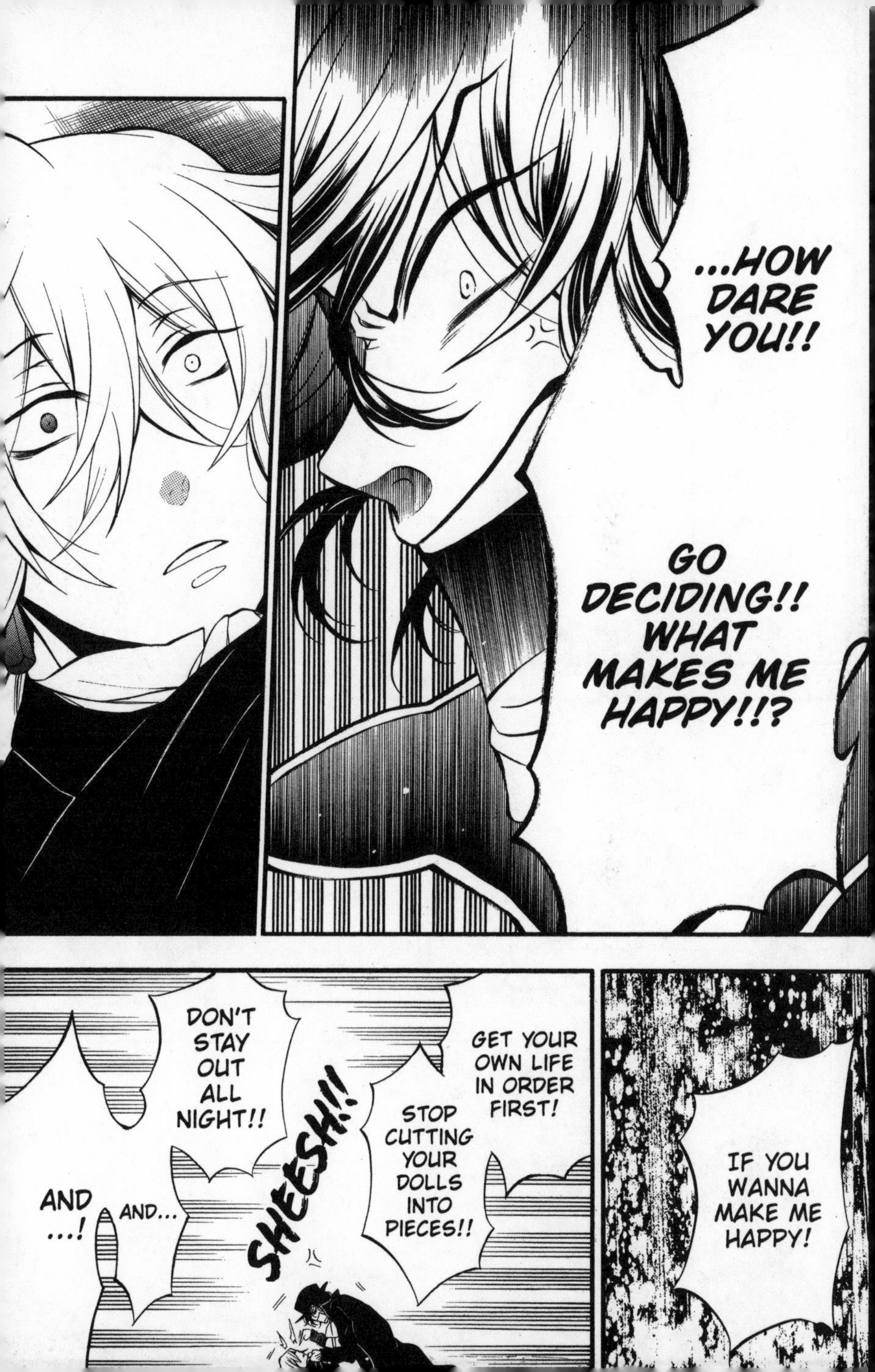
...HOW DARE YOU!!
GO DECIDING!! WHAT MAKES ME HAPPY!!?
IF YOU WANNA MAKE ME HAPPY!
GET YOUR OWN LIFE IN ORDER FIRST!
DON'T STAY OUT ALL NIGHT!!
STOP CUTTING YOUR DOLLS INTO PIECES!!
SHEESH!!
AND...
AND ...!

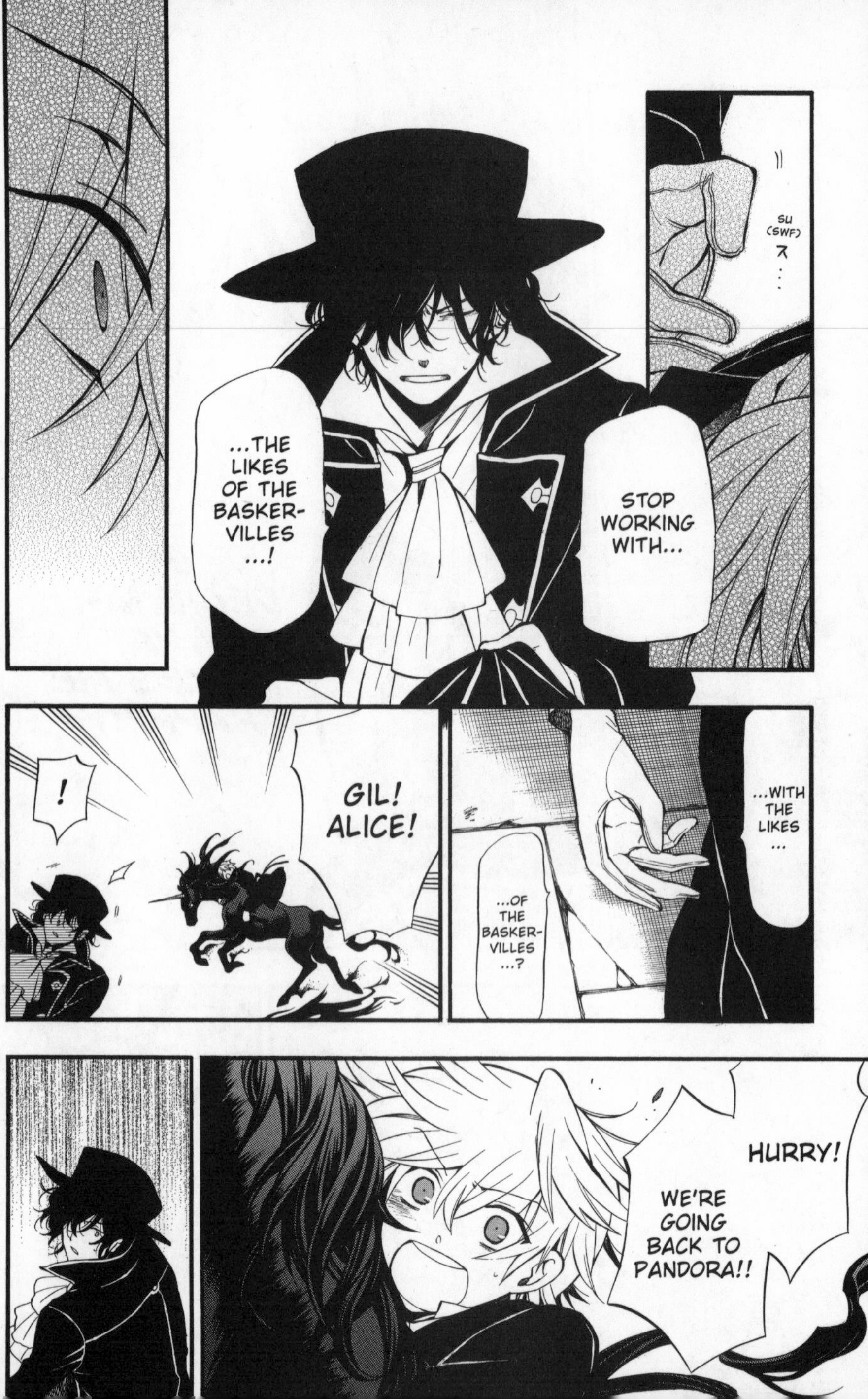
SU (SWF)
ス…
STOP WORKING WITH...
...THE LIKES OF THE BASKER-VILLES ...!
...WITH THE LIKES ...
...OF THE BASKER-VILLES ...?
GIL! ALICE!
!
HURRY!
WE'RE GOING BACK TO PANDORA!!

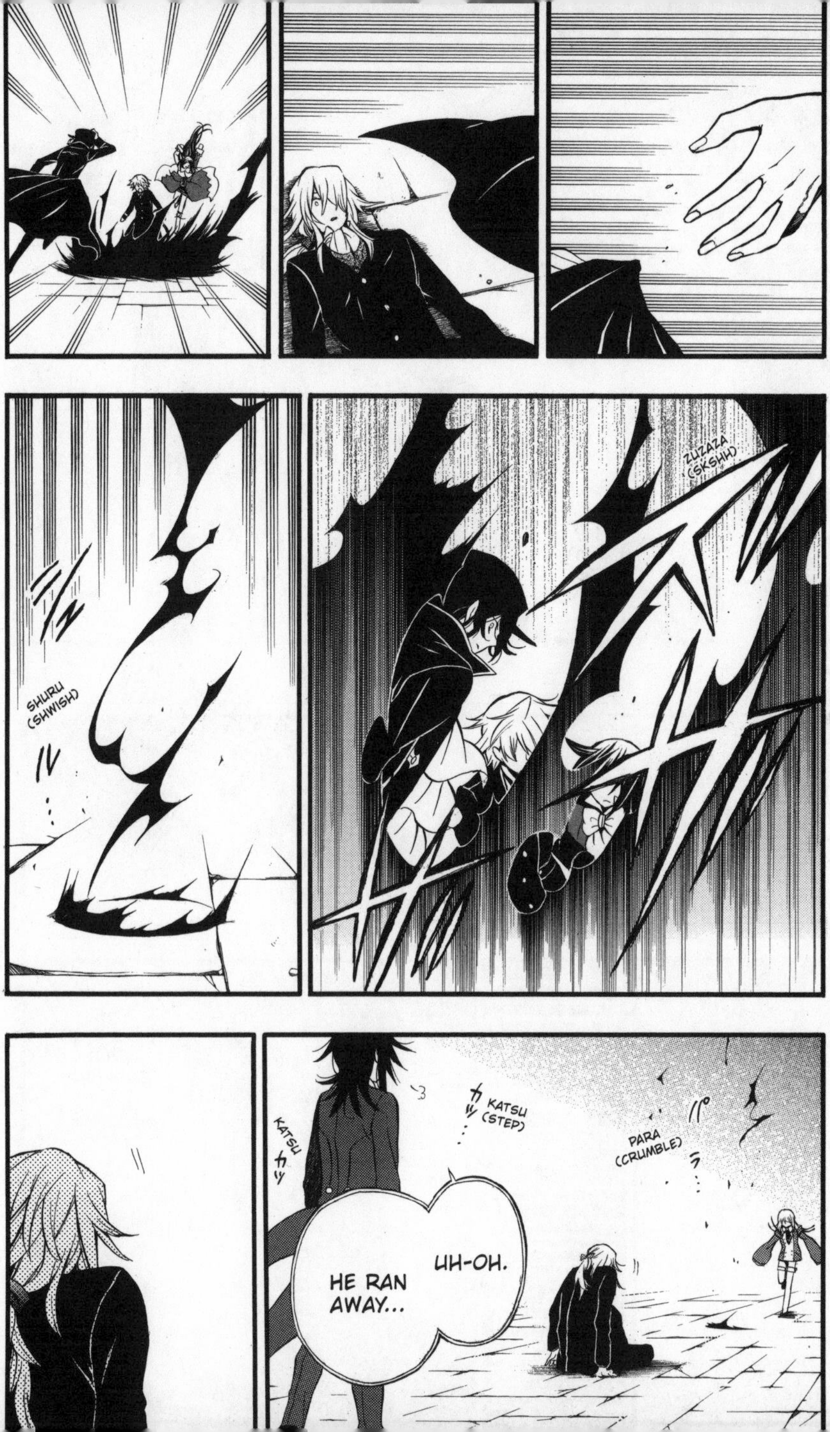
ZUZAZA (SKSHH)
SHURU (SHWISH)
PARA (CRUMBLE)
KATSU (STEP)
KATSU
UH-OH. HE RAN AWAY...

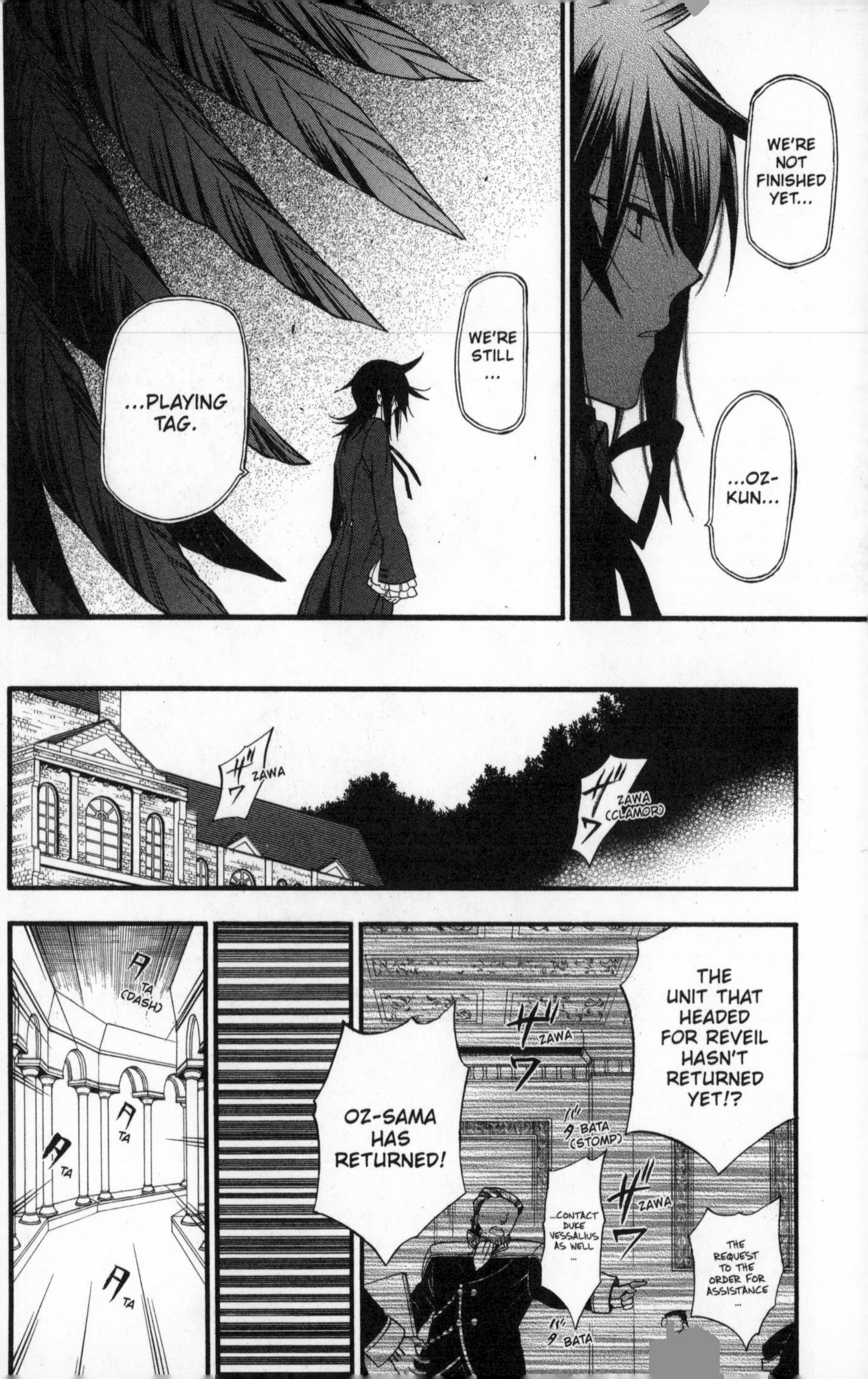
WE'RE NOT FINISHED YET...
...OZ-KUN...
WE'RE STILL ...
...PLAYING TAG.
ザワ ZAWA (CLAMOR)
ザワ ZAWA
THE UNIT THAT HEADED FOR REVEIL HASN'T RETURNED YET!?
ザワ ZAWA
OZ-SAMA HAS RETURNED!
バタ BATA (STOMP)
ザワ ZAWA
...CONTACT DUKE VESSALIUS AS WELL ...
THE REQUEST TO THE ORDER FOR ASSISTANCE ...
バタ BATA
タ TA (DASH)
タ TA
タ TA
タ TA

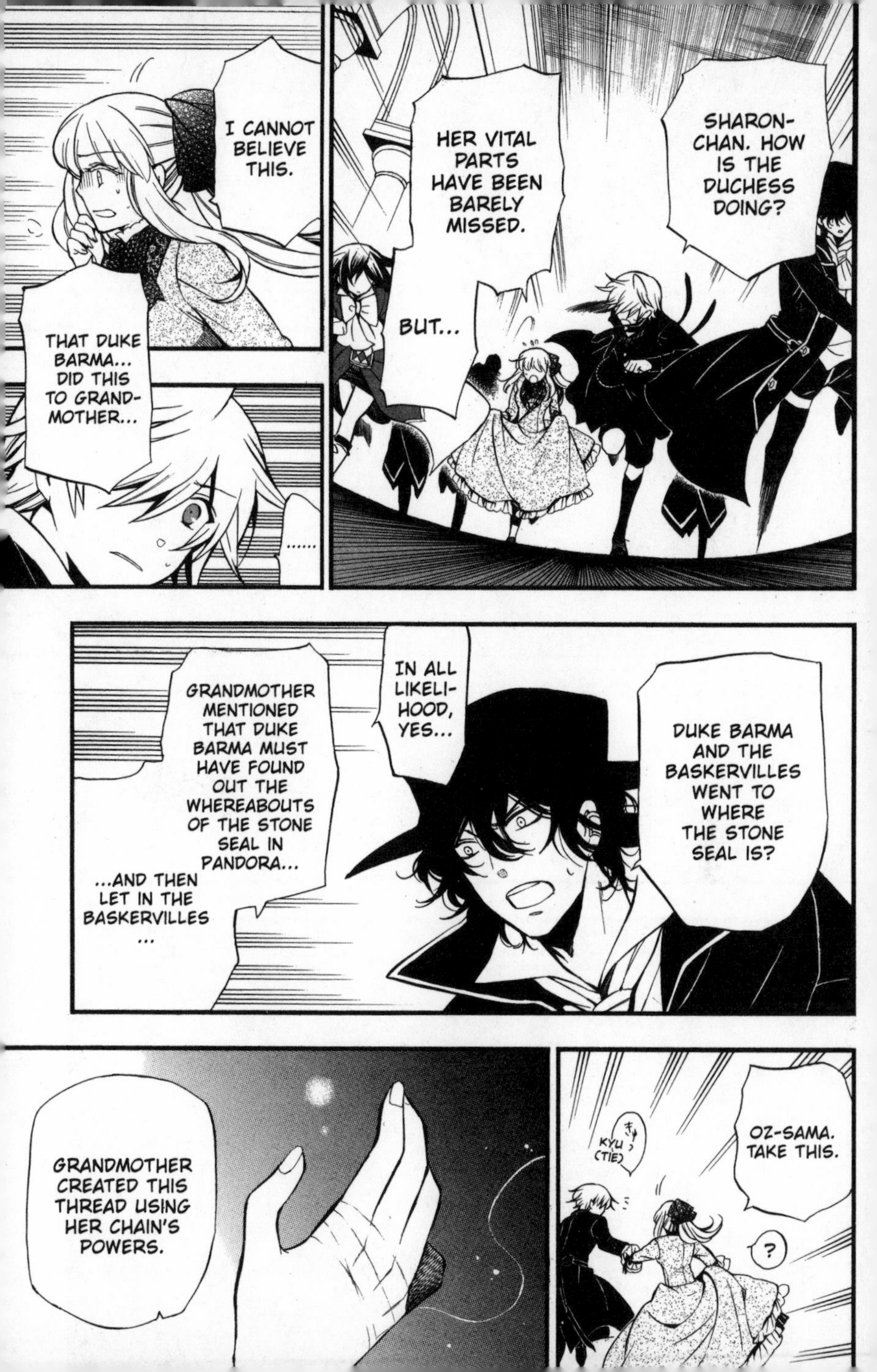
SHARON-CHAN. HOW IS THE DUCHESS DOING?
HER VITAL PARTS HAVE BEEN BARELY MISSED.
BUT...
I CANNOT BELIEVE THIS.
THAT DUKE BARMA... DID THIS TO GRAND-MOTHER...
......
DUKE BARMA AND THE BASKERVILLES WENT TO WHERE THE STONE SEAL IS?
IN ALL LIKELI-HOOD, YES...
GRANDMOTHER MENTIONED THAT DUKE BARMA MUST HAVE FOUND OUT THE WHEREABOUTS OF THE STONE SEAL IN PANDORA...
...AND THEN LET IN THE BASKERVILLES ...
OZ-SAMA. TAKE THIS.
きゅっ
KYU (TIE)
?
GRANDMOTHER CREATED THIS THREAD USING HER CHAIN'S POWERS.

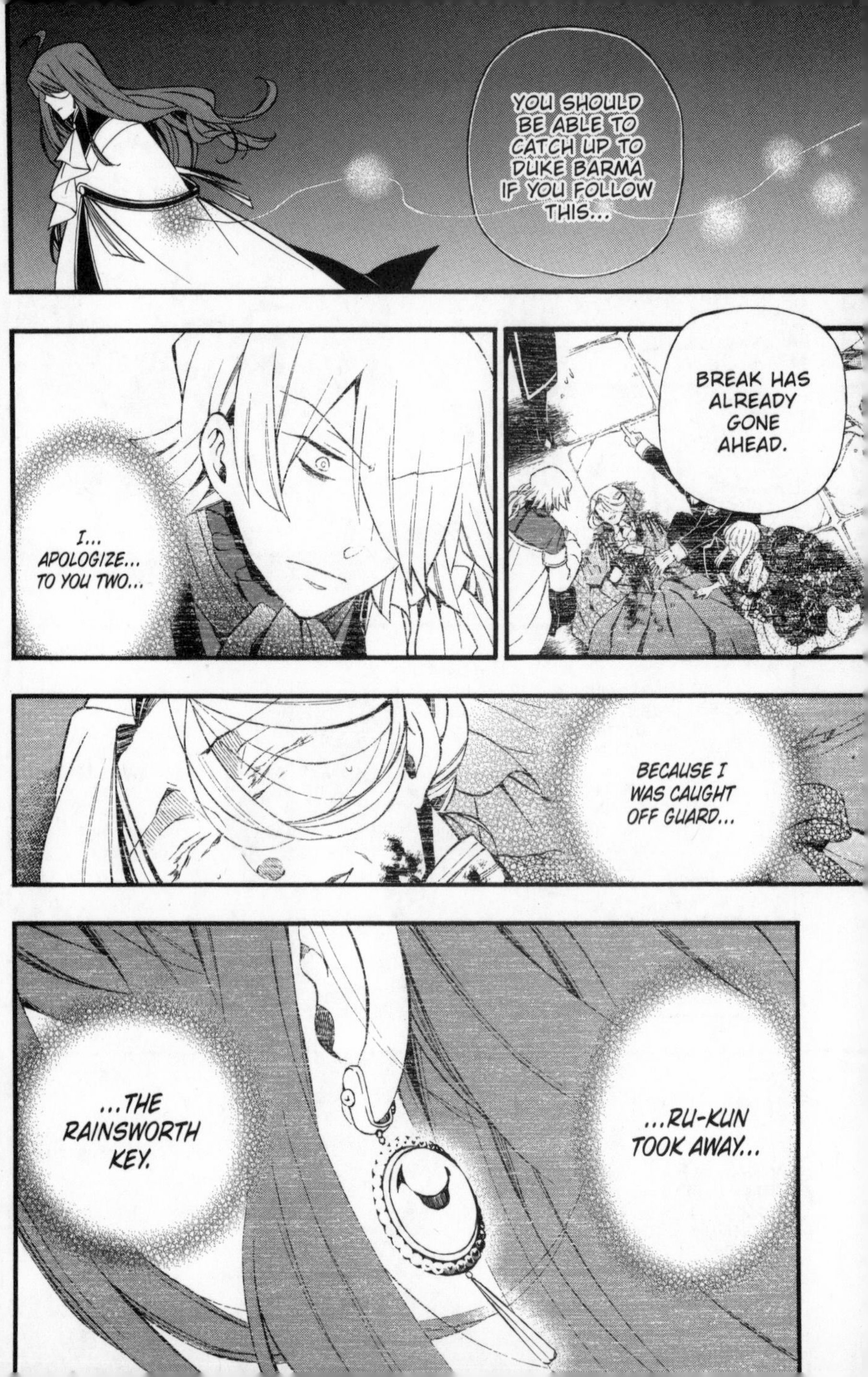
YOU SHOULD BE ABLE TO CATCH UP TO DUKE BARMA IF YOU FOLLOW THIS...
BREAK HAS ALREADY GONE AHEAD.
I... APOLOGIZE... TO YOU TWO...
BECAUSE I WAS CAUGHT OFF GUARD...
...RU-KUN TOOK AWAY...
...THE RAINSWORTH KEY.

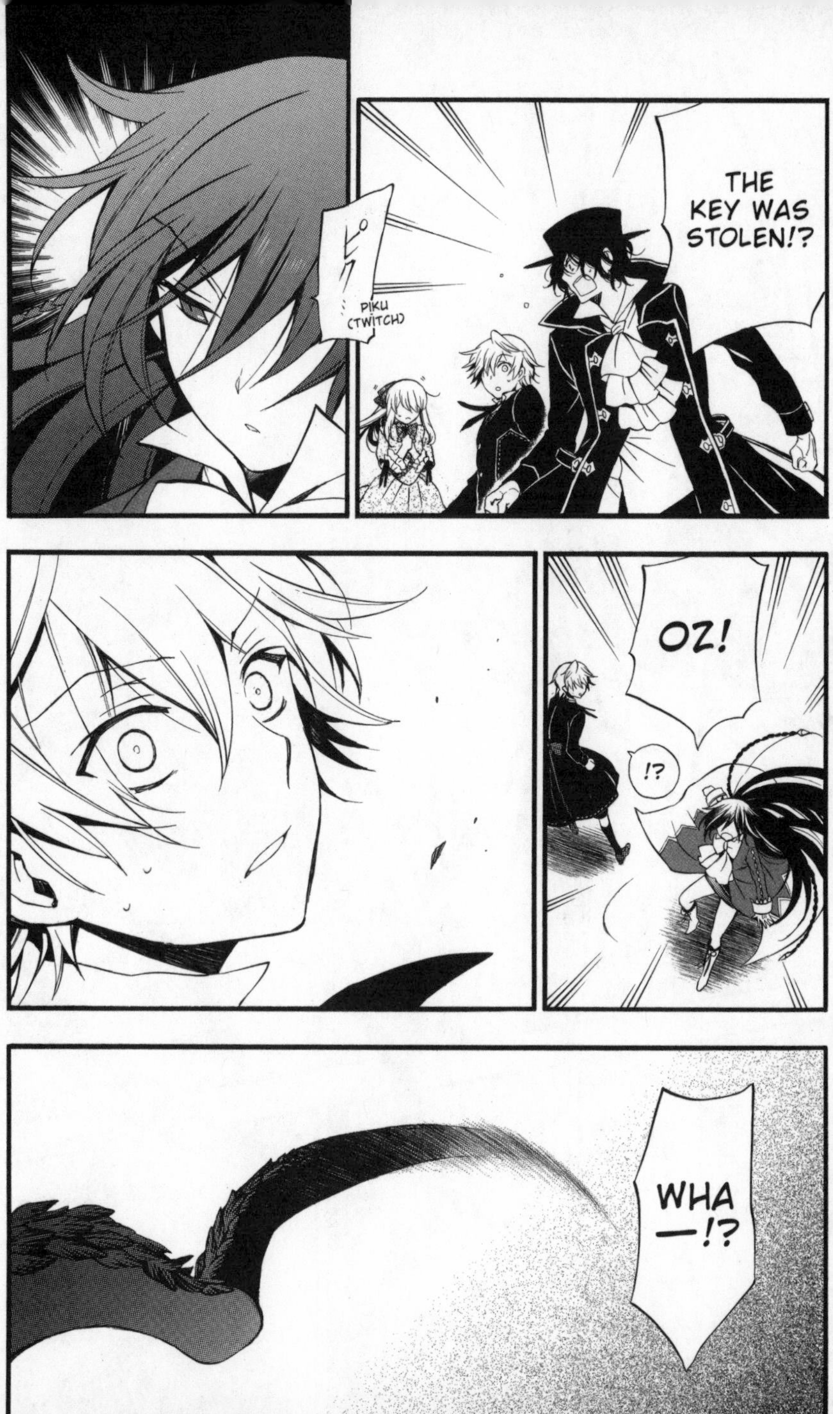
THE KEY WAS STOLEN!?
ピク…
PIKU (TWITCH)
OZ!
!?
WHA—!?

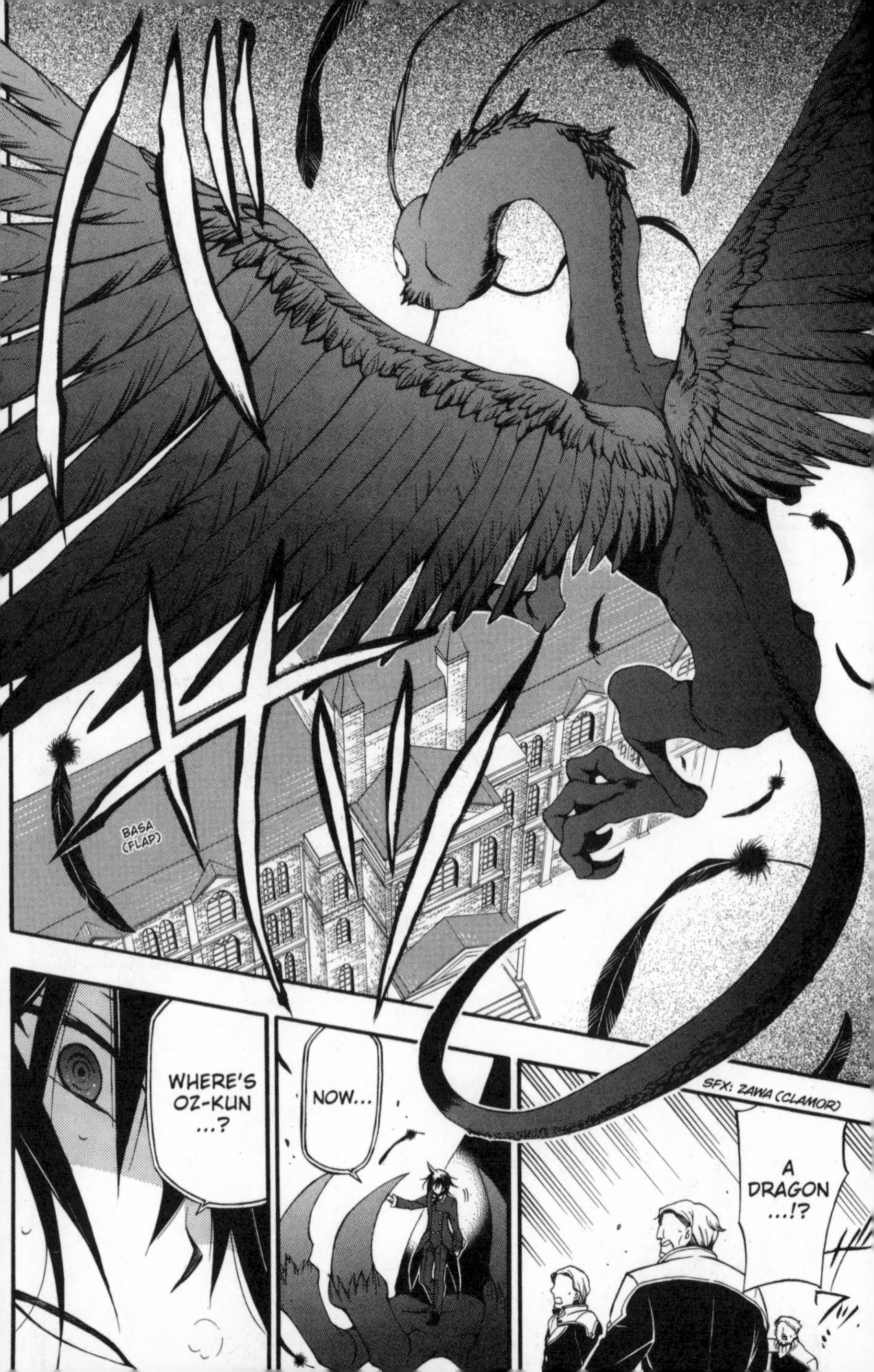
BASA (FLAP)
SFX: ZAWA (CLAMOR)
A DRAGON ...!?
NOW...
WHERE'S OZ-KUN ...?

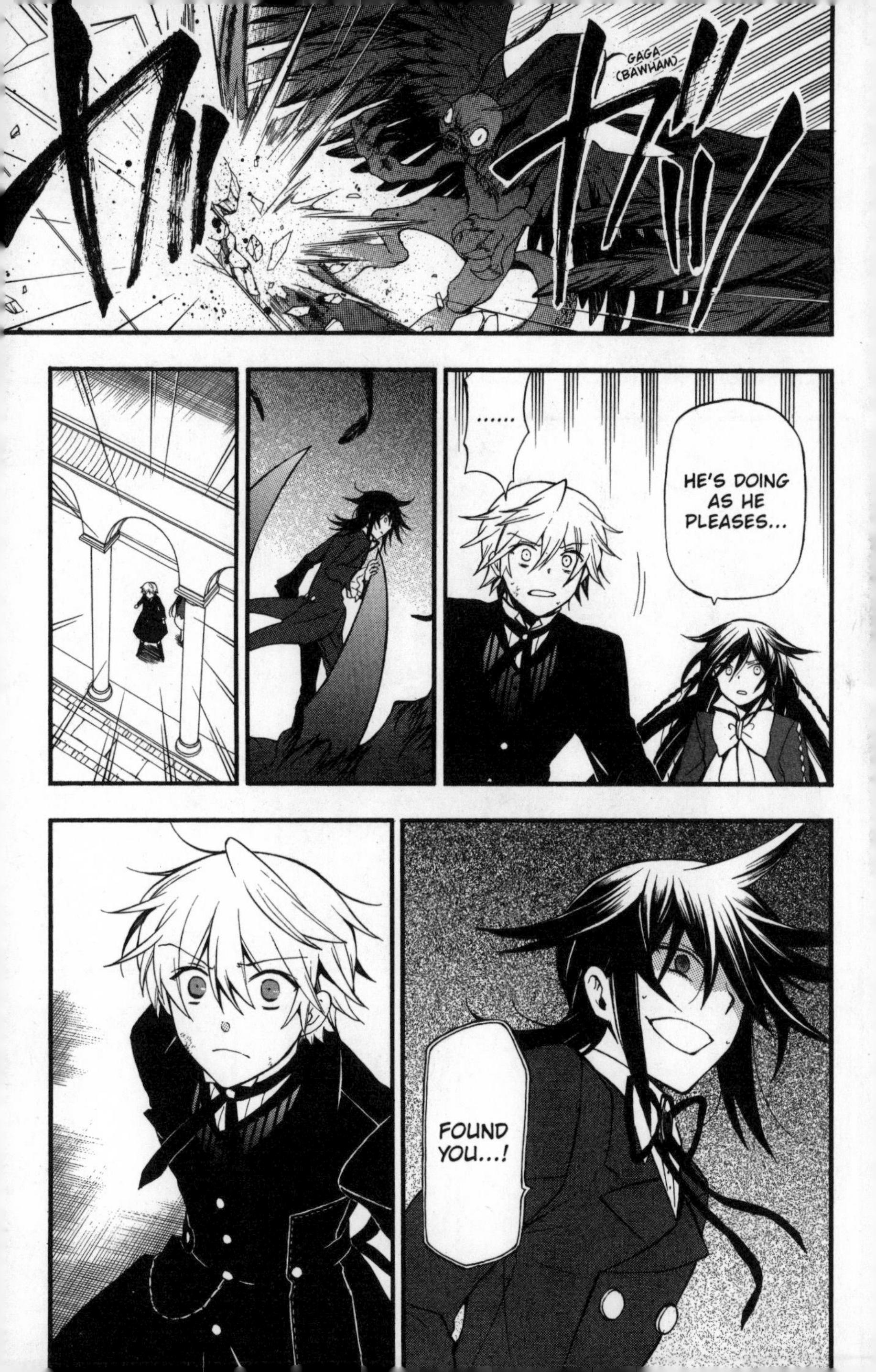
GAGA (BAWHAM)
HE'S DOING AS HE PLEASES...
......
FOUND YOU...!

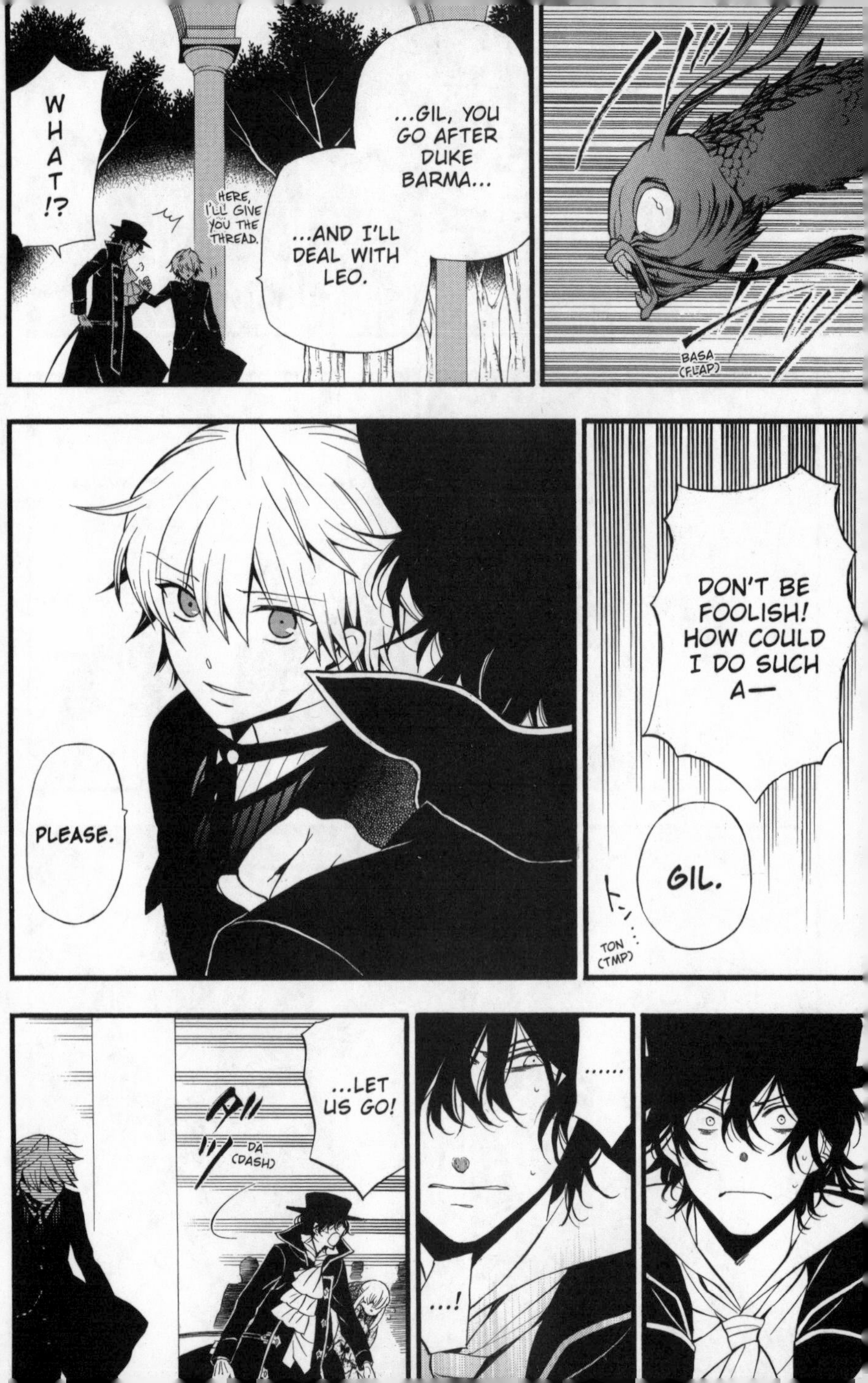
BASA (FLAP)
...GIL, YOU GO AFTER DUKE BARMA...
...AND I'LL DEAL WITH LEO.
HERE, I'LL GIVE YOU THE THREAD.
WHAT!?
DON'T BE FOOLISH! HOW COULD I DO SUCH A—
GIL.
TON (TMP)
PLEASE.
......
...!
...LET US GO!
DA (DASH)

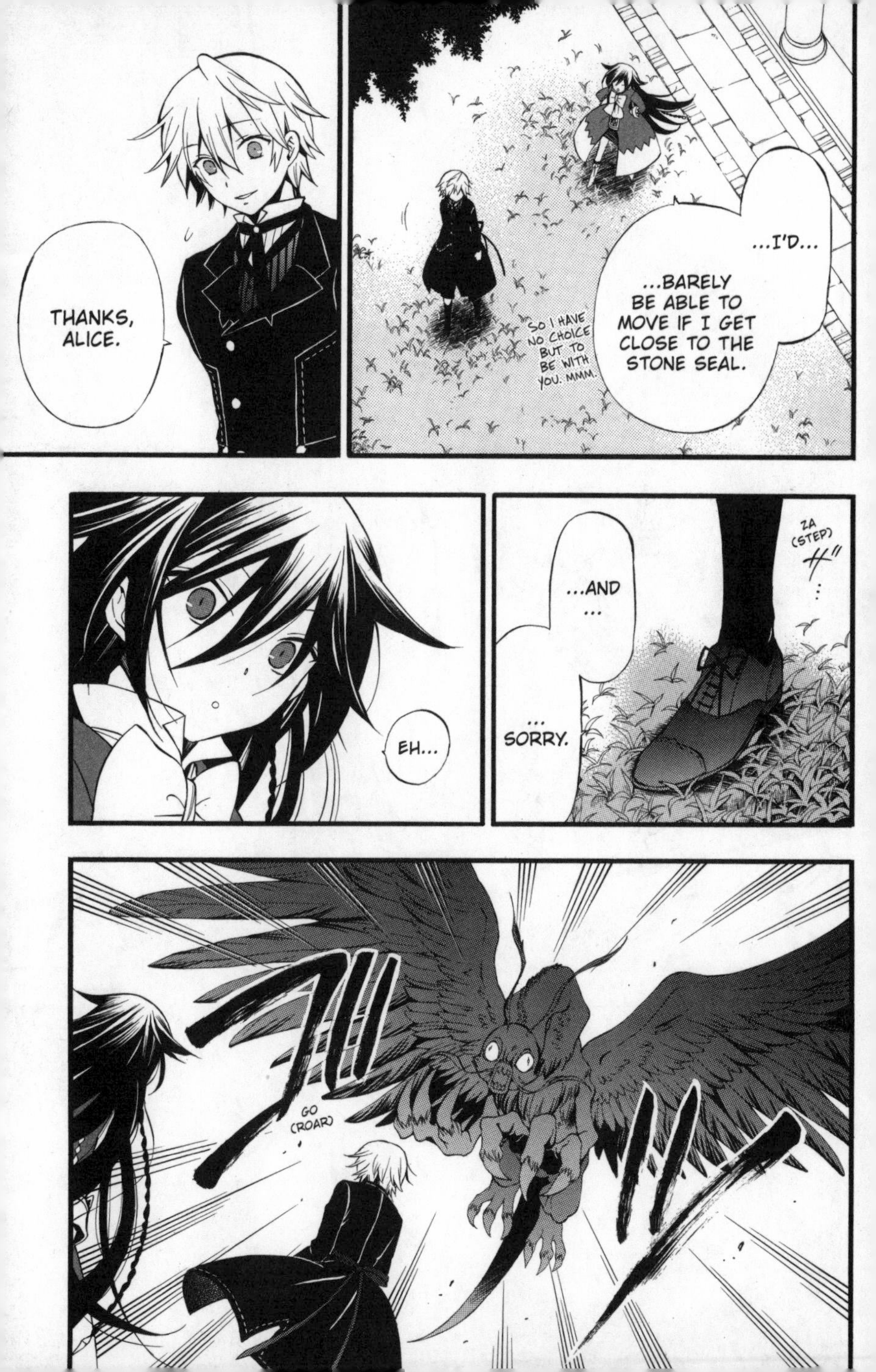
...I'D...
...BARELY BE ABLE TO MOVE IF I GET CLOSE TO THE STONE SEAL.
SO I HAVE NO CHOICE BUT TO BE WITH YOU. MMM.
THANKS, ALICE.
ZA (STEP)
...AND ...
... SORRY.
EH...
GO (ROAR)

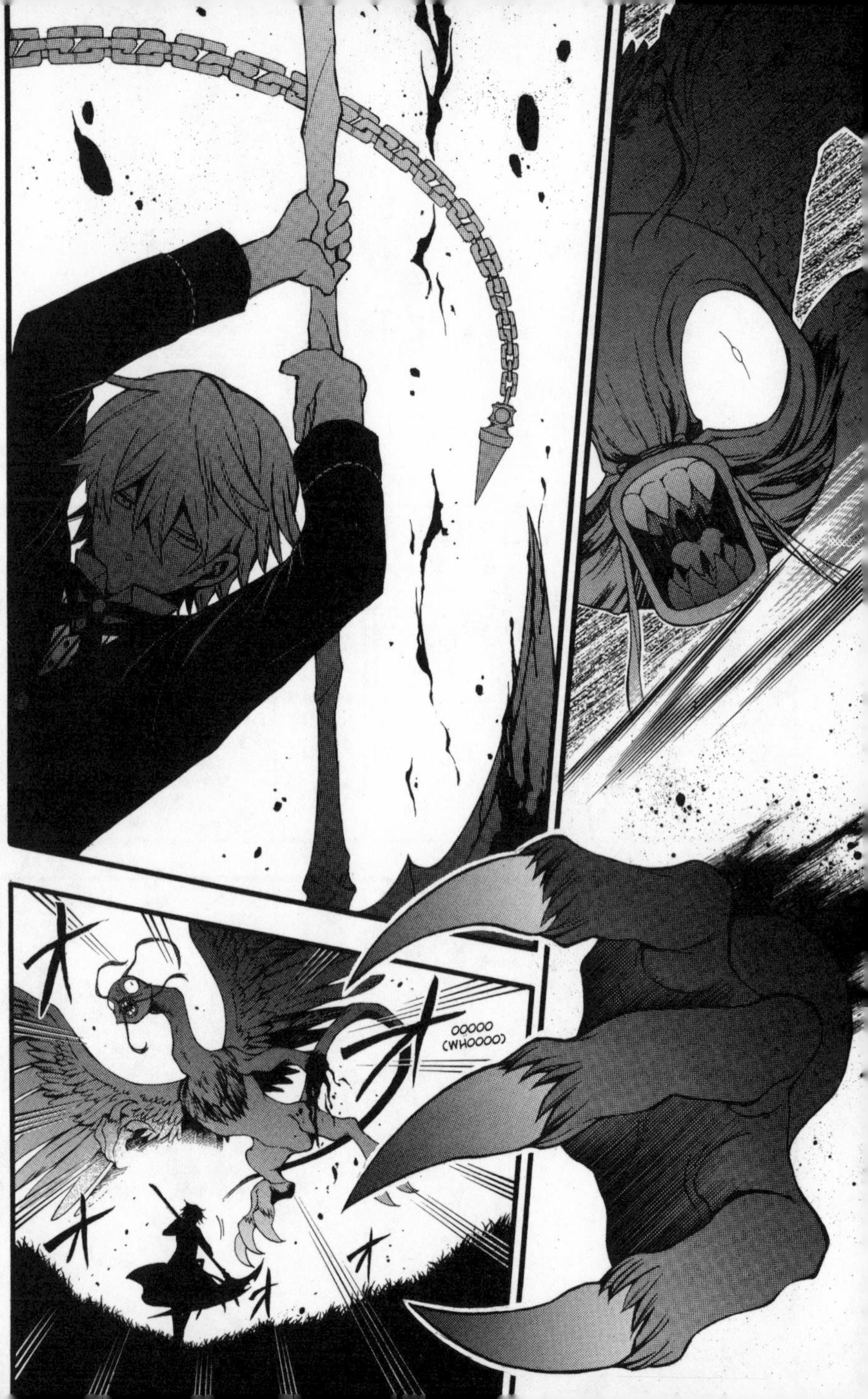
OOOOO
(WHOOOOO)

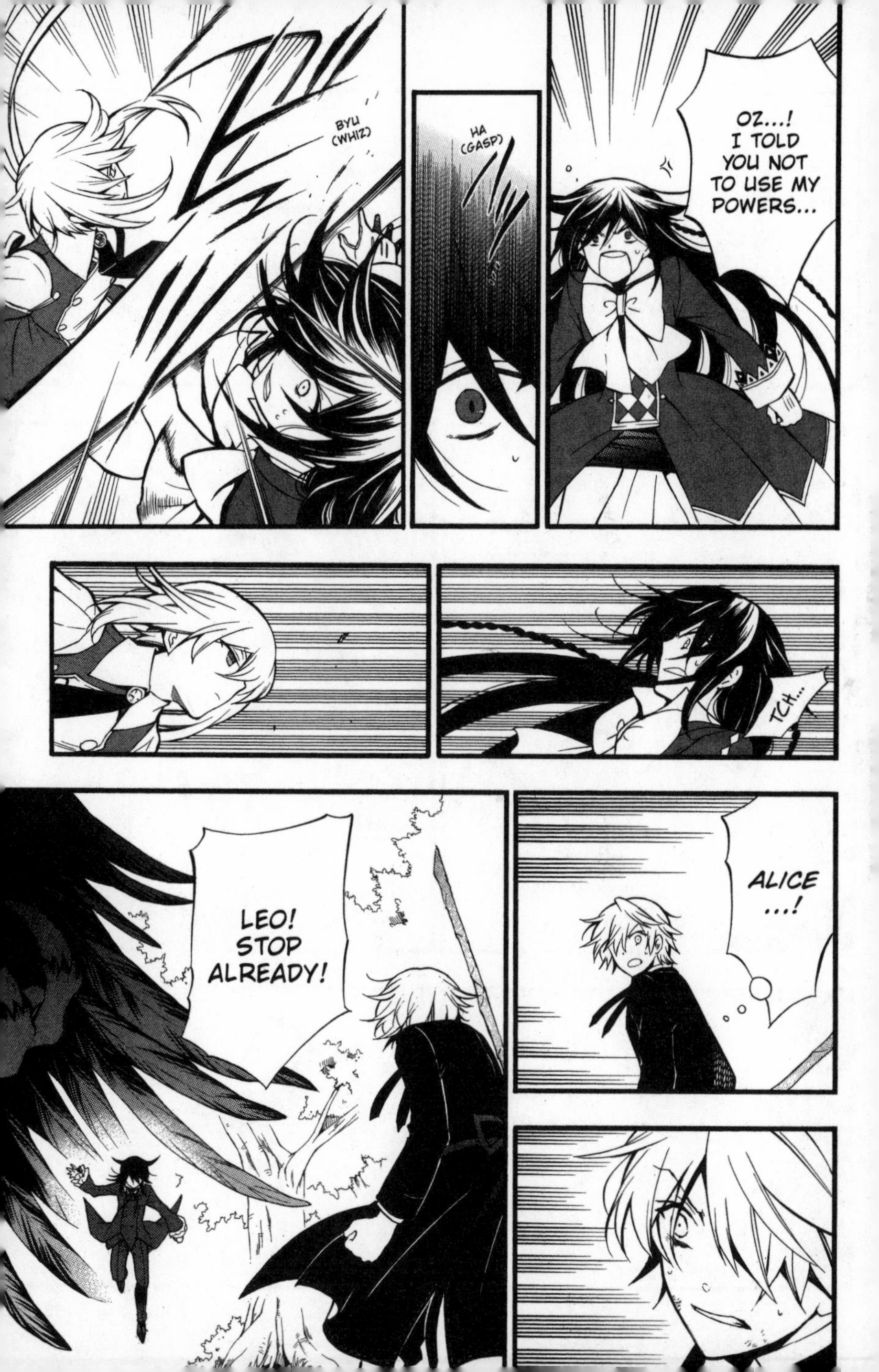
OZ...! I TOLD YOU NOT TO USE MY POWERS...
HA (GASP)
BYU (WHIZ)
TCH...
ALICE ...!
LEO! STOP ALREADY!

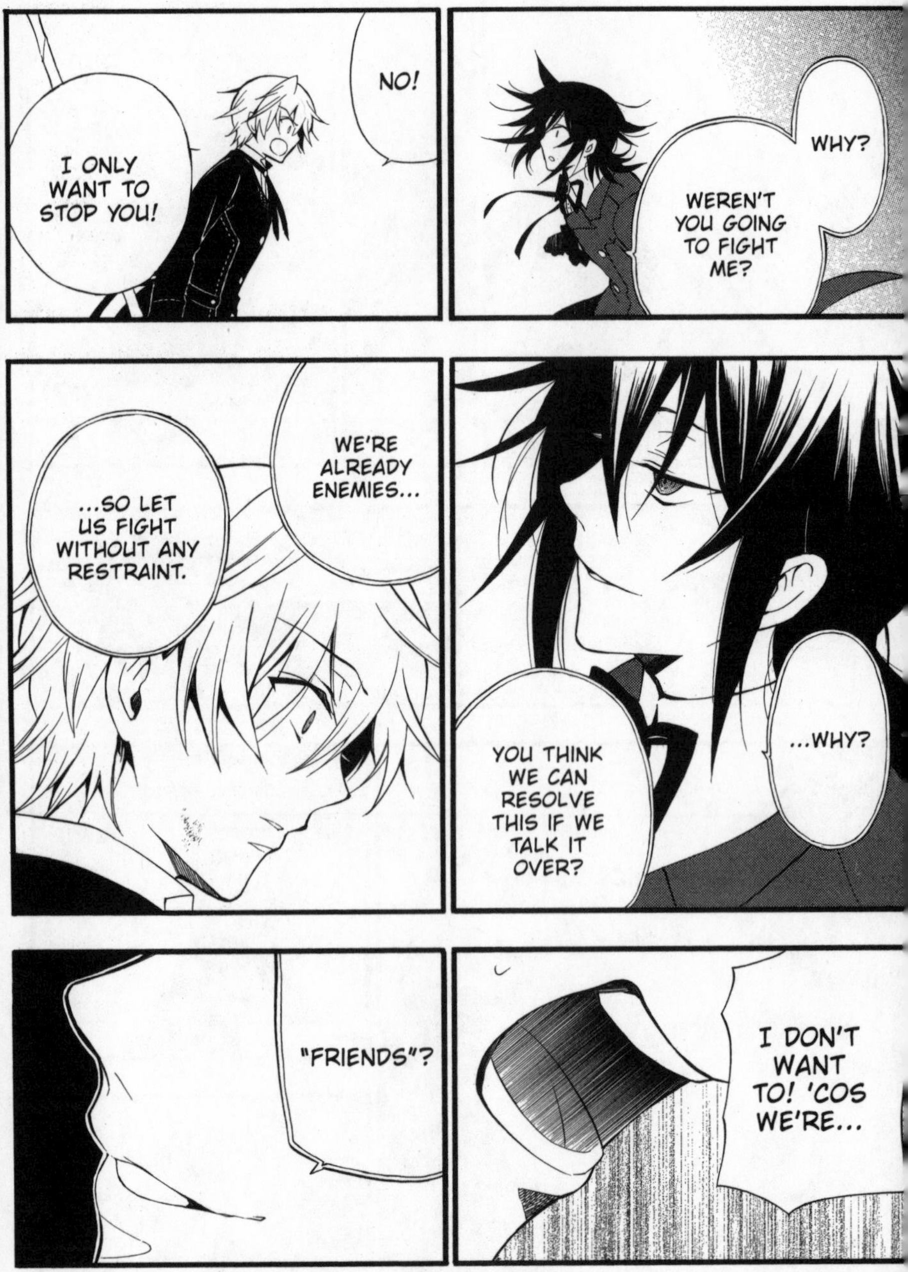
WHY?
WEREN'T YOU GOING TO FIGHT ME?
NO!
I ONLY WANT TO STOP YOU!
...WHY?
YOU THINK WE CAN RESOLVE THIS IF WE TALK IT OVER?
WE'RE ALREADY ENEMIES...
...SO LET US FIGHT WITHOUT ANY RESTRAINT.
I DON'T WANT TO! 'COS WE'RE...
"FRIENDS"?

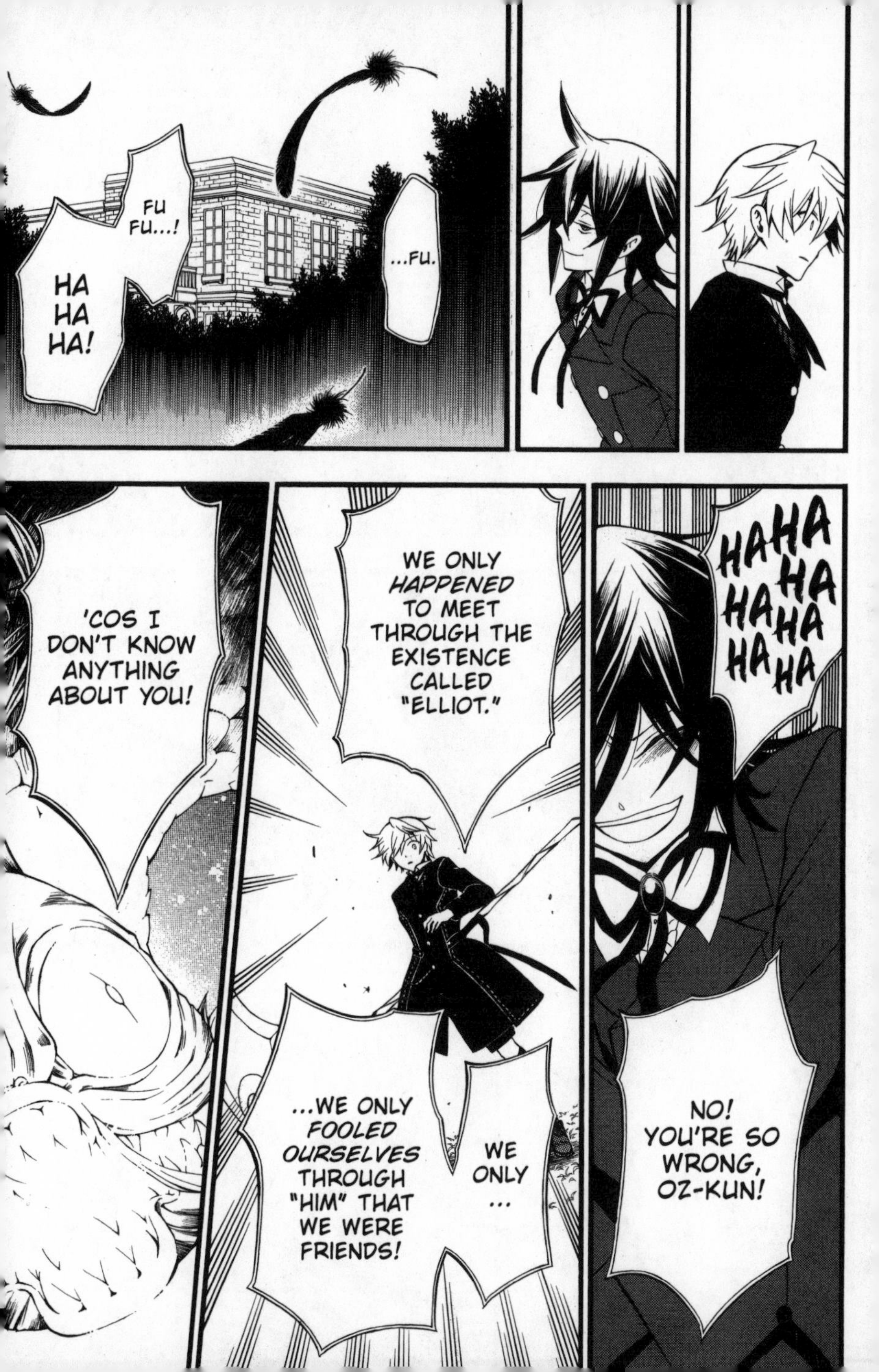
...FU.
FU FU...! HA HA HA!
HAHA HAHA HAHA HAHA HA
NO! YOU'RE SO WRONG, OZ-KUN!
WE ONLY *HAPPENED* TO MEET THROUGH THE EXISTENCE CALLED "ELLIOT."
WE ONLY ...
...WE ONLY *FOOLED OURSELVES* THROUGH "HIM" THAT WE WERE FRIENDS!
'COS I DON'T KNOW ANYTHING ABOUT YOU!

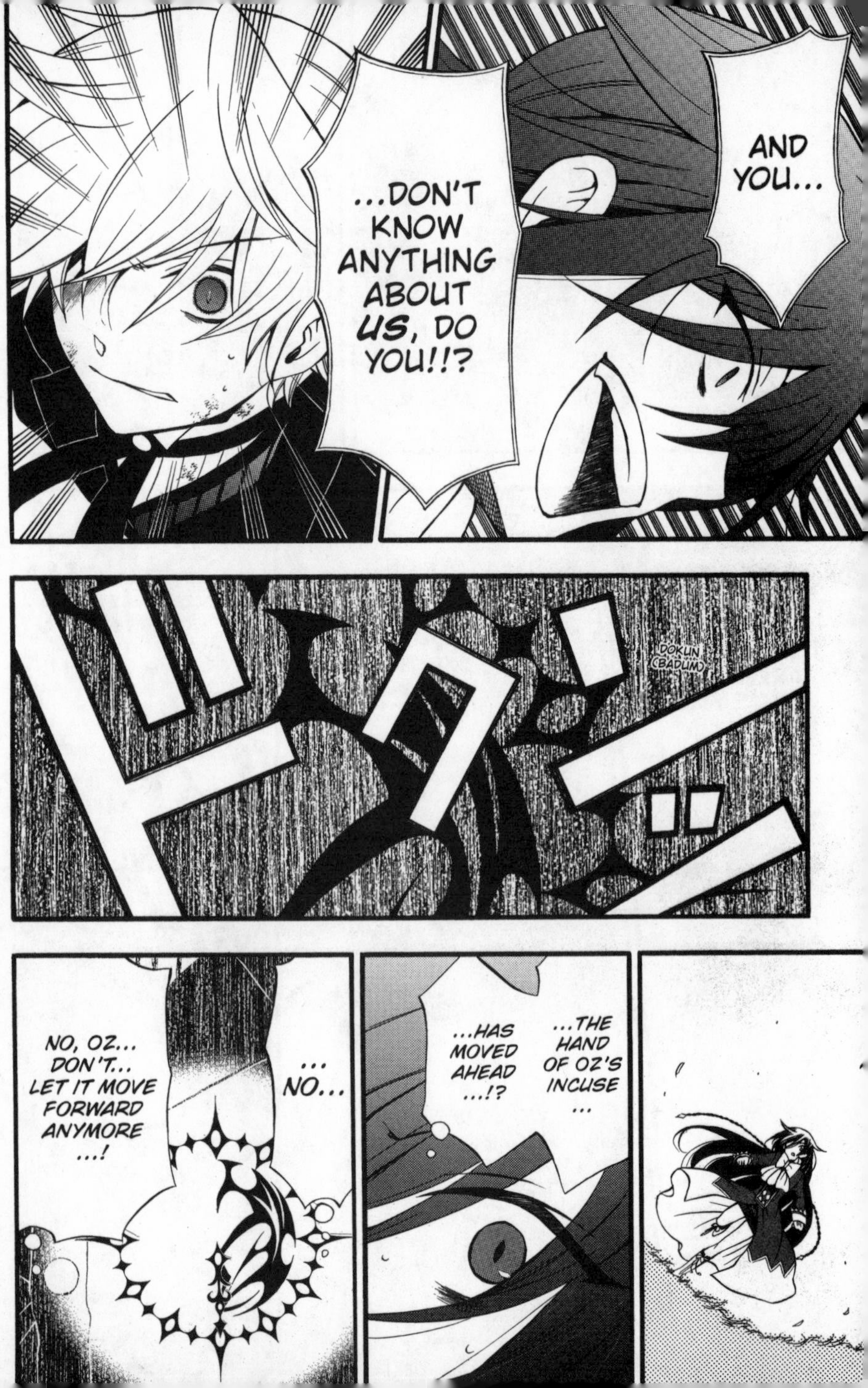
AND YOU...
...DON'T KNOW ANYTHING ABOUT US, DO YOU!!?
DOKUN (BADUM)
...THE HAND OF OZ'S INCUSE ...
...HAS MOVED AHEAD ...!?
... NO...
NO, OZ... DON'T... LET IT MOVE FORWARD ANYMORE ...!

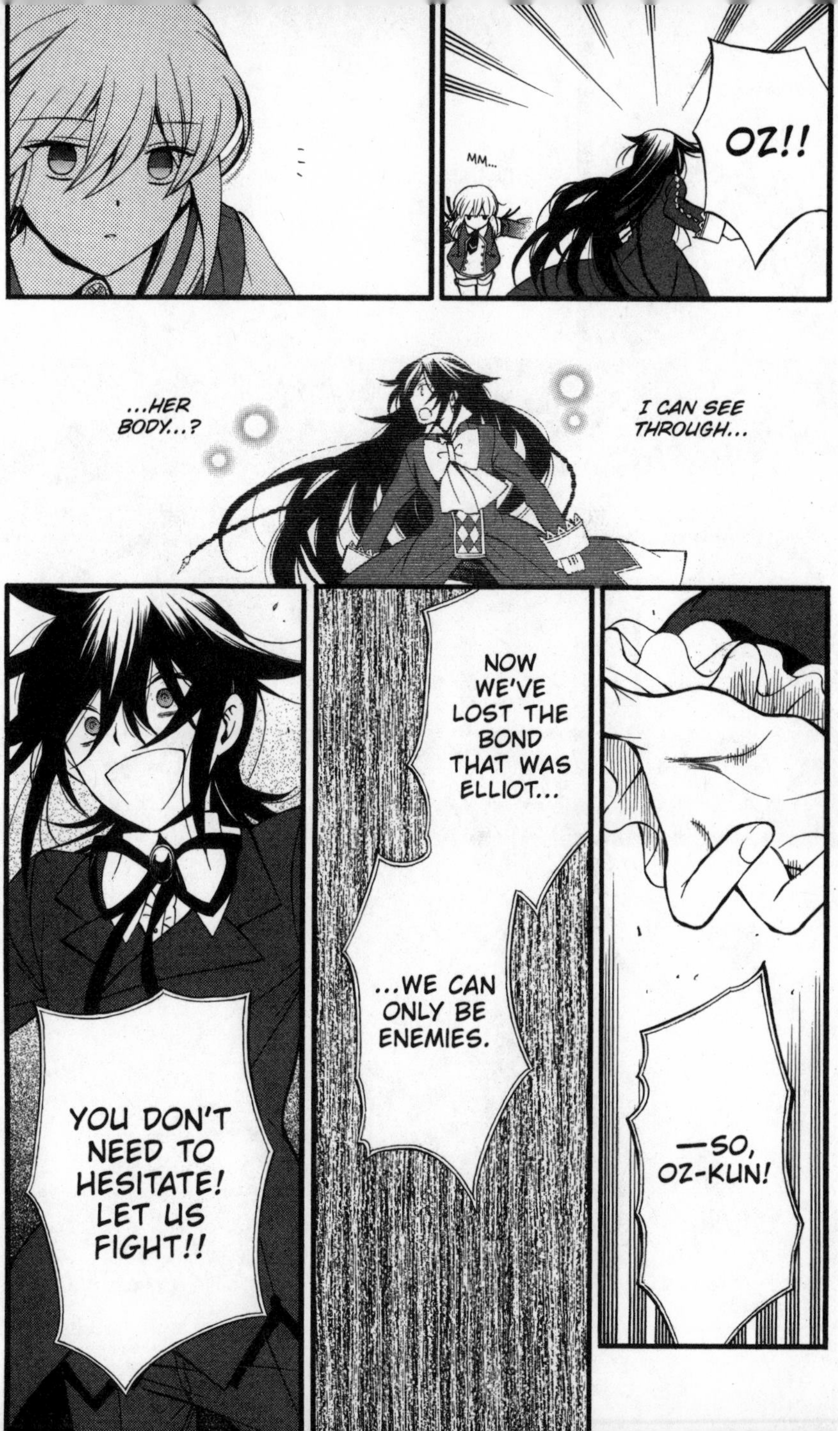
OZ!!
MM...
I CAN SEE THROUGH...
...HER BODY...?
—SO, OZ-KUN!
NOW WE'VE LOST THE BOND THAT WAS ELLIOT...
...WE CAN ONLY BE ENEMIES.
YOU DON'T NEED TO HESITATE! LET US FIGHT!!

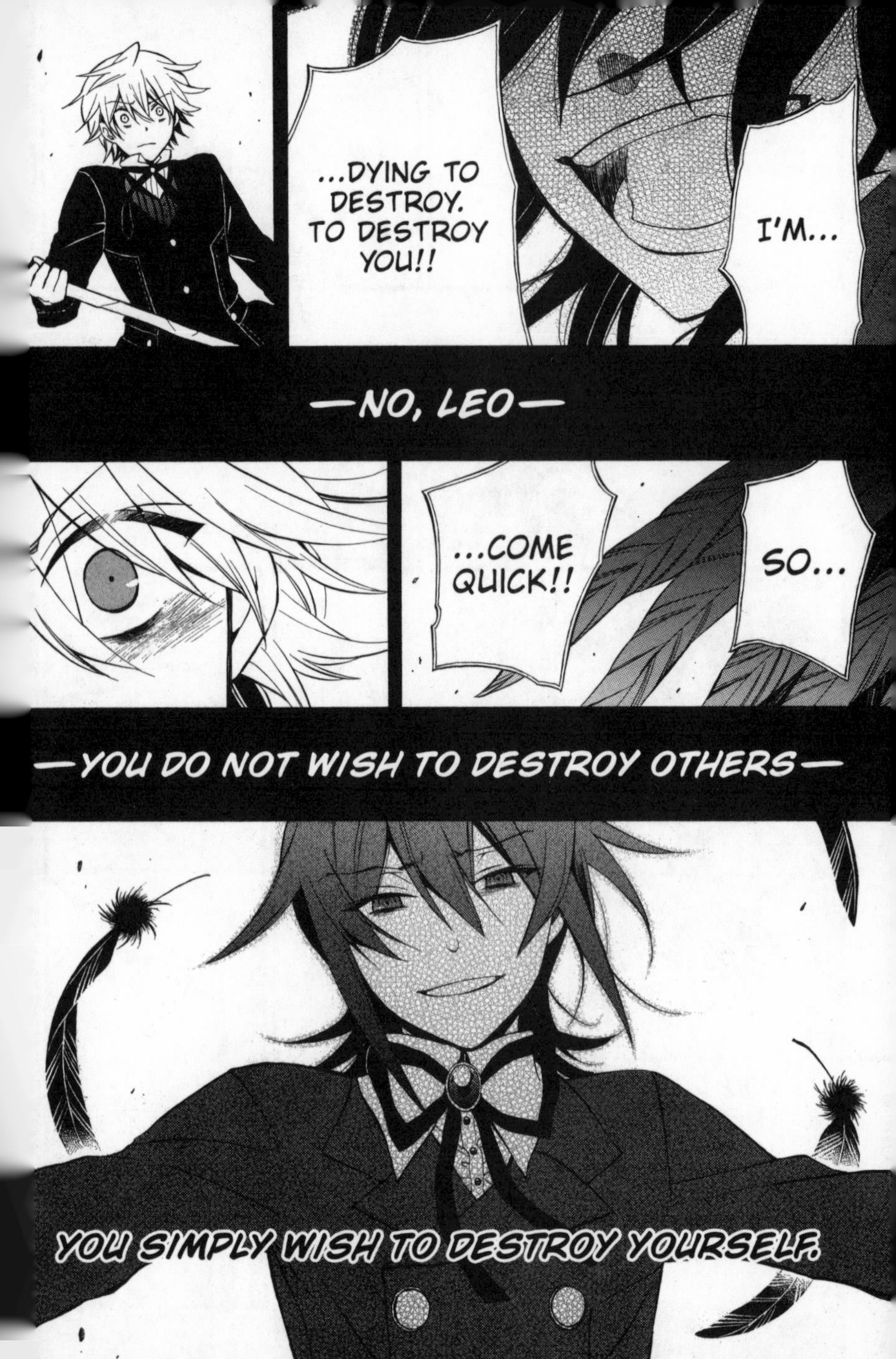
I'M...
...DYING TO DESTROY. TO DESTROY YOU!!
—NO, LEO—
SO...
...COME QUICK!!
—YOU DO NOT WISH TO DESTROY OTHERS—
YOU SIMPLY WISH TO DESTROY YOURSELF.

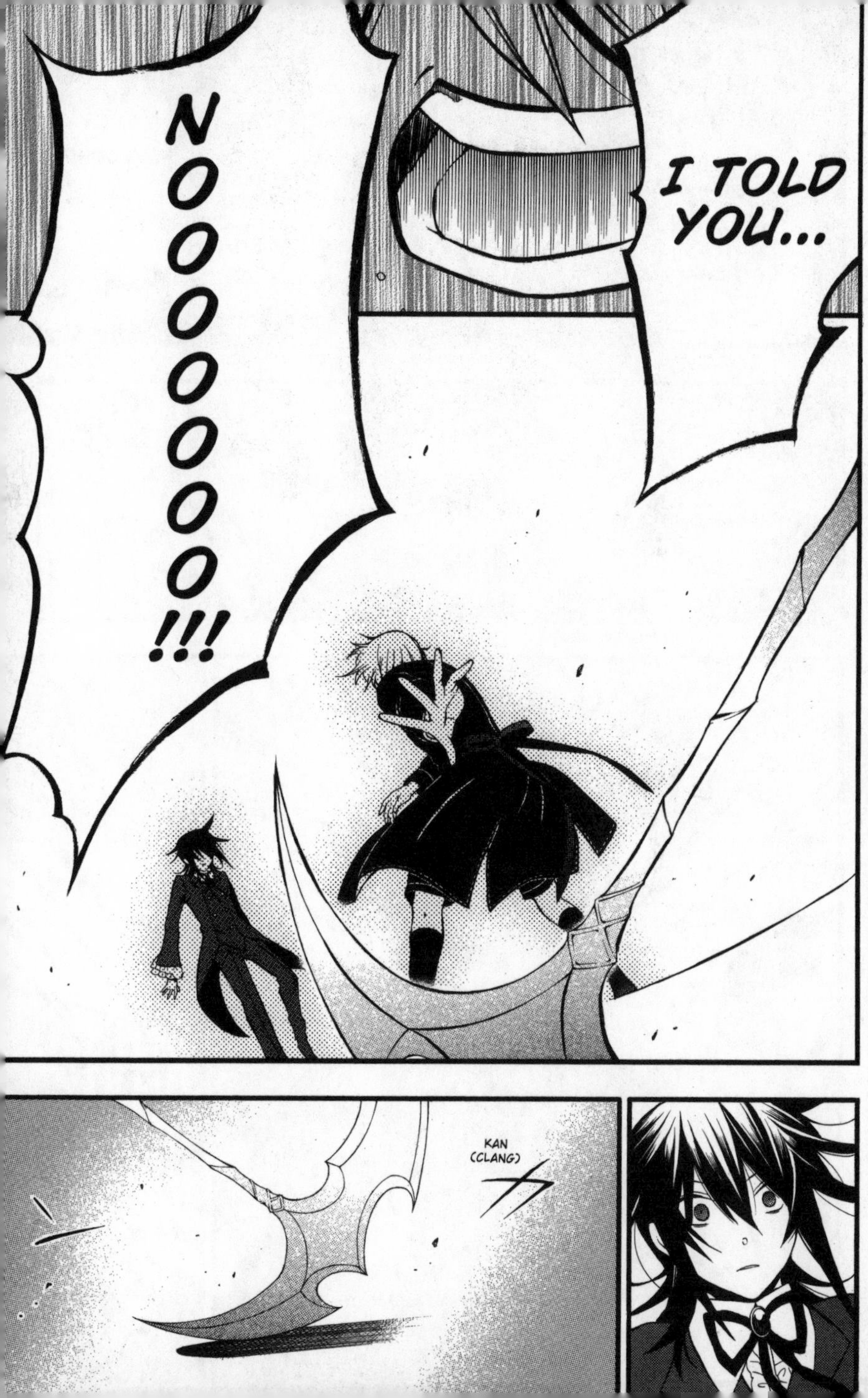
I TOLD YOU...
NOOOOOOO!!!
KAN
(CLANG)

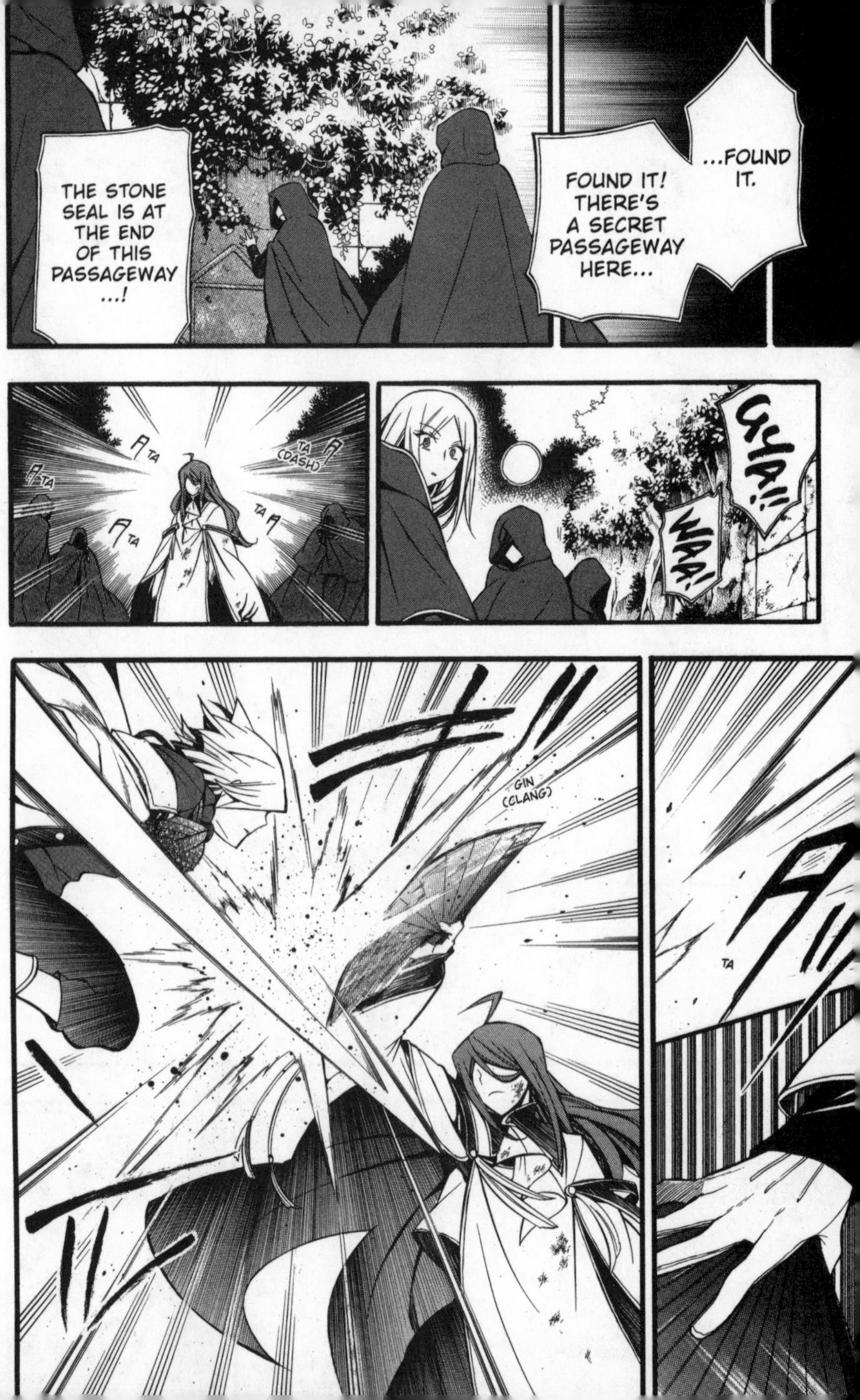
...FOUND IT.
FOUND IT! THERE'S A SECRET PASSAGEWAY HERE...
THE STONE SEAL IS AT THE END OF THIS PASSAGEWAY ...!
GYAA!!!
WAA!
TA
TA (DASH)
TA
TA
TA
TA
GIN (CLANG)

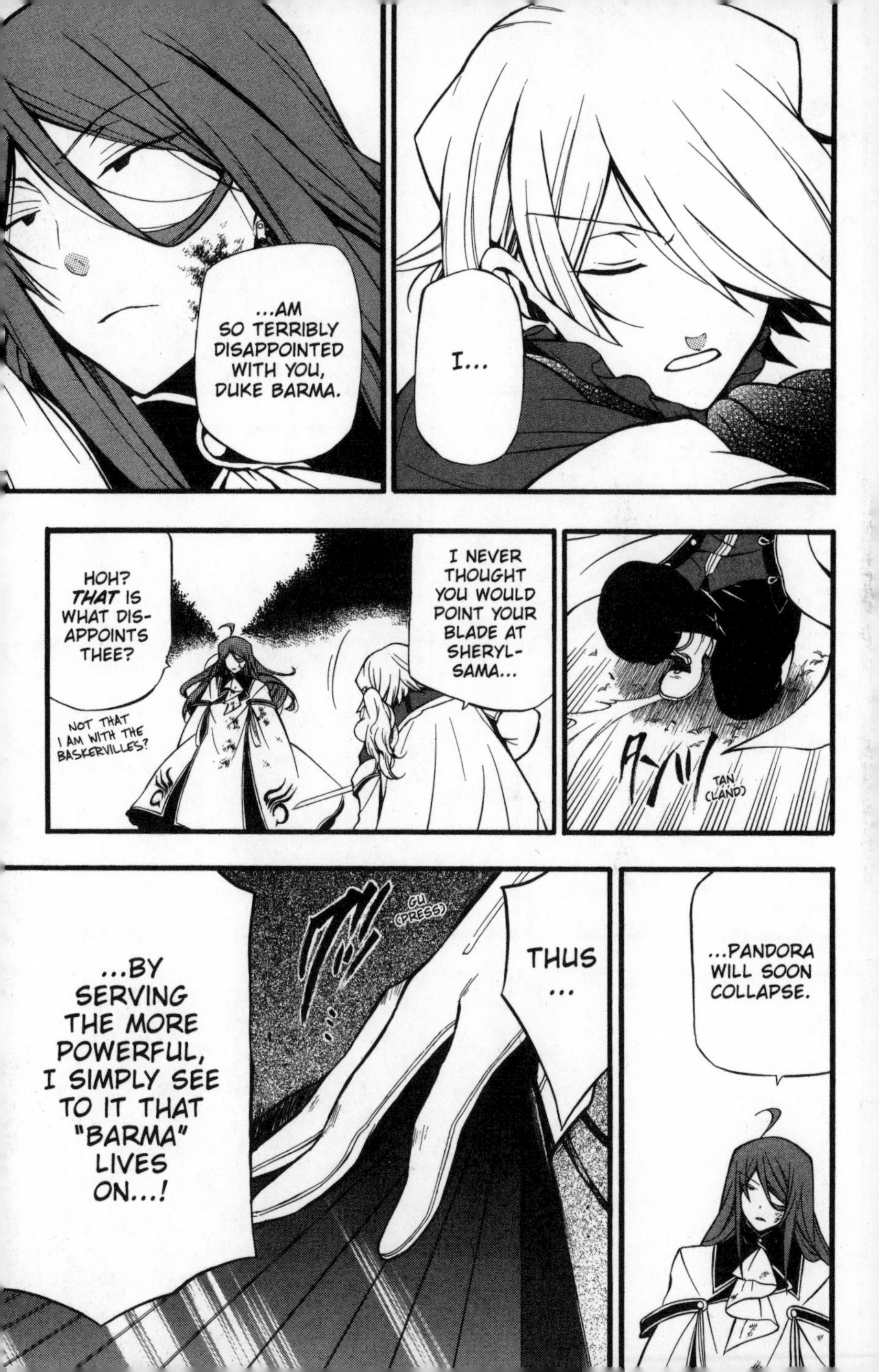
I...
...AM SO TERRIBLY DISAPPOINTED WITH YOU, DUKE BARMA.
TAN (LAND)
I NEVER THOUGHT YOU WOULD POINT YOUR BLADE AT SHERYL-SAMA...
HOH? *THAT* IS WHAT DIS-APPOINTS THEE?
NOT THAT I AM WITH THE BASKERVILLES?
...PANDORA WILL SOON COLLAPSE.
THUS ...
GU (PRESS)
...
...BY SERVING THE MORE POWERFUL, I SIMPLY SEE TO IT THAT "BARMA" LIVES ON...!

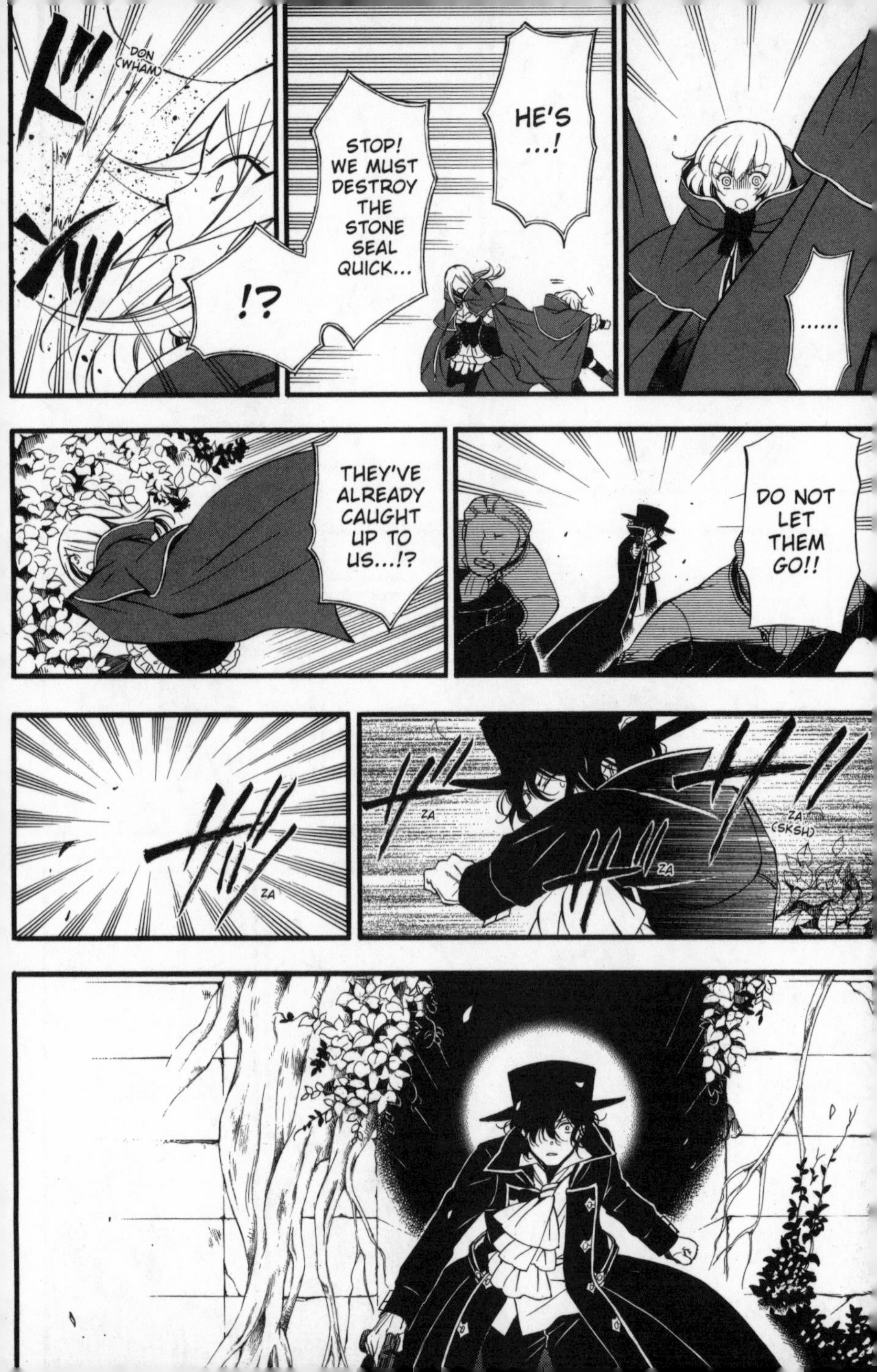
......
HE'S ...!
STOP! WE MUST DESTROY THE STONE SEAL QUICK...
DON (WHAM)
!?
DO NOT LET THEM GO!!
THEY'VE ALREADY CAUGHT UP TO US...!?
ZA (SKSH)
ZA
ZA
ZA

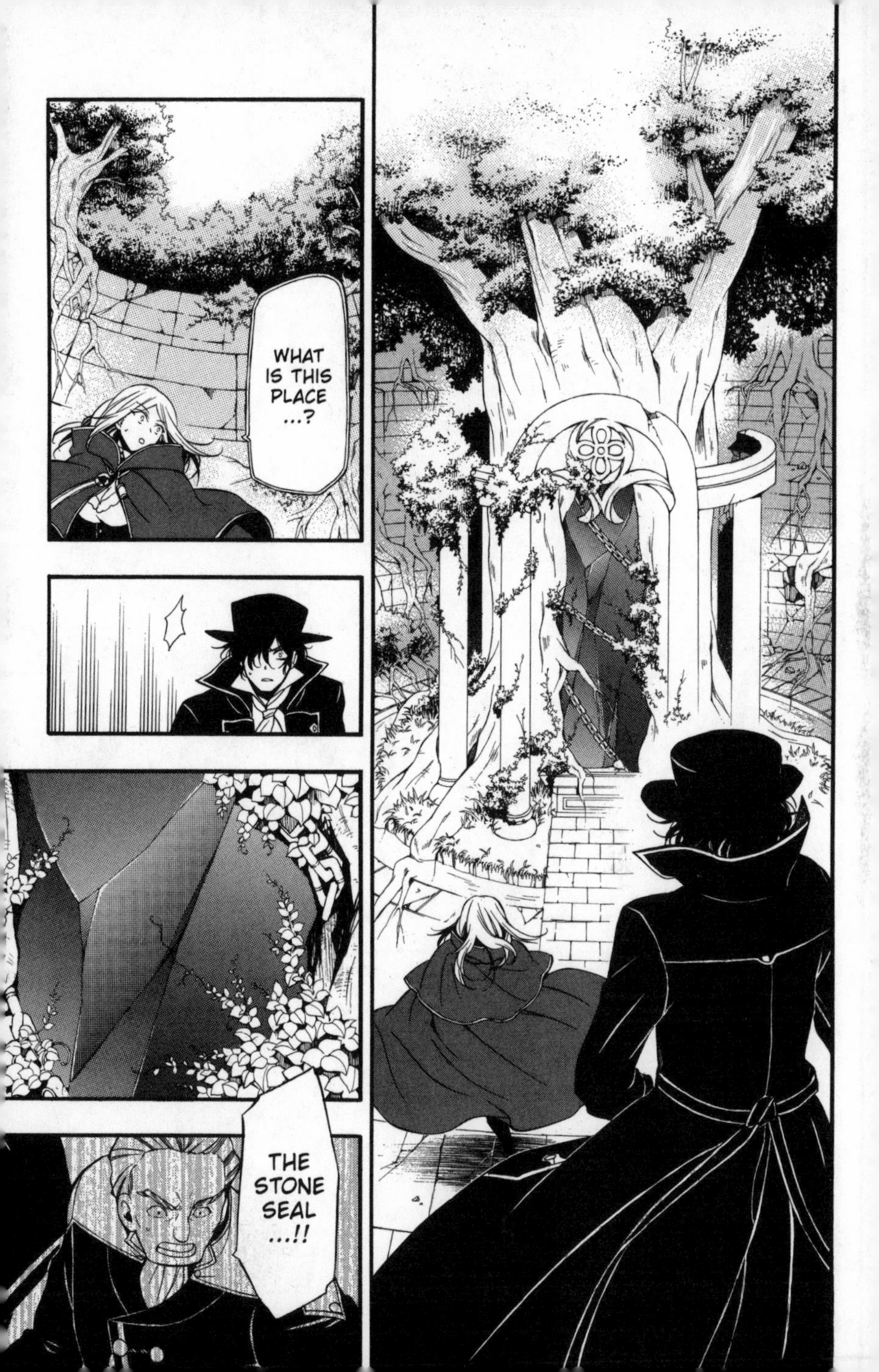
WHAT IS THIS PLACE ...?
THE STONE SEAL ...!!

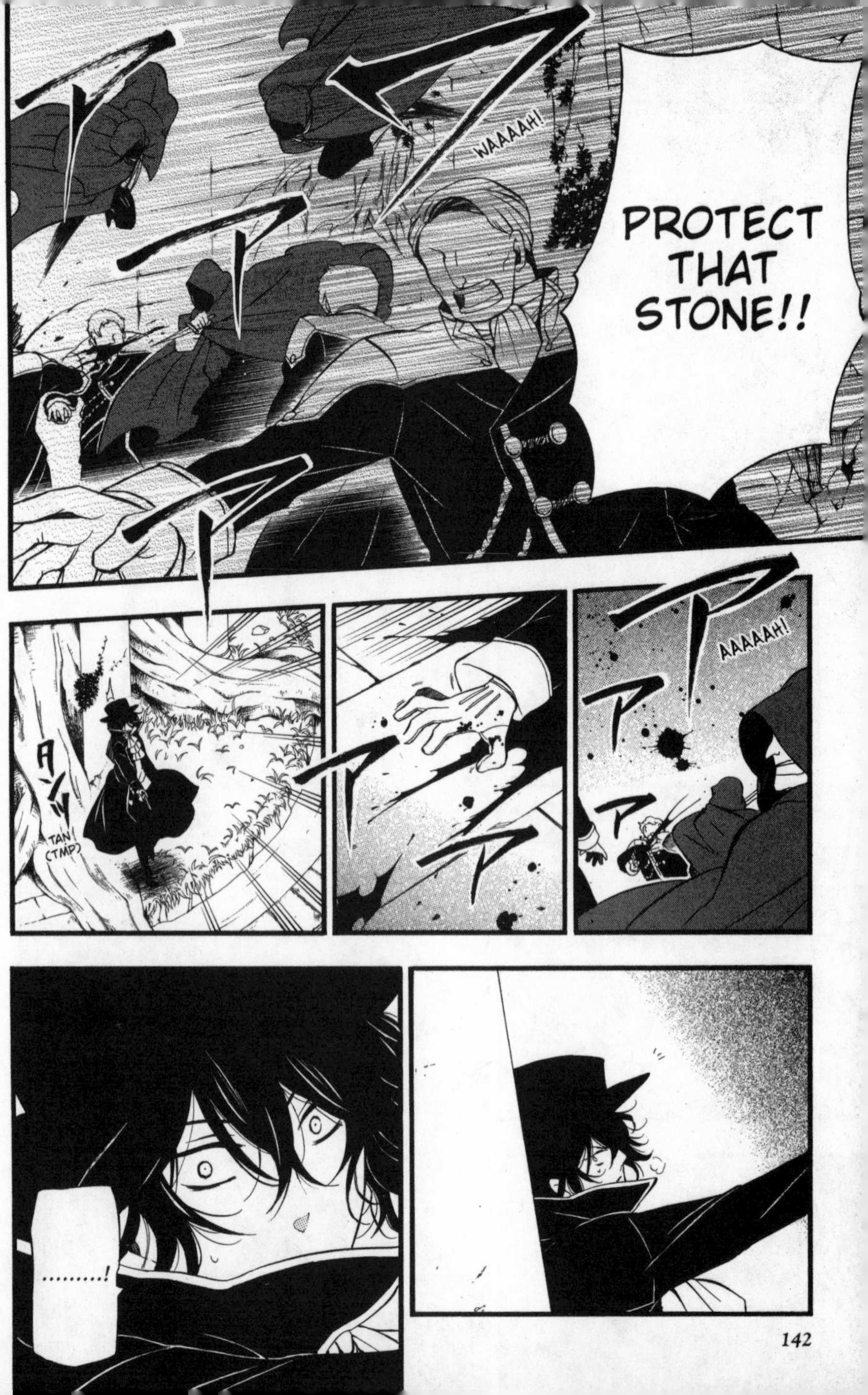
PROTECT THAT STONE!!
WAAAAH!
AAAAAH!
TAN (TMP)
.........!

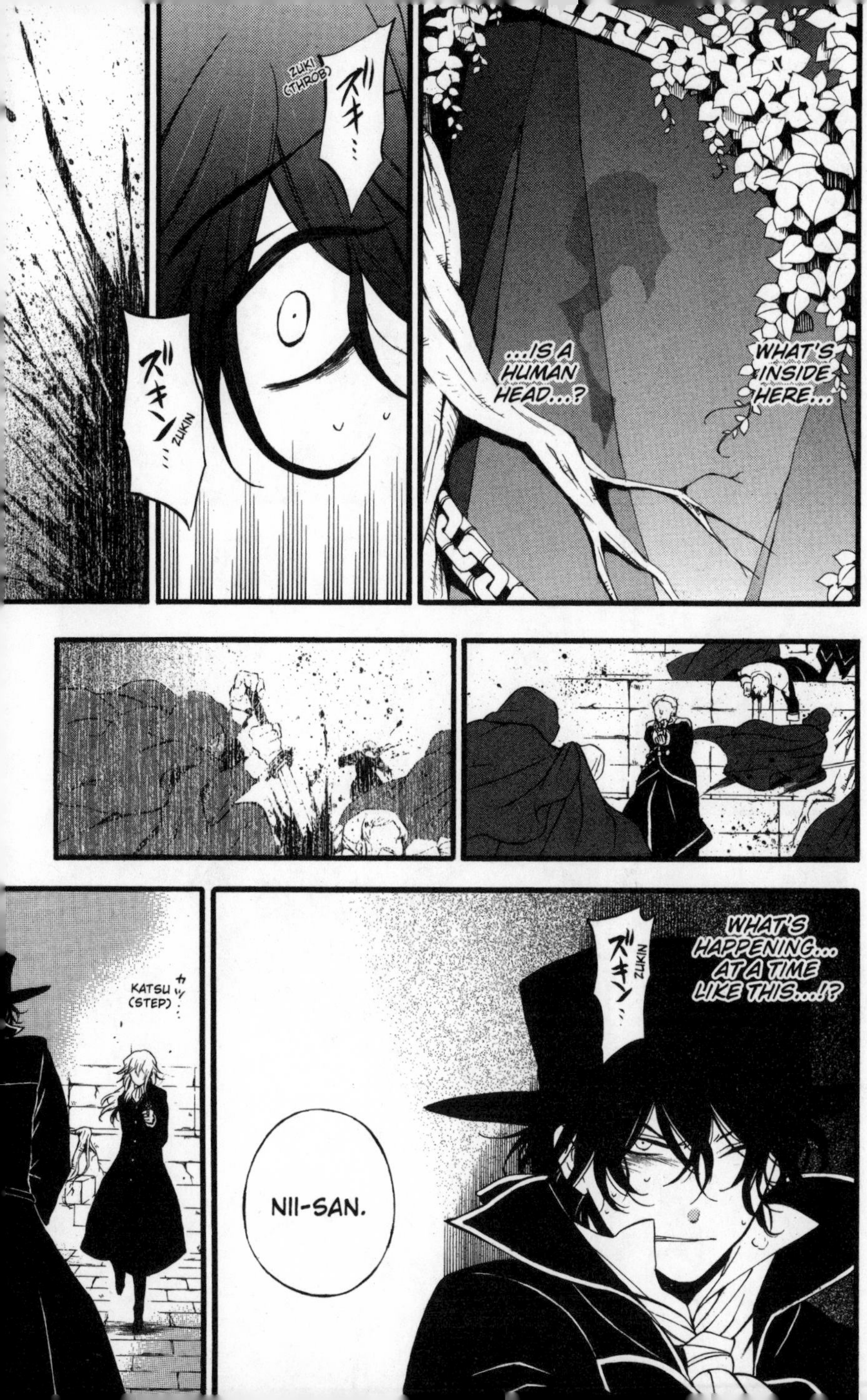
WHAT'S INSIDE HERE...
...IS A HUMAN HEAD...?
ズキ…
ZUKI (THROB)
ズキン…
ZUKIN
WHAT'S HAPPENING... AT A TIME LIKE THIS...!?
ズキン…
ZUKIN
NII-SAN.
カッ…
KATSU (STEP)

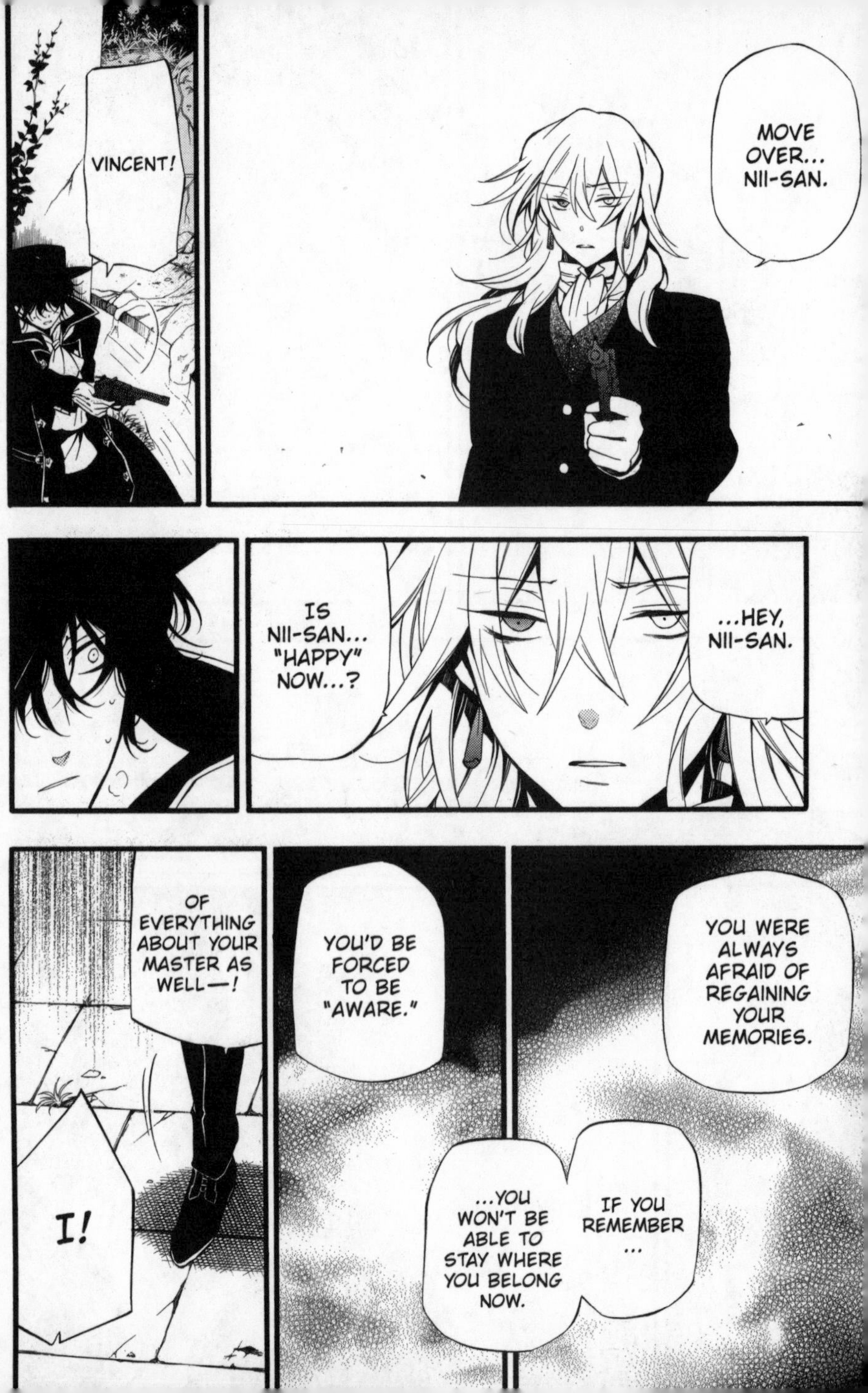
MOVE OVER... NII-SAN.
VINCENT!
...HEY, NII-SAN.
IS NII-SAN... "HAPPY" NOW...?
YOU WERE ALWAYS AFRAID OF REGAINING YOUR MEMORIES.
IF YOU REMEMBER ...
...YOU WON'T BE ABLE TO STAY WHERE YOU BELONG NOW.
YOU'D BE FORCED TO BE "AWARE."
OF EVERYTHING ABOUT YOUR MASTER AS WELL—!
I!

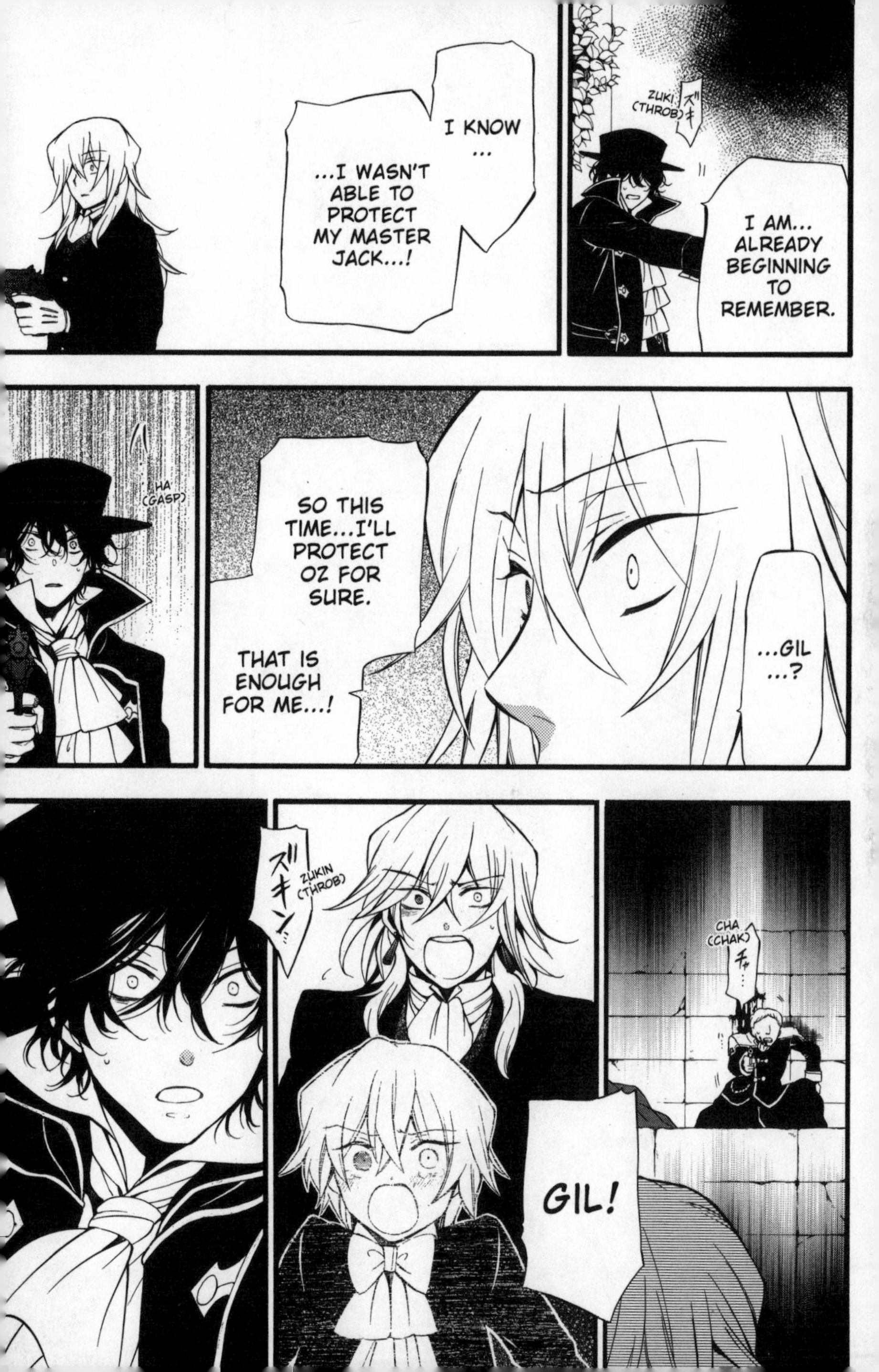
ズキ
ZUKI (THROB)
I AM... ALREADY BEGINNING TO REMEMBER.
I KNOW ...
...I WASN'T ABLE TO PROTECT MY MASTER JACK...!
...GIL ...?
SO THIS TIME...I'LL PROTECT OZ FOR SURE.
THAT IS ENOUGH FOR ME...!
HA (GASP)
CHA (CHAK)
チャ…
ズキン
ZUKIN (THROB)
GIL!

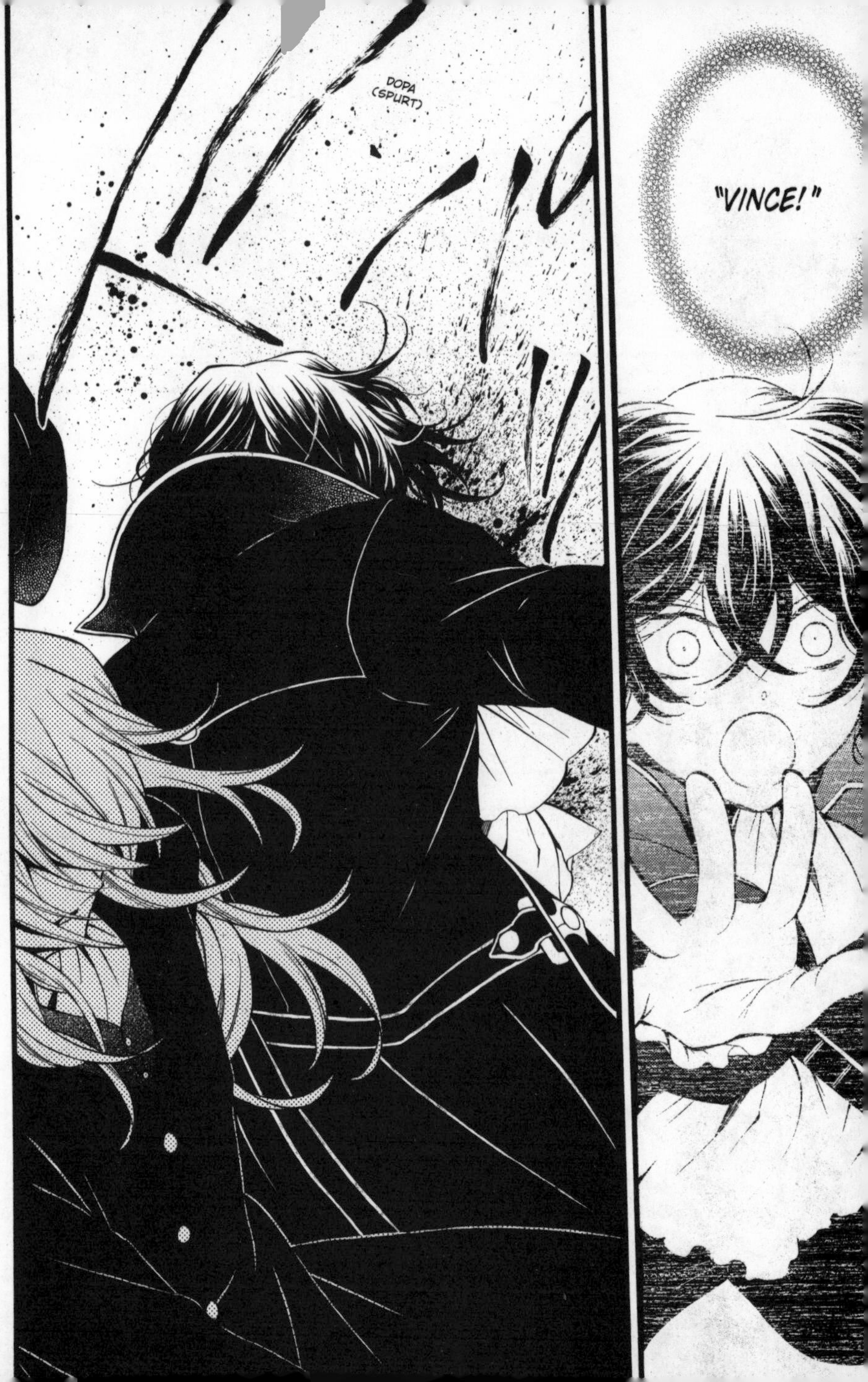
"VINCE!"
DOPA
(SPURT)

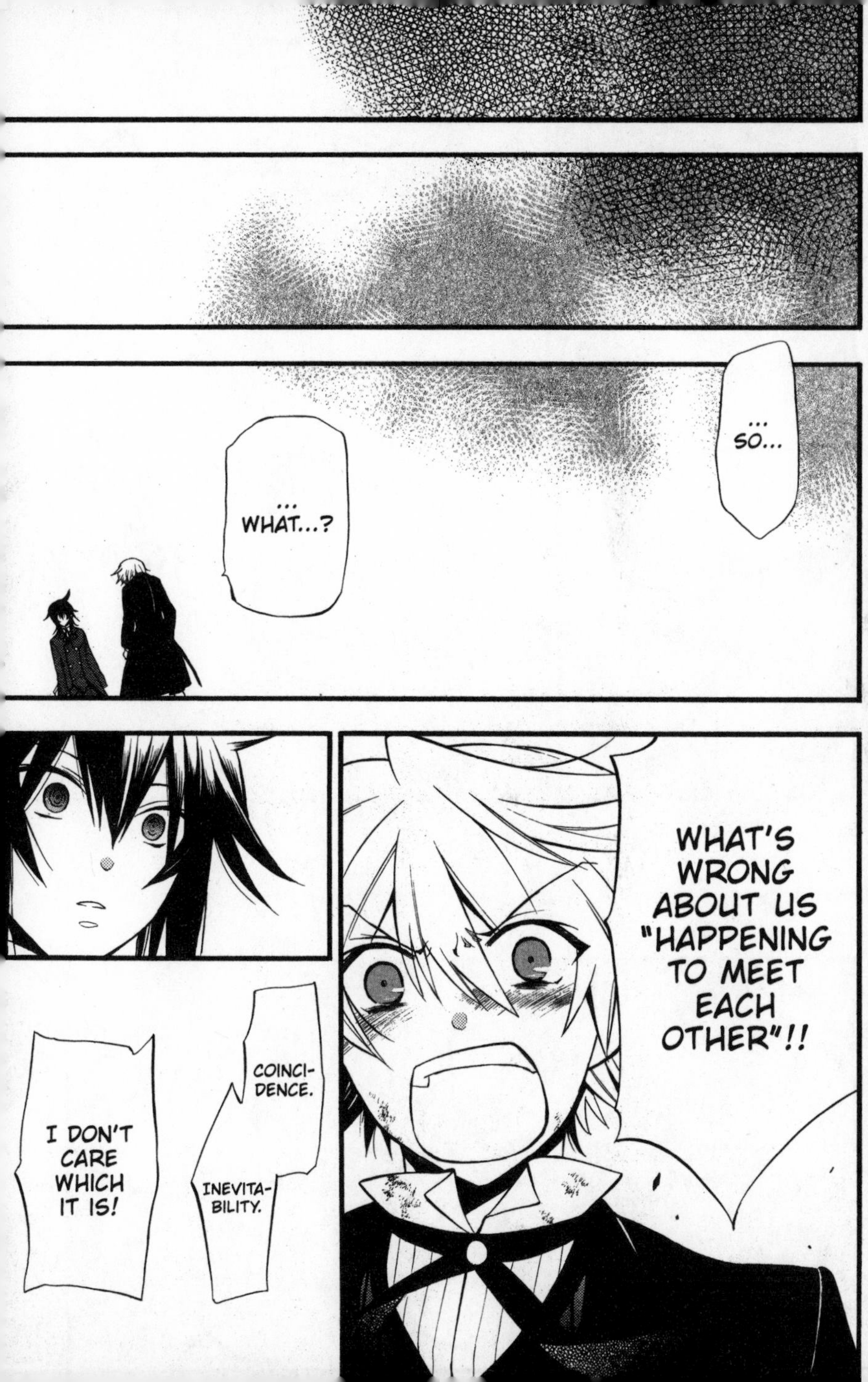
... SO...
... WHAT...?
WHAT'S WRONG ABOUT US "HAPPENING TO MEET EACH OTHER"!!
COINCI-DENCE.
INEVITA-BILITY.
I DON'T CARE WHICH IT IS!

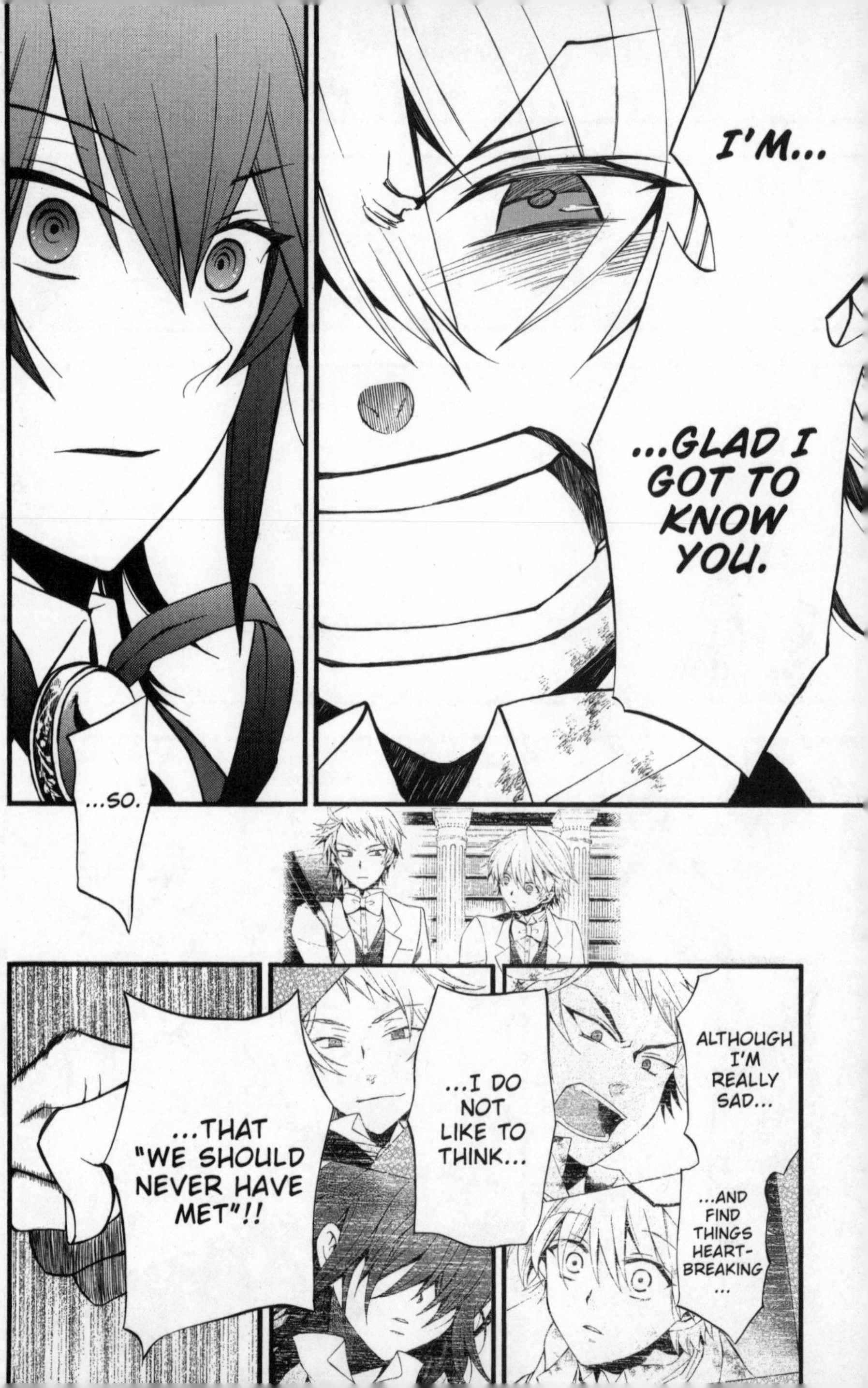
I'M...
...GLAD I GOT TO KNOW YOU.
...SO.
ALTHOUGH I'M REALLY SAD...
...AND FIND THINGS HEART-BREAKING ...
...I DO NOT LIKE TO THINK...
...THAT "WE SHOULD NEVER HAVE MET"!!

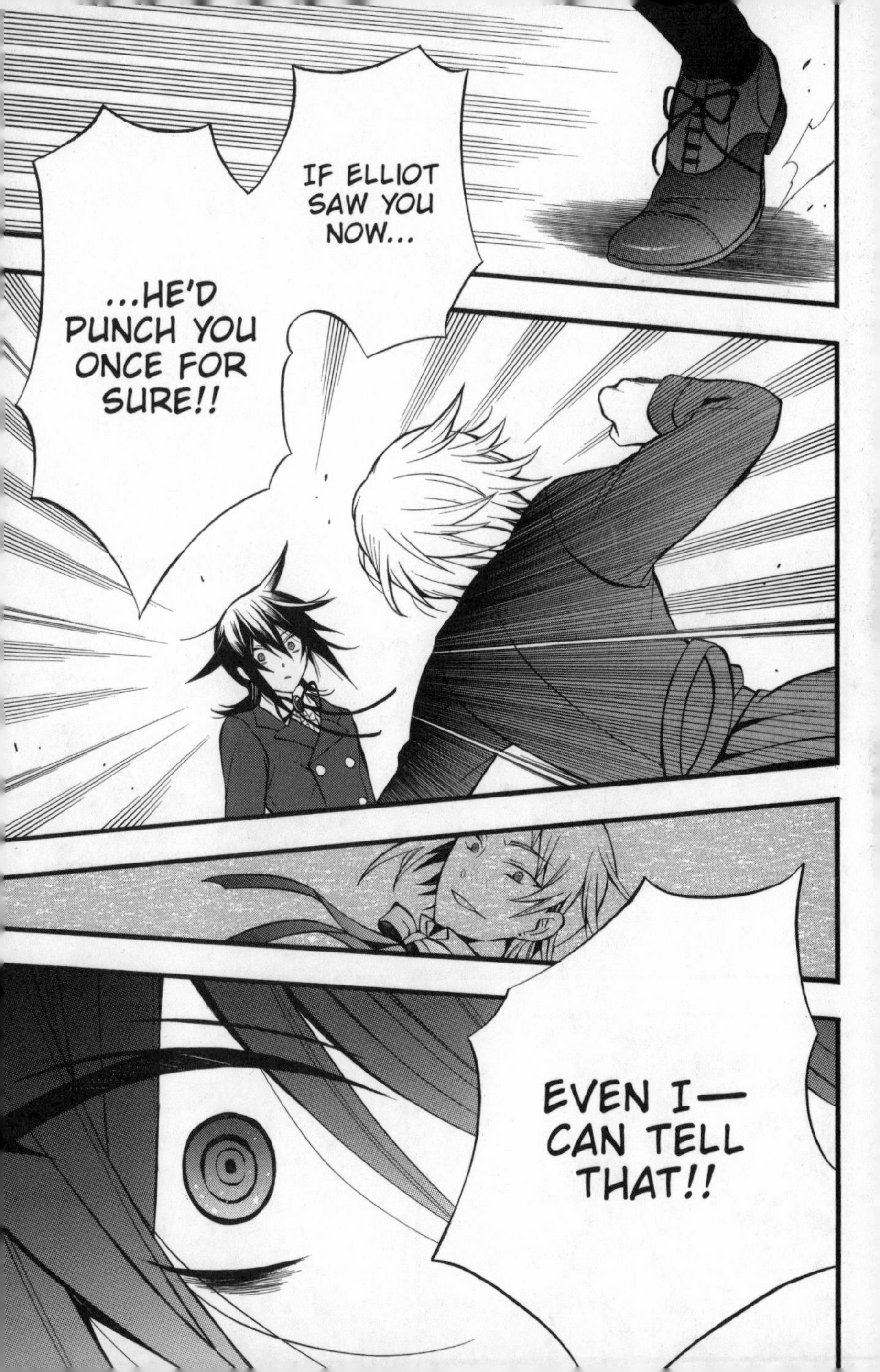
IF ELLIOT SAW YOU NOW...
...HE'D PUNCH YOU ONCE FOR SURE!!
EVEN I— CAN TELL THAT!!

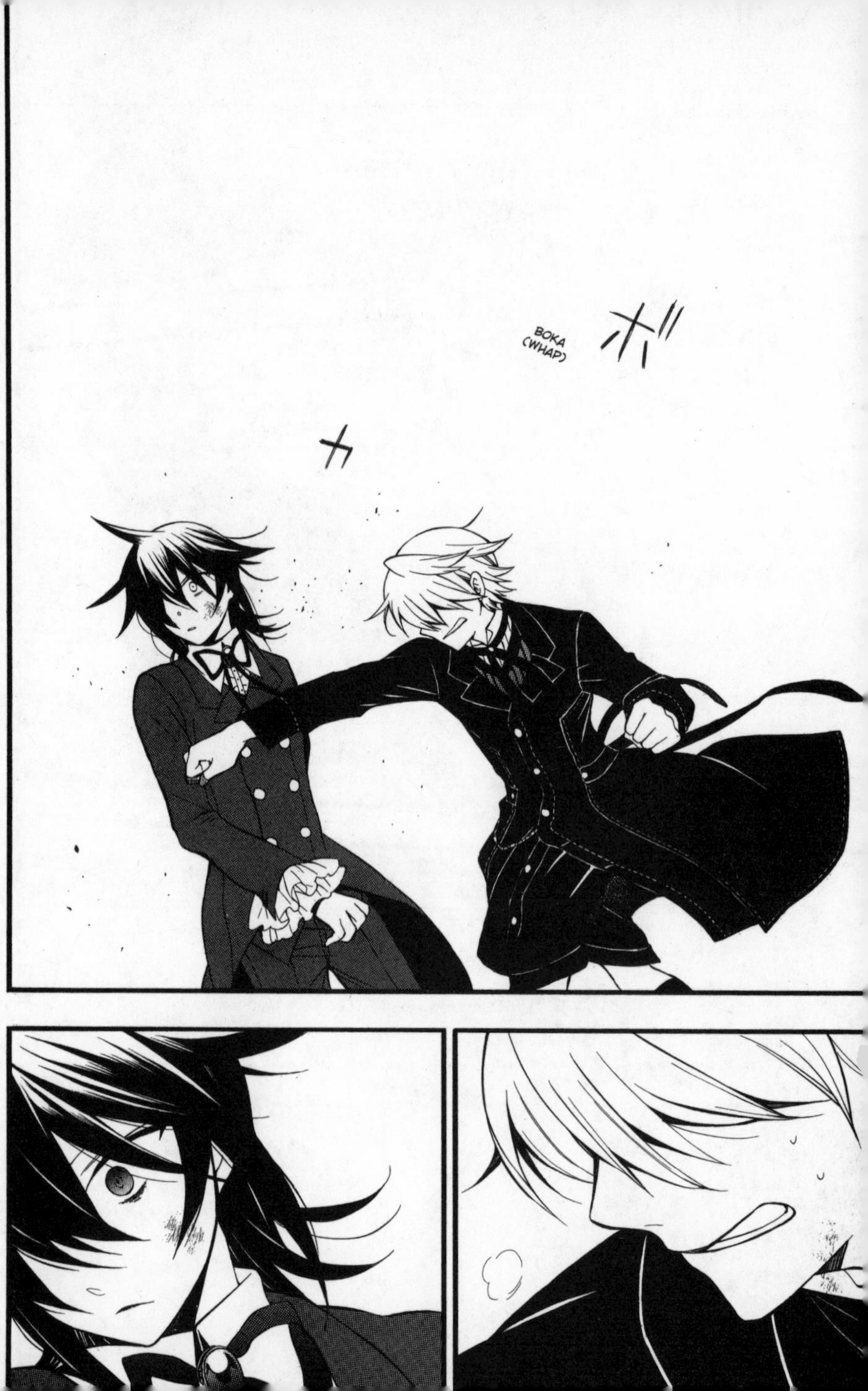
ボカ
BOKA
(WHAP)

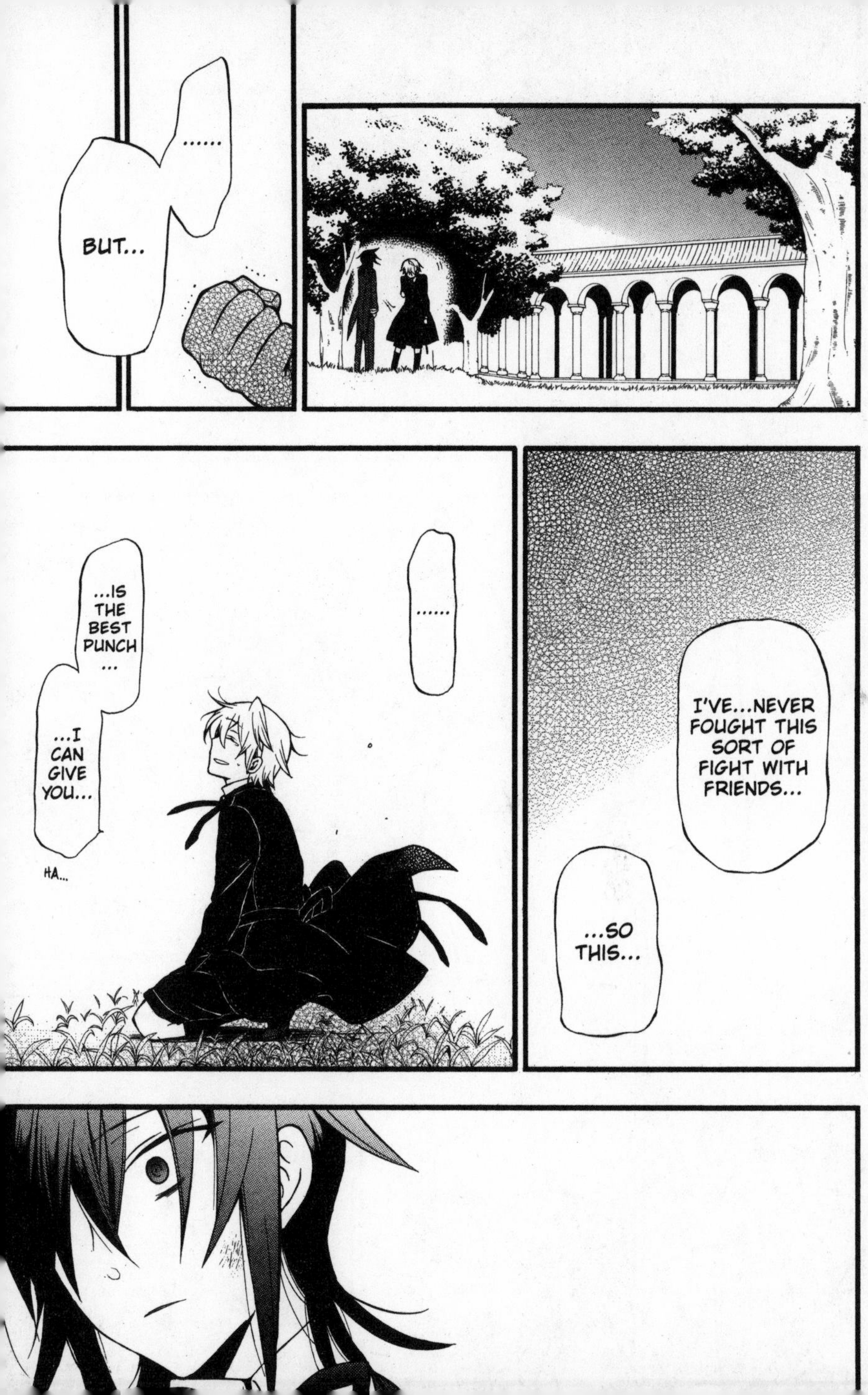
......
BUT...
I'VE...NEVER FOUGHT THIS SORT OF FIGHT WITH FRIENDS...
...SO THIS...
......
...IS THE BEST PUNCH...
...I CAN GIVE YOU...
HA...

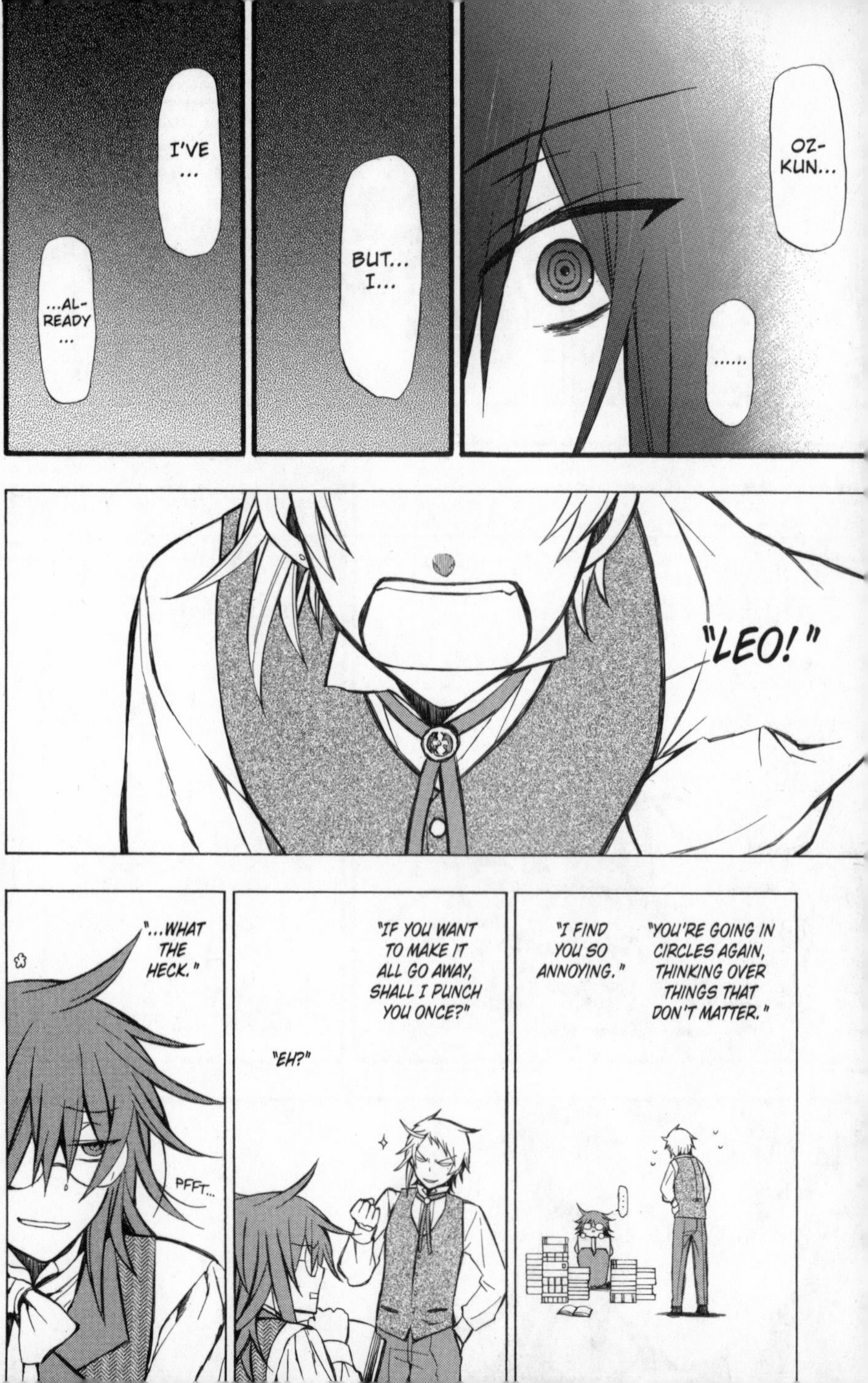
OZ-KUN...
......
BUT... I...
I'VE ...
...AL-READY ...
"LEO!"
"YOU'RE GOING IN CIRCLES AGAIN, THINKING OVER THINGS THAT DON'T MATTER."
"I FIND YOU SO ANNOYING."
...
"IF YOU WANT TO MAKE IT ALL GO AWAY, SHALL I PUNCH YOU ONCE?"
"EH?"
"...WHAT THE HECK."
PFFT...

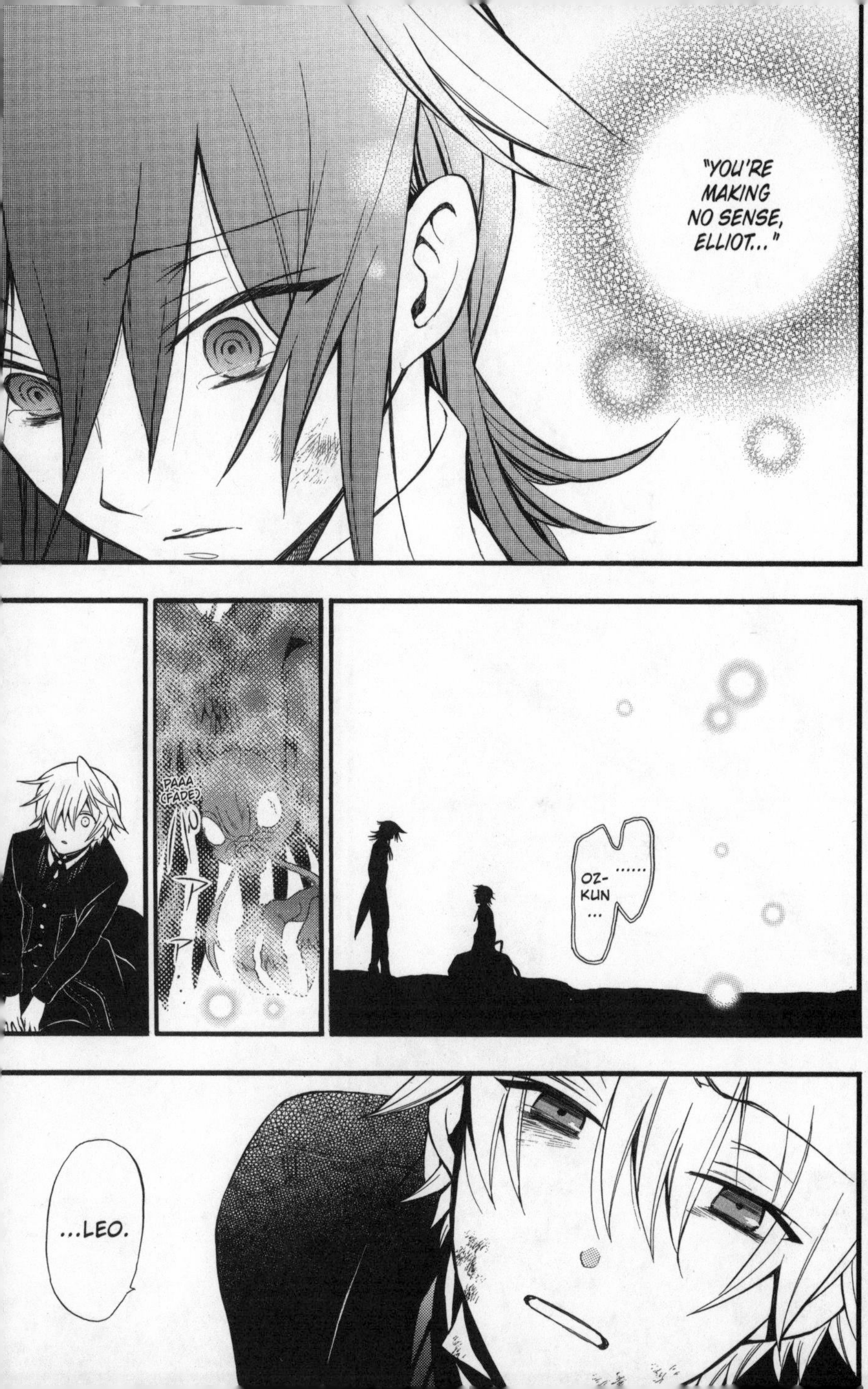
"YOU'RE MAKING NO SENSE, ELLIOT..."
...... OZ-KUN ...
PAAA (FADE)
...LEO.

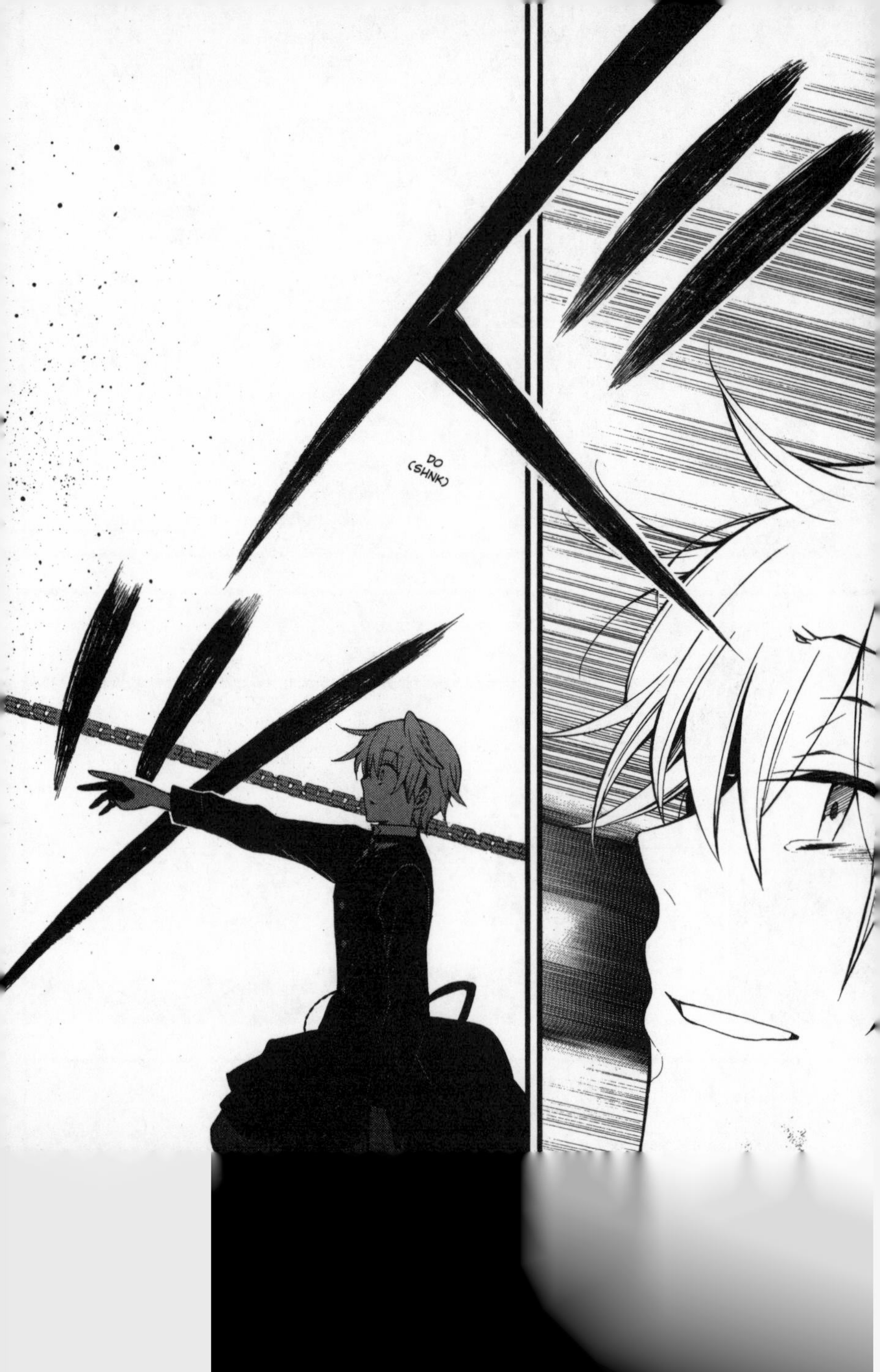
DO
(SHNK)

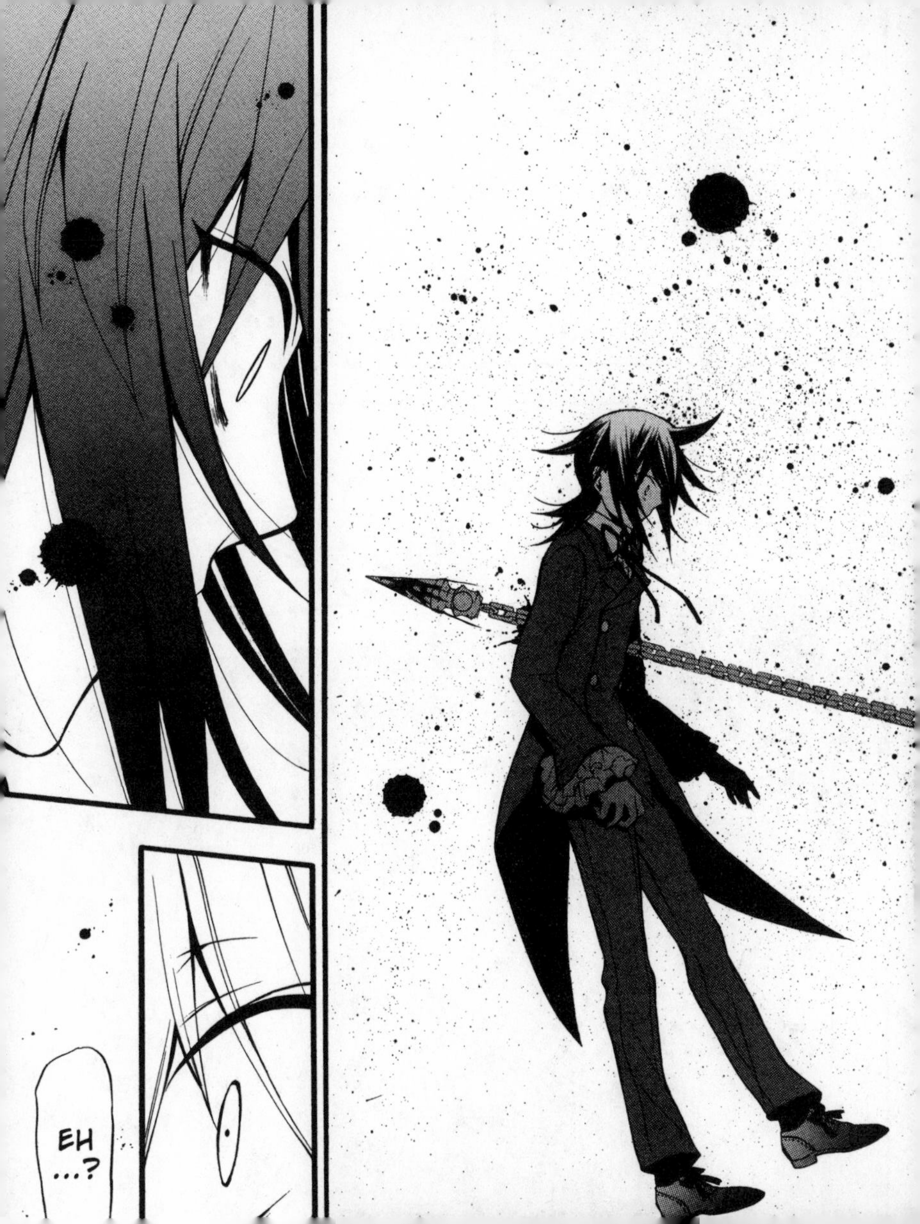
EH ...?

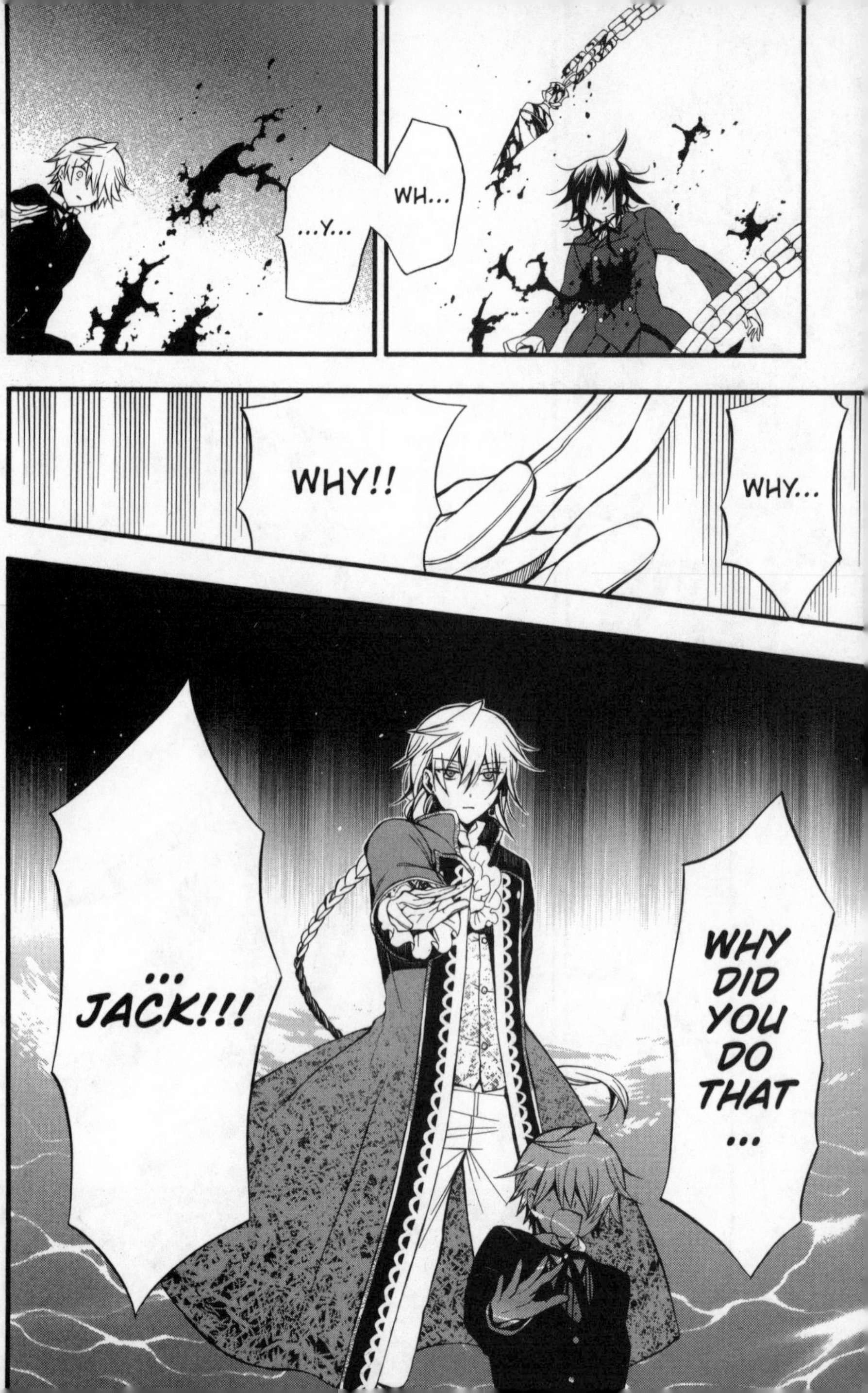
WH...
...Y...
WHY...
WHY!!
WHY DID YOU DO THAT ...
... JACK!!!

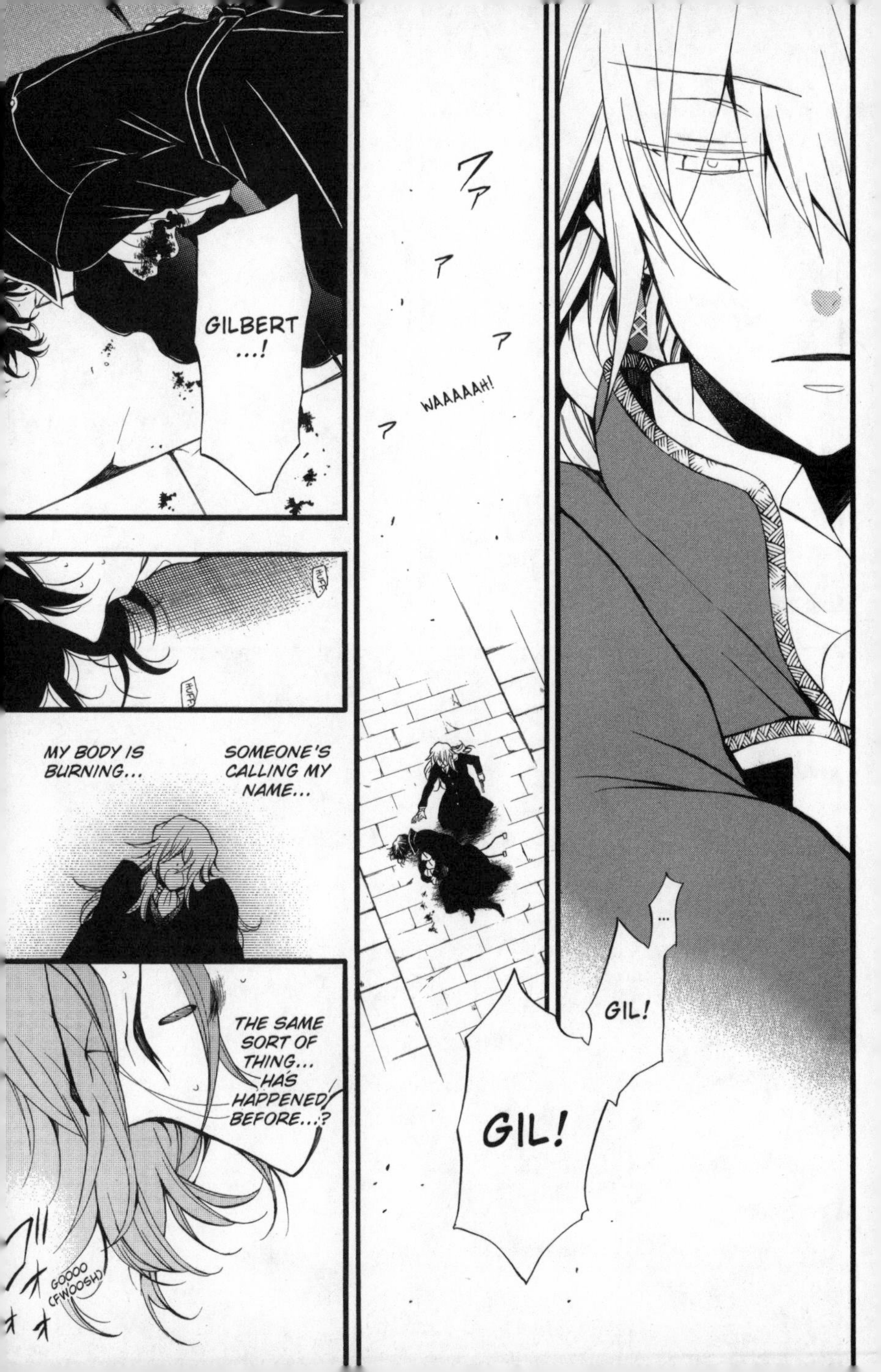
...
GIL!
GIL!
WAAAAAH!
GILBERT ...!
HUFF
HUFF
SOMEONE'S CALLING MY NAME...
MY BODY IS BURNING...
THE SAME SORT OF THING... HAS HAPPENED BEFORE...?
GOOOO (FWOOSH)

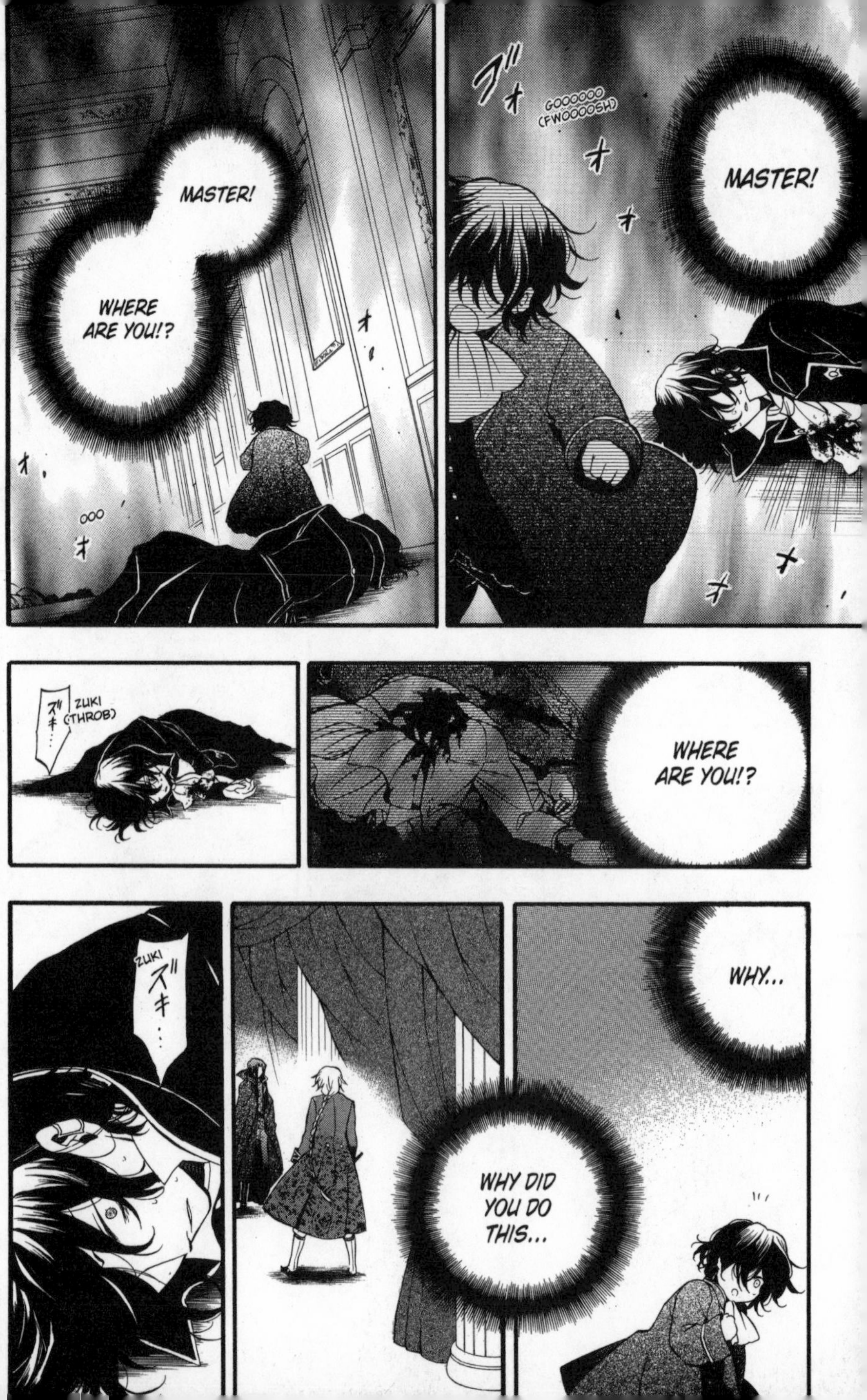
GOOOOOO (FWOOOOSH)
MASTER!
MASTER!
WHERE ARE YOU!?
OOO
WHERE ARE YOU!?
ZUKI (THROB)
WHY...
WHY DID YOU DO THIS...
ZUKI

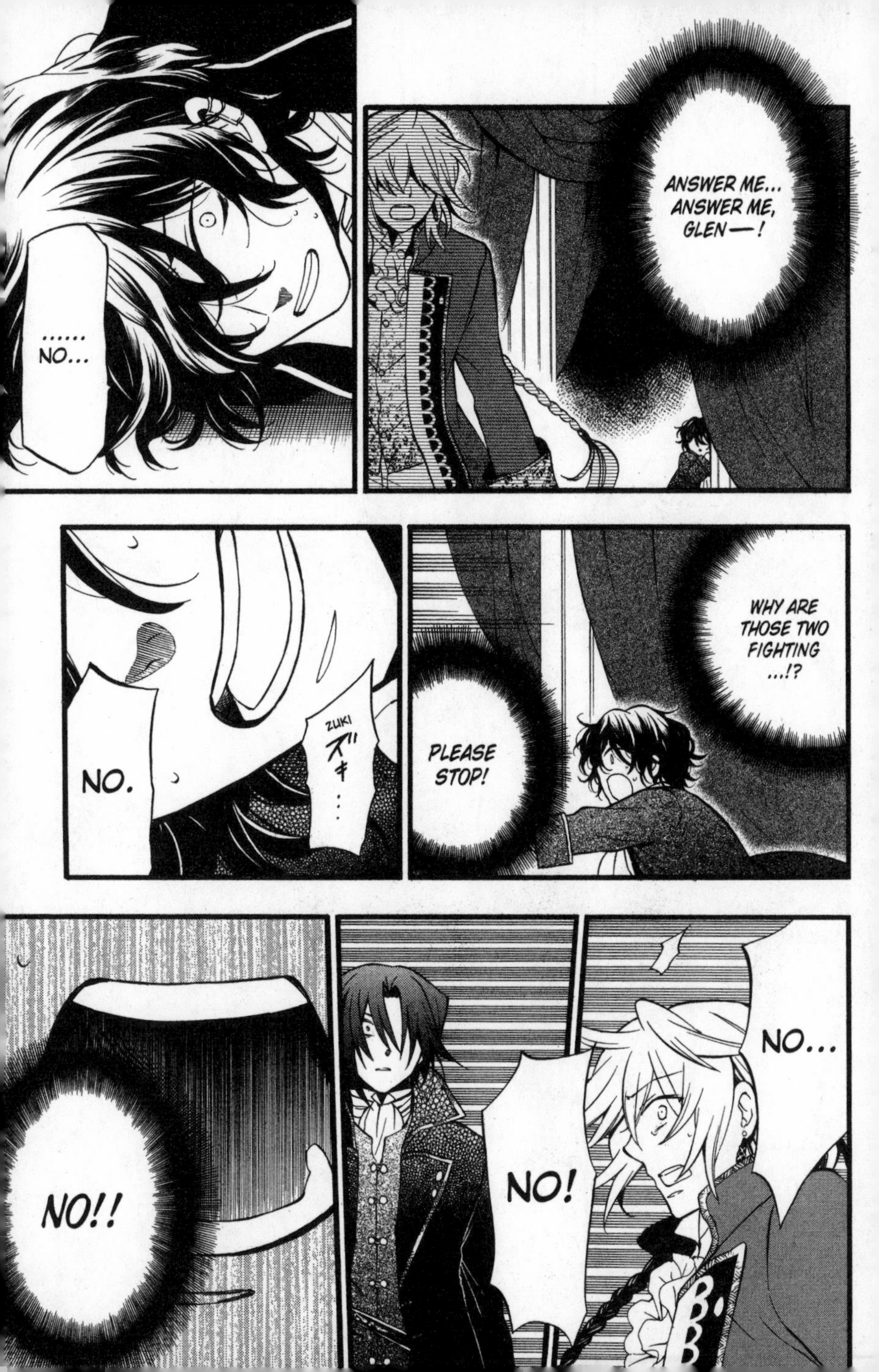
ANSWER ME... ANSWER ME, GLEN—!
...... NO...
WHY ARE THOSE TWO FIGHTING ...!?
PLEASE STOP!
ZUKI
ズキ...
NO.
NO...
NO!
NO!!

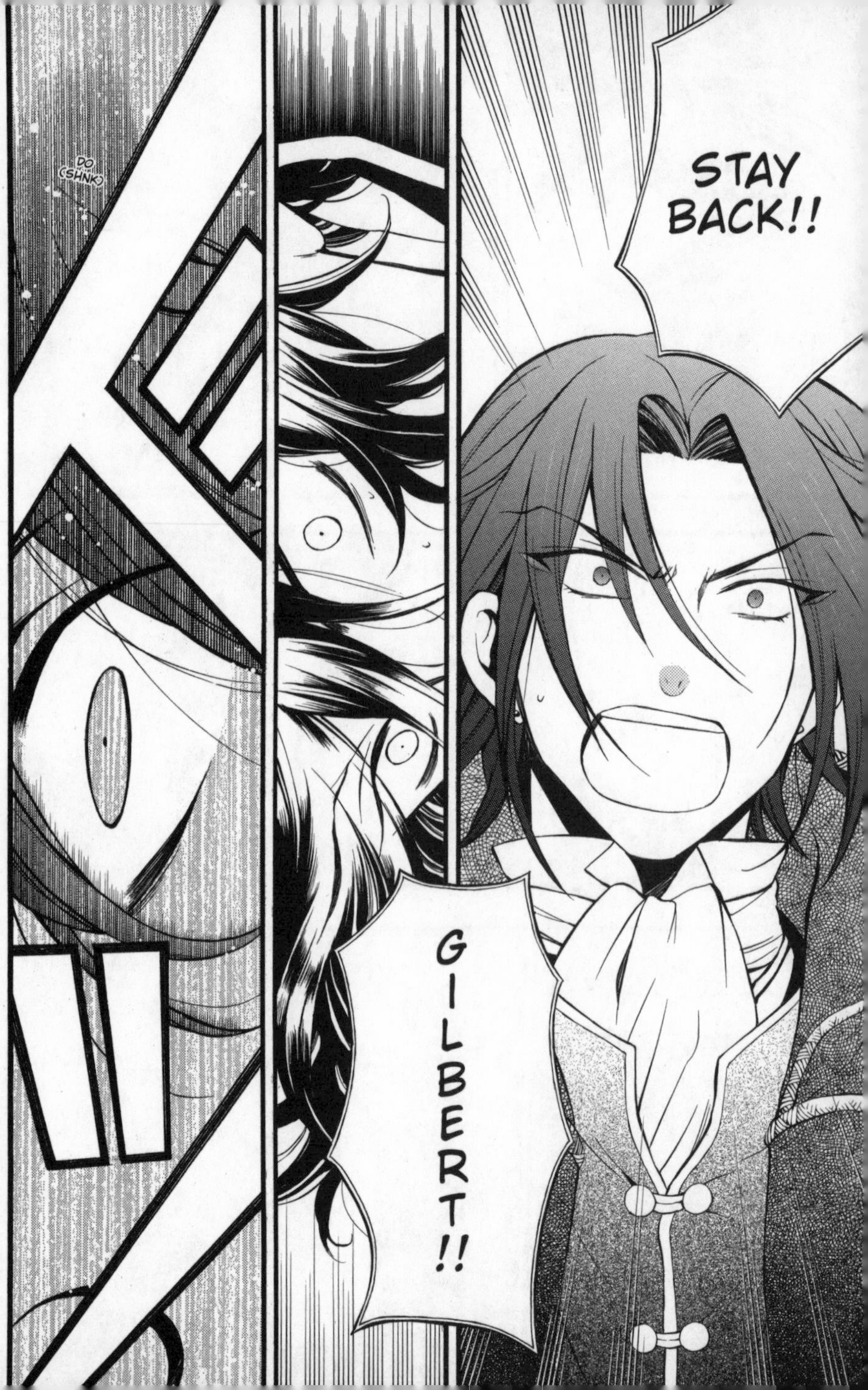
STAY BACK!!
GILBERT!!
DO (SHNK)

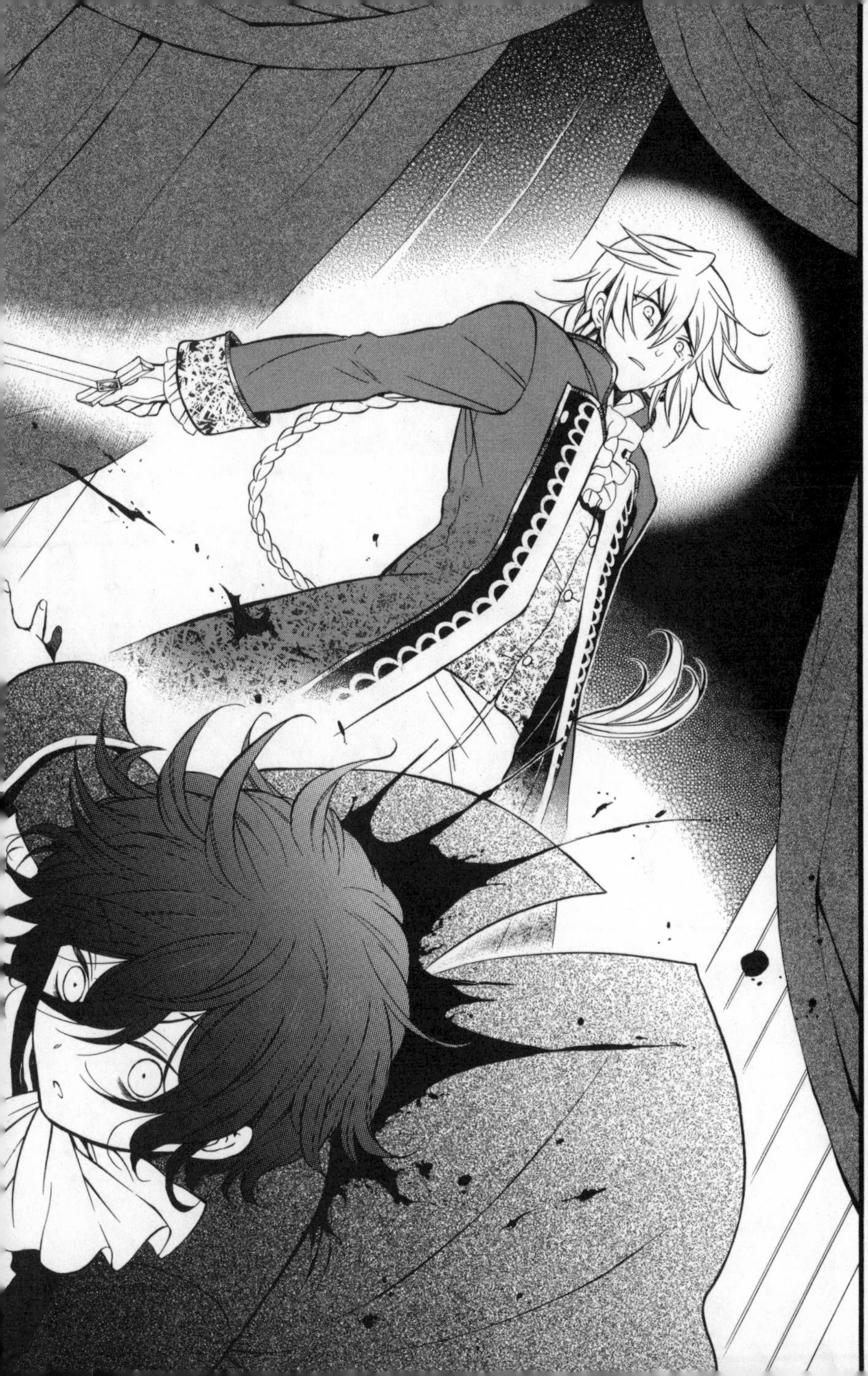

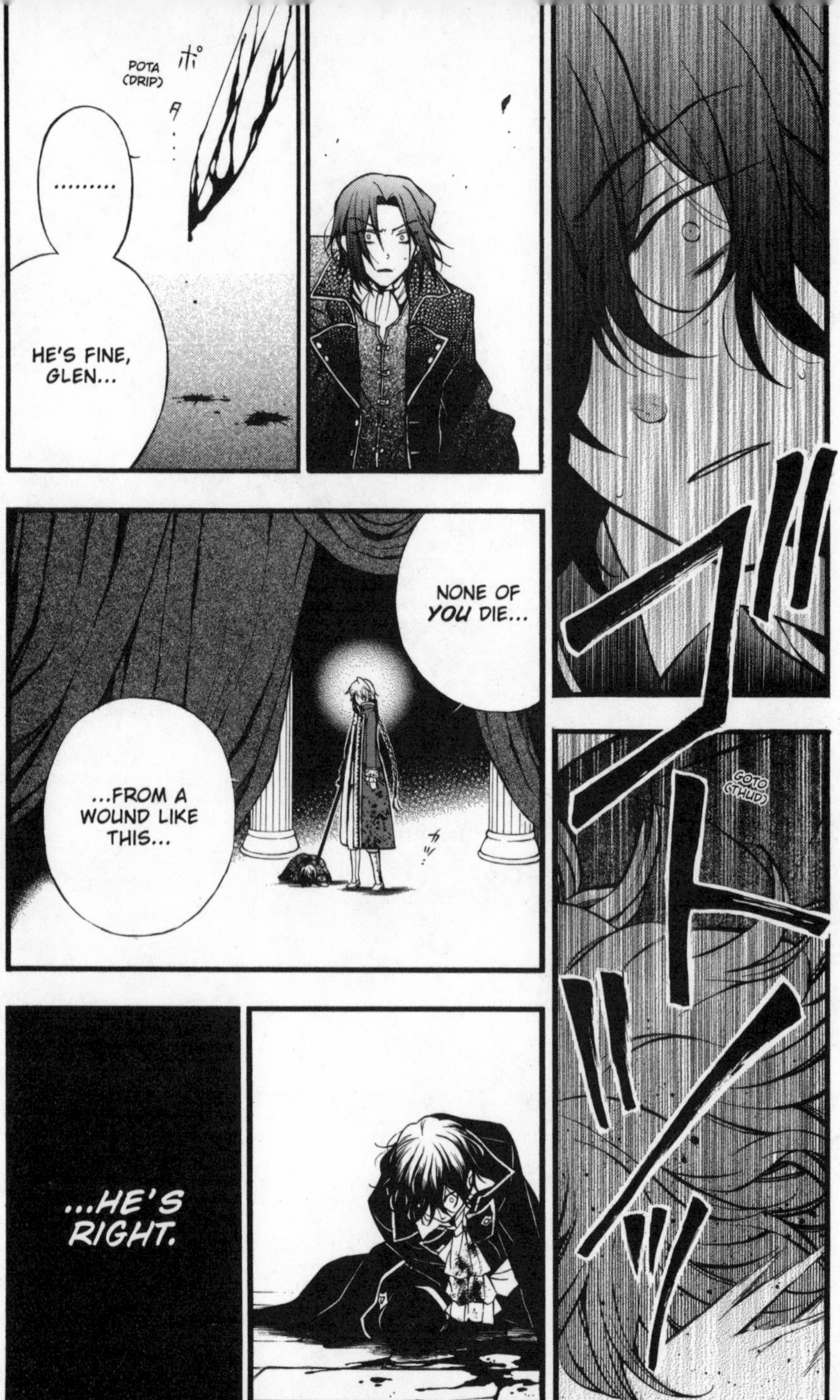
GOTO (THUD)
POTA (DRIP)
....
HE'S FINE, GLEN...
NONE OF *YOU* DIE...
...FROM A WOUND LIKE THIS...
...HE'S RIGHT.

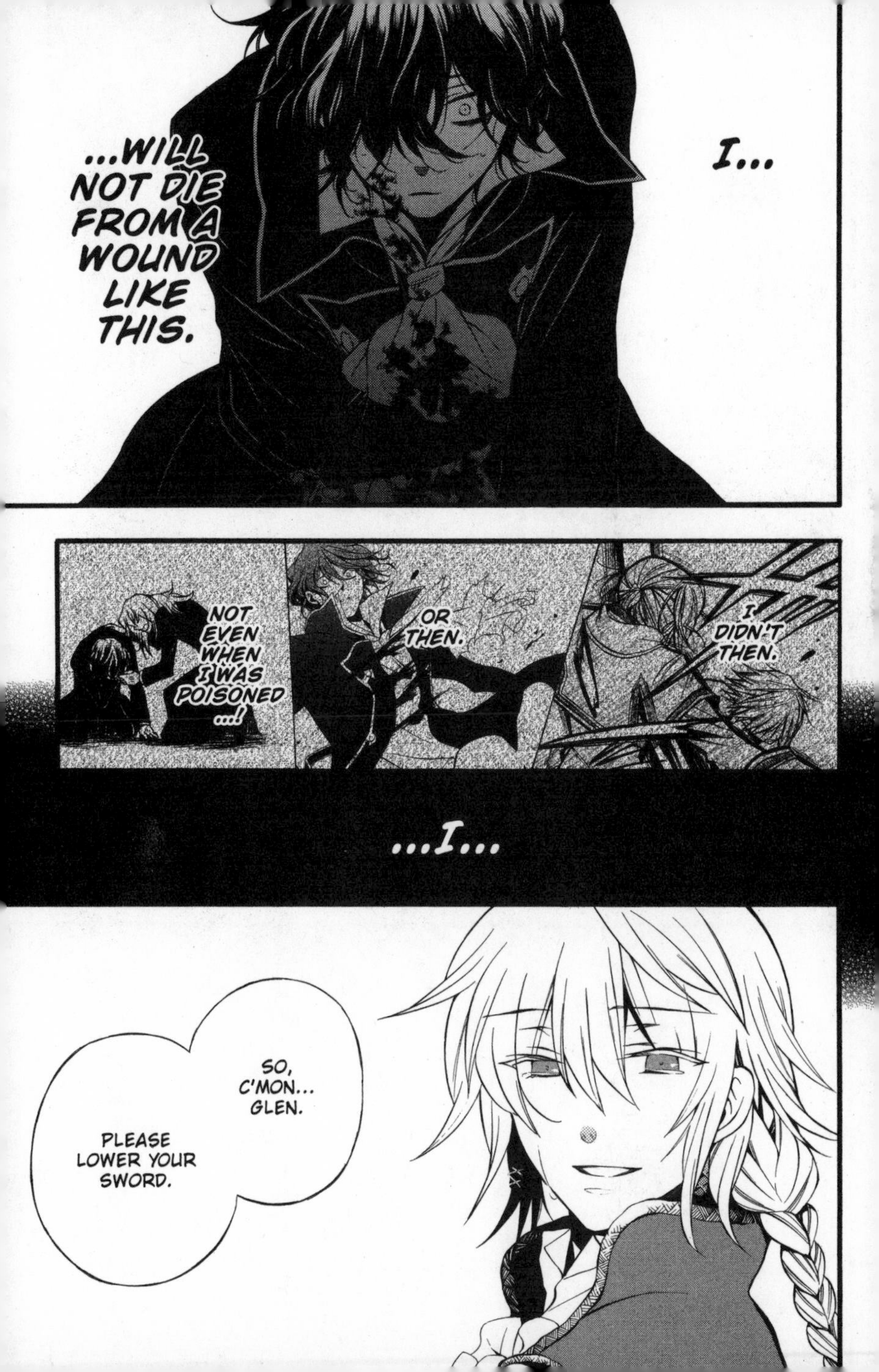
I...
...WILL NOT DIE FROM A WOUND LIKE THIS.
I DIDN'T THEN.
OR THEN.
NOT EVEN WHEN I WAS POISONED ...!
...I...
SO, C'MON... GLEN.
PLEASE LOWER YOUR SWORD.

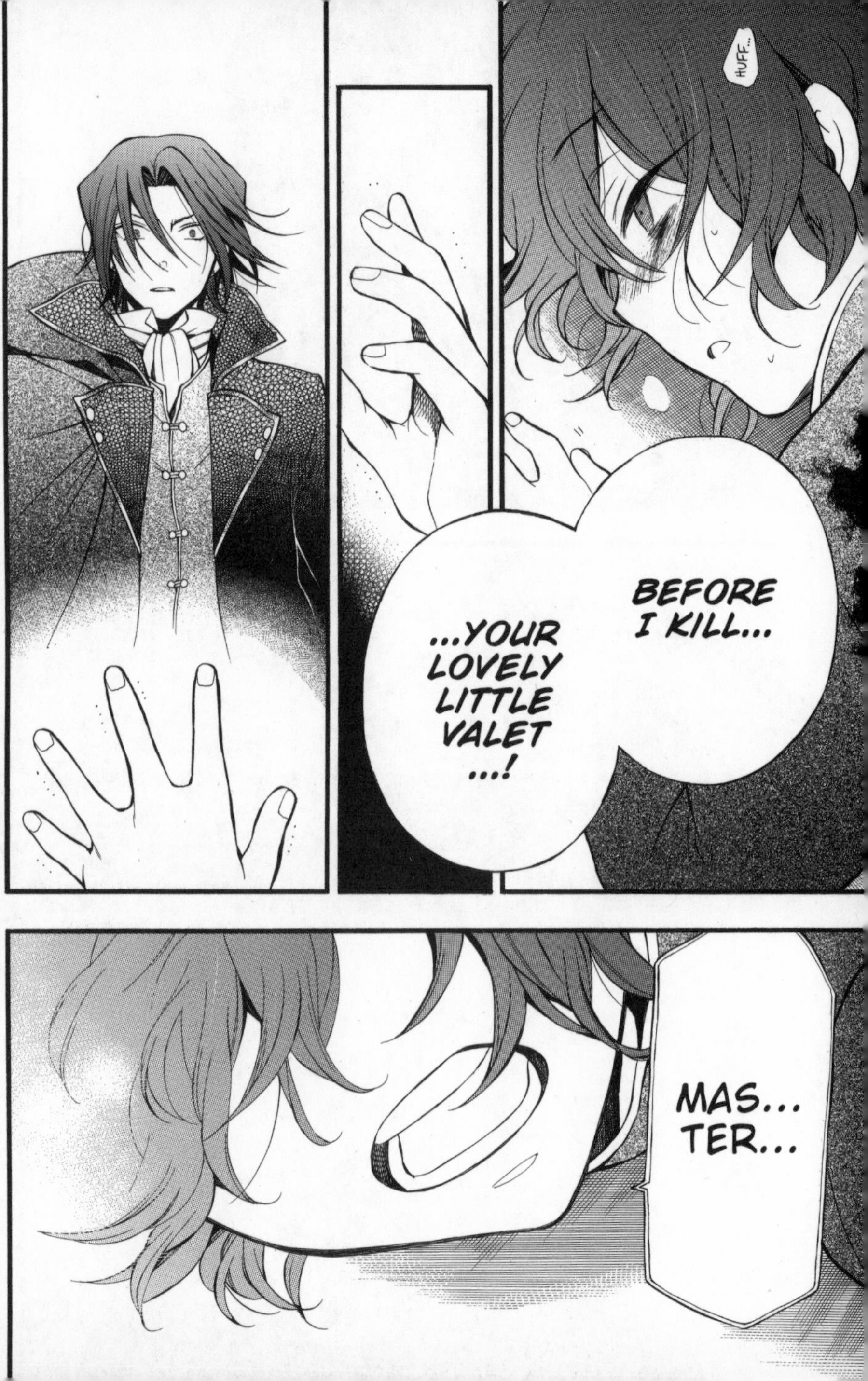
HUFF...
BEFORE I KILL...
...YOUR LOVELY LITTLE VALET ...!
MAS... TER...

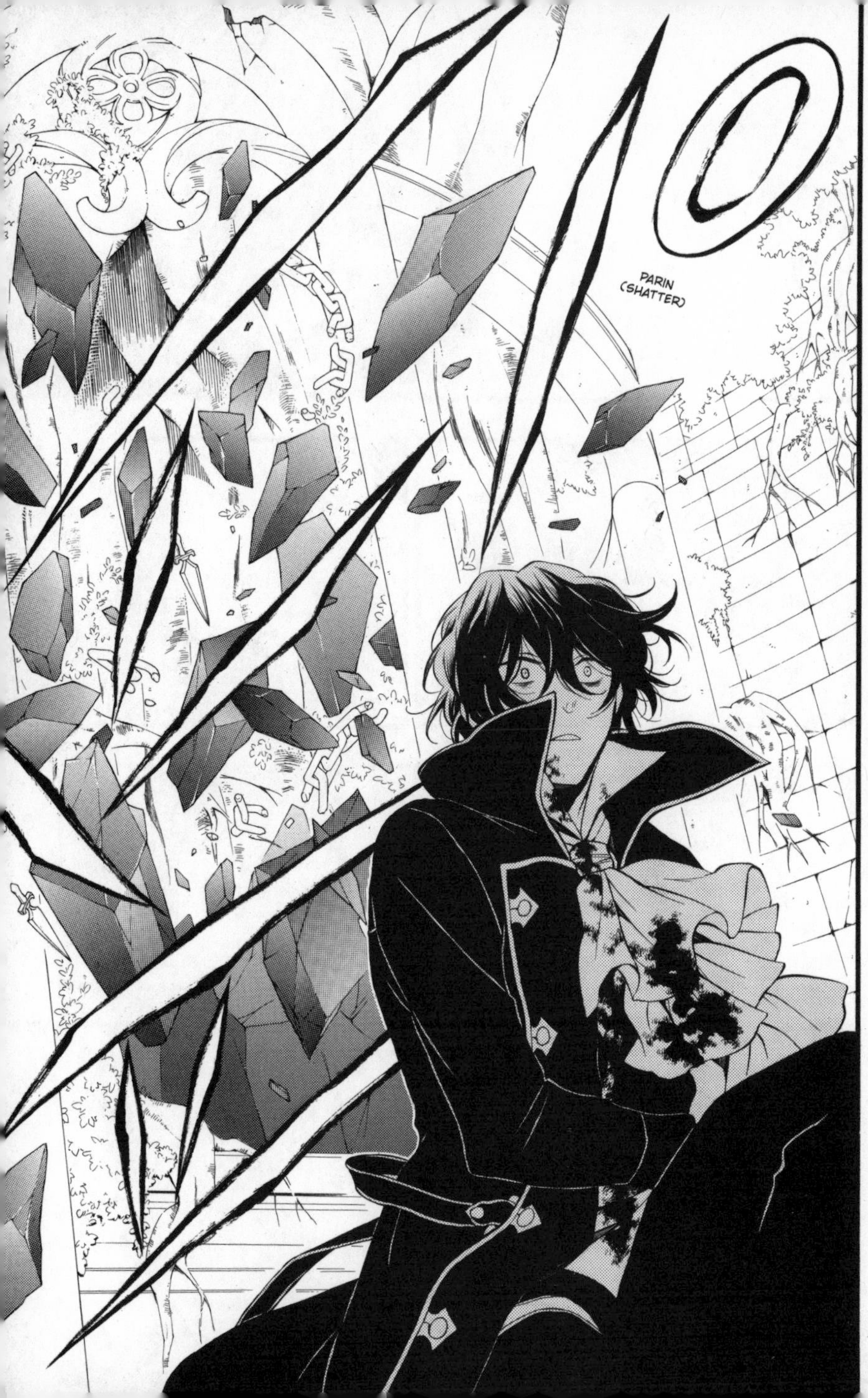
PARIN
(SHATTER)

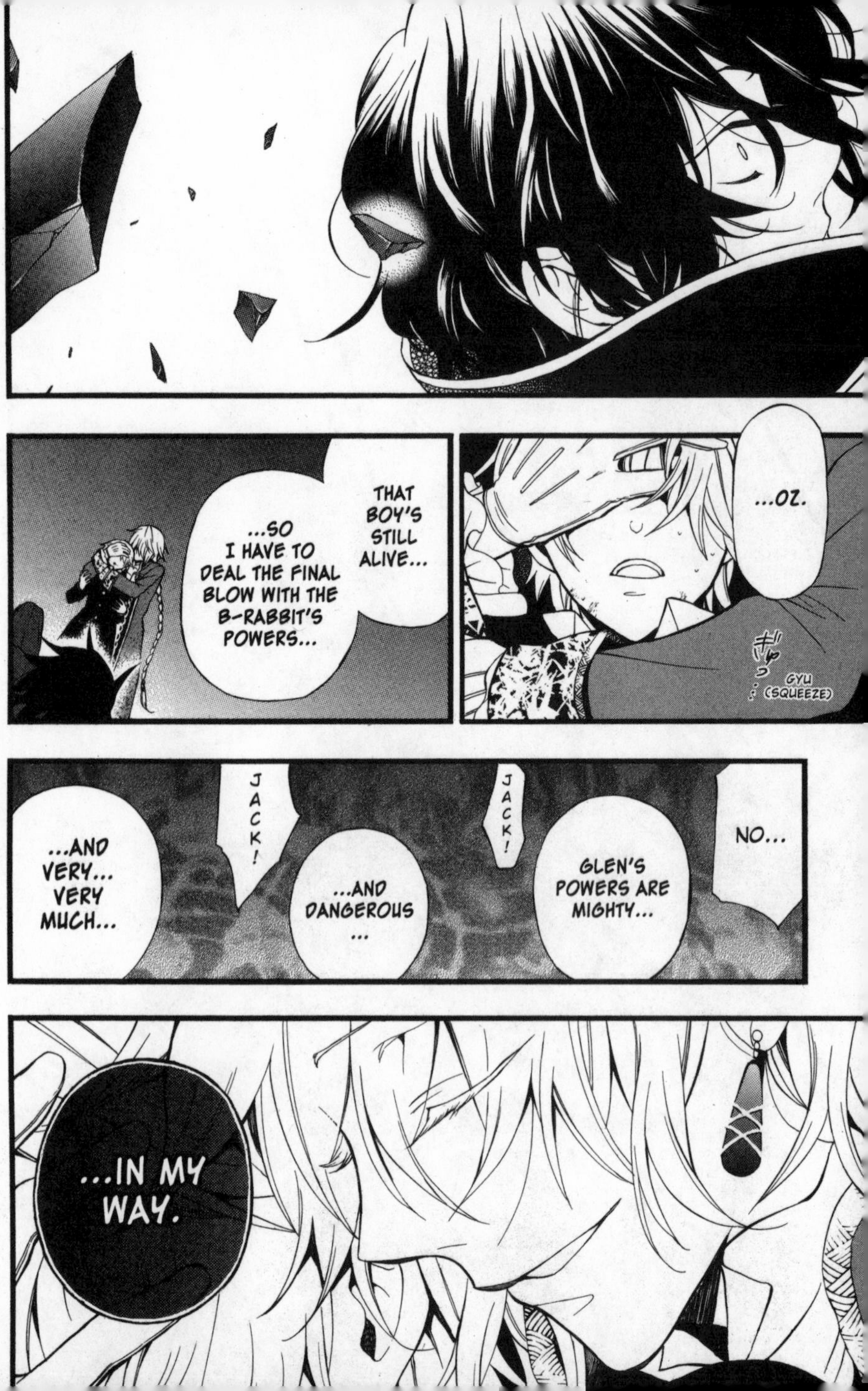

...OZ.
ぎゅっ
GYU (SQUEEZE)
THAT BOY'S STILL ALIVE...
...SO I HAVE TO DEAL THE FINAL BLOW WITH THE B-RABBIT'S POWERS...
NO...
GLEN'S POWERS ARE MIGHTY...
JACK!
...AND DANGEROUS ...
JACK!
...AND VERY... VERY MUCH...
...IN MY WAY.

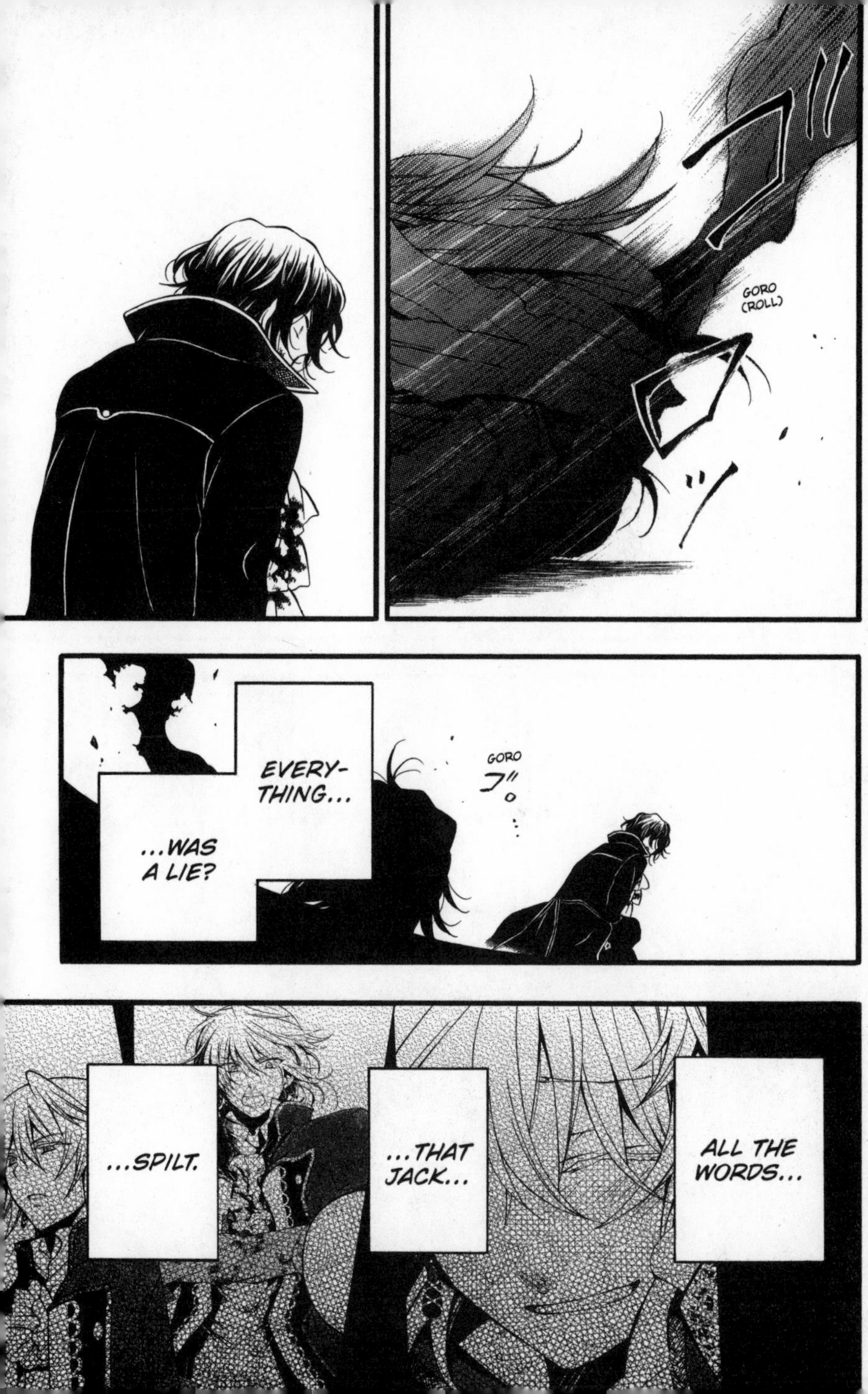
GORO (ROLL)
GORO
EVERY-THING...
...WAS A LIE?
ALL THE WORDS...
...THAT JACK...
...SPILT.

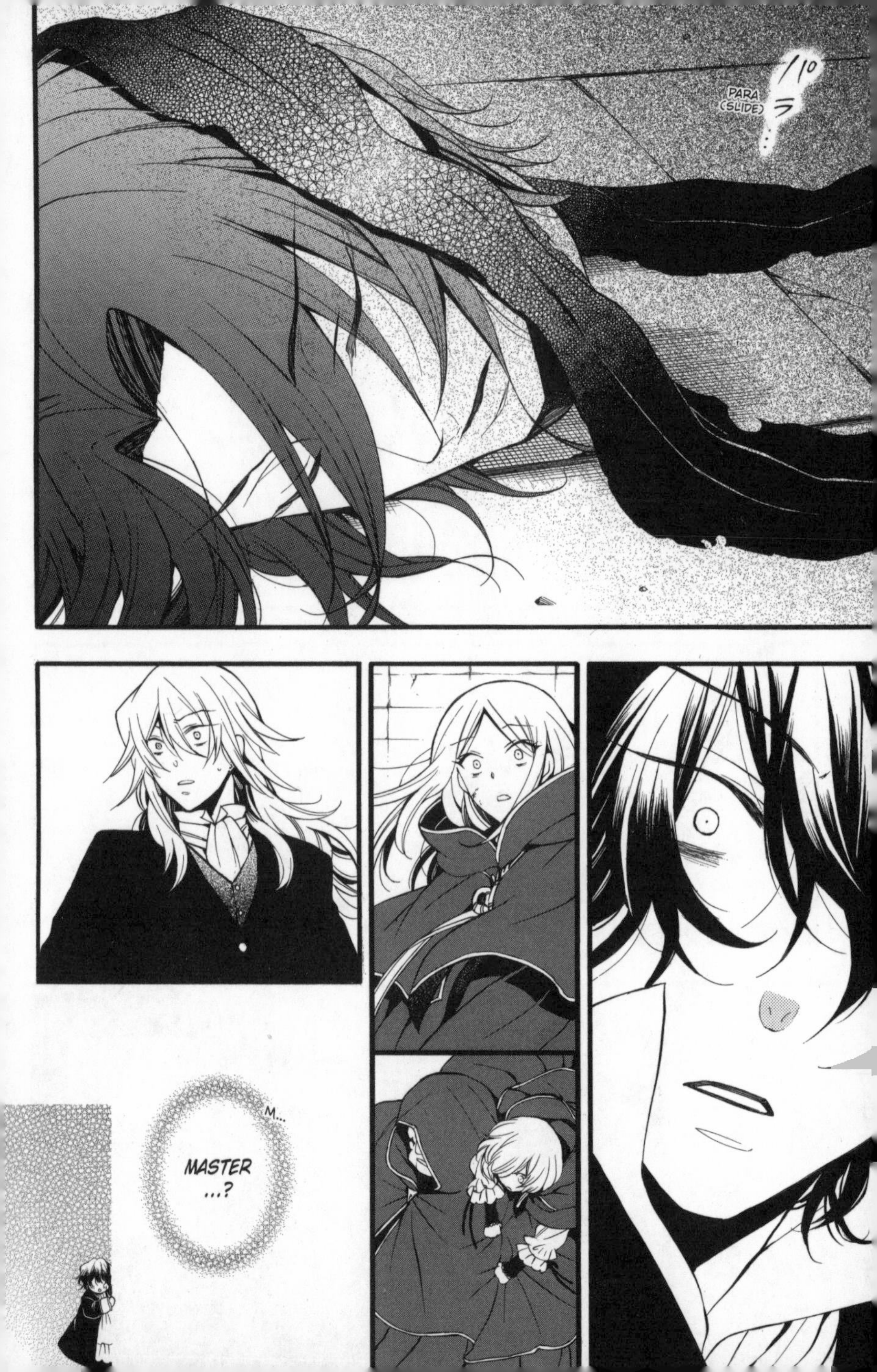
パラ
PARA (SLIDE)
M...
MASTER ...?

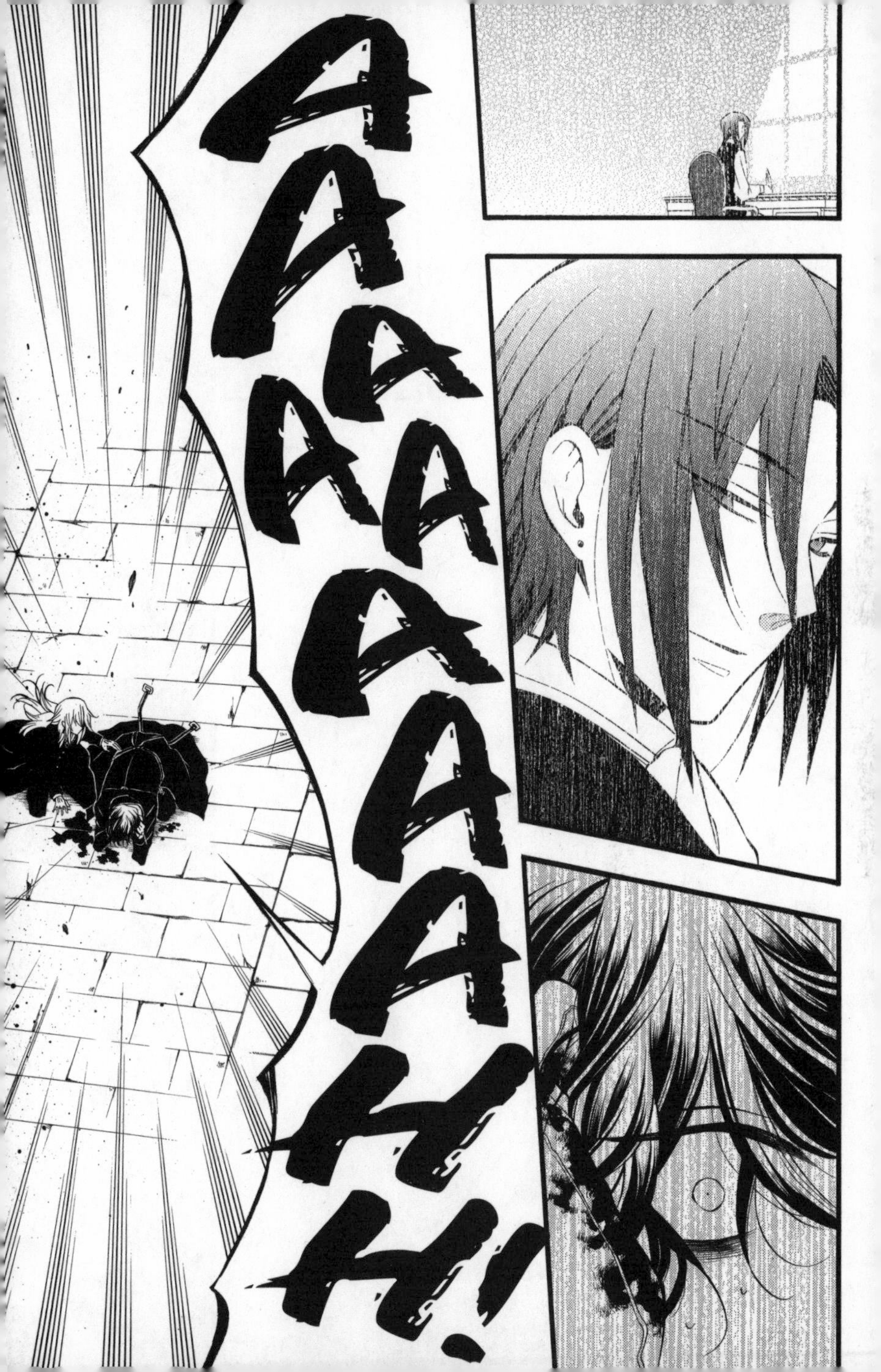
AAAAAAAAHH!

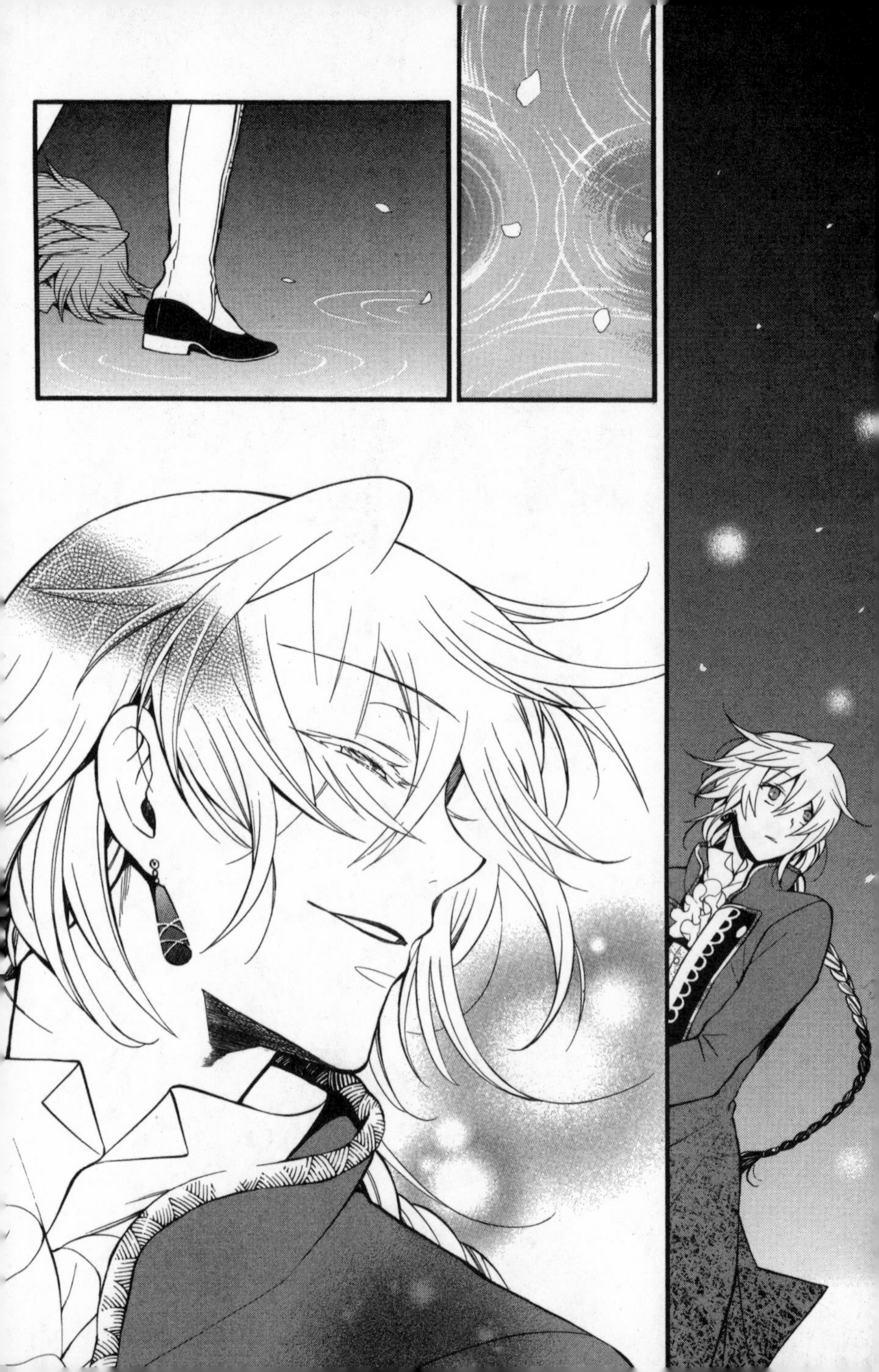

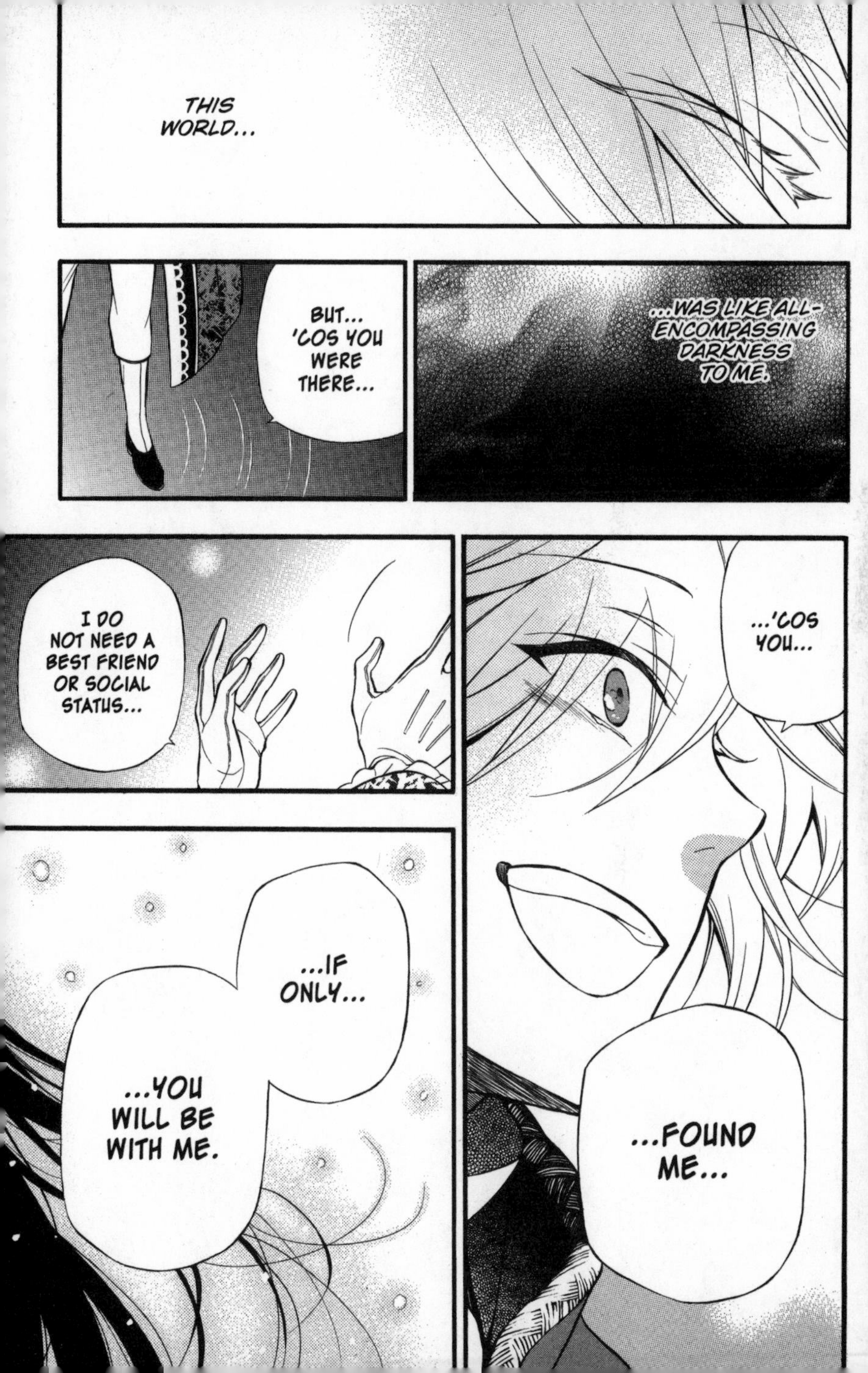
THIS WORLD...
...WAS LIKE ALL-ENCOMPASSING DARKNESS TO ME.
BUT... 'COS YOU WERE THERE...
...'COS YOU...
...FOUND ME...
I DO NOT NEED A BEST FRIEND OR SOCIAL STATUS...
...IF ONLY...
...YOU WILL BE WITH ME.

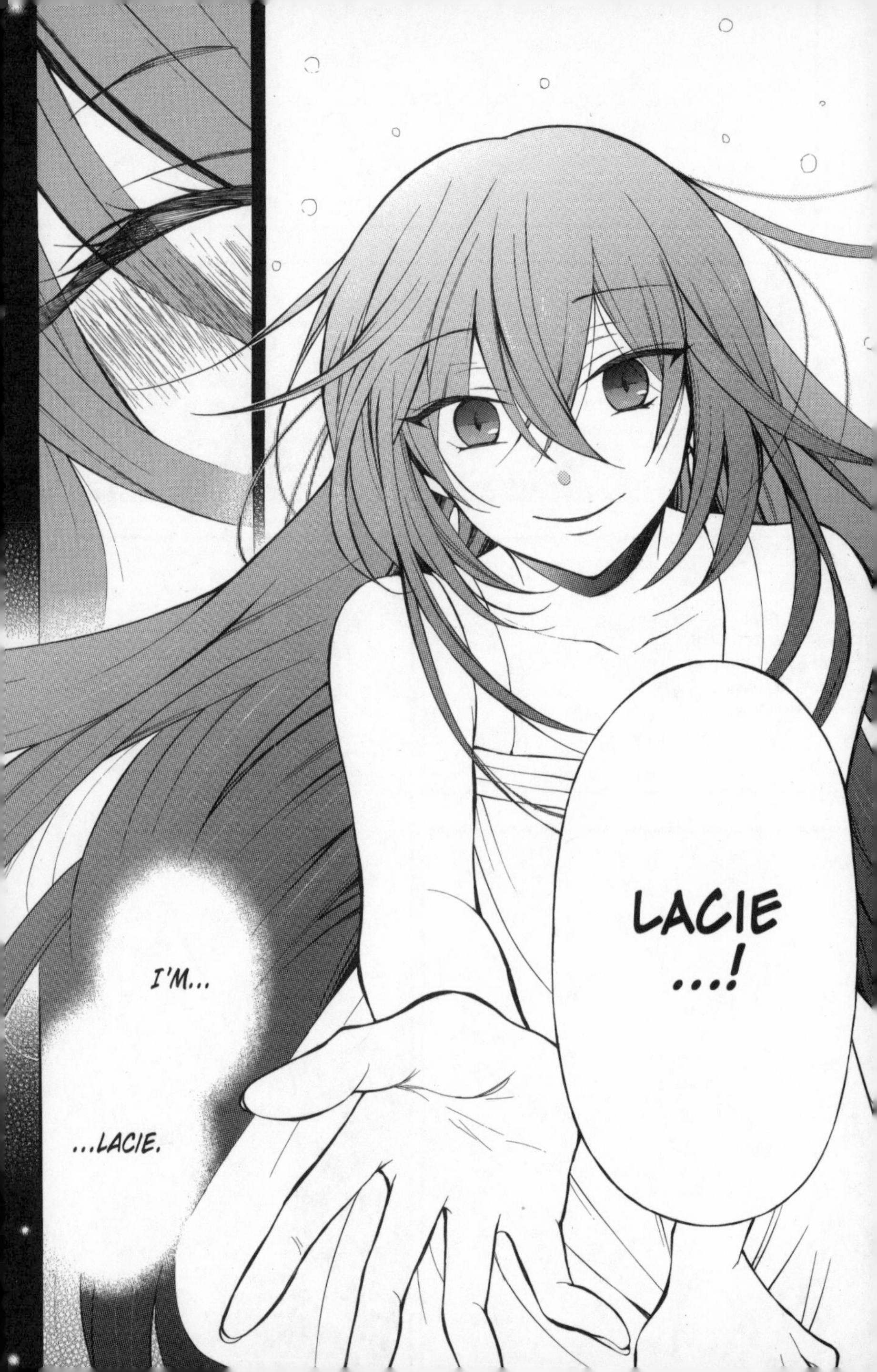
LACIE ...!
I'M...
...LACIE.

WHAT'S YOUR NAME?

WELL?

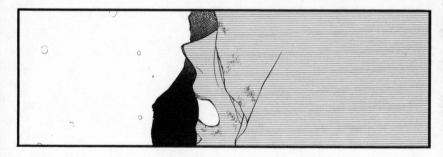

...AM... I...

....

...JACK.

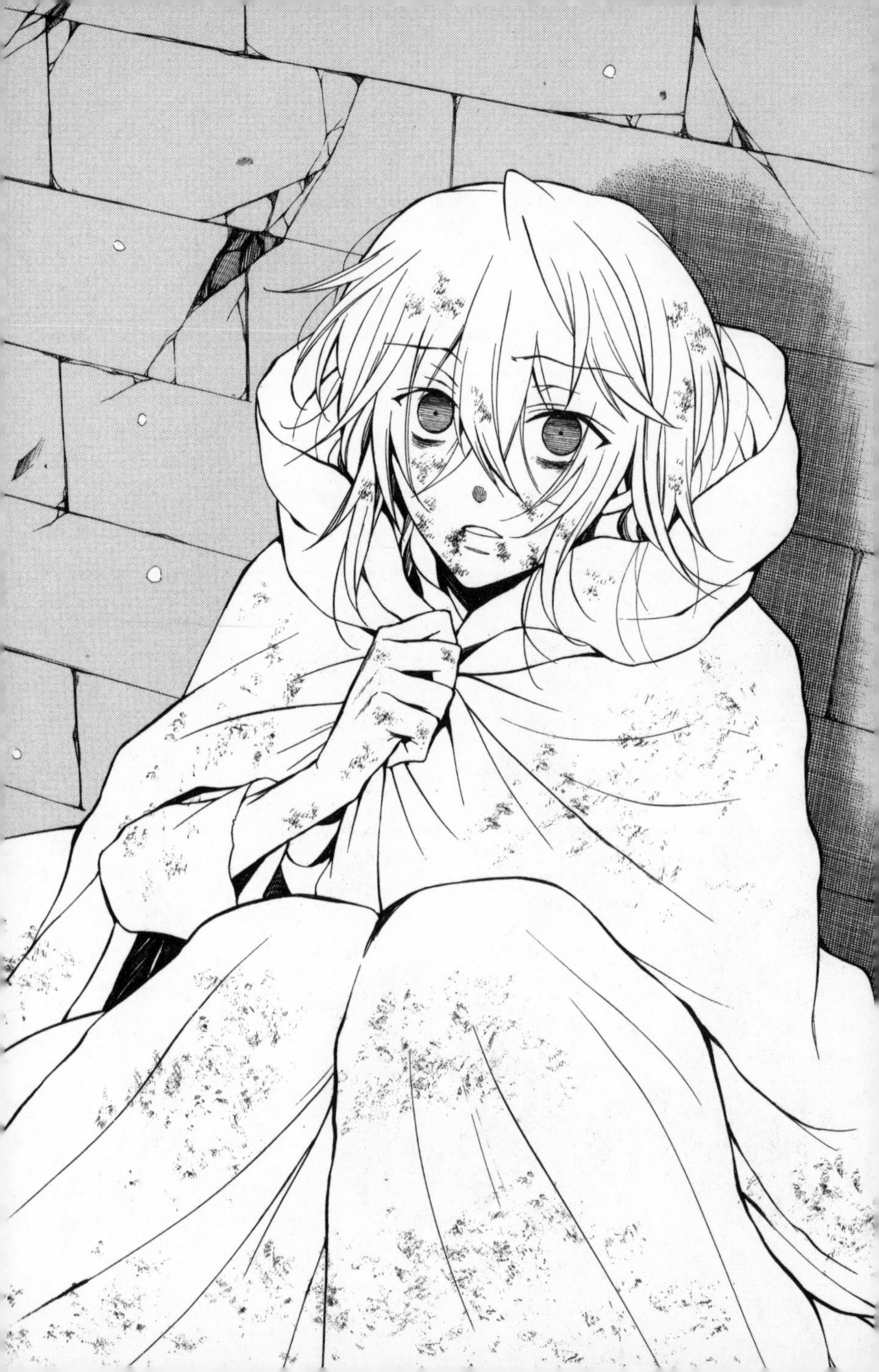

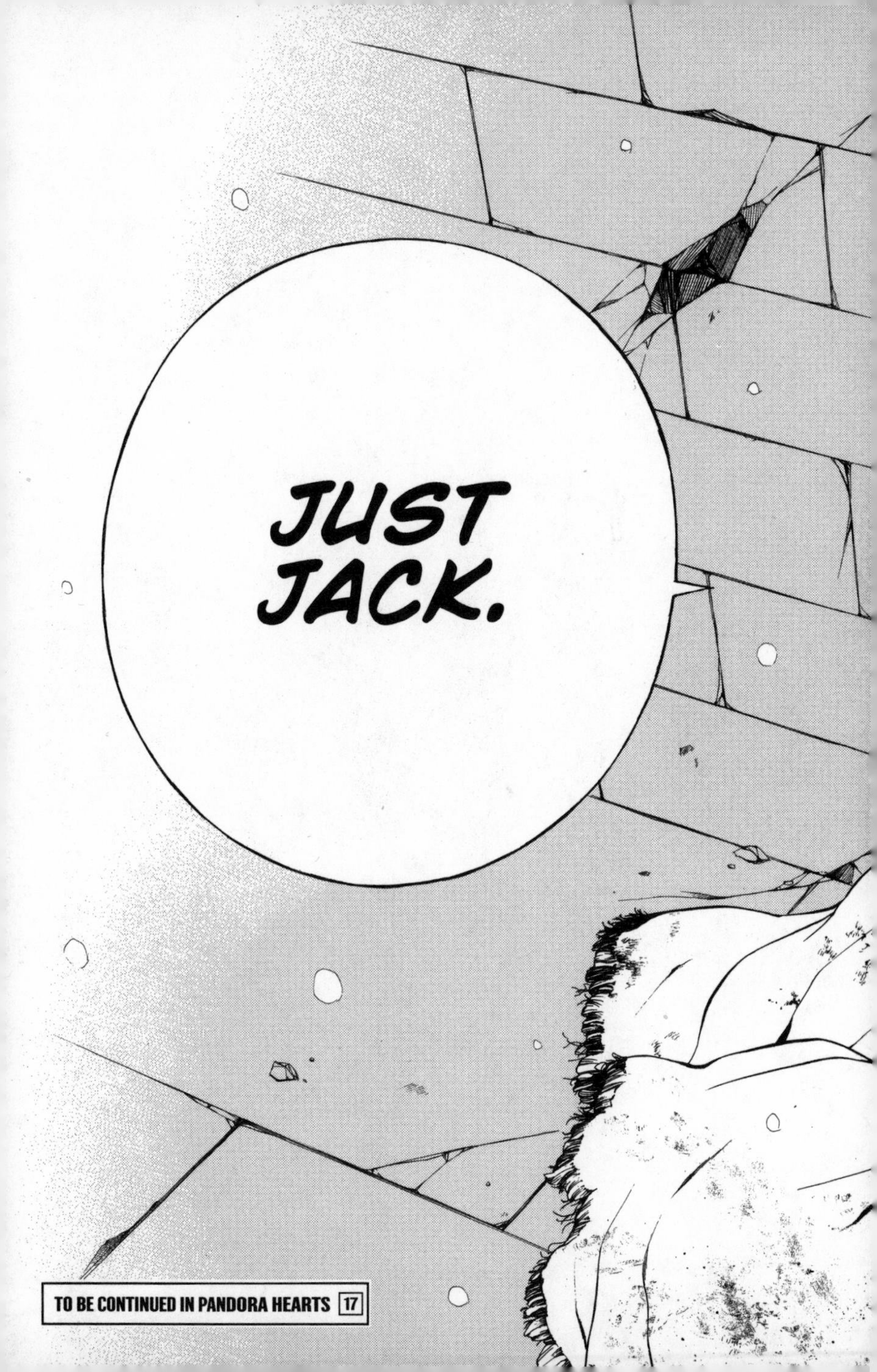
JUST JACK.

TO BE CONTINUED IN PANDORA HEARTS 17

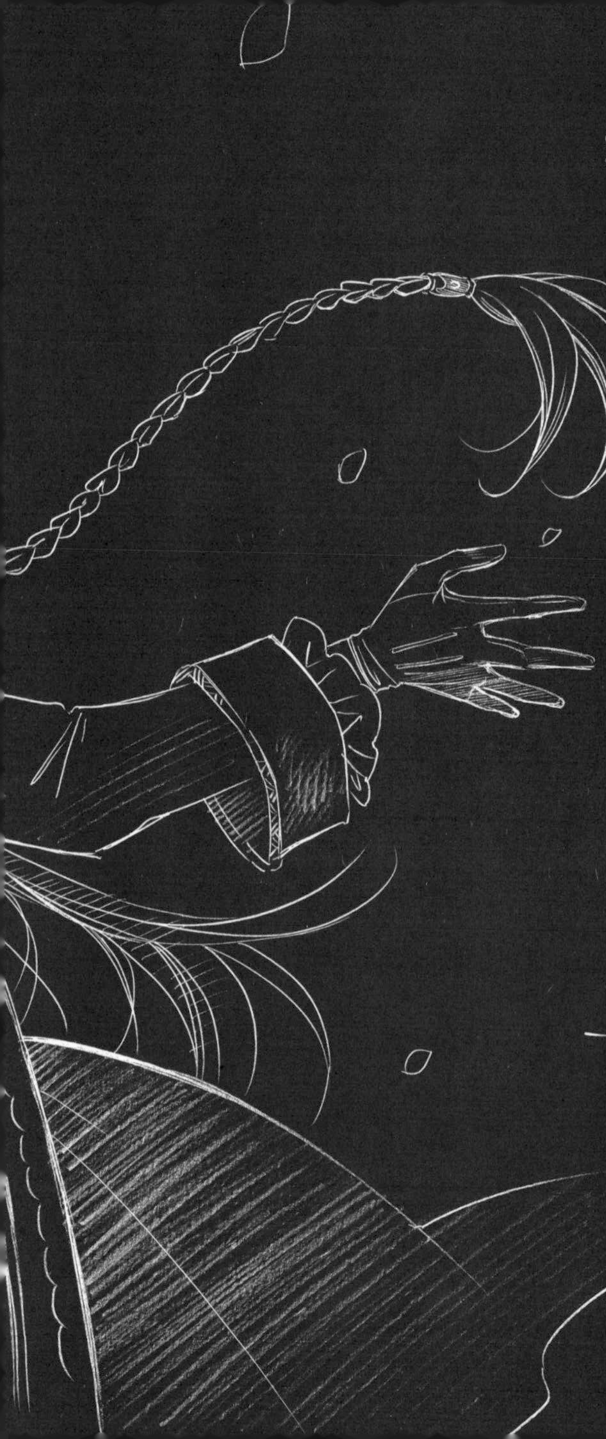

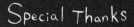

Special Thanks

FUMITO YAMAZAKI
FASHION LEADER AT THE WORKPLACE.
WHAT'S MY SCORE TODAY? EEP.

SAEKO TAKIGAWA
SAEKO, THE FATTY-FLESH-OF-PORK EATER.

KANATA MINAZUKI
A SANTA CLAUS WEARING A
BRIGHT RED PONCHO.

YUKINO
DO YOU STILL LIKE THE UNION JACK?

RYOOO
CONGRATULATIONS! RABBITS, RABBITS!

YAJI
COME BACK QUIIIIIIICK!

MIZU KING
YOU'LL BE YAJI'S SUCCESSOR!
(DRAWING ANIMALS AND PLANTS.)

TADUU
LET'S HAVE YOU DRAW LOTS AND
LOTS OF BACKGROUNDS!

AYANA SASAKI
LET'S GO SING KARAOKE. UFUFU!

BIG BROTHER (2)
+ YUKKO-SAN
I'LL COME VISIT & YOU VISIT US!

FATHER, MOTHER, BIG SISTER,
BIG BROTHER (1)
THANKS FOR ALWAYS TAKING CARE OF ME.

MY EDITOR TAKEGASA-SAMA
THANKS FOR ALWAYS TAKING CARE OF ME.

— and You!

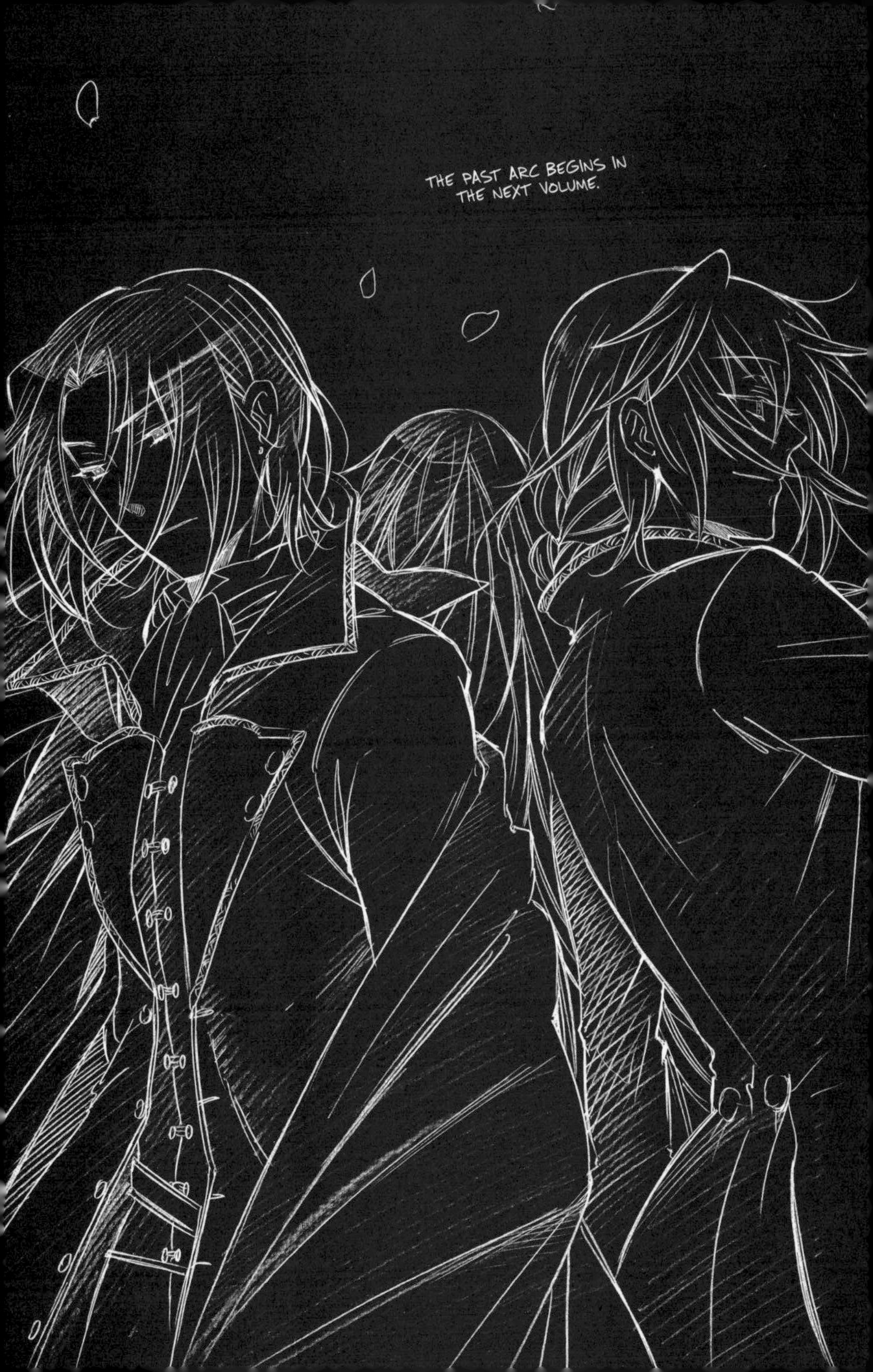
THE PAST ARC BEGINS IN THE NEXT VOLUME.

NOW I REMEMBER. IN VOLUME 1, AN ORDINARY BONUS MANGA WAS HERE!!

MY IDEAS HAVE RUN AWAY FROM HOME, SO I RETURN TO MY ORIGINAL INTENTIONS FOR NOW.

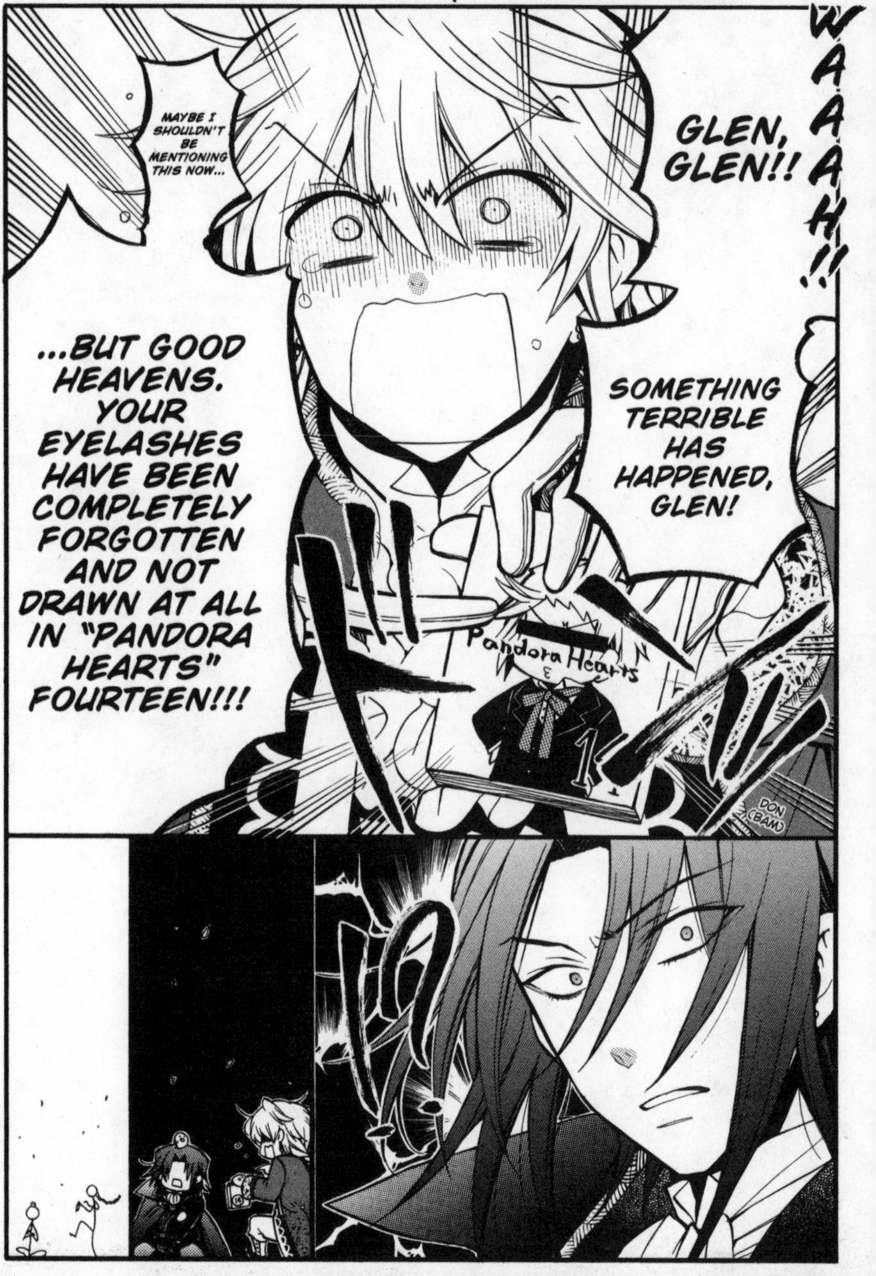
WAAAAH!!
GLEN, GLEN!!
MAYBE I SHOULDN'T BE MENTIONING THIS NOW...
SOMETHING TERRIBLE HAS HAPPENED, GLEN!
...BUT GOOD HEAVENS. YOUR EYELASHES HAVE BEEN COMPLETELY FORGOTTEN AND NOT DRAWN AT ALL IN "PANDORA HEARTS" FOURTEEN!!!
Pandora Hearts
DON (BAM)

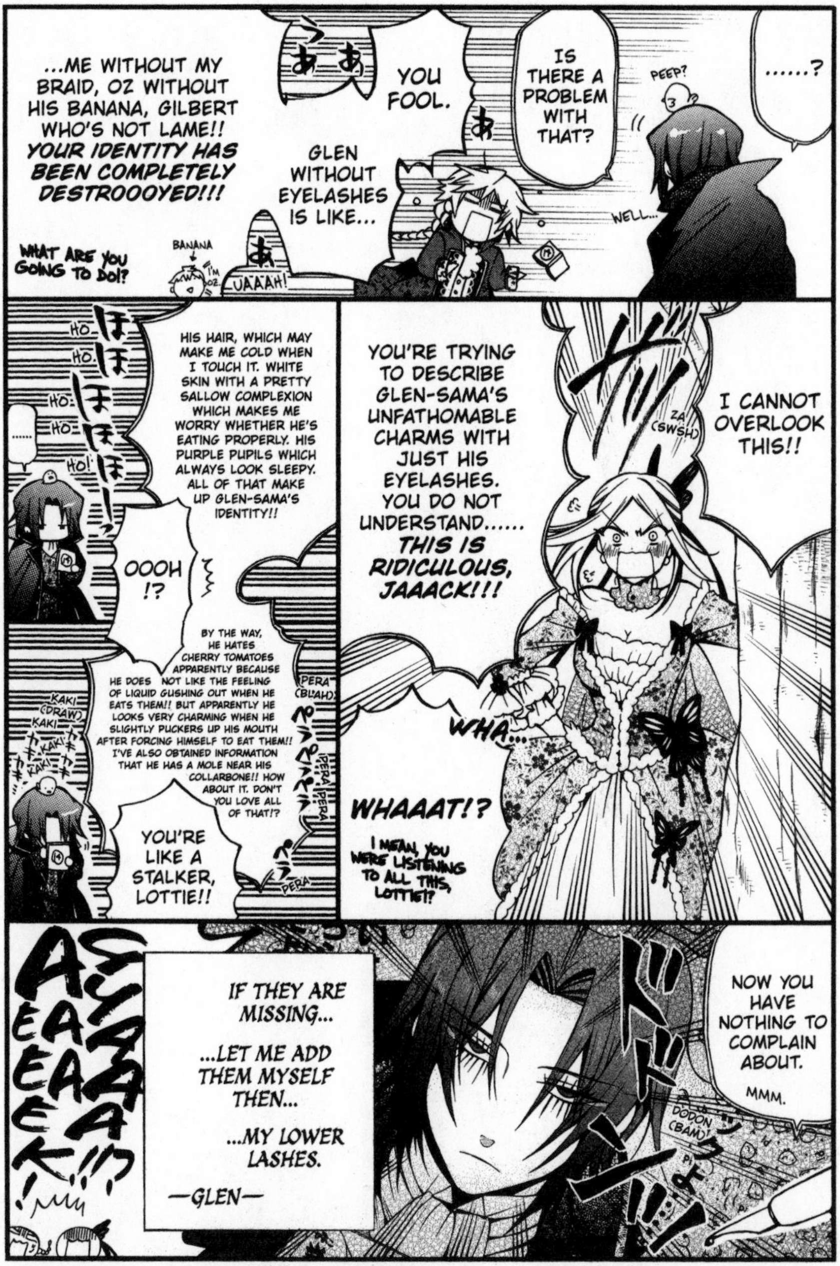
......?
PEEP?
IS THERE A PROBLEM WITH THAT?
WELL...
YOU FOOL.
GLEN WITHOUT EYELASHES IS LIKE...
...ME WITHOUT MY BRAID, OZ WITHOUT HIS BANANA, GILBERT WHO'S NOT LAME!! YOUR IDENTITY HAS BEEN COMPLETELY DESTROOOYED!!!
UAAAH!
I'M OZ.
BANANA
WHAT ARE YOU GOING TO DO!?
I CANNOT OVERLOOK THIS!!
ZA (SWSH)
YOU'RE TRYING TO DESCRIBE GLEN-SAMA'S UNFATHOMABLE CHARMS WITH JUST HIS EYELASHES. YOU DO NOT UNDERSTAND...... THIS IS RIDICULOUS, JAAACK!!!
WHA...
WHAAAT!?
I MEAN, YOU WERE LISTENING TO ALL THIS, LOTTIE!?
HIS HAIR, WHICH MAY MAKE ME COLD WHEN I TOUCH IT. WHITE SKIN WITH A PRETTY SALLOW COMPLEXION WHICH MAKES ME WORRY WHETHER HE'S EATING PROPERLY. HIS PURPLE PUPILS WHICH ALWAYS LOOK SLEEPY. ALL OF THAT MAKE UP GLEN-SAMA'S IDENTITY!!
OOOH!?
HO HO HO HO HO!
......
BY THE WAY, HE HATES CHERRY TOMATOES APPARENTLY BECAUSE HE DOES NOT LIKE THE FEELING OF LIQUID GUSHING OUT WHEN HE EATS THEM!! BUT APPARENTLY HE LOOKS VERY CHARMING WHEN HE SLIGHTLY PUCKERS UP HIS MOUTH AFTER FORCING HIMSELF TO EAT THEM!! I'VE ALSO OBTAINED INFORMATION THAT HE HAS A MOLE NEAR HIS COLLARBONE!! HOW ABOUT IT. DON'T YOU LOVE ALL OF THAT!?
PERA (BLAH) PERA PERA PERA
YOU'RE LIKE A STALKER, LOTTIE!!
KAKI (DRAW) KAKI KAKI KAKI
NOW YOU HAVE NOTHING TO COMPLAIN ABOUT.
MMM.
DODON (BAM)
IF THEY ARE MISSING...
...LET ME ADD THEM MYSELF THEN...
...MY LOWER LASHES.
—GLEN—

I CANNOT DO ANYTHING ABOUT WHAT'S ALREADY BEEN PUBLISHED, SO I DECIDED TO TAKE ADVANTAGE AND MADE FUN OF IT.

COMMON HONORIFICS

no honorific: Indicates familiarity or closeness; if used without permission or reason, addressing someone in this manner would constitute an insult.

-san: The Japanese equivalent of Mr./Mrs./Miss. If a situation calls for politeness, this is the fail-safe honorific.

-sama: Conveys great respect; may also indicate that the social status of the speaker is lower than that of the addressee.

-kun: Used most often when referring to boys (though it can be applied to girls as well), this indicates affection or familiarity. Occasionally used by older men among their peers, but it may also be used by anyone referring to a person of lower standing.

-chan: An affectionate honorific indicating familiarity used mostly in reference to girls; also used in reference to cute persons or animals of either gender.

PandoraHearts

I used to take only showers because I thought, "It's a waste of time to be in the bathtub since I can't do anything in there!" But after I started reading in the tub, I've come to feel at ease (?) with taking long baths.

I'm beginning to steadily make my way through the reference books that have piled up.

MOCHIZUKI'S MUSINGS

VOLUME 16

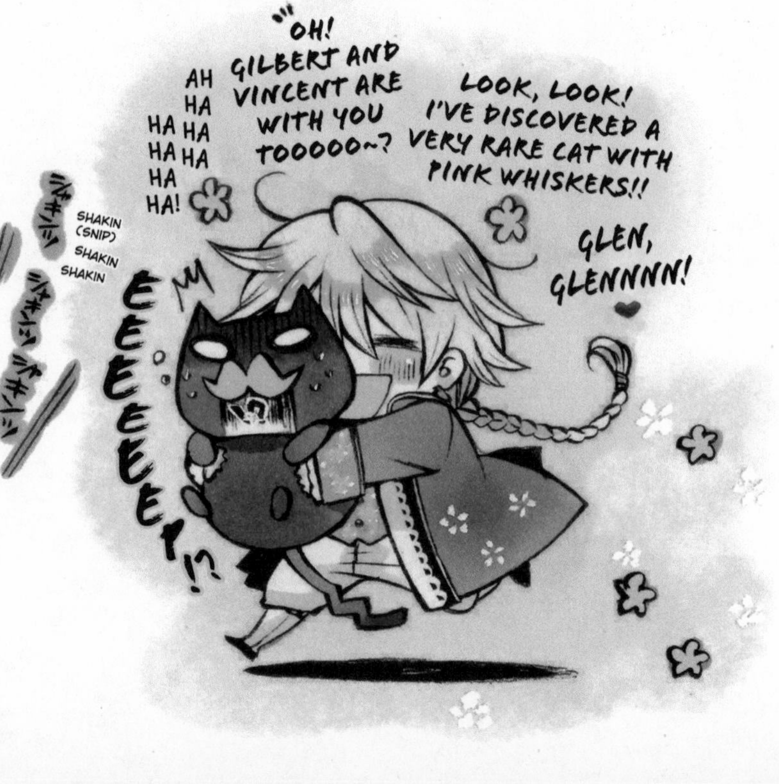
LOOK, LOOK! I'VE DISCOVERED A VERY RARE CAT WITH PINK WHISKERS!!
GLEN, GLENNNN!
"OH! GILBERT AND VINCENT ARE WITH YOU TOOOOO~?
AH HA HA HA HA HA HA HA HA!
EEEEEEEEEY!?
SHAKIN (SNIP) SHAKIN SHAKIN

PandoraHearts

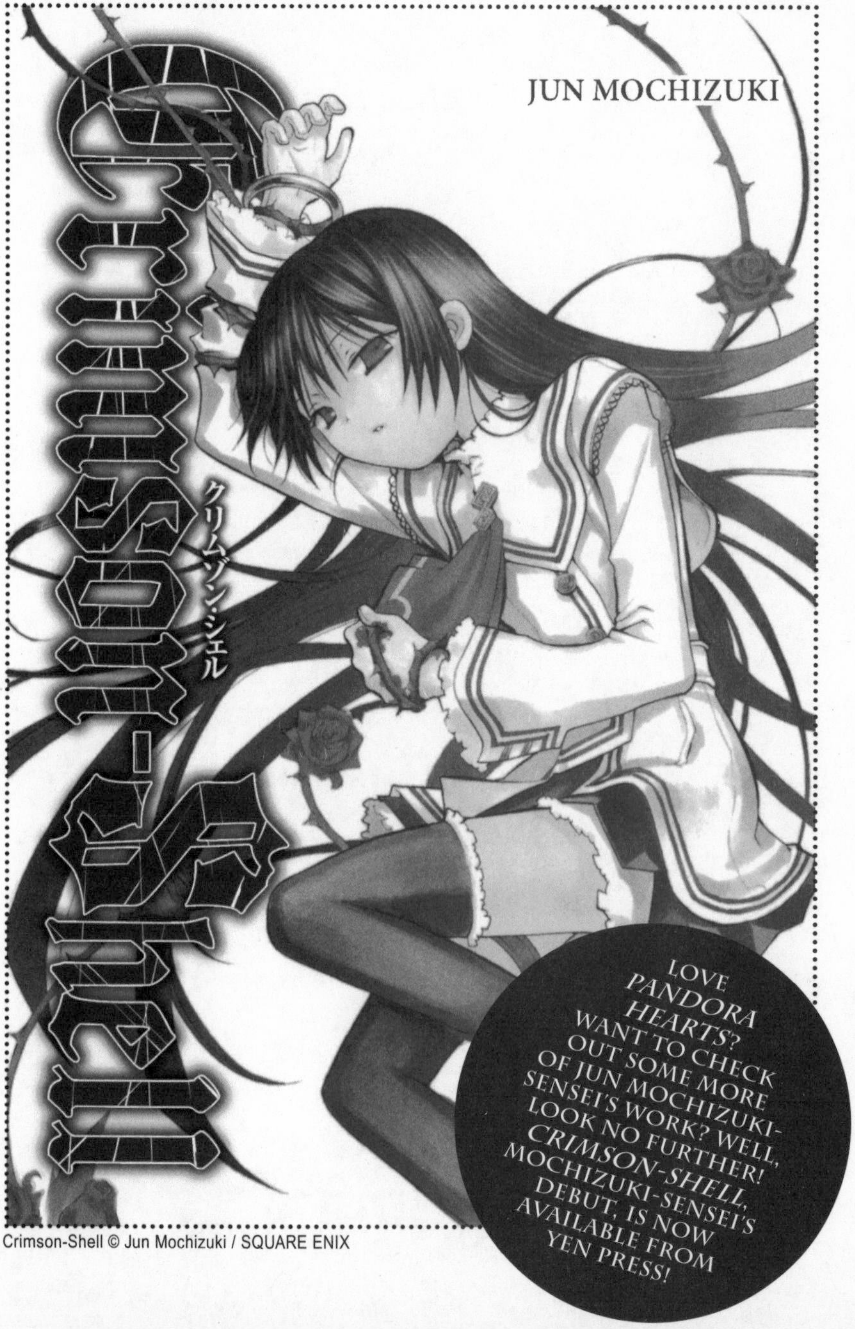
Crimson-Shell
クリムゾン・シェル
JUN MOCHIZUKI

LOVE *PANDORA HEARTS*? WANT TO CHECK OUT SOME MORE OF JUN MOCHIZUKI-SENSEI'S WORK? WELL, LOOK NO FURTHER! *CRIMSON-SHELL*, MOCHIZUKI-SENSEI'S DEBUT, IS NOW AVAILABLE FROM YEN PRESS!

PandoraHearts

Can't wait for the next volume? You don't have to!

Keep up with the latest chapters of some of your favorite manga every month online in the pages of YEN PLUS!

READ IT THE SAME DAY AS JAPAN!

Visit us at www.yenplus.com for details!

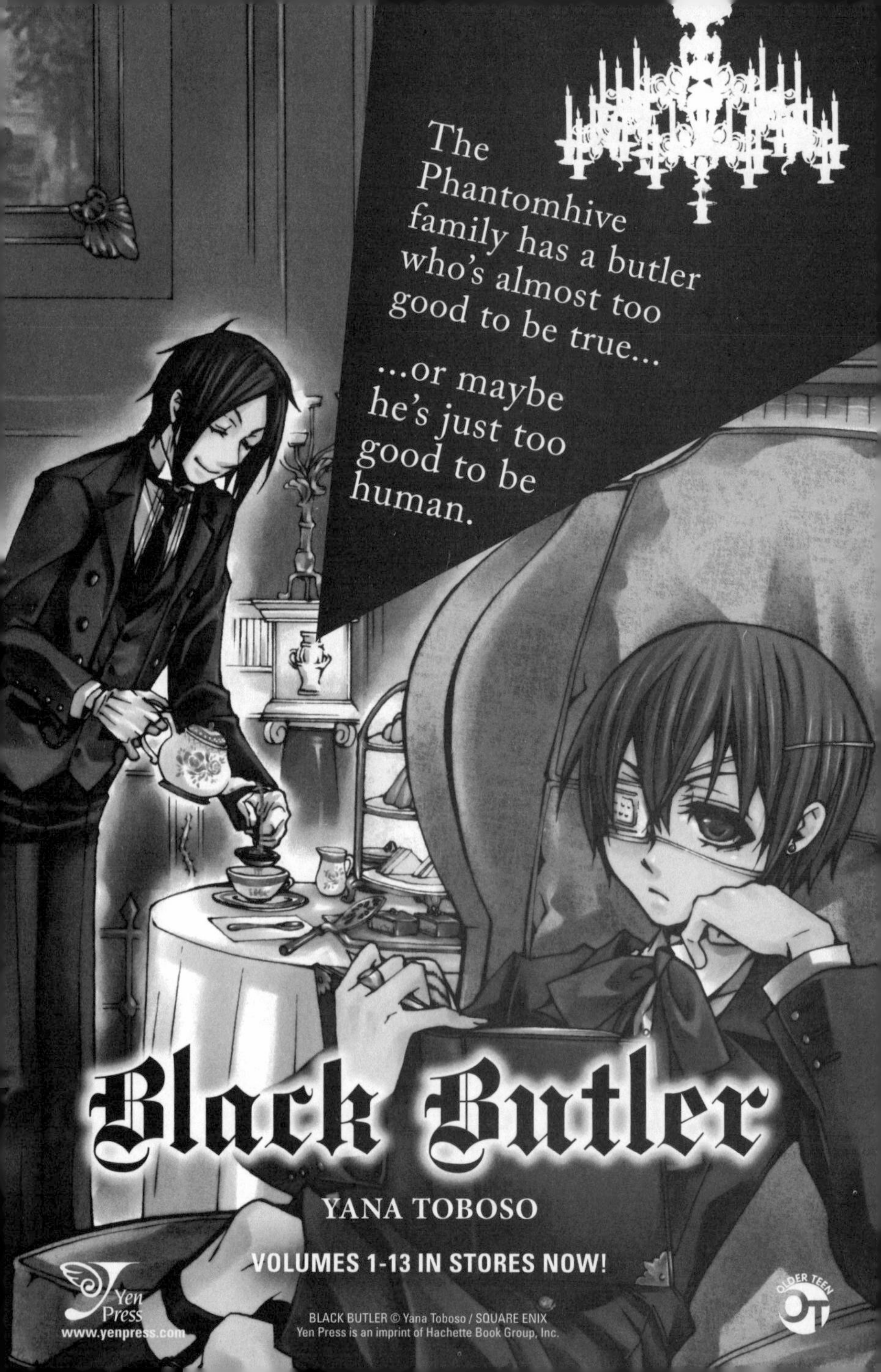

The Phantomhive family has a butler who's almost too good to be true...
...or maybe he's just too good to be human.
Black Butler
YANA TOBOSO
VOLUMES 1-13 IN STORES NOW!
Yen Press
www.yenpress.com
BLACK BUTLER © Yana Toboso / SQUARE ENIX
Yen Press is an imprint of Hachette Book Group, Inc.
OLDER TEEN
OT

WELCOME TO IKEBUKURO, WHERE TOKYO'S WILDEST CHARACTERS GATHER!!

AS THEIR PATHS CROSS, THIS ECCENTRIC CAST WEAVES A TWISTED, CRACKED LOVE STORY...

AVAILABLE NOW!!

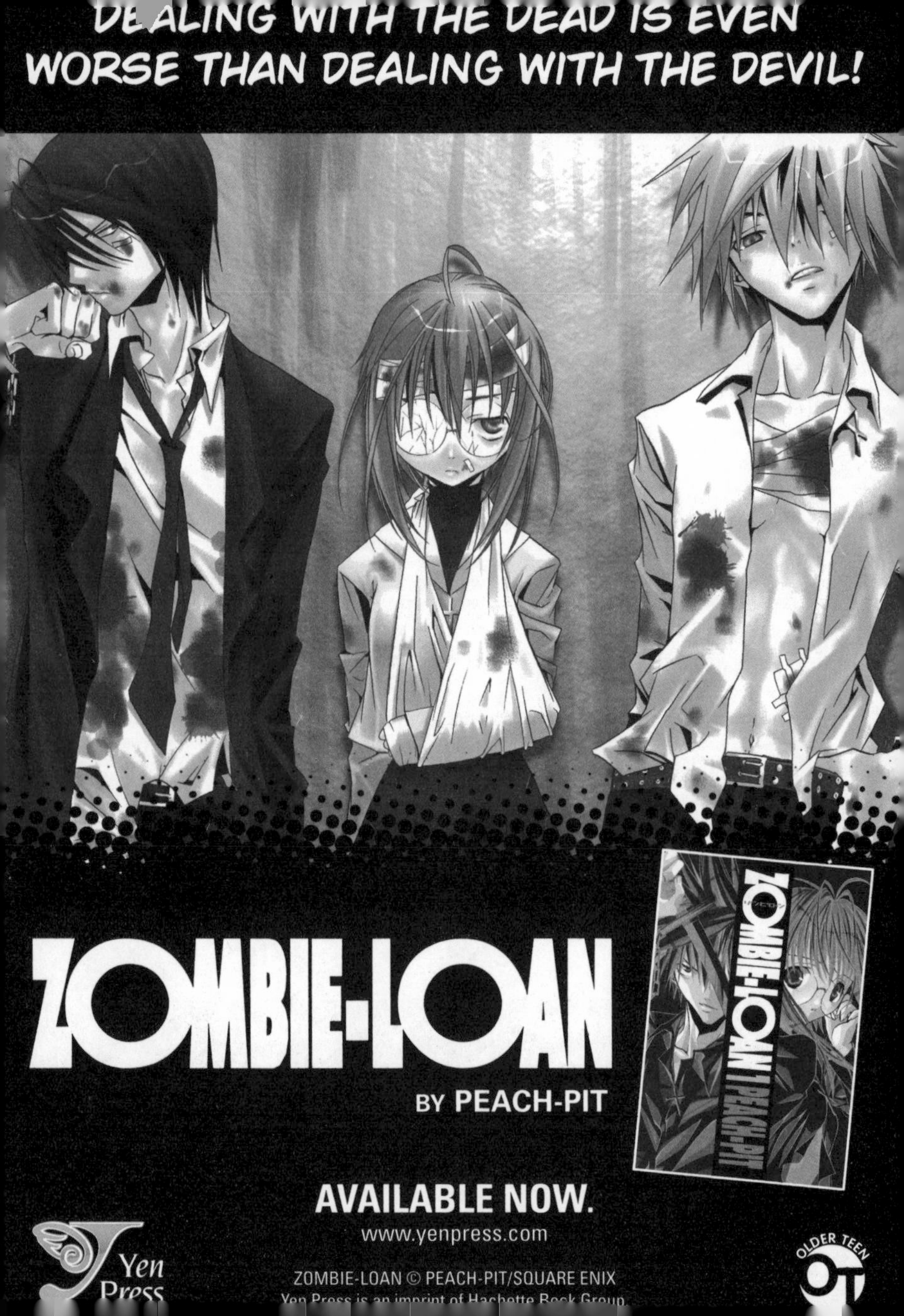
DEALING WITH THE DEAD IS EVEN
WORSE THAN DEALING WITH THE DEVIL!
ZOMBIE-LOAN
BY PEACH-PIT
ZOMBIE-LOAN PEACH-PIT
AVAILABLE NOW.
www.yenpress.com
Yen Press
OLDER TEEN
OT
ZOMBIE-LOAN © PEACH-PIT/SQUARE ENIX
Yen Press is an imprint of Hachette Book Group.

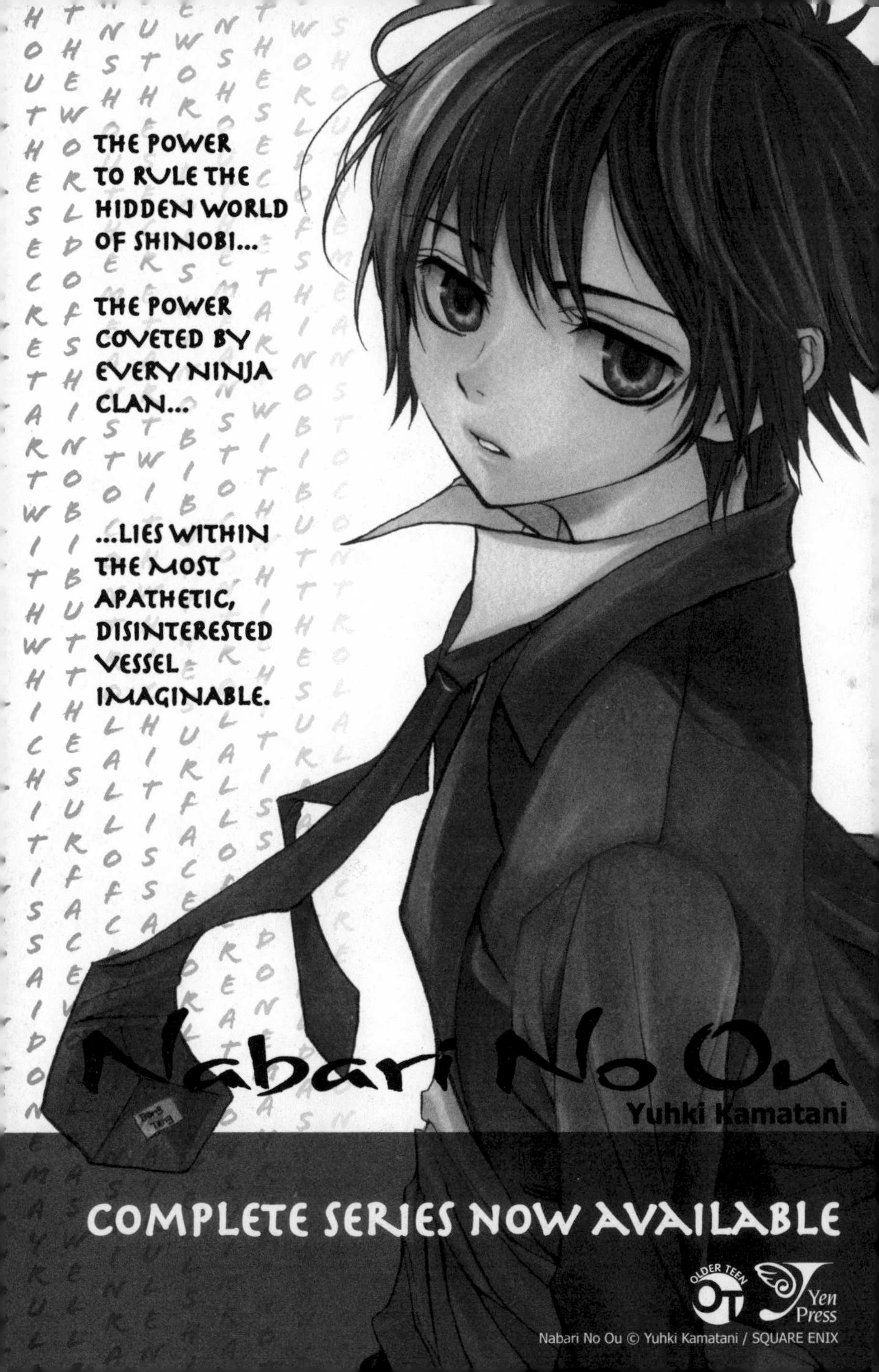
THE POWER TO RULE THE HIDDEN WORLD OF SHINOBI...
THE POWER COVETED BY EVERY NINJA CLAN...
...LIES WITHIN THE MOST APATHETIC, DISINTERESTED VESSEL IMAGINABLE.
Nabari No Ou
Yuhki Kamatani
COMPLETE SERIES NOW AVAILABLE
OLDER TEEN OT
Yen Press
Nabari No Ou © Yuhki Kamatani / SQUARE ENIX

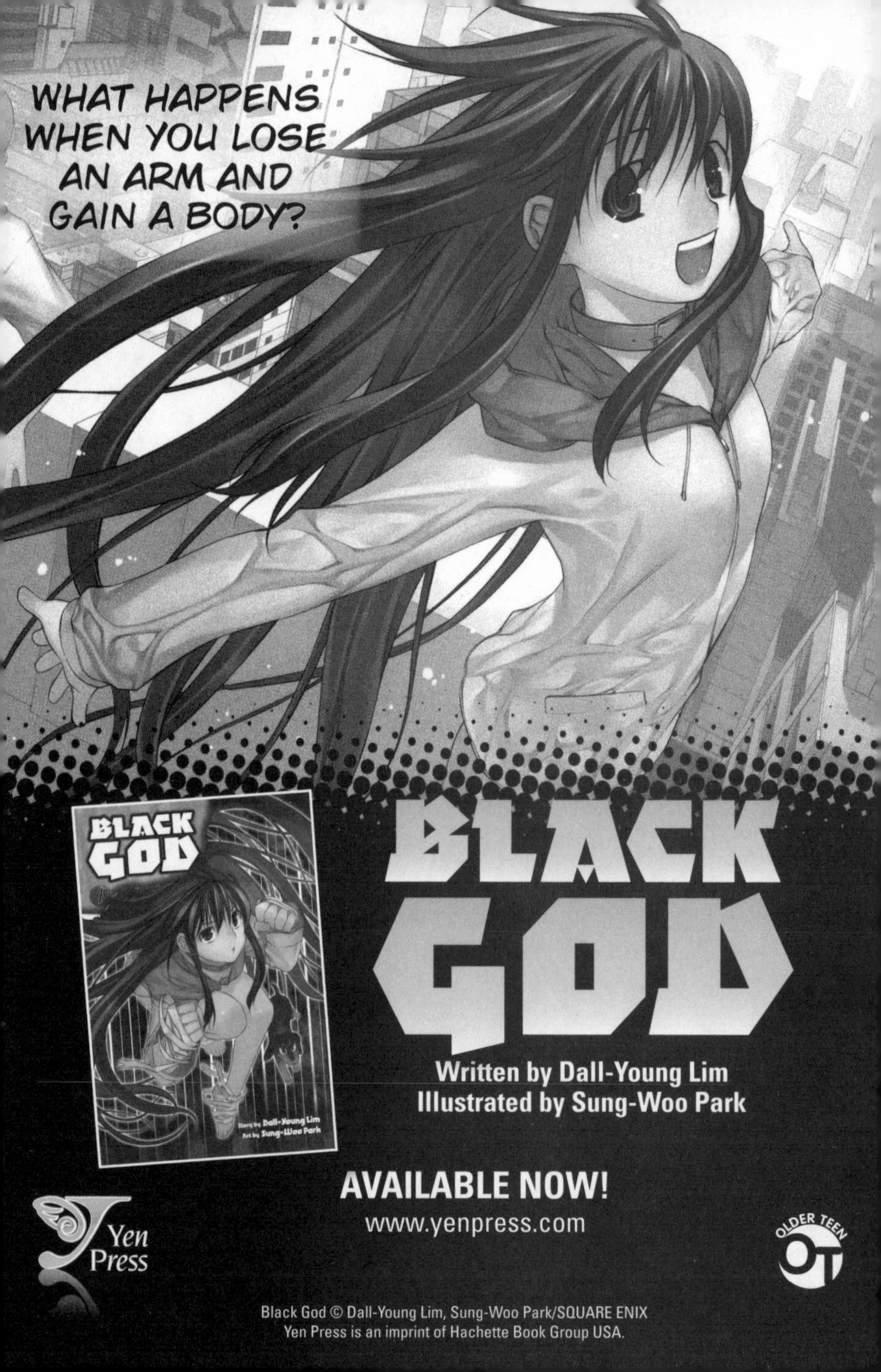
WHAT HAPPENS WHEN YOU LOSE AN ARM AND GAIN A BODY?
BLACK GOD
Story by Dall-Young Lim
Art by Sung-Woo Park
BLACK GOD
Written by Dall-Young Lim
Illustrated by Sung-Woo Park
AVAILABLE NOW!
www.yenpress.com
Yen Press
OLDER TEEN
OT
Black God © Dall-Young Lim, Sung-Woo Park/SQUARE ENIX
Yen Press is an imprint of Hachette Book Group USA.

PandoraHearts ⑯

JUN MOCHIZUKI

Translation: Tomo Kimura • Lettering: Alexis Eckerman

PandoraHearts Vol. 16 © 2011 Jun Mochizuki / SQUARE ENIX CO., LTD. All rights reserved. First published in Japan in 2011 by SQUARE ENIX CO., LTD. English translation rights arranged with SQUARE ENIX CO., LTD. and Hachette Book Group through Tuttle-Mori Agency, Inc.

Translation © 2013 by SQUARE ENIX CO., LTD.

Yen Press
150 West 30th Street, 19th Floor
New York, NY 10001

www.HachetteBookGroup.com
www.YenPress.com

Yen Press is an imprint of Hachette Book Group, Inc. The Yen Press name and logo are trademarks of Hachette Book Group, Inc.

First Yen Press Edition: June 2013

ISBN: 978-0-316-22538-0

10 9 8 7 6 5

WOR

Printed in the United States of America